D1099777

IN SEARCH OF
TOTAL PERFECTION

By the same author
Family Food
In Search of Perfection
Further Adventures in Search of Perfection
The Big Fat Duck Cookbook

IN SEARCH OF
TOTAL PERFECTION

Heston Blumenthal

B L O O M S B U R Y

LONDON · BERLIN · NEW YORK · SYDNEY

First published in Great Britain in two volumes:
In Search of Perfection (2006) and *Further Adventures in Search of Perfection* (2007).

Copyright © 2009 by Heston Blumenthal
Written in cooperation with Pascal Cariss

Photography: pages 6, 31, 37, 112, 114, 120, 146, 234, 266, 269, 396, 407, 423 © Simon Wheeler;
pages 48, 56, 59, 82, 85, 163, 181, 189, 214, 277, 282, 284, 339, 343, 352, 429, 440, 449, 463
© Andy Sewell; page 306 © Pascal Cariss.

Plate section photography: pages 1, 4, 5, 8, 9, 11, 13 (right), 14 © Simon Wheeler;
pages 2, 3, 6, 7, 10, 12, 15, 16 © Andy Sewell; page 13 (left) © Dominic Davies.

The moral right of the author has been asserted.

No part of this book may be used or reproduced in any manner
whatsoever without written permission from the Publisher except
in the case of brief quotations embodied in critical articles or reviews.

Bloomsbury Publishing plc, 50 Bedford Square, London WC1B 3DP
Bloomsbury Publishing, London, New York, Berlin and Sydney

www.bloomsbury.com/hestonblumenthal

By arrangement with the BBC
The BBC logo is a trademark of the British Broadcasting
Corporation and is used under licence. BBC logo © BBC 1996

The Silver Chair by C.S. Lewis copyright © C.S. Lewis Pte. Ltd 1953:
extract reprinted by permission.
Extracts from *Italian Food* by Elizabeth David reprinted with
permission from the Elizabeth David estate.
Extract from *Harry Potter and the Order of the Phoenix* copyright © J.K. Rowling 2003
Extract from *In Taste: Proceedings of the Oxford Symposium on Food & Cookery*
reprinted by permission of Prospect Books

Every reasonable effort has been made to contact copyright holders
of material reproduced in this book. If any have inadvertently been
overlooked, the Publisher would be glad to hear of them and make good
in future editions any errors or omissions brought to their attention.

A CIP catalogue record for this book is available from the British Library.

ISBN 978 1 4088 0244 1

10 9 8

Designed by Grade Design Consultants www.gradedesign.com
Printed and bound in Great Britain by Clays Ltd, St Ives plc

Contents

Introduction

When *In Search of Perfection* first aired on BBC2, I had no idea how it would be received. Of course there had been plenty of talk about the food 'revolution' sweeping Britain, and I was certain that we'd produced a series of programmes that made a genuinely innovative contribution to that revolution, but still the question nagged at me: would people go for an approach to cooking that involved not just techniques and a passion for food but also history, folklore, nostalgia, science and sensory perception? I watched the first programme in a state of elation and trepidation, and then nervously awaited the following day's ratings and reviews.

It turned out that I needn't have worried. There was, it seemed, a huge audience out there with an appetite for a cookery programme that went beyond lists of ingredients and a bit a skilful pan-handling. And the success of the show paved the way for all sorts of other fascinating projects, such as Channel 4's *Big Chef Takes on Little Chef* – in which we sought to transform the menu at a branch of Little Chef, hoping to revive the culinary fortunes of this very British institution – and *Feast*, in which I explored the food of the past and created modern versions of some strange and spectacular dishes. The same loyal audience also bought *The Big Fat Duck Cookbook* when it was finally published, even though, in order to accurately capture the restaurant's complex menu and personality, it was 530 pages long and weighed as much as a car battery!

In each of these projects there is a sense of being on a journey, be it into the past, into the mind, into the complexities of culinary techniques or into the physics of everyday things. In the *Perfection* series, however, that journey was often a very physical one, with passports and suitcases and itineraries. In the pages that follow you'll zigzag the globe, from New York to Delhi and from Beijing to Milan, in order to meet some extraordinary artisans: a visionary pasta-maker who sees his day job merely as funding for his true calling, creating a golden pasta that tastes better than any other; a master butcher who is introducing different and unfamiliar (but delicious!) cuts of meat to the British public; a brother and sister determined to create the perfect chocolate; and a car park full of chilli enthusiasts battling to make the best bowl of red. You'll come across scientists who are saving the Scottish fishing industry and historians who cook to unlock the past; have Sunday dinner (on a Thursday) with a French chef in his *village gourmand*; and hunker down with a very patriotic chicken. Many of these people have spent decades pursuing their own ideals of perfection, and the results are truly inspiring. This book's title is, in part, an acknowledgement of that, and a tribute to them.

Perfection is, of course, an incredibly subjective thing. Even the seemingly simple task of choosing which dishes to include in the series turned out to be a nightmare, and I knew I was bound to upset many people by leaving out their particular favourite. 'Where's steak and kidney pie, toad in the hole, bread and butter pudding? Where's prawn cocktail?' I could imagine people saying. Nonetheless, after holing up in a meeting room and vowing not to emerge until we had thrashed out a viable running order, the BBC team and I eventually had a list that seemed to have something for everyone – a range of undeniably popular meals that also offered lots of interesting challenges in the kitchen. Sixteen dishes that people could really get their teeth into.

Even so, there was heated discussion among us. Roast beef or roast chicken? Italian or American pizza? Trifle or tiramisu? There were fierce advocates of all points of view. It reinforced my opinion that, ultimately, there's no such thing as perfection. What's perfect for one is not going to be perfect for all – one man's meat really is another man's poison. Each of us has our own idea of what constitutes perfection, drawing heavily on a potent and highly personalised mix of emotions, memories and surroundings. Despite the book's title, I knew from the outset that I wouldn't be claiming my recipes were in any way 'definitive'. But I reckoned that, by using my technical skill and scientific knowledge, by talking to producers and artisans and chefs and their customers, I could pin down some of the things that made these dishes work.

While the dictionary defines 'perfection' as 'the state of being perfect', it also offers a second definition that is equally important to this book: honing through continual experimentation. Trying out ideas and then revising and retrying them until you've got something special, unique. The TV series gave me the opportunity to get out and try my hand at all sorts of things I'd never encountered before, and I was as excited about this as I was about the chance to explore memory and nostalgia in food because that's exactly how I started in the restaurant business.

Although I've had help and advice from many people, I'm a self-taught chef. My passion for cooking began at sixteen when my parents took me and my sister to L'Oustau de Baumanière, a Michelin three-star restaurant. None of us had ever been anywhere like that before, and I was totally knocked out by it – not just the fabulous food but the whole multisensory experience: the sound of fountains and cicadas, the heady smell of lavender, the sight of the waiters carving lamb at the table or pouring lobster sauce into soufflés.

I knew at once that I wanted to be part of it.

For the next ten years – like a car enthusiast dedicatedly stripping down and reassembling a vintage TR7 or Morris Minor – I took apart and examined every aspect of classic French cuisine, trying to perfect the kind of experience I had had in France. As the results of my cooking got better and my confidence grew, I began to explore how I might create dishes that matched up to my own ideals of perfection – meat in which the robust, earthy, browned surface gave way to a gratifyingly soft and velvety inner texture, for example, or a parsley mousse whose silky airiness seemed too fragile to contain any strong taste, so that when it melted in your mouth the depth of flavour came as a distinct and pleasurable surprise. And, mindful of how much the power of the Oustau experience lay in its appeal not just to my taste-buds but to all of my senses, I sought to capture that multisensory effect in the dishes I created. As you'll see, this has become a crucial part of how I approach the creation of a recipe.

At the Fat Duck the technical demands of many of the dishes mean they take days to prepare and require the attention of a huge number of people: there are more staff in my kitchen than there are customers in the restaurant. Although the dishes in this book represent a different sort of cuisine, exploring their potential proved equally challenging. Searching out the best ingredients took me to dubious backstreets in London and New York, and on several wild-goose chases in various parts of Europe (I was taken, with great solemnity and assurance, to a canning factory that turned out to be processing completely the wrong sort of tomato, and visited a dairy farm whose standards fell so far short of perfection that we couldn't film there). Refining the culinary techniques for each recipe, I ended up hand-milking a cow and then using dry ice to turn it into ice cream, smoking a fish in a squirrel cage, putting chicken breasts in an MRI scanner and nearly burning down my house in an effort to get the oven hot enough for a proper Neapolitan-style pizza!

It was a hectic but fascinating undertaking, and I hope that what follows conveys something of the sheer enjoyment I experienced while doing it – the problem-solving no less than the exotic locations. The end result is a set of recipes that I'm really proud of. I hope that you have fun trying them out, but more than that, I hope that the people, places and encounters in these pages will inspire you on your own quest for perfection.

Heston Blumenthal
Bray, 2009

Conversion Tables

Conversion is not an exact science, and it's best always to consult the tables below when translating any measurements rather than doubling or tripling a known amount. For ultra-accurate conversion from Celsius to Farenheit, use a thermometer or multiply the Celsius figure by 9, divide it by 5, then add 32. (Note that the recipes in this book were cooked in a conventional oven. If you have a fan-assisted oven, you will need to decrease oven temperatures in the recipes by 20°C/68°F, and you may find that the cooking times need to be reduced slightly.)

If you don't have a convection oven, the best way to achieve the lowest temperatures is to turn your oven to its lowest setting, then prop the door open and use an oven thermometer to regulate the heat.

TEMPERATURE

30°C	85°F	
40°C	105°F	
50°C	120°F	
60°C	140°F	
70°C	160°F	
80°C	175°F	
90°C	195°F	
100°C	212°F	
110°C	225°F	Gas ¼
130°C	250°F	Gas ½
140°C	275°F	Gas 1
150°C	300°F	Gas 2
170°C	325°F	Gas 3
180°C	350°F	Gas 4
190°C	375°F	Gas 5
200°C	400°F	Gas 6
220°C	425°F	Gas 7
230°C	450°F	Gas 8

LENGTH

5mm	¼in	10cm	4in
1cm	²/₅in	20cm	7¾in
2.5cm	1in	50cm	1ft 7½in
5cm	2in	1m	3ft 3½in

VOLUME

5ml		1 teaspoon	
10ml		1 dessertspoon	
15ml	½fl oz	1 tablespoon	
20ml			
25ml		5 teaspoons	
30ml	1fl oz		
40ml	1½fl oz		
50ml		⅕ cup	
55ml	2fl oz		
60ml			
70ml	2½fl oz		
80ml			
90ml	3½fl oz		
100ml			
115ml	4fl oz		
130ml	4½fl oz		
140ml	5fl oz		¼ pint
155ml	5½fl oz	⅔ cup	
170ml	6fl oz		
185ml	6½fl oz		
200ml	7fl oz		
225ml	8fl oz		
285ml	10fl oz	1 cup	½ pint
400ml	14fl oz		
425ml	15fl oz		¾ pint
565ml	20fl oz	2 cups	1 pint
710ml	25fl oz		1¼ pints
850ml	30fl oz		1½ pints
1 litre	35fl oz		1¾ pints

WEIGHT

10g	½oz
20g	¾oz
25g	1oz
50g	2oz
100g	3oz
150g	5oz
200g	6oz
250g	9oz
300g	10oz
400g	14oz
450g	1lb
500g	1lb 2oz

LIQUID AND DRY MEASURE EQUIVALENTS

2 tablespoons	1fl oz	25ml	30g
1 cup	¼ quart	250ml	225g
2 cups	1 pint	500ml	450g
4 cups	35fl oz	1 litre	
4 quarts	1 gallon	3.75 litres	

Ounces to grams	multiply by 28.35
Teaspoons to millilitres	multiply by 5
Tablespoons to millilitres	multiply by 15
Fluid ounces to millilitres	multiply by 30
Cups to litres	multiply by 0.24

MEASUREMENT OF DRY GOODS BY VOLUME

Butter, shortening, cheese and other solid fats

1 tablespoon	⅛ stick	15g	½oz
2 tablespoons	¼ stick	30g	1oz
4 tablespoons (¼ cup)	½ stick	60g	2oz
8 tablespoons (½ cup)	1 stick	115g	4oz (¼lb)
16 tablespoons (1 cup)	2 sticks	225g	8oz (½lb)
32 tablespoons (2 cups)	4 sticks	450g	16oz (1lb)
50g = 3½ tablespoons	100g = ½ cup minus 1 tablespoon		

Flours (unsifted)

1 tablespoon	8.75g	¼oz
¼ cup (4 tbsp)	35g	1¼oz
⅓ cup (5 tbsp)	45g	1½oz
½ cup	70g	2½oz
⅔ cup	90g	3½oz
¾ cup	105g	3¼oz
1 cup	140g	5oz
1½ cups	210g	7½oz
2 cups	280g	10oz
3½ cups	490g	1lb

100g = ¾ cup minus ½ tablespoon
250g = 2 cups minus 3 tablespoons
400g = 3 cups minus 2 tablespoons
500g = 3½ cups minus 1 tablespoon

Granulated sugar

1 teaspoon	5g	$^1/_6$oz
1 tablespoon	15g	½oz
¼ cup (4 tbsp)	60g	1¾oz
⅓ cup (5 tbsp)	75g	2¼oz
½ cup	100g	3½oz
⅔ cup	130g	4½oz
¾ cup	150g	5oz
1 cup	200g	7oz
1½ cups	300g	9½oz
2 cups	400g	13½oz

250g = 1 cup plus 3 tablespoons plus 1 teaspoon
500g = 2½ cups

Brown sugar

1½ cups	450g	1lb

Confectioners' sugar

4 cups	450g	1lb

Breadcrumbs

Dry	¾ cup	115g	4oz
Fresh	2 cups	115g	4oz

Egg whites

1	2 tablespoons
8	1 cup

Egg yolks

1	1 tablespoon
16	1 cup

Fruit, dried and pitted

Plumped	2⅔ cups	450g	1lb
Cooked and puréed	2⅓ cups	450g	1lb

Fruit, fresh

Raw and sliced	3 cups	450g	1lb
Cooked and chopped	2⅓ cups	450g	1lb
Puréed	1¼ cups	450g	1lb

Nuts

Chopped	¾ cup	115g	4oz
Ground	1 cup, loosely packed	115g	4oz

Vegetables

Carrots & other roots, sliced	3 cups	450g	1lb
Carrots & other roots, puréed	1⅓ cups	450g	1lb
Onions, sliced or chopped	3 cups	450g	1lb
Potatoes, raw/sliced/chopped	3 cups	450g	1lb
Spinach & other leafy greens	1½ cups	450g	1lb

Roast Chicken
————————————
& Roast Potatoes
————————————

'I gotta thing about chickens.'
Mickey Rourke in *Angel Heart*

History

CHICKEN

Charles Darwin first identified the red jungle fowl of southeast Asia as the original ancestors of the modern chicken because they showed the ability to breed with domestic birds and produce fertile offspring. The chicken's domestication seems to have taken place early in human history, with some archaeologists – perhaps following Darwin's lead – dating it to around 3000 BC, in India. Others argue that domestication happened in Burma or the Malay peninsula. Remains discovered in China confirm that, no matter where domestication first took place, it was certainly under way by the second millennium BC, though it's not clear whether these birds were raised for food – or for fighting.

The chicken's progress westwards was gradual and meandering. It was probably introduced to Europe via Egypt: Greek writings from the fourth century BC refer to the Egyptians not only keeping chickens but incubating them as well. The Greeks also kept domestic fowl – there are texts referring to chickens as *alektryones*, which means 'awakeners', a description with which anyone who has ever slept near a farmyard will agree.

From Greece the chicken went to Rome (there are many references to chickens being served up at symposia, and several recipes appear in the classical cookbook *Apicius*; the physician Galen recommended chicken soup for regular bowel movements), but when the Romans reached Britain, they discovered that the chicken had beaten them to it, probably brought there by Celtic tribes.

For centuries chickens remained little more than farmyard scavengers. Towards the end of the 1700s, however, attitudes began to change. The selective-breeding theories of Robert Bakewell (who created Longhorn cattle and shire horses), along with Darwin's ideas about genetic transmission, alerted agriculturalists to the breeding potential of chickens. The fuse of more widespread enthusiasm awaited only a match – which came in the form of Queen Victoria. In 1843 Sir Edward Belcher presented her with Cochins from what is now Vietnam.

When they were displayed at the Dublin Show three years later, they sparked a national mania for poultry breeding and exhibition. By 1865 the Poultry Club of Great Britain was drawing up the world's first Standards of Excellence, and the Victorian era had become recognised as 'the Golden Age of Rare Breed Poultry'.

That we have gone from the chicken's golden age to its opposite in less than 150 years is just one of the many shocking features of modern-day intensive poultry-farming.* In the scramble to produce birds with the maximum amount of white meat, everything else has been sacrificed – taste, health concerns (for both the chickens and those who consume them), ethics and, above all, humanity.

Broiler chickens (i.e. those raised for their meat) spend their scant six weeks of life crammed in an unclean shed with 10,000–40,000 other birds, each of which has a living space about the size of an A4 sheet of paper. The mortality rate is high: anything between 6 and 30 per cent. Those that survive often spend their final weeks on their knees, enfeebled by drugs and poor diet, unable to carry the abnormal weight of their artificially fattened bodies. This is the life of 98 per cent of broiler chickens in the UK – some 735 million chickens every year.

POTATOES

Potatoes were cultivated at least two thousand years ago in Peru, and possibly up to six thousand years earlier. Archaeological excavations suggest that their history extends even further back: in southern Chile there is evidence that wild potatoes were being gathered in 11,000 BC. They undoubtedly became a central part of Andean culture: potato designs have been found on shards of Nazca and Chimu pottery, and South American Indians measured time by how long it took to cook potatoes to various consistencies.

The transformation of the potato from knobbly, somewhat bitter tuber to universal staple began in 1537 in what is now Colombia. It was

* Poultry's sorry tale has taken a new twist with the worldwide advance of the H5N1 virus, commonly known as 'avian flu'. Poultry sales have collapsed as a result, even though H5N1 is not a food-borne virus. While the effects of the outbreak of the virus should not be under-estimated (millions of birds have died from it in the last decade), they need to be kept in perspective. Up to March 2009 the World Health Organisation has confirmed 256 deaths from the virus. In each case it is believed to have been caused by close contact with sick birds.

a by-product of conquest: the Spanish forces of Gonzalo Jiménez de Quesada discovered the potato while in search of the golden city of El Dorado. (It is not recorded whether Jiménez de Quesada was disappointed that, instead of the wonders of gold, he found the Golden Wonder.) Within twenty years it was cultivated in Spain and Italy.

The potato's history continued to be linked to various adventurers, though it's impossible now to unravel the truth of these stories. Sir Walter Raleigh, it is said, brought the potato to the British Isles around the 1580s and planted it on his estate at Youghal, in Ireland. Others claim that Sir Francis Drake obtained some roots in Cartagena, or that the potato was part of the booty from a wrecked Armada vessel. What is certain is that, despite its dramatic arrival in Europe, and its mass aceptance in modern times, people didn't at first take to the tuber. As part of the nightshade family, it was considered poisonous or liable to cause leprosy or syphilis. Protestants refused to plant it because it wasn't mentioned in the Bible, and it was still viewed as a delicacy in England some eighty years after its introduction. Despite the Royal Society's recommendation in 1663 that it be grown as a precaution against famine (a cruelly ironic fact, given the famine caused by potato blight in Ireland 200 years later), the potato only really became available to all classes in the early eighteenth century.

The spud was always going to win through. Born of conquest and adventure, it was a suitable cultivation for troubled times. As an under-ground crop it was difficult for soldiers to destroy: it couldn't be razed to the ground like a field of corn. It was also easier to grow than oats or barley. With each poor cereal harvest in Britain in the eighteenth century, potatoes grew in popularity until, by the end of the next century, it was the main vegetable crop in the country. (The Second World War gave the potato a further boost: the 'Dig for Victory' campaign in Britain – an initiative designed to compensate for lack of imports by means of home-growing – led to a doubling of the acreage devoted to production.) It is now the staple food of two-thirds of the world's population and, along with rice, wheat and maize, one of the most important food crops on the planet.

The early Peruvian farmers worshipped a potato goddess, depicted with a potato plant in each hand. It seems that their faith was well placed.

The Quest for the Best

CHICKEN STOCK

We researched what are considered to be the best chickens you can buy in the UK and came up with five: Label Anglais, Ark Chicken, Linda Dick, Ellel free-range and Waitrose organic free-range. Even before cooking, the differences between them were marked: one was a monster almost as big as a turkey; another had the attractive mellow yellow skin of a corn-fed bird. Some had a long breast shape, others a fat one. They all went in the oven for five hours at a low temperature, though at this stage the temperature wasn't the key detail: they just needed to be cooked to the same degree so that I was testing like for like, with the aim of finding the right combination of flavour, juiciness and texture.

These chickens were unlikely to taste like any of the usual fare. A properly reared bird has done a lot of running around, searching for stuff to eat. It has worked for its food and the workout gives it muscle, which results in a denser, tougher bird with a much gamier flavour. It can come as a surprise if you're not used to it (some people prize chicken precisely because it's bland: another example of how subjective perfection is), but for me it's how chicken is supposed to taste – and I reckon it's a far better eating experience.

My expectations were borne out in the tasting. All the chickens were superior to most of what you find on supermarket shelves: they had a genuine flavour, a decent meatiness to them. One even had a touch of almond in the flavouring, which was enjoyable, if a little weird. Tasting made it clear to me that it was the combination of flavour and texture that was important: the flesh of some of the birds tasted great but was too loose. Label Anglais had neither the strongest flavour nor the densest flesh, but in combination it proved the most satisfying to eat.

So, Label Anglais was our benchmark, but this test was always going to be a game of two halves. I'd wanted to try out British chickens partly because it's important to seek out and support local producers

– that's how a good food culture grows – and partly because it's always worth exploring beyond the products with an established reputation. Sometimes you stumble across something little known but truly exceptional. Nonetheless, I'd always known that, no matter which chicken impressed the most in our taste test, there would still have to be a showdown between it and the titan of the chicken world – the legendary Bresse. Now the moment had come. I had to travel through the countryside around Lyon to find out more about a chicken widely considered to be the very best.

THE CULT OF THE CHICKEN

The queen of chickens, the chicken of kings.
Jean-Anthelme Brillat-Savarin

I'd visited the area where Bresse chickens are reared, and I'd cooked and eaten them loads of times. It is undoubtedly a superb chicken. But either things had changed since I was last here, or maybe I'd simply underestimated the *poulet*'s pull. The cult of the chicken seemed to be growing …

This came home to me as we pulled off Autoroute 39 into a service station and were confronted by a chicken sculpture four storeys high in tubular steel. It was both monumental and surreal. (Imagine exiting the M5 near Cheddar Gorge and coming face to face with a gigantic fibreglass wedge of cheese.)

The same level of devotion continued inside. The place was decorated with photographs of Bresse chickens happily running through green fields. In the shop you could buy the chicken in many forms – on T-shirts, oven gloves, aprons, candlesticks, tea towels, or in the flesh, ready for cooking. There was even a postcard of the tubular steel chicken, as though it had already become a tourist sight to tell the folks back home about.

As it turned out, this service station really is on the tourist trail. The A39 is a major route south for Swiss, Germans and Belgians, and many deliberately plan their journey so that their lunchbreak falls in the department of Ain and they can get their fill of the fabled Bresse chicken. (It's the only stop on the motorway that sells it.) The area manager, Laurent Berthelin (his blue tie was printed with little chickens; I wondered if you could get that in the shop too), told me that they sell 15,000 chickens a year – more than any other place in France.

'It's one of those ideas that now seems such an obvious winner, but when we started selling Bresse chickens in our cafeteria a few years ago, we had no idea if it would take off or not. Even though the chicken is far cheaper here than in Britain, it's still an expensive bird, and we had to gamble on whether people would pay that bit more for a quality product. Now we're selling forty to fifty a day.'

Although L'Arche cafeteria had the same inexpensive furnishings and signage of motorway service stations everywhere, exposed beams gave it a homely, rustic look. The food on offer also marked it out as being different from most such places: there was a wide range of cheeses, a well-made *crème brûlée* and several sorts of bread. I caught sight of the baguettes as I joined the chicken queue and was instantly transported back to childhood memories of picnics in Windsor Great Park, the high point of which was roast chicken slipped into a buttered baguette. I bought bread and chicken and, as the hot, savoury aromas tormented me, set about recreating that memory. It may not have been the best-cooked chicken I've ever had, but it was a wonderful reconnection to the past. How often does a service station manage that?

COQ AU CHAUVIN

I want there to be no peasant in my kingdom so poor that he is unable to have a chicken in his pot every Sunday.
Henri IV of France

Part of the Bresse chicken's appeal comes from the packaging with which nature has obligingly furnished it. With its red comb, snowy white feathers and blue legs, it is decked out in the colours of the *tricolore*. What Frenchman (or, for that matter, foodie or Francophile) could resist? It certainly looks good, but I wanted to find out why it tastes so good, so I visited Christian Chotard's farm near the village of Viriat.

As I arrived I passed a line of men in green army fatigues with shotguns slung over their shoulders and bright orange caps on their heads (presumably to make sure they didn't end up in the guns' sights by accident). They were farmers hunting boar and, had they seen any, they might have made a mockery of the otherwise peaceful scene. As it was, they simply stood waiting for hours at the forest's edge, patient and impassive, as dusk gradually faded them to grey. They were a reminder that I was on different territory: country rules applied here, where the death of animals is a way of life.

However, Christian's farm, Bon Repos, was far from forbidding. There was, of course, a sculpture of a chicken in the front garden, though this one was carved from wood and quite manageable in scale. The buildings had a pleasing lopsidedness to them that suggested great age. Clusters of sweetcorn hung from the balconies, and bushy wisteria twisted up the sturdy beams. The neatly tended plots of geraniums and marigolds marked this out as a well-run farm that paid attention to details. No space was wasted: in the earth around the outbuildings both curled and flatleaf parsley were cultivated.

Like the hunters, Christian was dressed in military green. He has been rearing Bresse chickens for twenty-five years, as did his father and grandfather before him, and he often wins prizes at Les Glorieuses, the Bresse chicken farmers' equivalent of the Oscars. Standing on the stony track that runs through his property, I asked him what gave the chicken its marvellous flavour.

'The Bresse area is small – maybe 100 kilometres by 50 – but unique,' he said. 'There's almost no chalk in the ground here, so the birds' skeletons are thinner and lighter. You get more meat for your money but a more fragile bird. And there's a lot of acid in the soil which acts like a bleach, whitening the feathers and making the feet pale blue.'

He opened the door of a roomy plywood shed strewn with straw. Panicky chatter filled the air as chicks scattered at our intrusion. Too young to have acquired their patriotic colouring, they were pale yellow with a slightly unkempt look, as though they'd just woken up, but already they looked energetic.

'These birds are two weeks old,' Christian told me. 'They'll stay in here another two weeks because they're still little babies and can't stand the cold. Then they'll go outside.'

'They look pretty healthy already. What are they fed on?'

'While they're inside they get a standard chicken feed. Then comes a big change – they eat what they can find in the grass.'

We looked over to where chickens wandered around tussocky fields, alongside long-bodied, creamy-coloured Charolais cattle. The fencing was deliberately set high enough that the chickens could wander where they liked. They stayed here because they wanted to.

'An unusual landscape like this one creates a very particular ecosystem,' continued Christian. 'The soil that the birds peck in, the herbage, the insects – it's all very different from the neighbouring areas, and it's what gives the Bresse chicken its distinctive taste.'

In acknowledgement of the formative interplay of bird and environment, the Bresse chicken was awarded *appellation d'origine contrôlée* (AOC) status in 1957, and its production is now regulated as rigorously as that of any wine or cheese. 'Each bird must have plenty of space to strut around in – at least 10 square metres,' Christian explained, 'and they must spend the majority of their life outdoors, to grow up healthy and get the benefits of the Bresse soil. Chicks have to be put out at five weeks old at the latest, and stay out for a minimum of nine weeks. So, except at night, when they're shut in to protect them from foxes, the chickens roam free. The only supplement to their diet is maize plus a little wheat and milk. Nothing else. Certainly no antibiotics, chemicals or hormones. Then, at the very end, the last one or maybe two weeks, we put them in wooden coops – *épinettes* – to fatten them up.'

The chicken that fulfils this regime ends up decorated like a war hero: an identity ring on the left leg bears the name and address of the rearer; the coveted AOC red diamond label adorns its body; and a tricolour metal seal with the name of the dispatcher is attached to the neck. There are about 400 farmers rearing birds in this fashion, producing about 1,500,000 per year, most of which are sold in France (export accounts for a mere 5 per cent).

LES HALLES DE LYON

Later, I got to see plenty of these extravagantly bedecked chickens in Lyon's foremost food market, Les Halles.

I had been here before, of course. Before I opened the Fat Duck I spent years teaching myself the principles of classic French cuisine, and I would visit France each summer to build on what I'd learned. With its famous chefs – Alain Chapel, Paul Bocuse and Georges Blanc – and its reputation as one of the gastronomic capitals of the world, Lyon had been an important stopping-off point for me during my summer travels. I had fond memories of the fantastic range of produce on offer in Les Halles, particularly at Mère Richard, which sold some of the best cheese in the country. I wondered whether it would all be as good as I remembered.

The area had another special significance for me: barely an hour from here was L'Oustau de Baumanière, the restaurant that had first opened my eyes – and tastebuds – to the wonders of cooking. Nestling at the foot of a tower of rock, amid olive groves, with the air carrying wafts of lavender and the whirr of cicadas, it had offered total sensory overload. Waiters poured sauces into soufflés, carved legs of lamb at the table or crunched over the gravel wheeling chariot-sized cheese trolleys. The sommelier, a formidable figure with a handlebar moustache and leather apron, presented the wine list as though it were a stone tablet from Cecil B. DeMille's *The Ten Commandments*. As if to match this solemnity, the wine glasses were a foot high. I'd never experienced anything like it. Perhaps that's why it had such a dramatic, life-changing effect on me: as far as fine dining went, I was a blank canvas. L'Oustau sketched out my future. On that day, cooking got into my blood, and there was nothing I could do about it.

Les Halles is situated in a bland, unprepossessing part of Lyon, between a Guggenheim-style car park and the anonymous tower blocks of hotels and banks. The squat two-storey concrete building with its sliding glass doors gives no indication of the wonderland within. Even so, it seemed somehow tidier and trendier than I remembered. But as I wandered up and down the market's three long passageways, I could see that the place still had the air of an Eastern bazaar. A jumble of small premises – bakers, butchers, game merchants, charcuteries, pâtisseries – were squeezed in together, each vying for attention and setting out elaborate displays of produce to tempt you. Pyramids of Pouligny and Valençay cheese gave way to the crescent curlicues of langouste-tail halves or the iridescent green of ducks' heads. Different aromas – aniseed, cumin – waxed and waned enticingly as I walked. La Mère Richard was still there, as were some of the quirkier places that add to the market's character: Chez Georges appealed to me, with its six types of oyster and counter in the form of a boat.

This wasn't just a trip down memory lane, however. I was here to visit the Boucherie Trolliet. Maurice Trolliet is a master butcher who really knows his craft: in 1986 he won the hugely prestigious Meilleur Ouvrier de France award. His was the place to buy a Bresse chicken – and perhaps pick up some advice as well.

Maurice's shop is professional, formal and discreet. On the façade ornate neon handwriting picks out his surname. Below it, five butchers wearing long white aprons and black tunics with *tricolore* edging trimmed meat with the speed and precision of surgeons, placing it on the counter wrapped in folds of thick waxy paper. They were all busy, and their customers knew a thing or two about meat as well. Transactions were accompanied by passionate, informed discussion about the quality of the produce and how it should be prepared.

Maurice got down to business in brisk, no-nonsense fashion, reaching across the counter to put a dead bird in my hands. The head lolled over the end of my palm; it still had its fan of white plumage topped by a brilliant red comb. There was no doubting this had once been a bird: it was about as far from the supermarket's anonymous, pale, prepacked meat-blob as you are likely to get.

'The female chicken has a finer flesh,' Maurice advised. 'Less *ramasse*. How do you say that in English?'

'Dense?'

'Yes, compact. The males toughen up as they chase the women around. So here we sell only the female.'

The bird I was holding had tell-tale yellow spots beneath its skin – signs of fat deposits that had built up and spread through the flesh. They would give a marvellously rich texture to the meat.

I handed over 50 euros and Maurice wrapped the bird in paper and popped it in a natty Trolliet bag. It was certainly expensive, and it would be much dearer in Britain. But it's a very special product, and proper care costs money. It's an animal, not a mass-produced bit of plastic. You're paying for the time and care, the passion and humanity and history that go into the farming of a perfect chicken.

And there's no substitute for that.

By now the queue around the *boucherie* was several deep and the hubbub of voices had increased. Everyone seemed to know everyone else, as though this were a small village within the city. The customers were all sorts: old couples for whom this had become a ritual part of each day's entertainment, fastidiously dressed gourmets, families with kids larking about or sucking lollipops. The children might look a little bored but, without even realising it, they were gaining a valuable education in food: seeing the proud care and knowledge of the retailers; hearing their parents' confident negotiations for exactly what they wanted. This was how they, in their turn, would be able to come to the market and partake in passionate, informed discussion with master butchers and fishmongers and cheesemakers. This was how the great French culinary tradition stayed alive. It was encouraging to watch, and I could only hope that kids were getting equally bored in farmers' markets all over Britain.

THE BLANC GENERATION

I'd followed the chicken from green field to butcher's slab. It seemed right to finish what I'd started and track it to the table. And although there are many famous and talented chefs in and around Lyon, there was really only one person to talk to about cooking the Bresse chicken: Georges Blanc.

The Blanc family enjoys a 130-year-old tradition of gastronomy and has practically become a national institution. In 1872 Jean-Louis Blanc and his wife, Virginie, created a small *auberge* catering mainly to the poultry dealers who came to Vonnas every Thursday for the market. It was their daughter-in-law, Elisa, who put the town on the map, creating food that drew in people from miles around and earning two Michelin stars in the process. By the early 1930s the name Mère Blanc was famous throughout France, and the celebrated gastronome Curnonsky had called her 'the best cook in the world'. Georges Blanc's parents, Jean and Paulette, maintained both the quality and the tradition before handing over to him in 1968. Georges has since not only earned a third star but also embarked on a magnificently ambitious historical building project based around the *auberge*.

In Lyon it had been raining fit to bust, so the camera crew wrapped early and we headed over to Vonnas to check in to Blanc's Résidence des Saules hotel. From the balcony of my room I had a great view of some of Georges's achievements. Before me lay the market square – a patch of sandy earth that I could imagine was a favourite with boules players – bordered by two stately ranks of plane trees and a small river. At the far end was the solid brick of the original 1872 *auberge*, now transformed into the Restaurant Georges Blanc. This was just one of fifteen buildings around the square that Georges had lovingly restored to create the spirit of a *village gourmand*: '*Vivant, gai, harmonieux et protégé, illustrant "l'art de bien vivre".*' It's a kind of living museum and homage to the past – a little insight into the way life was lived. And I'd say that the sense of context and tradition that Georges manages to evoke serves only to increase your enjoyment and appreciation of the food he cooks.

LIKE MAMA USED TO MAKE

The following morning I got another small insight into the way life was once lived – at least in the Blanc household while Georges was growing up. He had generously agreed to show me the *poulet à la crème* that his mother used to make every Sunday. And, in concession to British tastes and traditions, he'd agreed to prepare a roast chicken as well.

It had stopped raining. I walked across the square and entered the restaurant a few minutes early so that I could have a look round. As befits a great chef who is part of a long-standing tradition, Georges's establishment is covered with testimonials from satisfied customers. In the lobby black and white photos of Catherine Deneuve, Jean-Paul Belmondo, Alain Delon, Yves Montand and Johnny Halliday graced the walls, along with handwritten words of praise. Rowan Atkinson and Nicole Kidman were there as well. Richard Burton declared, soberly, 'Many thanks for your wonderful hospitality.' There was a photo of Bill Clinton, who, though I didn't realise it at the time, was to become a kind of leitmotif for my travels; wherever there was good food to be had, Bill had got there first, and had his picture taken for good measure. In Georges's case the Clinton connection came about when he was asked to cook for a G7 meeting in Lyon and came up with Bresse chicken with roast garlic and a foie gras sauce. The president apparently asked for seconds, which Georges claims as his finest moment.

I turned to discover I'd been caught snooping by Georges himself. He has a schoolboyish air, and the glint in his eye suggested he enjoyed catching me off guard. He led me through to his kitchen, a spacious warren of interconnecting white-tiled rooms, where chefs in tall pleated hats were frying ceps and snipping bay leaves into more pleasing shapes.

'For you, Heston, Sunday dinner is roast chicken and roast potatoes.' As if to illustrate this point, Georges put an onion into a chicken's cavity and placed the bird in a pot, which he then slid into an oven preheated to 160°C. 'But I'm from a different culture. Of course, we too had the family meal on Sunday. It was a great ritual, and *poulet à la crème* was the main course. When I was young, every Sunday was this. Do you want to see how it was done?'

Hmmm … did I want a three-star chef to cook his traditional Sunday dinner for me – a dinner that was part of his heritage and had many memories for him, that had been enjoyed and perfected by four generations of legendary French chefs, and that contained possibly the world's finest chicken?

It wasn't a tough call.

Georges put butter in a copper pan and let it froth before adding the two parts of each leg plus salt and pepper. 'I don't support an excess of salt,' he declared, 'but I do like a lot of pepper.' The legs began to brown. 'It's very important to have the right coloration because … how do you say in English, *le sucre*?'

'The sugars?'

'Yes, in this recipe the caramelised sugars give the sauce its flavour. I use no stock.'

The butter was foaming vigorously around the panful of chicken pieces. They were already a lovely shiny brown colour, like the patina on polished pale wood. Georges had kept back the neck and wingtips because they'd take less time to cook. He added them now. 'To give more *sucre*.'

Half an onion studded with a clove or two went in the pan. A head of garlic with the top lopped off. Then more onions, this time cut into smaller pieces. A little flour was spooned in, along with some chopped mushrooms.

Georges is softly spoken and gentle but his voice acquires a sharp edge of authority when he's in the kitchen. Instructions were rapped out whenever an ingredient wasn't to hand. There was a brief, tense moment when someone mislaid the white wine, but it was soon found. A glass or so was poured into the pan, sending up a marvellous smell of caramelised chicken and alcohol. By now the chicken had a darker patina. The onion and garlic were flecked with brown too. Georges turned the pieces, leaned low over the pan and wafted the aromas towards him – perhaps having his own Proustian madeleine moment.

'Has this recipe changed over time?' I wondered out loud.

'Never. Less flour maybe, so the dish is less heavy,' Georges said. But cooking the dish is a kind of revisitation of the past, and he kept remembering details he'd forgotten, little changes that he and others had made.

'There didn't used to be mushrooms or white wine. They'd cook the chicken pieces with the roux, then drain them and add cream. Cream mixed with a yolk. And a drop of lemon. Now it's different. The acidity is introduced at the beginning, with the white wine. We don't use lemon at all.'

He picked up a big glass jug of cream and poured in the lot. 'No water or stock. Just white wine and cream. Very natural. So the sauce has only the taste of the chicken and its aromas.' He slurped a couple of spoonfuls. *'Oui, c'est bon.'*

A touch more seasoning and it was left to cook for thirty-five minutes.

In the meantime, the roast chicken was ready. It sat there, a beautiful pale gold, with its blue legs sticking up out of the pot in undignified fashion. It still had the ring on its leg, as if to remind me that, even when cooked, this bird was an aristocrat.

Georges lifted it respectfully out of the pot and let the juices drain off before setting it down on the chopping board. He carved and placed the pieces artfully around the plate: leg, two slices of breast and one of the 'oysters'. He ladled over some juice and a handful of girolle mushrooms. 'For me, it's important to use a male bird. The leg is more interesting – less tender but with more meat; a more interesting texture.'

Sharing memories of roast chicken with French chef Georges Blanc.

'What is it about the Bresse chicken that makes it so special?' I asked.

'The price,' Georges deadpanned. 'OK, seriously. The marbling – the fattiness – gives it taste, just as it would in red meat. In the Bresse chicken the fat is nicely spread out rather than in big deposits. And the fact that it has been running around means it has nice dense flesh. The diet too is good: what it gets from the ground gives it more flavour.'

'And roast chicken is such a wonderful family dish,' I said. 'It stirs up emotions and memories of sitting around a table together. Everybody has strong opinions – male or female bird, leg or breast, white meat or dark, skin on or off – often for no apparent reason, they've just developed over time and out of habit. It's great.'

'Yes,' Georges agreed, 'and the quality and taste are perfect for me. It's a simple dish. That's the beauty of it. Even the juice to go with it is simple – no stock, just a drop of vinegar at the last moment.'

Georges was right: simplicity was the key here. He backed up a conviction that had been growing in me since we first arrived in Lyon to investigate the Bresse chicken. Many farmers and butchers devoted their lives to a careful rearing and preparation of the bird, taking great pains to avoid a production-line approach, in the belief that it benefited both the chicken and the consumer. In this context, I felt, the recipe I developed should be an extension of their efforts, celebrating the basic flavours they had worked hard to produce. In other contexts I might attempt something extremely complicated, but here it seemed right to keep it simple, keep it pure. Let the chicken speak for itself.

We turned our attention back to *poulet à la crème*. Georges took a carving fork and fished out the pieces, giving each a final sloosh around in the juices before placing it in a heavy black cast-iron pot. He grabbed a ladle and a conical sieve, which he held over the pot. The thick creamy sauce was scooped into the sieve and allowed to trickle gradually over the chicken pieces.

'You know, Heston, it's very interesting for me to revisit the tradition in my cuisine, and to change little things. People come to my restaurants for the local specialities and for authenticity. It's very important for me – as I hope it will be for my sons, Alexandre and Frédéric, who are both chefs too, and for my grandson, who already shows an interest in cuisine – to preserve the classic traditions of the area. Because we have our roots here in the Bresse region, where people are still very close to the land and its products, the good cuisine that comes from it.'

It was a beautiful sentiment. French cuisine is in good hands with people like Georges around. I too hoped that an awareness of tradition would inform the cooking of his sons and grandson.

The sauce had made its way through the sieve. It was time to sample Sunday dinner in the Blanc household. *Poulet à la crème* – a real example of what Georges was talking about: good cuisine that comes from the region.

He set out two white plates and placed a leg on each. Cream was gently spooned over each piece. It ran down the meat and spread out across the plate – simple, decorative, tasty-looking and very rich. You'd need some form of potato with it or, better still, bread, to mop up every last drop.

'With this dish,' said Georges, 'it's important that the meat doesn't colour too much or it starts to harden and ends up dry.'

The first plunge of my knife told me there was no danger of that here. The flesh simply fell away as I cut. The sauce had a lovely natural aroma, almost a perfume to it, and it did indeed contain a marvellous roasted flavour, the result of Georges's careful browning of the chicken in butter. We both put far too much in our mouths at once, and the director complained that he couldn't understand what we were saying.

'So, Heston,' said Georges, once he'd swallowed, 'now you know not only how the Bresse chicken feeds, but how he cooks as well. In that spirit, to finish with, I'd like to show you what we offer in my restaurant. I call it "La Bresse en Fête", a celebration of the chicken to show that every part of it is good. This is what a third of our customers order.'

He laid before me a sequence of six beautifully presented dishes. I especially liked *Le sot l'y laisse et l'huitre creuse, dans une nage mousseuse et iodée avec des soissons* – a preparation of oysters and chicken oysters – and *Le poulet et la grenouille: duo de cuisses entre Bresse et Dombes 'façon blanquette' sans crème, au vin jaune et cerfeuil* – in which chicken and frogs' legs were cooked together. I was attracted by the play on words that underpinned each dish, but they were more than just witty flourishes. Both were light and beautifully balanced, and enshrined the respect for the region that Georges was so passionate about (the frogs are a speciality of neighbouring Dombes). It was marvellous cuisine – playful, informative and precisely executed.

SPUDS-I-LIKE 1

What I say is that, if a fellow really likes potatoes, he must be a pretty decent sort of fellow.
A.A. Milne, *Not That It Matters*

I'd got some way towards sourcing the perfect chicken. Now I needed roast potatoes to go with it. For most of us, potatoes can be divided into two groups according to use. You need a dry, floury variety for mash, roast and chips, and a waxy, creamy one for salads, gratins and purée. So Maris Piper and King Edward for mash; Charlotte and Belle de Fontenay for purée. *Sorted.*

When I first became obsessed with the idea of the perfect chip, however, I'd had to go into more detail. I spent years researching complicated questions such as starch conversion and dry matter (I even persuaded my wife, Susanna, to sneak around the local supermarket with a bucket of water, testing the dry-matter content of different varieties). Eventually I'd come up with what I wanted, and other people seemed to like them too. Even so, I felt as though I'd barely tapped the potato's potential, so the fact that I had to develop recipes for chips, mash and roast seemed like a good excuse to take a fresh look at this versatile vegetable.

I drove over to the Norfolk distribution centre of MBM in Little Snoring. (How many times had someone described it as a sleepy little village, I wondered. I decided not to try it out on my hosts.) MBM is one of the biggest suppliers of potatoes in the country and, to judge by the commitment of its staff, one of the best. Peter Pattrick, Tom Dixon and Claire Harrison have a passion for potatoes that at first seems almost comic, but their enthusiasm quickly wins you over. (It's strange that when an Italian waxes lyrical about a tomato it seems fitting and dramatic, whereas vaunting the humble spud only gets a laugh. We've no real vocabulary for talking about food in this country; we've not argued and defended and deliberated over the dinner table the way Europeans have. It's surely one of the reasons our cuisine has comparatively little fixed identity or tradition.)

The boardroom table at MBM was covered with crates containing different sorts of potato. The huge variety in shape, size and colour was a sorry reminder of how small the choice is at any local supermarket. Alongside the familiar, golden-globed King Edwards and Maris Pipers were menhir-like Pink Fir Apples and finger-sized Anyas with their pitted skins. Juliette, a smoother version of Anya, lay next to Purple Star – with its purple veining – and the deep-red flesh of Highland Burgundy Red. The names seemed determined to add a lustre of romance to the spud, and often sounded more like exotic butterflies than potatoes: there was a Blue Belle and a Pentland Dell, not forgetting Lady Claire, Lady Rosetta and Lady Olympia. (This naming isn't always successful: BF15 sounds to me more like a fighter-jet than a potato, and the Dutch have created a variety called Arsey, which may have limited success in English-speaking markets …)

Before long, Peter, Tom and Claire were trying to convert me to their particular favourites, filling me in on the ducal history of the Highland Burgundy Red or brandishing a Juliette and insisting, 'This'll make a wonderful Joël Robuchon mash.' But there was more to consider here than just varieties. We all donned heavy Day-Glo reflective jackets and stepped outside to explore the equally tricky question of storage.

We were surrounded by pine trees and silence, interrupted occasionally by the yelp of a pheasant. Tom Dixon and I walked between towers of slatted wooden crates towards the metal freight containers where varieties for testing were kept, and he outlined some of the complexities involved in keeping potatoes.

'You've got to remember that a potato's a living thing. Put it in the ground and it'll grow new ones. It's not dead, it's just dormant. And that's how we've got to keep it. To achieve this we need to consider, first and foremost, the temperature. Keep them too warm and potatoes'll sprout or go bad. Keep them too cold, though, and the starch in them begins to break down into its constituent parts, mainly the sugars sucrose and glucose. Naturally, if you roast potatoes with a high concentration of sugars, caramelisation will occur, browning the spuds and making them bitter. So you need to store them at 7–9°C.'

On shelves running along one side of the container were plastic trays holding new types of potato. 'We're constantly testing new varieties to see if they'll give as good quality as the established types,' said Tom. 'One of the most important considerations is what is known as "dry matter". Although it looks like a solid lump, most of a potato – about three-quarters – is water. The rest is dry matter, most of which is starch. The dry matter is what gives a potato its flavour, and managing the starch content during cooking is what makes the difference between good or bad roast, mash and chips. Floury potatoes have a high dry matter, waxy ones have less.'

Tom told me that many things contribute to the amount of dry matter in a spud: the soil and climate – especially the rainfall – are influential, as are the amount of light and irrigation. Potatoes take on a particular character depending on where they're farmed.

Since dry matter gives a potato more flavour, I was hoping to be able to roast one with a high dry-matter content. So we went over to the labs to see if Tom could find me something suitable by weighing the dry matter of various potatoes on MBM's special scales. He explained that, in order to get an accurate reading, we had to rumble the spuds to remove their skins.

'OK,' I said. 'Let's get ready to rumble.' (I couldn't resist.)

The machine kicked into life – a throaty barrage of noise that sounded as though someone had filled a washing machine with rocks and turned it on. Once skinned, the potatoes were placed in a basket suspended from the scales and lowered into water.

Using Tom's matchless advice and his magic scales, I arrived at a quintet of potatoes that held the promise of a good roast and would allow me to experiment with dry-matter content as well. The final five looked like this:

	% dry matter
Lady Claire	21.8
Daisy	21.1
Maris Piper	21.9
King Edward	20.5
Yukon Gold	20.3

ROAST TEST

With roast potatoes, as with chips, I was looking for a crust with a delicate crunch, and a fine fluffy centre. I asked two chefs at the Hind's Head, Mary-Ellen McTague and Dominic Chapman, to roast the five contenders; then the three of us tasted them.

Lady Claire had a good-looking crust but it was just too tough, even a bit leathery. It didn't give way with the kind of ease you need in a perfect roast potato. It turned out to be the first of several to be let down by their crust. Daisy too was tough and chewy on the outside, and had a starchy centre. Its flavour was bland and had no character.

Even at first glance, it was quite obvious that the roasted Maris Piper was in a league of its own. The crust had fissured a little round the edges, allowing the oil to penetrate the surface and produce a

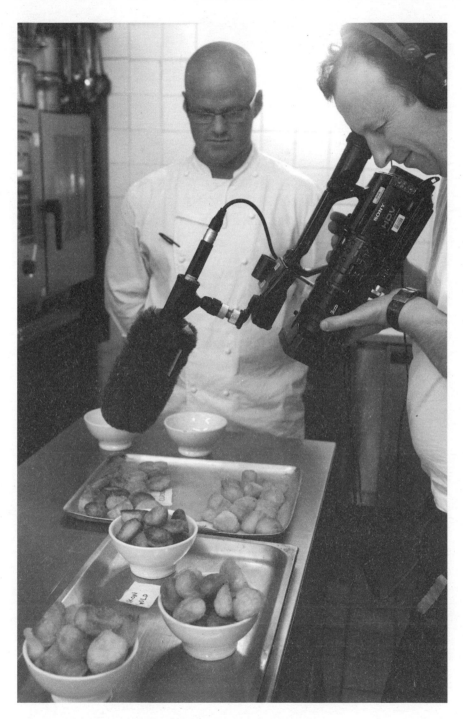

My potato taste test comes under the scrutiny of the director.

deliciously crunchy, glass-like crust. And so it proved to be. The oil gave the potato a real juiciness that was the perfect contrast to the flavourful inside. This was the benchmark the others had to beat.

King Edward was close: it probably had a better overall flavour than Maris Piper. But a perfect skin is part of the point of a roast potato and the King Edward just didn't have it. There was none of the Maris Piper's juiciness, probably because the skin had broken up less. It was altogether chewier – the wrong kind of textural companion to a fluffy interior.

Yukon Gold's crust had gone off-puttingly dark, far darker than any of the others, and had a slight bitter note, as though the potato was almost scorched. Since there was virtually nothing to choose between its dry-matter content and that of the King Edward, something else had to be at work here. I wondered whether this example of Yukon Gold had developed a high glucose content, perhaps due to bad storage. In any case, the result was a crust with no crunch – a disaster in a roast potato. It would be Maris Piper calling the tune.

Roast Chicken & Roast Potatoes Serves 4

A raw chicken is about 80 per cent water. Cooking it is basically a battle to hang on to some of that moisture, so that you end up with a deliciously succulent bird. In this recipe, two techniques help achieve that aim: brining and low-temperature cooking.

Brining is a great way of tenderising the flesh and helping it to stay moist at the same time. The salt alters the proteins in such a way that they hold on to moisture more effectively. The result is a much juicier chicken – especially if, as here, some of the bird's own juices are injected back into its body.

The higher the cooking temperature, the more water is lost. (Think of how water leaves a sponge when it's squeezed: heat has a similar effect on protein fibres, causing them to contract and crowd together, forcing out the water between them.) A chicken that has reached an internal temperature of 70°C/160°F will have lost a large percentage of its water. Even at 60°C/140°F, a lot of water will be gone, but this lower temperature manages the best balance of juiciness and a superbly tender texture. It takes a little longer, but it's worth it.

A third technique – inspired by the ducks hanging up to dry in the windows of Chinese restaurants – adds something special to the chicken's texture. Blanching the bird and then letting its surface dry out leads to a marvellous crispy skin when cooked.

My Sunday lunch would team chicken with broccoli and glazed carrots, so I've included recipes for these as well, which can be adapted to other vegetables. The broccoli recipe is also suitable for leeks, green beans and Romaine lettuce, while the carrot recipe is great for many root vegetables – celeriac, swede, parsnips – as well as asparagus.

Special equipment
Oven thermometer, digital probe, large tongs, baster with a needle attachment

Timing

This needs to be begun the day before, but mainly in order to sit the chicken in a pot of brine for six hours and then quickly blanch it and leave overnight in the fridge. On the day, the long, slow cooking and resting of the chicken gives plenty of time to prepare the veg *and* mingle with your guests or family.

For the chicken

1.5kg poulet de Bresse or good-quality free-range chicken _ approx. 350–375g table salt _ 100g unsalted butter _ 2–3 tbsp groundnut oil _ freshly ground black pepper

For the potatoes

1kg large Maris Piper potatoes _ olive oil (enough to fill the roasting tray to a depth of just under 1cm) _ 4 cloves of garlic _ 1 generous bunch of fresh rosemary _ table salt

For the carrots

12 large carrots (about 500g) _ 50g unsalted butter _ table salt and freshly ground black pepper

For the broccoli

1 large head of broccoli _ 50g unsalted butter _ table salt and freshly ground black pepper

BRINING AND ROASTING THE CHICKEN

1. First, prepare a brine for the chicken. Get a large saucepan or casserole that the chicken can sit in comfortably, and place the chicken in it. Measure how much water you would need to cover the chicken, then weigh out 8 per cent of that volume in table salt.* Remove the chicken and refrigerate. Tip out the water and refill the pot with the same amount of fresh water. Add the salt, then place the pot over a high heat until the salt has dissolved. Leave the brine to cool completely.

---

* Generally, grams and millilitres are interchangeable, so if, for example, it takes 500ml of water to cover your chicken, think of this as 500g, then calculate 8 per cent of that and weigh out that amount of salt. (Where pinpoint accuracy is required – as in the water for pizza dough – it's best to measure in grams.)

2. Meanwhile, remove the chicken's wings at the first joint. Trim away the neck and feet, if present, and discard. Reserve the wings to make a buttery juice for the finished bird (see step 9).

3. Remove the chicken's wishbone, in order to make carving easier (unless its removal is going to disappoint children who are looking forward to the fun of tugging it for luck!). To do this, lift up the flap of skin covering the neck cavity, then run the blade of a small, sharp knife along the wishbone on each side of the V-shaped cavity. It can then be eased away from the breastbone and carefully pulled off the chicken.

4. Put the chicken back into the pot of brine. Cover and refrigerate for 6 hours.

5. Remove the chicken from the fridge and pour off the brine. (Brining makes the skin quite fragile, so handle it gently.) Rinse the chicken under running cold water. Return it to the pot and fill with fresh cold water. Leave it to soak for an hour, changing the water every 15 minutes to wash off the salt.

6. Lift the chicken from the pot. Wash out the pot, then refill it with fresh cold water and bring to the boil. Fill a large bowl or basin with cold water and ice. Dunk the chicken in the boiling water for 30 seconds. Remove and plunge into the ice-cold water. Bring the pot of water back to the boil and repeat both steps. The skin will now look puckered and slightly webbed.

7. Dry the chicken with kitchen paper. Place on a cooling rack with a tray underneath. Loosely cover with a breathable fabric, such as muslin or even a new J cloth, and leave in the fridge overnight to dry.

8. Preheat the oven to 60°C/140°F, using an oven thermometer to check it. Sit the chicken in a roasting tin and cook until the internal temperature of the bird when probed has reached 60°C/140°F. (This should take about 4–6 hours.) At this point, the chicken will have a pale white, slightly anaemic appearance. It won't look browned.

9. Remove the chicken from the oven and leave it to rest for 1 hour. Meanwhile, roughly chop the reserved chicken wings. Heat the butter in a small pan over a low to medium heat, add the chopped wings and fry until the butter smells nutty and has turned dark

brown. Pass the wings and butter through a fine sieve into a bowl. Discard the wings and reserve the buttery juices.

10. To brown the chicken, heat a large frying pan over a high heat for 10 minutes. Add the groundnut oil and, when it starts smoking, the chicken. Use a pair of tongs to turn the chicken so that it browns all over. (Be careful not to burn yourself.) Remove from the pan.

11. Use the baster to suck up some of the buttery juices. Push the needle through the skin, into the flesh of the chicken, and release the juices. Carefully remove the needle and refill. Repeat at several points around the chicken – be really generous with this – after which it is ready to carve, season and serve.

ROASTING THE POTATOES

1. Preheat the oven to 190°C/375°F/Gas 5.

2. Wash the potatoes thoroughly and then peel them. Reserve the peelings and tie them in a muslin bag. Cut the potatoes into quarters (the quartering's important because it's the edges that get nice and crunchy: that's why reasonably large potatoes are needed for this recipe) and leave them in a bowl under running water for 2–3 minutes (or put in a bowl of water for 15 minutes, changing the water every 5 minutes).

3. Bring a pan of salted water (10g of salt per litre of water) to the boil, add the potatoes and toss in the bag of peelings (they contain lots of flavour). Cook for 20 minutes, or until the potatoes are very soft: take them as far as you can without ending up with potato soup. (It's the fissures that form as the potato breaks up that trap the fat, creating a crunchy crust.)

4. Meanwhile, pour the olive oil into a roasting tray (it needs to be large enough to hold all the potatoes in one layer) and place in the oven.

5. Once the potatoes are soft, drain them in a colander and discard the bag of peelings. Give them a gentle shake to roughen the edges and drive off any remaining drops of water.

6. Put the potatoes in the hot roasting tray and roll them around so that they are completely coated in oil. Roast for an hour or so, until crisp and a lovely golden brown, turning every 20 minutes. Add the garlic and rosemary after 50 minutes.

7. Season with salt and serve.

COOKING THE CARROTS

1. Top, tail and peel the carrots, then cut each one lengthways into 4 long batons. Keep the pieces together and cut diagonally into chunks.
2. Place the carrots in a sauté pan large enough that they can sit in one layer. Season well, add the butter and cover. Place over a low heat and cook for 30–40 minutes, or until the carrots are soft and nicely coated in the butter (which now contains many of the flavour molecules that have leached out of the carrots). Shake the pan regularly to prevent the carrots sticking. If the butter gets too hot and there's a risk of the carrots frying, add a dessertspoon of water.

COOKING THE BROCCOLI

1. Bring a medium-sized pan of salted water to the boil. Prepare a large bowl of ice-cold water.
2. Cut the broccoli into small florets (as far as possible, they should all be the same size), then drop them into the boiling water, bring back to the boil and cook for 1 minute.
3. Remove the broccoli and plunge into the ice-cold water to halt the cooking process. (At this point the broccoli can be stored in the fridge and reheated – as below – just before serving.)
4. To reheat, put the broccoli in a pan along with the butter, salt and pepper and cook over a medium heat for 3–4 minutes or until the stalk yields slightly when a knife is pushed through. Remove from the heat, adjust the seasoning and serve.

Chicken

Tikka Masala

'Chicken tikka masala is now a true
British national dish ... '

Robin Cook, British Foreign Secretary, 19 April 2001

History

It is often said that Indian food in British restaurants bears little resemblance to the real thing: it's a hybrid, concocted by Bangladeshi chefs to cater to British tastes. This line of argument usually presents chicken tikka masala as Exhibit A. Chicken tikka is an Indian dish in which chunks of chicken are marinated in yoghurt and spices, then skewered and cooked in a tandoor oven. Masala, on the other hand, means simply 'a mixture of many spices'. According to *The Oxford English Dictionary*, it got yoked to chicken tikka on British menus in the mid-1970s.

The arranged marriage of tikka and masala is claimed by a number of places – Birmingham, Glasgow, London and, indeed, almost anywhere with a sizeable Asian immigrant population – and explained in a number of ways, ranging from the pragmatic (it's a way to recycle leftover kebabs) to the gastronomic (it's an inventive adaptation of Indian techniques). I particularly liked the suggestion that a troublesome diner demanded gravy with his tandoori chicken, and got a sauce made from a can of tomato soup simmered with various spices.

That story smacks of myth-making: it presents a memorable image that doesn't really stand up under scrutiny. Would a man ask for gravy in an Indian restaurant and, were he that ill informed, would he really have enjoyed what he got? However, disentangling fact from fiction in the tale of chicken tikka masala turns out to be extremely difficult. (And travelling to India, as we'll see, only complicates things further.)

Some dates, however, provide parameters. The Moti Mahal restaurant in Delhi was the first to have a tandoor oven, in 1947. The Gaylord restaurant in Mortimer Street, London, is reported to have had one by 1968, when *The Good Food Guide* stated it was using a 'proper mud oven' to make 'tandoori chicken masal'. Not long after, there was a large influx of Bangladeshi refugees from the 1971 civil war, causing a dramatic growth in the Indian restaurant trade. So from this point an environment existed that was conducive to the evolution of chicken tikka masala. And, although sources insist that CTM is a British dish, it clearly draws its inspiration from Indian dishes such as murg makhani (butter chicken), in which pieces of tandoori chicken are finished off in a buttery tomato sauce.

More than anything else, the debate about chicken tikka masala's creation and cultural identity shows how far it has become big business. Its ascent to the status of British national dish is often attributed to the efforts of Sir Gulam Noon, who began supplying supermarkets with frozen, readymade Indian meals in 1989, and now produces 10 tonnes a day to satisfy demand. Sainsbury's sells more than a million readymade meals each year. Add this to the 23 million portions of CTM cooked and served by Indian restaurants and you have a truly phenomenal output – not bad for a dish often dismissed as inauthentic.

The Quest for the Best

DELHI BELLY

As the plane landed at Indira Gandhi International Airport, I took off my watch and strapped it back on with the six where the twelve should be, neatly converting it to Indian time – five and a half hours ahead. I had never been to India before, and I wondered how much of the experience might need a similar reorientation before it made sense.

Certainly, the drive to the city centre seemed to confirm that a kind of topsy-turviness was at work. Delhi was in the grip of a record heatwave, which meant that, although it was two in the morning, the temperature was still a sweltering 37°C. It was dark, but it felt like day. The traffic too seemed to have ignored nightfall: all around us a maelstrom of trucks, motorbikes, buses and auto-rickshaws surged forward on all sides. In Salman Rushdie's *Haroun and the Sea of Stories* rhymed posters warn of the perils of speed: 'ALL THE DANGEROUS OVERTAKERS END UP SAFE AT UNDERTAKER'S' was my favourite. It wasn't advice that was heeded in Delhi. Everyone drove as though their vehicle was surrounded by some kind of protective forcefield.

Rickshaws and bubblecars puttered in the dead centre of the road, as if the median strip was their sightline, and no amount of headlight-flashing or horn-beeping would budge them. This (I thought to myself later, luxuriating in the embrace of crisp cotton sheets and the hotel's air-conditioning) is a place that won't be confined by demarcation lines. It sprawls – and that's got to add some excitement to researching chicken tikka masala.

TIKKA TUCKER

It has been said that going to Delhi without visiting the Moti Mahal is like going to Agra and not seeing the Taj Mahal, and it's certainly true that the place is a landmark in the history of Indian cooking. Soon after he acquired that tandoor oven in 1947, Kundan Lal Gujral spotted the potential of its fierce, dry heat for cooking not just bread but marinated meat dishes too. The spice mix for tandoori chicken was invented there, as was murg makhani. Clearly, if I wanted to find out about chicken tikka masala, this was the best starting point.

Leaving the time-warp opulence of the Imperial Hotel, the film crew and I crammed into two cars and orbited Connaught Place at speed before slingshotting off down one of its arterial roads. Eventually we pulled in abruptly between a wheeled cart selling shirts and a tricycle with a piled pyramid of melons. Brightly painted buses and rickshaws thundered past me down Netaji Subhash Marg. I left the street's horn symphony and stepped into Moti Mahal's oasis of calm. Overhead, the rippled spears of ashoka leaves provided welcome shade. Beyond, a large courtyard opened out, with flares of bushy Rangoon creeper up the walls and wonky, marble-topped trestle tables set out in rows. The peeling, pistachio-green walls gave an impression of seaside-town optimism, which was reinforced by the pebbled fountain at the centre of the courtyard, reluctantly giving out a thin spray of water. Before this stood the owner, Vinod Chadha. Despite the unbelievable heat, he looked dapper in formal black trousers and a carefully pressed pink shirt.

'Welcome, Heston. Please come and see the kitchen where butter chicken was born.' He put an arm around my shoulders and led me across the courtyard to a small, white-tiled hangar.

If the air outside was like an oven, in here it was genuinely oven-heated – significantly, almost unbearably, hotter than outside. Nonetheless, at three squat, blocky, stone-topped workstations chefs were diligently dicing a scree of purple onions or trimming chickens. In the corner two manned the tandoor, pummelling dough on a board made out of three floor planks. Their tall toques were pieces of white corrugated cardboard wrapped around the head and crudely taped at the back. Sweat was already beginning to shred and frill the card across their foreheads. I thought they looked pretty funny until I realised that I looked as though I'd been swimming fully clothed.

Vinod's head chef, Ajay, had a chicken on a chopping board surrounded by several metal bowls containing pale liquids and pastes, and a couple of red powders. He took a knife to the chicken.

'We are removing the fat from this bird,' Vinod said. 'Then we make cuts right down to the bone.'

The irrepressible Vinod Chadha gives me his personal take on chicken tikka masala.

'That'll let the flavourings get right into the chicken, I guess, and remove some of the moisture?'

'Yes. It'll become tender. Once the slits are done, a paste of raw garlic and ginger is rubbed in.' Ajay flicked five teaspoons of paste on to the bird and smoothed them into the skin. 'Then fine-ground chilli powder.' This was sprinkled all over to give a fine red snowfall, followed by similar sprinkling of salt.

'How hot is the chilli?'

'Oh, it's quite mellow.' A red colouring mix was being scattered on top of the chilli and salt. The chicken looked as if it was covered by a thick layer of volcanic ash. 'Salad oil is now added for basting. It will make it taste better.' Ajay spooned on the oil and began massaging the bird with practised, intrusive hands, making sure every crevice was coated in the lumpy orange paste.

'Why do you do all this separately rather than mixing it all together and applying it in one go?'

'We have to remove the smell of the raw chicken. So it has to be done in stages. The next step is to add some fresh lime.' This was dribbled over the chicken, giving the marinade a slushier appearance. 'And then vinegar on top.'

'What kind?' Vinod passed over the bottle. Delco Non-fruit Vinegar. It had a malty note. I passed it on to Ajay, who poured some into his hand and trickled it over the chicken, then began another vigorous massage. 'So once this is rubbed in, what happens next?'

'It goes in the fridge for twenty-four to thirty-six hours.'

'Have you got one already prepared? Can I see it?'

Eventually, I did get to see the marinated chicken, but only after a series of misunderstandings, which meant that we kept filming the chef retrieving from the fridge the same chicken he had just put in it. 'NO!' the director would admonish each time. The translator would be brought in to explain, in different words, what we wanted. And the whole thing would start all over again. Maybe it was the heat – even Vinod's chin was pearled with water droplets. Maybe something did get lost in translation (though our translator, Neelima, was a 5-foot firebrand who generally got her message across). Maybe, too, self-preservation was at work. On the front of the Moti Mahal was a sign that declared 'We Have No Other Branch'. I had seen the same notice outside several restaurants. It seemed that decent Delhi establishments felt vulnerable to cheap imitators trading off their good name, and that fostered a certain wariness about telling all. Perhaps that was what caused the Keystone Cops chaos that surrounded the filming session.

A day in the fridge gave the chicken a bright orange appearance. 'Now we coat it in a yoghurt batter with sugar, garlic, red chilli and lime juice.' As Vinod talked, Ajay dropped blobby teaspoons of the batter on top and started working them in. The chicken began to look as though it had been in a mud-wrestling match.

'Does the massaging help to tenderise it?'

'Yes.'

'And then it's returned to the fridge?'

'For maybe a quarter of an hour, after which it goes in the tandoor. Why don't you pick up one of those skewers over there, Heston?' He pointed to a row of what looked like shepherds' crooks hanging from a metal rafter. 'And we will get cooking.'

The oven was a wide-bellied hole sunk into one of the workstations. I handed over the skewer so that Vinod could thread on the chicken, while I used a tea towel to nudge aside the wrought-iron bowl that acted as a lid. 'How hot is it?'

'I would declare it to be 370°C.'

I was sure the tandoor was crucial to the dish (and not only because, when it was built, it would have been seasoned with spinach, curd, salt and mustard oil, then fired up with cow dung cakes), so I wanted to find out exactly how hot it was. I pointed the thermometer's infra-red beam into the haze of air that rippled in the oven's belly. The readout's digits scrambled furiously, then settled on 380°C.

'And I told you 370! Hey, hey!' Vinod cried out in delight. (There was something of the boisterous schoolboy about him, which I found charming and amusing, though it drove the film crew nuts. The director was forever begging him: 'Don't look at me. Look at Heston,' while, during cutaway shots, the translator was constantly hissing at him to keep quiet.) He lowered the skewer into the oven and edged the lid back in place.

'How long will it take to cook?'

'Oh, six to eight minutes.'

'I expect that's another virtue of the slashes made in the meat at the start. The heat can work its way through the flesh very quickly.'

As the chicken came out of the oven, it had a lovely chargrilled look, and its colour had calmed down to a mellow orangey-brown. Ajay took a cleaver and cut through the joints, releasing a fantastic spicy smell that engulfed the kitchen. The meat was separated into pieces and set out on a metal salver.

'And now the butter sauce,' announced Vinod, the master of ceremonies.

A chef ladled lots of runny tomato sauce into a heavy frying pan, along with a little sugar, chilli powder and fresh green chilli, and let it bubble furiously for a few moments before emptying in the salver of chicken pieces. The sauce was scooped over the chicken, and the pan constantly shaken back and forth. Butter was lobbed into the pan – a good four or five dollops – then there was more shake 'n' scoop. After ten minutes cream was poured in and the sauce became bright orange. It was ladled into a metal bowl and topped with half a lime and two halved green chillis arranged in a cross. Vinod handed over a spoon, mock-serious.

The chicken was very tender with a big mouthfeel – rich, full, spicy; the flavours nicely balanced. The heat too was balanced: delicate enough to add complexity to the dish without blowing your head off.

OLD SPICE

I wandered along the narrow alleyways of Gadodial, the wholesale spice market in Old Delhi. On either side of me was a series of small, square, tiled rooms covered by sagging canvas awnings. The merchants sat cross-legged drinking *chai* – milky, impossibly sweet tea – in earthenware cups, or lay slumped against the walls, their faces impassive, unimpressed by the commotion the cameras were causing and the sudden crowd of onlookers. I liked to think these were their business faces – the ones they used to haggle with clients, giving nothing away.

They were hemmed in on all sides by their wares. Fat hessian sacks sandbagged entrances and buttressed back walls, their handpainted flanks advertising things such as 'Super Bold Stoneless Sterilized Black Pepper'. The tops had been cut open and rolled back to show off dusty green cardamom seeds, black peppercorn balls, gnarled fingers of ginger and pink, feathery blades of mace that looked like some form of sea creature. Most eyecatching of all was the turmeric, coaxed into tall piles of knobbly, bright yellow nuggets.

I was nudged aside by a stick-thin Indian bent almost double by the sack on his back, kept in place by the S-shaped hook gripped tightly by the hand that reached over his shoulder. There was a constant flow of porters through the market, transporting huge, unwieldy loads through the throng. Dodging them became a necessary part of the market's choreography. Despite the narrowness of the alleys, spices were also transported on long, heavily bolted wooden trolleys that were see-sawed clumsily around tight corners and often picked up too much speed on the incline leading out of the market. They would careen wildly into the sea of people, cows and macaques on Khari Baoli, the trolley-pullers desperately hanging on to slow the momentum, and occasionally ending up in a collision and a shouting match.

I have often said that food is a multisensory business, and the market was a great reminder of this. As well as the bustle, the colours and the calls of the porters, I was hit by a succession of pungent, fragrant aromas that mingled to produce a wonderfully subtle but complex perfume – the nutmeggy woodiness of mace overlaying cardamom's lemony scent accentuated by peppery turmeric that mixed with the bitter nutty earthiness of cumin crossed with cinnamon's exotic sweetness and cloves' dusky warmth. It was almost suffocating, especially when I reached the corner where the chilli sacks were stacked. The spice's heat wafted invisibly into the nostrils and caught at the back of the throat – as it sometimes does when chilli is heated in a pan, sending the home cook scurrying to open the kitchen window. I felt seared, scoured inside, and couldn't stop coughing. Nor could the camera crew and producer. Nor even could the vendors, lolling on top of the sacks, who have to deal with this insidious physical assault every day. I wondered how they stood it. The market echoed with the harsh staccato barks of people trying to loosen chilli's grip on their throats. The spice's power was impressive – no wonder it had become such a crucial feature of Indian cookery: it must have been gratifying to harness and tame that power by adding it to dishes.

I staggered towards the exit, sucking in spice-free air. Even a cup of oversweet chai would have been welcome now. Before me the commerce of Khari Baoli continued in all its surging, chaotic, well-meaning, good-humoured, smelly, sticky, shouty, crowded, ramshackle, resourceful, brightly coloured splendour. I have always insisted that context is crucial to a dish. I wondered how I was going to get all of this into chicken tikka masala.

MASALA MIX-UP

The fact that India is a land of profound contradictions has long been the novelist's stock-in-trade, but the confusion surrounding chicken tikka masala was making my head spin. In India I met several people who insisted it was an Indian dish. 'Spices belong to India, not England,' the owner of Karim's had declared gruffly, and Vinod Chadha had even produced his own version for me to try. He used leg meat, loads of chopped onions and just a touch of tomato, finished off with a little 'chicken curry gravy' to produce a dry, almost condiment-like sauce – very different from what we in Britain think of as chicken tikka masala (which, to add to the confusion, looks and tastes similar to murg makhani). Now that I was back in Britain, it was time to get some grounding. It was time to revisit Malik's.

The chef's working hours make it difficult to eat with family and friends. My own way round this is to make certain meals sacrosanct. One of these is Sunday dinner. The other is Monday's curry night. There are lots of fantastic places to go to in London – Atul Kochhar's Benares, Vineet Bhatia's Rasoi or Sanjay Dwivedi's Zaika – and all of these have shaped my flavour memories of Indian food (and Sanjay would later give lots of advice to me and my team). However, more often than not, I end up renting a video and ordering in from my favourite local curry house, Malik's in Cookham, so for me his food is a major frame of reference. (Conveniently, my local is also the winner of a prestigious British Curry Award.) At the start of my research the BBC had filmed me in Malik's eating chicken tikka masala. Now I was back for another.

It had an orange colour similar to that of butter chicken. The meat was bite-sized pieces of breast, soft and delicately chargrilled. Mild, balanced, not at all oily, it didn't sit heavily on the stomach. The butter chicken I'd had in India had a flavour strongly reminiscent of tinned tomato soup, which threatened to overwhelm the dish. Here that flavour was kept in check, coming through subtly towards the end. It was strange: although I had been coming to Malik's for years, I had never really analysed what was put in front of me (after all, Monday is my day off). I hadn't consciously noticed before how much I liked the use of coconut in the dish.

'How is it, my friend? Good?' Malik appeared at the table. I was keen to ask him a few questions and invited him to join me.

'Delicious, as always. The coconut is what really makes it for me. Is that a Bangladeshi thing? I was hoping that might be a way in to the origins of chicken tikka masala. It's supposed to have been invented in the 1970s, and I think of coconut as a very characteristic taste of the period. Bounty bars, that sweet tobacco for kids called "Spanish Gold", the marshmallow things with little flakes of desiccated coconut on top ... '

'Well, Bangladesh certainly has a korma tradition that uses coconut. When I was growing up in Sylhet, chunks of it would be added to the dish. Over here, of course, korma has developed differently. In the past there would have been very little access to fresh coconut, so desiccated coconut was used instead, taking the dish in a different direction. I think many dishes in British-Indian restaurants, including chicken tikka masala, have developed in this way, adapting to ingredients, to market forces, to the customers' palate.'

'So it's almost as if there are two separate and distinct traditions – one Indian, the other British.'

'Indeed.' Malik nodded vigorously. 'Nowadays, most of the chefs working in Indian restaurants were born here and learned their trade here. A style of cooking has grown up and been handed on from one generation to another. It has its own identity, and it's no use tying oneself up in knots trying to establish whether it's authentic or not.'

'It's part of the beauty of cooking – the way things change and adapt and renew.'

'We have a green curry on the menu that was inspired by a marvellous Thai meal I had. I played around with the ingredients, altered the spicing, and came up with an Indian version of a classic Thai dish. Now lots of the curry houses round about are serving something similar. Food has a life of its own, beyond historians' attempts to pin it down.'

'What, then, do you think about the historians' view that chicken tikka masala originated in Britain?'

'All I can say is that when I first came here in the 1970s, it wasn't on the menu in any Indian restaurant that I worked in. So it seems unlikely that it was a dish the first generation of chefs brought over with them from Bangladesh.'

'Several places I went to in India insisted that it is in fact an Indian dish.'

'That's not surprising when it has become such a lucrative business. I hear that the dish is becoming very popular over there.'

'Yes, though it's not at all like this.' I pointed to the scrapings left on the plate in front of me.

'The chefs over there have made it their own,' said Malik. 'Just as you will make it your own. I'm very much looking forward to seeing – and perhaps tasting – what you come up with!'

TANDOOR LORE

The camera rolled and my research chefs, Chris and Kyle, loped across the gravel towards the far end of the Hind's Head's car park, each with a spade slung over his shoulder, as though off for a spot of grave-digging. 'Cue slo-mo and *Reservoir Dogs* music,' murmured the director.

I had sent them off to dig a hole. My experiences in India had shown me that the tandoor was essential to the character and flavour of chicken tikka masala and, above all, the naan bread that accompanied it. So I was going to start by building my own tandoor oven. And to build a tandoor, you need a hole.

Half an hour after Chris and Kyle's gravel-stride, I walked over to check on their progress. They had taken their role as builders to heart and were perched on upturned crates drinking tea and reading the *Sun*. Beside them was a vague indentation about 60 centimetres deep.

'We hit rock,' Chris explained.

I decided my assistants were more suited to labwork than scutwork. 'OK, that's it. I'm going to call in the big boys.'

'I thought we were the big boys,' said Kyle. He looked crestfallen.

Digging a hole for a tandoor oven. (Note that my chefs have already downed tools.)

Some hours later the Big Boys arrived with a mini-digger on the back of a flatbed truck. I was disappointed to see that the bucket – the thing at the business end of the digging arm – was a small scoop rather than the metre-wide, metal-toothed job I had been hoping for. The truck's ramps were lowered and the digger manoeuvred slowly forward on its rubber caterpillars. I climbed into the cab. Boyd took me through the array of levers at far too fast a pace for me to make sense of it, and then I was on my own. Driving wasn't too bad, but digging took careful angling and coordination. At first, each plunge of the bucket made the cab rear backwards alarmingly, as though I were doing a wheelie.

'You're not on a mission,' advised Boyd. 'You don't have to fill the bucket full.'

But I did. Like most chefs, I'm competitive and I like to get stuff right. I like to master technical details and practical problems. I kept at it till I could dig dirt and discard it in what looked like a vaguely competent manner (and could lurch the cab in Kyle and Chris's direction in such a way that it wiped the smiles from their faces), and then I handed it back to Boyd. I noticed that he immediately repositioned the digger in a sneaky side-on position that he hadn't told me about, and began pivoting back and forth at speed, the pile of earth growing by the minute. The first stage in making a tandoor was well under way.

'C'mon, you two,' I said. 'You can scoop quenelles instead.'

MORE TANDOOR

The Big Boys gibe seemed to have hit a nerve with Chris. He had spent hours in Boyd's hole building a ten-brick-deep circular shaft complete with carefully crafted air hole. Now he and Kyle were backfilling it with earth to create a truly traditional sunken tandoor. They presented an unlikely picture, slaving away, not least because Kyle continued to wear chef's whites as he ferried earth back and forth. Now, though, they both looked pleased with themselves as they invited me to place the last brick, as though I were the Queen. I hoped I was laying the cornerstone of a great chicken tikka masala, but one thing worried me about the oven's construction. In India the tandoors weren't straight-sided: they narrowed towards the top, like an old earthenware storage jar or amphora (which I guess was the inspiration for the tandoor in the first place). I was sure this would make a difference to cooking in it, but it seemed churlish to point this out now, when they had worked so hard.

Chris lit a fire and began feeding the shaft bags of charcoal. It would take several hours for it to build up the kind of residual heat we needed.

In an oven, there are three ways that heat transfers to food: conduction, convection and radiation. Conduction relies on the fact that when two substances with different temperatures come into contact, heat will travel from the hotter object to the cooler one. When air is the medium in which this takes place, it's an inefficient form of heat transfer because air is a poor conductor. The molecules in air are relatively far apart, so they come into contact with the food infrequently.* Convection

---

* Water is a more efficient medium because its molecules are closer together. That's why you can put your hand in a 100°C oven for a few seconds without fear of burning it, but you can't put it in boiling water. Metal is more efficient still: put a piece of chicken in the oven on a skewer and the metal will soon heat up and begin to cook the centre of the chicken.

can be a more effective way of transferring heat. We all know that hot air rises and cooler air falls. That's how radiators work, creating a constant circulation of air known as a 'convection current'. The same process is at work in the oven, and the circulation allows far more hot air molecules to come into contact with the food. (The fan in a convection oven increases this circulation and further enhances the heat transfer: that's why it usually needs to be set 15°C lower than a conventional oven.)

Both these processes are at work in the tandoor, but a key mechanism here is radiation. All hot material emits infra-red radiation – electromagnetic waves that are of the right length to be absorbed by molecules, making them more energetic and hotter. Stone tends to take that energy and reflect it right back. The result is a relatively even, steady heat that penetrates the food's surface particularly effectively. It's perfect for that charred effect.

Four hours and ten big bags of charcoal later, the oven was ready. I'd checked it with the temperature gun and the readout had flashed out HI: its way of saying the oven had topped 500°C. I brushed five chicken pieces with ghee (clarified butter), threaded them on to a tandoor skewer – a metre long with a curved hook at one end – and leaned into the fierce cloud of heat that mushroomed around the oven's opening just long enough to place the skewer vertically in the hole.

'In India,' I told Chris, 'the chicken took six minutes, so let's aim for the same.'

After a couple of minutes, however, the lowest chicken piece was already golden brown, while the upper ones were still a pale caramel colour. It appeared that the narrowed neck of the traditional tandoor helped to hold in and circulate the heat, which otherwise spread unevenly in the oven. Ours was much hotter at the bottom than the top. I pulled out the skewer and took off the lowest chicken leg after three minutes. It looked exactly right – a rich brown colour with nicely charred edges from the intense heat of the oven, and the flames and smoke caused by dripping ghee.

It tasted exactly right too. That charred note is absolutely essential to tandoori chicken, mixing with the other flavours to give the characteristic taste. It also retained its moisture incredibly well. When we took out the other pieces – which had browned but not blackened – they

The oven was finished – but would it be hot enough to give the right flavour? I aimed the temperature gun and held my breath.

were undoubtedly delicious but, lacking that charred note, they simply weren't tandoori chicken.

I'd learned something else from this fieldwork as well. We had chosen leg meat (because it has more fat, which keeps it juicy and increases the char) and marinated it in ginger and garlic. But tasting the meat and appreciating that range of taste supplied simply by the oven, I realised that I didn't want to compromise it by overspicing. That tandoor flavour had to come through. It gave a radiant-heat char that was very different from a flame char – less aggressive, less bitter – and really suited the combination of chicken, ginger and garlic.

I would have to strip any marinade to its bare essentials. Start simple and build it up slowly and gently. That was the next problem I had to solve in the lab.

That and the fact that I could hardly ask home cooks to build a tandoor in their back garden.

MORE THAN MEETS THE MRI

'OK, let's do an MRI scan.' The phrase is familiar from countless hospital dramas on television, usually requested alongside a CT, CBC, Chem-7 and chest X-ray. But in my case the patient was a chicken breast.

I wanted to know whether a marinade really penetrated the meat or just coated the surface, so I went to the Magnetic Resonance Research Centre in Cambridge to find out. I was met at the door of the wooden A-frame building (with four super-powerful magnets inside, there is as little metal as possible in the construction) by Dr Mick Mantle, who led me upstairs to the conference room and advised me to remove my watch and take keys and coins out of my pockets. I noticed that his cufflinks bore an image of Chef, the cafeteria cook in *South Park*. Mick was clearly a scientist with a sneaky sense of humour.

This was probably just as well, since I'd asked him to apply three different rubs – garlic; ginger; garlic + ginger – to chicken breasts, MRI them for five hours, then add a marinade of yoghurt, garlic, chilli and spices to one of the pieces and leave them in the machine for another ten hours. A decade or so ago, trying to get scientists to take this kind of culinary experimentation seriously was often like wading through treacle.* Nowadays, thankfully, chefs and scientists are far more receptive to each other's ideas, but there's still a leap of faith involved, especially when something as high-tech as a magnetic resonance imaging scanner is used on a humble piece of chicken.

We were joined by Professor Laurie Hall, who pioneered the use of MRI in analysing food, and Mick took us to the room housing the scanner. It looked above all like a large airing cupboard tank, albeit one with a lot of complicated pipes coming out of it and sectioned off by black and yellow hazard tape. 'Our MRIs have a vertical bore rather than the horizontal one you see in hospitals, so they're loaded vertically,' he told me.

'How does an MRI work?'

'In techspeak we're altering the rate at which magnetisation returns to equilibrium following interrogation by MRI. Put more simply, the magnet in the scanner causes the hydrogen atoms in water

---

* At 20°C/68°F water's viscosity is 1 centipoise; treacle's is 20,000.

to align in the direction of the magnetic field. The atoms are knocked out of alignment by a pulse of radio waves, then allowed to return to the aligned state. The rate at which they do this will be affected by the presence of molecules from the ginger, etc. By recording the rate of return to equilibrium, we can see where the water's environment has changed.'

'Which, given that the body – human or chicken – is 60 to 70 per cent water, can be very revealing,' added Laurie.

'I suppose a good analogy,' Mick continued, 'would be taking three different grades of toothbrush, bending over the bristles, then letting them go. By watching how they spring back, you can establish which is hard, soft or medium.'

'OK, so talk me through the results.' On the screen I could see four kidney-shaped orangey blobs, like a geographer's diagram of a cluster of islands. One had a thick pale band around its edge, as though that were the one with a beach.

'That's the ginger rub. The band is where it has had some effect on the water. And if you look at the garlic and ginger rub,' Mick said, pointing his pen, 'there's a band there too, though not as distinct. So we can unequivocally say that ginger affects the meat in some way. The garlic rub, on the other hand, seems to have made very little difference. There's almost no change in colour. It looks much like the control, which has had no rub at all.'

'Can we tell if aroma is going in, though?'

'No. What the apparatus detects is changes to the water content, not the passage of flavour molecules.'

'But there is a whole family of other tests you could do,' cut in Laurie, ever the champion for MRI's potential, 'to explore structural questions, such as the texture and tenderness of the marinated chicken, or how the marinade travels along the fibres.'

'That could be invaluable for the cook, if you were to find that the meat surface should be exposed so that the marinade can penetrate efficiently.'

'The MRI would be a very non-invasive way of doing this. You could film over hours or even days.'

'Exactly,' Mick agreed. 'Here we've done a timed series of images – one every seven minutes – to look at the marinating process in action.'

He hit a key and the screen filled with the outline of two islands. 'The chicken on the left is covered in rub and the yoghurt marinade. The chicken on the right is covered with rub on one side with nothing on the other as a control.' He hit another key and the film began: a vague lightening danced around one edge of the right-hand island. 'The rub seems to have had no further effect. It's as though it's done all the work it's going to do after five hours. The next ten have made little difference.'

The left-hand island, on the other hand, provided a bit of movie magic. A pale band gradually spread inwards from the edge of the island until all but the very middle had lightened up, rather as if the tide had risen, leaving only a central ridge exposed. We watched it several times over, mesmerised by the evidence of molecules at work. 'Look at that,' Mick finally declared, as impressed with his work as I was. 'It's pretty conclusive that yoghurt has an effect.'

'Well done!' said Laurie. 'This is most exciting. It shows that some of those old recipes calling for an overnight marinating are right after all. The MRI proves it.'

'Yes, so often we don't know if food lore is fact or fiction. It's great to get the opportunity to test it. But the next question is what effect that marinating actually has. I need to find out what flavours have been created, what reactions have occurred to create new compounds. That film of the yoghurt marinade shows it affecting water's environment virtually to the centre of a piece about 1 centimetre thick. Perhaps that's an optimum size that can be used to advantage, especially if cutting the grain in a particular way also makes a difference.'

'The next step is to take the science and see how it translates into flavour development,' Laurie said. 'A lot of cooking and tasting. That's your end of things, Heston, back at your own lab.'

Chicken Tikka Masala **Serves 4**

Following up the MRI results turned out to be extremely interesting. Using the same preparations as in the scanner – chicken breasts left for fifteen hours after being coated in rub, or rub followed by marinade, or rub and marinade all together – the chicken was cooked on a barbecue, then trimmed of its outer flesh (the knife wiped clean between each cut to prevent it transferring flavour from the outside to the inside) and tasted. Then the same procedure was performed again, but with the meat placed in a water bath to ensure that each piece of chicken was cooked in exactly the same way.

The second tasting confirmed what we'd found in the first: the piece of chicken that had a rub for five hours followed by a yoghurt marinade for ten had a noticeably better texture and flavour than the other two. Although scientists have yet to establish exactly what's happening and how, something beneficial definitely comes about during the process, backing up thousands of years of Indian tradition that probably began simply as a way of preventing the meat from becoming contaminated.

Special equipment
Kettle barbecue, 6 bricks, 2 bags (5kg) lumpwood charcoal (the flavour imparted by this is superior to that of briquettes – a light smoky note rather than a petrol one), pressure cooker, square of muslin, 16 long metal tandoor skewers, long-armed tongs, spice grinder, food processor, 2 square pizza stones

Timing
Preparation takes 2 hours, plus 21 hours for marinating. Cooking takes approximately 4 hours.

For the brined chicken
2kg water _ 160g table salt _ 8 chicken thighs, skinned

For the rub
6 bulbs of garlic _ 150g olive oil, plus extra for drizzling _
200g (about 2 pieces) fresh root ginger, peeled and roughly
chopped _ 15g table salt _ reserved brined chicken thighs

For the yoghurt marinade
100g coriander seeds _ 65g green cardamom pods _ 35g black
cardamom pods _ 100g cinnamon sticks _ 75g black peppercorns _
25g cloves _ 125g cumin seeds _ 20g mace _ 5 dried bay leaves _
25g ghee _ 25g chickpea flour (available from Indian and Middle
Eastern grocers) _ 50g olive oil _ 10g Kashmiri chilli powder
(lends an authentic character to the dish) _ 450g Greek-style
yoghurt _ ½ tsp ground fenugreek leaves (available through
thespiceshop.co.uk) _ reserved chicken thighs, coated with rub

For the cashew nut butter
50g whole cashews

For the toasted melon seeds
1 tsp ghee _ 20g charmagaz (dried melon seeds, available at
spicesofindia.co.uk) _ salt, as needed

For the masala sauce base
5g coriander seeds _ 5g cumin seeds _ 1kg vine-ripened tomatoes _
100g water _ 50g ghee _ ½ tsp Kashmiri chilli powder _ 2 large
onions (about 400g), finely diced _ 5cm piece (about 25g) fresh root
ginger, peeled and minced _ salt, to taste _ 40g tomato purée _
10g roasted garlic purée (reserved from the rub) _ ½ tsp reserved
garam masala _ ½ tsp ground fenugreek _ 1½ tsp ground turmeric

For cooking the chicken
100g melted ghee _ reserved chicken in yoghurt marinade

For the finished dish
reserved chicken tikka masala sauce _ 50g Greek-style yoghurt _
35–80g coconut milk (according to taste) _ reserved cooked chicken _
100g unsalted butter _ reserved cashew nut butter _ table salt _

reserved toasted melon seeds _ 1 green chilli, seeded and finely diced

For the naan
750g self-raising flour _ 20g sugar _ 10g salt _ 6g baking powder _ 230g water _ 230g whole milk _ 100g whole eggs _ ghee

BRINING THE CHICKEN
It is always best to use organic, free-range chicken thighs. The quality of a well-reared bird will really show through.

1. Combine the water and salt in a container and stir well from time to time to dissolve the salt.
2. Meanwhile, remove the bone from the thighs by cutting around the bone and drawing it away from the meat. Make three slashes across the thick side of each thigh so that the marinade will be better able to penetrate.
3. Add the chicken thighs to the brine, then cover and refrigerate for 6 hours.
4. Pour off the brine and rinse the thighs under cold running water. Fill the container with fresh cold water and leave the thighs to soak in it for 2 hours, changing the water every 30 minutes to wash off the salt. Drain the chicken and pat dry.

PREPARING THE RUB
1. Preheat the oven to 180°C/350°F/Gas 4. Trim the tops off three of the garlic bulbs to expose a little of the individual cloves. (Be sure not to cut the root end.) Drizzle a little olive oil over each bulb and wrap individually in squares of aluminium foil. Roast for 30–35 minutes, or until soft. Leave to cool completely.
2. Meanwhile, separate the three remaining garlic bulbs into cloves and peel them.
3. Unwrap the roasted bulbs and squeeze 50g (about 2 bulbs) of the garlic purée in a food processor, reserving the rest. Add the peeled garlic cloves, ginger, olive oil and salt. Blitz until the mixture has a paste-like consistency.
4. Generously coat the chicken in the rub, making sure to push it into the incisions. Cover and refrigerate for 5 hours.

PREPARING THE YOGHURT MARINADE

1. While the chicken is refrigerated, preheat the oven to 130°C/250°F/ Gas ½.
2. Prepare a garam masala by combining all the spices and the bay leaves. Scatter the mixture over a large baking sheet and roast for 1–1½ hours, shaking occasionally, until the spices become aromatic. Leave to cool.
3. Tip the spices into a grinder and grind to a powder. Pass the spices through a fine sieve to remove any husks or large unground bits. Transfer to an airtight container. This yields more garam masala than you need for this recipe, but it can be stored for several weeks and used in a variety of other recipes.
4. Melt the ghee in a small saucepan over a medium heat. When it starts to bubble, whisk in all the chickpea flour until it is fully incorporated. Continue whisking for 1 minute to cook the flour. Remove from the heat and allow to cool. (Incorporating this roux will help the marinade to stick to the chicken.)
5. Place a small frying pan over a medium heat. Pour in the oil, then add the chilli powder. Fry for 2–3 minutes, then leave to cool.
6. Tip the yoghurt, chilli/oil mixture and ground fenugreek into a large bowl. Add 10g of the garam masala and the chickpea roux. Stir to combine.
7. Remove the chicken from the rub and brush off most, but not all, of the ginger-garlic mixture. Place the chicken in the yoghurt marinade and toss to coat thoroughly. Cover the bowl and place in the fridge for 10 hours.

MAKING THE CASHEW NUT BUTTER

1. Preheat the oven to 180°C/350°F/Gas 4.
2. Spread the cashews out on a baking sheet. Roast for 10 minutes, or until golden brown.
3. Tip the cashews into a food processor while still warm and blitz to form a paste. (You might need to add 2 tsp of melted ghee to help this process along.)
4. Remove the mixture from the food processor and reserve for the finished dish.

TOASTING THE MELON SEEDS

1. Place a frying pan over a medium heat. Add the ghee and the melon seeds. Stir for 3–5 minutes, or until the seeds are nut brown.
2. Season with salt and leave to cool on a piece of kitchen paper.

PREPARING THE MASALA SAUCE BASE

1. Toast the coriander and cumin seeds. This should be done in a low oven, as the spices have been done for the garam masala blend.
2. Meanwhile, wash the tomatoes and remove the cores, keeping the tomatoes whole.
3. Bag the toasted spices in a square of muslin. Place the bag in a small pressure cooker with the water and tomatoes. Put on the lid and place over a medium heat. Bring to full pressure, then cook for 20 minutes. Set aside to cool.
4. Once cool, remove the lid and place the tomato mixture back on the hob. Cook over a high heat, stirring frequently, for 10–15 minutes, or until the sauce has reduced by half. Discard the bag of spices. Strain the tomatoes through a sieve.
5. Melt the ghee in a large saucepan over a medium heat. Add the chilli powder and fry for 2–3 minutes.
6. Turn the heat down to low. Add the onions, ginger and salt and cook for 10 minutes, or until the onions are soft but not coloured. Turn the heat back up to medium, and cook for a further 5 minutes, or until golden.
7. Stir in the tomato purée and the roasted garlic purée and cook for 2–3 minutes. Add the strained tomato sauce and cook for 10 minutes, stirring constantly.
8. Turn the heat down to low. Add the garam masala, fenugreek, turmeric and salt, and simmer for 5 minutes.
9. Allow the sauce base to cool while you cook the chicken.

COOKING THE CHICKEN

1. Light the barbecue and leave for 15–20 minutes, until glowing red. As the coal burns down, top it up, allowing for plenty of airflow through the vents.
2. Meanwhile, shake most of the marinade off the chicken and place on a board with the narrowest end towards you. Take a skewer and

hold it parallel to the right-hand, longer side of the thigh. Place it 1cm in from the edge and weave it in and out of the chicken. Weave another skewer along the left-hand side of the thigh in similar fashion. Push the chicken to the middle of the skewers, leaving about 15cm clearance between the chicken and the tip of the skewer. Repeat with the remaining thighs.

3. Using tongs, clear the charcoal from the centre of the barbecue. Place the first three bricks in a triangle in the base of the barbecue. Stack three more bricks on top of the first three, leaving a hole large enough to fit the chicken inside.

4. Build up new coal around the perimeter of the triangle so that it is almost level with the top of the bricks. (No coal should be on the bottom, or the fat will drip on to it and cause flaming.) Allow this new coal to burn until it is glowing and grey. This will take at least an hour, and it is important to wait so that the bricks have time to absorb enough heat to radiate into the chicken.

5. One by one, brush the skewered thighs lightly with ghee and place them inside the brick 'chimney'. Turn the skewers every minute until golden brown on both sides.

6. When an even char has developed, remove the skewers and set aside while you cook the remaining ones. Leave the cooked chicken to cool slightly before cutting into large chunks.

ASSEMBLING THE FINISHED DISH

1. Heat the masala sauce in a pan (this can be the same pan as it was made in provided it is large enough to hold all the chicken).

2. Add the yoghurt and the coconut milk and very gently simmer together for 1–2 minutes.

3. Add the pieces of cut chicken and simmer very gently for 10 minutes. It is then best to cool the mixture and store in the fridge for 6–12 hours, or until the next day, to develop both flavour and texture. However, this is not essential, and you can proceed directly to the next step.

4. Fold in the butter to finish the sauce.

5. Fold in some cashew nut butter according to taste, and adjust the seasoning with salt.

6. Serve with a sprinkling of melon seeds and the diced chilli.

MAKING THE NAAN

1. Sift all the dry ingredients together and place in the bowl of a mixer fitted with a hook attachment.

2. Add the water, milk and eggs, incorporating them on a slow speed.

3. Once all the liquid ingredients are incorporated, mix for 3 minutes on a low speed followed by 1 minute at a medium speed.

4. When the dough is well mixed, transfer it to a generously floured work surface and knead by hand for an additional 2 minutes.

5. Divide the dough into 100g portions (12 pieces), roll into balls and place on a floured baking sheet. Cover with clingfilm and refrigerate for at least 2 hours before using.

6. Remove all the racks from the oven and place 2 square pizza stones in the bottom in a V-shape: each stone should rest against the oven wall on either side and meet in the middle at a 45° angle. If your oven has room for only one pizza stone, you can use a small baking sheet or another metallic object to keep it against the oven wall at a 45° angle. Preheat the oven, with the top grill set at 100 per cent for 20 minutes.

7. Flour a work surface and place a floured ball of dough on it. Oil your hands and flatten the dough with the tips of your fingers until you have a disc approximately 20cm in diameter. Repeat with the other balls of dough.

8. Place 1 or 2 pieces of flattened dough on a floured pizza peel (or the back of a baking sheet) and brush lightly with melted ghee.

9. Put the sheet on top of the stones as far back in the oven as possible. Note: If you have 2 stones in the oven, you can bake 2 naan at a time. If not, you will have to bake 1 at a time.

10. Bake for 1 minute 40 seconds, then remove and bake the remaining naan in the same way. Serve immediately.

Peking Duck

'Peking duck is different from Russian caviar.
But I love them both.'

James Bond in *You Only Live Twice*

History

Domestication of the duck began in China more than 2,000 years ago, and roasting the bird also has a long history, although the breed originally used was a small, black-feathered variety of mallard called Nanjing duck. It is said that when the capital of China moved from Nanjing to Peking (now Beijing) in 1421, the local ducks got to feed on grain spilled from barges servicing the new capital, and gradually evolved into a new variety that was larger and plumper. This white-feathered bird, known as Pekin duck, was then forcefed to make it fatter still, and prepared according to the special techniques that give the dish Peking duck its particular appearance and flavours – pumping in air to separate the skin from the flesh, blanching and coating the outside with some form of sugar to give it a beautiful amber colour, and then roasting it vertically in a special oven.

It seems clear that Peking duck didn't simply come into being with the court's transfer to the capital. Many sources suggest that the dish can be traced back to the Yuan dynasty (1279–1368), and it is mentioned in a thirteenth-century book by the inspector of the imperial kitchen, Hu Sihui. However, it became a particular favourite of the imperial family during the Ming dynasty (1368–1644), which oversaw the move from Nanjing, and its complicated preparation meant that it remained an exclusive pleasure of their court. Elaborate cuisine had long been one of the ways in which Chinese dynasties chose to express and define themselves. Ming, the dynasty of the upwardly mobile (its founder, Chu Yüan-chang, has been described as a military deserter, drifter and petty criminal), made court cookery more aspirational and elitist than ever before. (In 1425 some 6,300 cooks were employed in the kitchens.) Peking duck was not so much a dish as a ritual. There was pomp in that pumping.

Social changes during the Qianlong period (1736–95) of the Qing dynasty meant that the dish became accessible to the upper classes. By 1870 it was being served in the Bianyifang and Quanjude restaurants in the capital, and beginning to acquire the international reputation that has given rise to the often-quoted tourist advice: 'There are two things you must do in Beijing – walk the wall and eat Peking duck.'

The Quest for the Best

CRISPY CRITTERS

It's funny that when the BBC are in Bray filming a tasting at midday, every member of the research kitchen seems to find an excuse to linger, usually with a prop in hand – graduated beaker, pipette clamp, magnet, rubber tubing – to show that they're on legitimate business and not just looking for lunch.

This time their hungry eyes were fixed on a crispy duck that lay steaming gently on the lab's central work surface, its back an inviting rich brown colour.

It wasn't Peking duck, of course. Crispy duck is a Szechwan dish in which the duck is steamed or boiled and then deep-fried. (In China it isn't served with pancakes and plum sauce either.) However, crispy duck is what most people in Britain have in mind when Peking duck is mentioned, and it's what they have most experience of. So before going to Beijing I wanted to taste a couple of crispy ducks to establish a benchmark for what I was looking for. I'd learned the hard way that it was often foolish to discount people's expectations of a dish, no matter how far they strayed from authenticity.

As the second crispy duck came out of the oven, a ring on the doorbell announced the arrival of a third, ordered from the local Chinese takeaway. I opened the box while Kyle carved chunks off the other two and then cut them into neat medallions. Eventually we had three plates of meat – from the local takeaway, the local supermarket and a trade supplier.

Overall each duck fell short of what I wanted, while offering valuable lessons in what to look for. The supplier's version was acceptable but bland, which was hardly surprising since it had almost certainly been pre-cooked before being packaged and then cooked again. The processing had effectively processed the life out of it, and a chef would have to work hard to disguise that.

I was much more impressed with the takeaway's offering. It looked the business, with a glistening, mahogany-coloured skin that was really enticing, but the beautiful lacquered finish was deceptive: it was disappointingly soft in the mouth. I was sure the duck needed a glass-like surface that shattered as you bit into it, much like the brittle pleasure of good crackling.

The supermarket version went to the other extreme. To prevent it drying out the producer had left on lots of fat, resulting in a duck that was claggy and had no crispness at all. But, despite this, it was still the driest of the three, requiring a spectacularly generous helping of cucumber strips and hoisin sauce to make it juicy and palatable. The meat had lost all its rosy pinkness and surrendered to a dull grey. I definitely wanted meat that had less fat and retained a bright pink tinge. The flesh had to be moist and tender, the skin crisp and glazed. How much of this, I wondered, was down to the duck itself – the breed and the conditions in which it was brought up? And, given that the cooking processes involved in achieving crispness and moistness were largely mutually incompatible, how was I going to manage to combine the two? Maybe I'd find out in Beijing.

NIGHT MARKET

It was already dark by the time I arrived at Beijing's airport, and the following two days would be taken up with filming in two sharply contrasting restaurants – regimented formality on a vast scale versus high-concept designer modernity – the old and new faces of the city. I would be too busy to walk the wall. However, there was one place I could go to get a little street-level insight into the place's culinary culture: the Wangfujing night market. I dumped my bags at the Crowne Plaza hotel and got the film crew to take a walk with me.

Even the short stroll down Wangfujing Daje showed just how Westernised Beijing had become. The wide boulevard was lined with the kind of high-rises that characterise every big city. International labels were proudly displayed on shopfronts – Tag Heuer, Nike, Chanel,

Armani. David Beckham stared down at me from a vast hoarding. I hoped that China's economic success story and its rush to modernise wouldn't turn Beijing into something blandly corporate, its rich history and individuality abandoned, forgotten. Glimpses down some of the alleyways and *hutongs* showed that a rawer, more knockabout version of life continued – clusters of card-players hunkered on the pavement; bicycle repairmen crouched over stacks of oily cogs and sprockets (even though the streets no longer swarmed with bicycles); washing strung between traffic signs. I wondered whether it would survive the sprucing-up that accompanied the city's push towards the 2008 Olympics.

We turned right at Dong'an Men Dajie. On the north side of the street, below the shaggy silhouettes of pagoda trees, eighty-eight red lanterns shimmered in the darkness, casting a romantic glow over the little stalls beneath them. Under jaunty red and white striped canopies, vendors in red aprons and sun visors tried to draw in onlookers by greeting them in English, though the clipped, singsong delivery made it sound Chinese. 'Hlo, hlo, hlo, hlo, hlo.'

Each stall had a stainless-steel table on which lay trays holding neatly set-out rows of produce, most of it skewered so that it could be eaten on the go – broccoli florets, oyster mushrooms, sweetcorn cobs, shiny red crayfish, roundels of lotus root, and slippery pink squid, their tentacles dangling over the edge of the stalls. It was strange to see customers striding along the street brandishing squid on sticks, as though in a surreal martial arts film. I handed over a couple of yuan for a skewer of smoked eel instead, and chewed on its rich, sticky flesh as I explored further.

The place was a real assault on the senses. There were the stall-holders' calls, the woks' hiss, and the stockpots' noisy boil. Fistfuls of spring onion, clumps of coriander. Crabs steamed in perforated stainless-steel troughs, their shells smooth and pink and striped with crimson, the exotic colours of tropical fish. And every once in a while a slightly faecal note would catch at the nose – the smell of simmering tripe.

Of course, there was the weird food too. Skewered cockroaches, beetles, scorpions, starfish and seahorses (which felt like it oughtn't to be legal, but this market is one of the few that are government-approved). What looked like fat, ridged brown dates were, I was told, silkworms.

The stall with the biggest crowd had a bright yellow sign that announced 'Centipede'. They could be purchased loose or on sticks; a tight fit which made their legs jut out at right angles to the body. I was pleased to see that it wasn't just Westerners who were gawking. This wasn't a regional delicacy: it was tourist trade – a photo opportunity with shock value; a meal to boast about to the folks back home.

I was more interested in *jiaozi*, the steamed or fried Beijing dumplings that resemble large tortellini and are usually filled with minced meat, ginger and Chinese leaf. As a child, my first 'favourite food' was wonton soup, and I was considering adding a dumpling to the soup that traditionally finished a meal of Peking duck. At Stall No. 79 I found some that were elaborately folded, like a nun's wimple, and handed over a few more yuan.

It was a deliberately sparse bowl of soup. The thin stock allowed each ingredient its place in the range of flavours – the rich, fatty pork balanced by the crisp sharpness of spring onions, plus the zing of ginger and the fruitiness of a dash or two of vinegar. The dumpling had a nice doughy chewiness and again that lovely touch of ginger. My first taste of China. It made me keener than ever to go duck-hunting.

On the way out of the market, I got another glimpse of how fast and how eagerly China is embracing the new. A few years ago, when I first advocated making ice cream with dry ice, I had come in for a fair amount of teasing from sceptical journalists. Yet here Stall No. 35 sold plastic beakers of liquid – some Guinness-dark, the others lemonade-yellow – that had a thick head of vigorously bubbling vapour, like the smoke off a witch's cauldron. The vendor was using pellets of dry ice to make the ultimate iced tea.

RINGING THE CHANGES

The black limo cruised down a seemingly endless twelve-lane highway hemmed in by geometrically intricate glass-and-steel office blocks that thrust towards the sky. Ultra-modern, ambitious, forward-looking, this was the new China. Cuisine reflects the society that creates it, so, not surprisingly, Chinese cooking is in the midst of reinventing itself too. I was about to meet one of its rising stars, Da Dong.

Our car pulled into a gated compound and came to a halt on a cobbled pathway lined with red lanterns. To one side was a low-roofed stone building that turned out to be the imperial granary during the Ming dynasty – the destination of those barges that spilled the grain that fattened up Pekin ducks. I doubted it was a coincidence that Da Dong's restaurant stood opposite. Here was a man who knew his history.

Red glass doors slid open as I approached, and I entered a space that wouldn't have looked out of place in an interior design magazine. Glass walls lit from below revealed a pattern of brush-stroked foliage. Other walls were painted gold and incised with Chinese characters. Behind the polished marble bar were high, open shelves housing ceramic pots and beautifully bound books. 'That's a complete set of *Si ku quan shu*, an ancient encyclopedia,' Da Dong explained as he shook my hand. 'The writing on the walls is from Chinese poetry. I want to place my food in a cultural context.'

'I've heard that you have created another fusion of old and new with your Peking duck.'

'Would you care to see?'

'Yes, please,' I said evenly, because I had learned that Chinese etiquette expected a measured response, but in truth I was extremely eager to see what Da Dong did to his ducks. I understood that he had spent five years reappraising every aspect of the dish, and had come up with a leaner, cleaner-tasting version to suit the contemporary Chinese palate.

We walked upstairs and along a corridor that had a phalanx of waitresses who chorused 'Nihao' as we passed. So much of China seemed to operate on this vast and formal scale – it often felt as if I were on the stage of an opera. It was a relief to discover that the kitchen, at least, was familiar territory – chefs in whites hunched over stainless-steel worktops finely slicing tofu or cleaning squid – though even here there were differences. The cleaver was used for every task, no matter how small, and the chopping boards were thick, heavy discs of wood, as though cut straight off a tree trunk. To catch the trimmings, each board had a kidney-shaped metal bowl that neatly fitted the curve of the wood.

'The ducks are forty-five days old when they are delivered,' Da Dong explained, balancing one on the palm of his hand. 'They have been forcefed to give them some fat, and they need to be young so that the fat is soft and will render easily.'

It had the freshness, the give, of a just-dead animal. The skin was smooth to the touch.

'The ducks are already plucked when they arrive. Our first job is to remove the innards. Can you guess how we do it, Heston?'

Normally, I knew, the end of the duck is cut off and the innards simply pulled out, but this duck seemed unblemished.

'See here, under the wing – that small incision? My chefs can hook out the guts through there in forty seconds.'

'Wow. It's like a new martial art. Tae kwak do.'

Generously, Da Dong ignored my terrible pun and ushered me past a rack of gumboots and rubber bibs into a gloomy, low-ceilinged room. 'After gutting, the skin is blown and then the ducks are blanched for thirty seconds, and the skin brushed with a sugar and water solution to help colouring during roasting. Then they come here – the drying room. The removal of water is very important for a crispy skin. Traditionally, drying is done outdoors, but I have developed my own special technique.' Ducks hung on four long racks, like coats in a locker room. The thunder of the air-conditioning unit and two large fans made it difficult to hear what Da Dong was saying. 'If the temperature stays constant, there's nowhere for the water to go, so we have to fluctuate it. The room warms up a little, causing evaporation, then cools to take the water away.'

'How long do you leave the ducks in here?'

'Seventy-two hours, but it's a three-stage process because I realised there was a way of getting rid of even more moisture from the birds. As water in their cells freezes, it expands, bursting open the cell walls and leaking out. I can then remove this water as well. So the ducks go from the drying room to a cold room and back again.' He opened a door that looked on to a room similar to the drying one, but without fans, and shrouded in a winter chill. 'It's set to minus 5°C. The ducks mustn't be in here too long or it damages them.'

Understandably, Da Dong was careful about which details he revealed of cooking processes that he had worked hard to discover, and had even patented in some cases. I tapped and examined the ducks: they were in the freezer for somewhere between four and ten hours, I reckoned.

'And then they're ready for cooking?'

'Yes,' Da Dong replied. 'Come, I'll show you the ovens. They're made to my own special design so that the hot air circulates properly.'

The ovens were housed in a glassed-in section at the front of the restaurant, emphasising the ritualistic, theatrical character of the dish. (There was even a marble counter and tall stools in front of it so that waiting customers could enjoy the spectacle of it all while enjoying a cocktail.) So we walked out of the cold room, back along the corridor with its line of waitresses – *Nihao. Nihao. Nihao* – and down the stairs.

Inside, the heat was formidable. I knew how crucial the oven was to the cooking of Peking duck. I was beginning to realise that, much like the tandoor, radiant heat played a significant part in this. Along one side of the room I could see six arched openings in a brick wall, through which chefs shoved quartered boughs of cherrywood, leaving the ends resting on the lip of each opening, to give a slight smoked effect.

'After firing up the ovens,' Da Dong told me, 'it takes two hours for them to reach the right temperature. The ideal is 350°C. We use only fruit tree wood. It retains its energy for longer, so there's less temperature fluctuation.'

'And it'll add a fragrance to the duck.'

'Certainly.'

I peered in through an opening. The ducks hung vertically, looking ghostly, disembodied in the flickering light. 'How do you control the effects of the heat on the ducks?'

'Oh, they're turned in a particular way.'

Perhaps this was patented, because Da Dong didn't elaborate. 'The chefs in here do only Peking duck, nothing else. After one hour and forty minutes the duck is removed from the oven and hung up on a rack above a drip tray.' He gestured towards what looked like several clothes rails. Each had a row of beautifully browned birds. 'These have less than half the fat of ducks prepared in the traditional way. I've had it analysed at the university.'

'Do you rest the meat at all before serving it?'

'No. Once it's ready, the faster it gets to the table the better. And that's yours on the rack there, Heston. So you'd better hurry up and sit down!'

I took my place at a black lacquered table stamped with Da Dong's ideogram in red. A chef wheeled over a slatted table and carved long slices of breast.

'It used to be that Peking duck was swimming in grease when carved at the table, but not now,' said Da Dong. 'The chef will cut 108 slices in all.'

'Why?'

'Just tradition.'

The slices were placed on a white oblong plate on top of a frill of bright green lettuce leaf. Dainty bits of skin were nicked off and placed on top of the meat. Next to this were small, shallow dishes – two black, two white – each of which had a partition down the middle. They contained radish and cucumber in both julienned and pickled form, garlic paste, sugar, plum sauce and strips of spring onion. It was all beautifully presented. I was keen to get stuck in, but there was a final ritual to be performed first. Da Dong plucked some skin from the plate and flung it at the table, where it shattered into pieces.

'See how crisp it is.'

'Absolutely. It's crispy but sort of melting at the same time. I've never had anything like it.' His process had resulted in skin that had taken on a kind of honeycomb effect.

It was undoubtedly a very original take on an old classic, and it was thrilling to see how scientifically Da Dong had approached the recipe. I didn't know if I wanted to remove quite so much of the fat – for me it was part of the dish's character – but it clearly found favour with Da Dong's customers. The restaurant was full, and there were as many Chinese diners as Westerners.

'Do people in Beijing accept culinary innovation?' I wondered. 'What do they think of your inventions?'

'Oh, they've no problem with new and unusual cuisine. We were so suppressed in the past that now we welcome change.'

It was going to be very exciting to see where that took Chinese cooking in the future.

Modern Peking duck at Da Dong restaurant in Beijing. It would be skilfully and surgically carved into exactly 108 slices.

DUCK SOUP

As the food was brought to my table, the waitress handed over a pink envelope stamped with Chinese characters. Inside was a card that announced:

> **Quanjude was established in 1864
> (the third year of Tongzhi, Qing Dynasty),
> enjoying a history over 140 years.
> [115 million 390636]
> The above number is the roast duck
> we have served from 1864 on.**

This part of my trip was as much about history as it was about food. I was partaking in a great tradition, as had millions (well, 115 million 390635) before me. Quanjude is one of the oldest Peking duck restaurants in Beijing. Legend has it that the owner paid off a court chef in order to get his hands on the imperial recipe. The branch I was visiting had been built on a site personally selected by premier Zhou Enlai, and could cater to 1,500 people in one sitting.

When I arrived, streams of visitors were making their way into the place, pausing only to get a picture of themselves in front of this famous establishment. The Chinese posed stiffly in front of the wide stone steps, making the photographer crouch and point the lens upwards so as to include the restaurant's name above the porch. Westerners preferred to have their photo taken hugging the plastic duck that stood incongruously by the golden revolving doors. I had joined the throng, walking through the entrance hall with its tasselled red lanterns, its gold, dragon-decorated pillars and its greeters in long red tunics slashed to the thigh, and taken the lift to the fourth floor.

The Grand Hall is the biggest of Quanjude's forty-one dining halls, and it lived up to its name. Before me stretched six long rows of tables for four, with red chairs and golden-yellow tablecloths. Golden pillars flanked the fretworked, frosted-glass windows that admitted a strange, watery light. Huge crystal chandeliers mushroomed from the ceiling. It was as if I had walked in on a dinner-dance on an ocean liner. There was even a raised stage at one end, flanked by gold curtains and red pillars, as though we might expect the oriental version of Joe Loss and His Orchestra. A waiter in a yellow tunic broke away from the parade line by one wall and ushered me to my seat. I ordered the All Duck Banquet, the first part of which arrived accompanied by that numbered card.

Three white plates of food were put on the table – pale frills of duck web, thick, meaty lobes of liver and dark chunks of gizzard. When duck is part of a meal, many Beijing restaurants make use of every bit of the bird, a practice that seemed to me to suit the ritualistic origins of the dish. I also appreciated the fact that it tapped into the gastronomic tradition of showcasing an ingredient's range and versatility. (I'd enjoyed an example of this when I tasted Georges Blanc's 'Bresse en Fête' menu, designed to show that 'every part of the chicken is good'.) The challenge and the thriftiness of doing this with Peking duck appealed to me, though I imagined I'd have to reinvent the first course. I like the texture of cartilage, especially when cooked as carefully as it was here, and served with a subtle mustard sauce, but gizzard and web would probably be a step too far for many people.

More plates came, filled with sugar and garlic, slivers of spring onion and cucumber, a sweet sauce and a stack of pancakes. There was a steady flow of ducks from the kitchen, wheeled out on metal trolleys like patients ready for surgery (the impression reinforced by the carvers, who wore paper masks over their mouths), and suddenly there was mine, its skin a lovely tan colour, like polished leather. The carver made an incision in the neck to allow steam to escape, then cut the duck into slices – longer, thinner ones than at Da Dong – working at getting an even balance of skin and flesh. Carving is truly an art here, and it was the work of a few minutes to transform the bird into a neat pile of oval medallions. The head was cut in two and placed on its own plate, with the special fillets from inside the breast laid on top – a ritual within a ritual. I reached for a pancake, horribly aware of how difficult it is to fill and fold it using only chopsticks, and how clumsy it would look on camera. I pincered in all the ingredients and prodded the pancake into a crude parcel shape, then bit into the soft dough.

The duck had leaked plenty of fat as the carver cut, and I was concerned that it might turn out too fatty. But in fact, although it needed the counterbalance of the spring onions and, especially, cucumber, I found I wanted that fat. It reminded me of crispy duck and even of the crackling on pork – a familiar and tasty flavour that had its place here. The sauce also brought something important to the dish, adding moisture without overpowering the other ingredients. I pestered the waitress for the recipe and was told it was soya bean and honey. It was less dominating than plum sauce, which made it a far better accompaniment for this dish. I earmarked it as something to experiment with back in Bray.

The end of the banquet was a rich broth made from the bones and emulsified duck fat – not good for cholesterol levels, but a nice way to finish the meal, using the last pieces of the duck and capturing its flavour in a last concentrated burst.

PUMP IT UP

Air pumps have improved dramatically since I was a kid. I'd been given a choice of a PowerZone Force – a matt black T-bar with bright red dial that looked like the sort of thing Wile E. Coyote would use on Road Runner – or a pillar-box red, foot-action job packing twin cylinders like miniature scuba tanks. I bought both and had just enough time to hide them away in a cupboard before Chris and Kyle brought the ducks into the lab.

I had researched dozens of suppliers and breeds to come up with four that I hoped would suit the specialised cooking techniques involved in Peking duck while maximising the flavours. Kyle lugged in the first of these, breathing heavily. The Moullard was a monster of a bird that took up half the space in the roasting tray (it's used for foie gras, so it's bred big and then fed even bigger). The Gressingham, by comparison, seemed almost puny, an impression reinforced by its particularly pale, smooth skin. The Muscovy and Aylesbury were in between these two extremes – well sized and well fed. I was particularly curious about the latter because in the nineteenth century Pekin ducks were crossbred with Aylesburys to improve the breed. I was about to cook these four and see whether they developed moist flesh and a crispy, lacquered skin. Maybe genetics would give the Aylesbury an edge.

'Getting the skin right is crucial to my recipe,' I told Chris and Kyle. 'And the key to that seems to lie in separating it from the flesh before cooking. I didn't get an opportunity to see this in action in Beijing, but I did get the next best thing – a photocopy of a 1957 recipe for Peking duck. It's the first ever published. I found it in Beijing National Library … '

Neither of them seemed very impressed – perhaps because the text was in Mandarin and the photos were so grainy that it looked as though the duck was being prepped in a snowstorm.

'Anyway, it's time to blow and blanch. Try these.' I handed over two drinking straws, and pointed Kyle in the direction of the Moullard and Chris to the Muscovy.

'I see we've got the short straws,' said Chris. 'What about you?'

I opened the cupboard, brandished my red footpump and set to work on the Gressingham.

It'll come as no surprise to discover that duck pumping isn't as straightforward as it looks. A couple of minutes' huffing and puffing hadn't blown any ducks, but it had given Chris and Kyle purple faces, and we ended up laughing so hard that we had to stop and try again.

'Maybe it's better if we go in the neck side,' Kyle decided after a long, squinted scrutiny of the fogged pictures in the photocopy. He started digging between the skin and flesh with a knife to encourage the two to part company. I doubted it was an approach sanctioned by the National Library document, but I too began pulling at the skin with my hand. My gamesmanship with the footpump had backfired because it proved far harder to keep the nozzle in place than to use a straw, but eventually one side of my bird ballooned out. I turned it around and began on the other side. This proved easier. The legs twitched upwards as the bird began to inflate, and with each pump it seemed to heave a laborious, ragged sigh. *Squawk–squawk–squawk.*

'I think the patient's coming back to life, doctor,' said Kyle.

In the end we managed to separate the skin on all four birds. It was something I had always wanted to do, and it was very satisfying to achieve that ambition. The most difficult part was starting off: once some headway had been made, once some of the skin's tension had loosened, it came away more readily. I didn't know how easily this would translate to home cooking, though. Maybe a stronger pump would do the job more efficiently. I'd have to take a duck to the local garage …

An unorthodox method of separating duck skin – using the local garage's air pump.

While I'd got caught up in pump envy, the ducks were getting blanched. Three times they had been dunked in a vat of boiling water for fifteen seconds, then plunged into a tub filled with iced water, after which they were hung up to dry on a length of twine that had been stretched across the lab at head height. Buckets were placed underneath, into which the ducks dripped. Kyle and Chris started painting them with maltose syrup, giving them a shiny, varnished look. The drips in the buckets turned brown.

Much later, once that maltose painting had given the ducks a sort of toffee-apple look, they were put in the oven and roasted at 65°C/ 150°F to see if we could get a crisp skin without overcooking them.

The results were disappointing. Even as I slit down the leg of the first duck, I could see that the flesh was far from moist and much too fatty, and the skin wasn't crispy at all. And each of the four was the same. I didn't know whether it was a conflict of techniques – maybe you couldn't have moist flesh and crisp skin – or whether these ducks, good as they were, weren't right for Peking duck. I knew that choosing the right type of potato for chips, mash or roast was absolutely essential to the success or failure of the dish. I was beginning to suspect that the same imperative applied here. The ducks I had seen in China were much younger and smaller. There wasn't much thickness on the breast. They were very different creatures from what I had in front of me.

There was no ducking the issue: I'd have to do some more research if I wanted perfect skin.

GOING OUT FOR A DUCK

Silver Hill Foods in Emyvale, County Monaghan, supplies 98 per cent of the Chinese restaurants in Britain. Walk through London's Chinatown and the glazed brown ducks hanging in the windows are almost certainly theirs. The company has won a clutch of awards, including two from the Irish Food Writers' Guild. If I wanted to get under the skin of Peking duck, Silver Hill seemed the best place to ask.

I was met at Belfast airport by the company's MD, Stuart Steele. As we thundered down the motorway and then wove our way around the drumlins of County Monaghan, he explained how his parents, Ronnie and Lyla, had started the company forty-five years ago – 'She wanted to farm chickens. He was set on turkeys. So they ended up with … ducks!' – and how competition from Thailand meant Silver Hill concentrated more than ever on quality rather than quantity. 'We can never compete on labour costs. One of our employees costs per day what an entire workforce costs per week over there. That's what we're up against. We've diversified into readymeals, duck down duvets, even organic duck manure.'

He seemed very organised, business-like and urbane, but precautions against bird flu are a great leveller. Once we'd donned white wellington boots, a white labcoat and a blue hairnet, we both looked like bit-part actors in a budget sci-fi movie. 'OK, Stuart. What is it that makes Silver Hill ducks so special?'

'I'll show you.' He led me past a series of factory buildings with green corrugated roofs and down a ramp to a small Portakabin. Inside, on small, angled stands, were two ducks. The stands held each bird's wings gently away from its body and loosely gripped the ankles, leaving the chest bared. Both eyed me in my extraterrestrial get-up and began quacking loudly.

'There are three things that make the Silver Hill duck what it is. And the first is breeding,' said Stuart, raising his voice to be heard. 'Our ducks are a cross between Pekin and Aylesbury. It's crucial that they have the right meat-to-fat ratio. We used to select breeders simply by feeling the birds. Now we use ultrasound.' He indicated the keyboard and screen, the latter with a long white tube extending from it. 'The breeding programme has really taken off since we cut out the guesswork.'

'So this is the same ultrasound as would be used for a pregnant woman?'

'Exactly the same. Watch the screen.' He smoothed a little oil on to the breast of a duck and nestled the head of the ultrasound among its feathers. 'There's the heart. And there's the breast in cross-section.' The grainy image showed alternating stripes of light and dark. Stuart pointed with his free hand at one of each. 'We measure from here to here to find the ones that have what we consider the correct ratio. The actual figure's a closely guarded secret. The ones that do – about 1 per cent of our ducks – go on to the breeding programme. It works on the same principle as two tall people creating tall offspring. Get the fat ratio of both parents right, and it'll probably be handed on to their children.'

The ducks had by now lost interest in us, and turned their bills away, disdainful of the TV camera. We walked back up the ramp, along a concrete balcony and through several passageways to a door marked 'Plucking and Waxing Rooms'.

Here was a part of the process that tested your commitment to eating meat. I have been to many killing floors: it's probably an experience every carnivore should have at least once, to see if they can stomach what goes into filling their stomach. No matter how benign the factory involved, organised death has a particular brutality. At head height, slung on metal frames, hundreds of dead ducks wound their way around a large, bare, concrete room. At intervals they were lowered and dragged through tanks filled with liquid, like witches undergoing Ordeal by Water.

'They're baths of wax,' Stuart told me, as we reached the first tank. 'This one is 120°C and they go in for about twenty seconds.' The puckered, pale-skinned birds proceeded in and out, acquiring a very pale caramel sheen and a form of blanching from the heat. We moved on, keeping step with the conveyor belt, the rattle of metal loud in our ears.

'The next wax-bath is kept as cool as possible while keeping it liquid.' The surface churned viscously. The ducks emerged from this transformed to a deep basted brown. 'The final tank is just cold water, to harden the wax.' Enclosed in their wax shrouds, the ducks were now conveyed upwards to a raised platform where two men stood, wearing red overalls, blue hairnet, ear defenders, disposable gloves and white rubber bib. As each bird passed, they unfolded the body from the frame to let it dangle upside down. In one swift, practised movement each man gripped a rump, tugged it gently forwards, then ran his hands down both sides of the animal. The duck trundled on, its skin now like parchment. In the plucker's hands was a creepy rubbery carapace, like some alien life-form. We were back in that sci-fi movie.

'The wax takes off the last of the feathers without damaging the skin,' Stuart explained. 'You can't have tears or blemishes in it or the bird won't cook properly. This is the best way to ensure that, though it's also important that the ducks are killed when they're forty-five to forty-eight days old. After that the feathers become too porcupine-like and are much more difficult to remove.'

We left the ducks to their indignity and stepped across to the Air Chill Room, the third of Silver Hill's key processes. It too had a *Brave New World* aspect to it. Overhead, in seemingly endless rows that reached to the ceiling, ducks suspended on a conveyor belt were shuttled around in the frigid air. 'The room's kept at 4°C,' Stuart shouted over the machine-rumble. 'Most places cool their ducks by putting them in water, but we find that air-chilling is better. The birds retain less water and the flesh ends up tender rather than spongy. And there you have it.' He took me out of the room's wintry grip. 'The three reasons why Silver Hill ducks are so good. "Succulent, tender and full of flavour", as our vans say.'

Succulent, tender and full of flavour – that and a glass-like crispy skin were exactly what I wanted. I wondered how I was going to get that without using specialised mechanical processes, and without access to a well-developed, tailor-made breeding programme.

SOUPED UP

There is a technique known as 'ice filtration', which produces an unbelievably pure, clear liquid that also has a powerful, concentrated flavour. At the Fat Duck I had found wonderful applications for it, such as venison and frankincense tea, and I was convinced that it could be used to create a lovely duck broth to finish the meal, something refined and, above all, cleansing.

The consommé in the graduated glass beakers confirmed my instincts. It was an enticing, deep golden yellow, the colour of a dessert wine. The clarity made its full-bodied, roasting-juice flavours all the more unexpected. A mouthful with a big mouthfeel. Now I had to finish it off: find the flavours that would enhance and enrich it, the top notes and heart notes that would give it depth and complexity.

With that big taste still on the tongue, I ransacked the lab for ingredients that might fit the bill, plucking dark soy sauce from the shelves, and Shao Xing rice wine, Chinkiang vinegar, Mizkan rice-flavoured distilled vinegar and toasted sesame oil. One of my first gastronomic experiences was going to eat at a Chinese restaurant in Paddington and drinking jasmine tea, so I added a packet of jasmine to the growing pile of condiments, along with some extraordinary lapsang souchong that could perhaps introduce a smoked flavour.

I sniffed and swirled and swilled, pipetting in drops of this, spooning in a little of that, until the flavours cancelled each other out or gave in to the most dominant, at which point I had to begin afresh. Soy sauce and sesame oil overpowered everything too quickly: I added the beakers to the growing debris of unstoppered bottles, lids, used spoons, half-drunk cups of Earl Grey (for refreshment rather than experimentation) and half-full pipettes. Distilled rice vinegar had a subtle, complementary flavour that worked well, and I decided to keep it simple. I warmed some consommé in a pan and flicked in a few green strands of jasmine, let the aroma rise, then sipped.

It was the sort of top note I had been looking for. There was still a lot of testing to do – jasmine leaves were too refined and had a wet-hay note to them: I would have to try essential oil instead – but my ideal of a full-flavoured, cleansing soup was starting to come together.

SKIN DIPPING

We had brined a duck, blanched it in sugar syrup, hung it for four days in the fridge to air-dry the skin, then roasted it for thirty minutes at 60°C. Now it hung from a chain above a vat of boiling oil – another bird undergoing a medieval interrogation. (This was in part inspired by a visit to China Tang at the Dorchester, one of London's best Chinese restaurants, where Ringo Chan had shown us his approach.)

Ladlefuls of oil were scooped over its head, provoking angry sizzles as they cascaded down the skin. I ignored the fact that it was splashing everywhere, that this technique wouldn't work well in a kitchen that didn't have a hood, that it looked more like an extreme sport than a cooking method, and simply hoped that it would achieve what had so far eluded me: a duck with moist, tender flesh and glass-like skin. The heat needed to crisp up the skin always made the meat too dry. We had already used up twenty ducks looking for the answer. Maybe this oil baste would be the solution.

Chris flopped the duck on to a chopping board. The skin was a beautiful glossy brown, but I had learned the hard way that this gave no clue as to how the bird had responded to cooking. I picked up a knife, carved a slice, took a bite and chewed.

The fact that it tasted fine didn't matter. The skin still wasn't crisp. We were no nearer the goal. I couldn't find a way to manage the moisture content so that it kept the meat juicy but didn't soften the skin. I didn't want to take the skin off and give it a final blast of heat on its own (as you might a pork roast) because I wanted the elegance of the skin remaining on the bird. But it was beginning to look like I had no choice.

Peking Duck Serves 4

Once the tasks of keeping the flesh moist and making the skin crisp were separated – with the skin stitched on a rack (a final form of medieval punishment for the beleaguered duck) – it proved easier to achieve both objectives. Although I would have liked to finesse an intact crispy-skinned duck, I like to think there's still an elegance to the recipe in the way that every part of the animal is used in the dish. The crown is the meat for the pancakes; a confit of legs and thighs is shredded for the stir-fry; and the breasts are blitzed with aromatic vegetables for the dumplings. Even the bits that we in the West often baulk at – the bones, heads, necks and feet – go into the stock for the consommé. Nothing is wasted, which seems in keeping with the Chinese attitude towards food.

The key to the consommé is ice filtration, an amazing and versatile technique discovered by the German scientist Gerd Kloeck. We use it at the Fat Duck to make a crystal-clear consommé with a really intense flavour, and I'm sure it will prove equally invaluable for the home cook. Ice filtration relies on the principle that if you freeze a block of gelatinous stock and then thaw it gradually, the smaller taste and aroma molecules are concentrated in the liquid that melts out of the frozen block of stock, while the larger molecules, such as gelatin and fat (which is what makes a consommé cloudy), are left behind in the ice.

Several steps are crucial to success. There must be enough gelatin in the stock to make it gel, and it should be frozen only after it has gelled. Most important of all, the stock has to be thawed very slowly in the refrigerator. If it thaws too quickly at a warmer temperature, the fat will melt back into oil droplets and fall into the consommé, making it cloudy.

In keeping with the nothing-is-wasted philosophy, the unfiltered stock that remains after thawing can still be used: it retains plenty of flavour.

Special equipment
Mandolin, pressure cooker, bamboo steamer, food processor, barding needle, butcher's string, kitchen shears, wire rack wrapped in muslin, oven thermometer, digital probe

Timing
DUCK: Preparation takes 15½ hours, including 12 hours for brining. Cooking takes 4 hours.
CONFIT: Preparation takes 45 minutes plus 12 hours to set aside. Cooking takes 24½ hours (most of this time is the confit process).
CONSOMMÉ: Preparation takes 30 minutes plus 24 hours for the ice filtration. Cooking takes 2 hours 15 minutes.
DUMPLINGS: Preparation takes 30 minutes plus 1 hour for meat to salt. Cooking takes 30 minutes.

For the ducks
2 whole ducks, preferably Silver Hill breed

For the consommé
750g reserved duck wings, chopped into small pieces _ 1.2kg pork spare ribs cut into 2.5cm pieces _ reserved duck carcasses, wing tips, necks, extra meat and trimmings, chopped into small pieces _ 40g thinly sliced ginger _ 60g sliced spring onions _ 90g Shao Xing wine or fino sherry

For the consommé infusion and ice filtration
1kg finished stock (reserve any extra for future use) _ 20g sliced ginger _ 2.5g (about 6) Szechwan peppercorns _ 2g Szechwan chillies, roasted _ 2g cinnamon _ 4g star anise _ 10g spring onions

For the duck confit
42g star anise _ 24g ground ginger _ 12g Szechwan peppercorns _ 12g cinnamon _ 6g cardamom _ 150g sel gris (coarse sea salt) _ zest from 1 mandarin orange _ 4 reserved duck legs _ rendered duck fat

For the pickled cucumber

50g water _ 75g white wine vinegar _ 25g sugar _ 1 English cucumber

PREPARING THE DUCKS

1. Remove the giblets from the ducks. Reserve everything except the livers for the consommé, then rinse the cavity of the birds.
2. Remove the head, neck and wing tips of both birds, cutting as close to the body as you can without damaging the skin on the breast. Reserve the head, neck and wing tips for the consommé.
3. To remove the skin from the birds, begin by using a paring knife to cut through the tendons at the bottom joint of the legs.
4. Working with one duck at a time, cut a slit through the skin on the back, running from the top to the bottom of the bird. Using a pair of kitchen shears, remove the parson's nose.
5. Use your knife to gently free the skin from the flesh. Begin by peeling back the skin on both sides of the long cut. When you reach the legs and wings turn the bird over on to its back and continue peeling the skin away from the wings and then from the legs. Do your best to keep the skin intact and in one piece. Repeat this process with the other duck.
6. Remove the legs from the ducks by popping each joint from its hip socket and then cutting it away from the body. Reserve the legs for the confit.
7. Remove the wings in a similar fashion – pop them from their sockets and then cut them away from the body. Reserve the wings for the consommé. Chop the bones and reserve for the consommé.
8. Take one duck and use kitchen shears to cut through the ribs, separating the breast from the back. Cut close to the breast and then cut through to the neck. The idea is to have a clean separation between the breasts on the bone and the ribs, back and neck. Reserve this 'crown' of breast and the back for the first course.
9. Remove the wishbone from the crown by carefully cutting along it with your knife, then using your fingers to prise it loose.
10. Take the other duck and remove the breast meat with your knife. Reserve 200g of this meat for the dumplings and use the rest in the consommé.
11. Reserve the butchered carcasses of the ducks for the consommé.

MAKING THE CONSOMMÉ

1. Put half of all the meats and trimmings, half the aromatics and half the Shao Xing wine in a pressure cooker and add 1.5kg of water.
2. Cook under full pressure for 1 hour, then remove from the heat and allow the pressure cooker to cool.
3. Strain the stock and repeat this process a second time with the remainder of the ingredients, but use the previously made stock instead of water.
4. Strain the finished stock and reserve.

INFUSING AND FILTERING THE CONSOMMÉ

1. Bring the finished stock back to a simmer.
2. Remove from the heat and add all the aromatics. Infuse for about 10 minutes.
3. Pour the stock into the largest flat-bottomed container you have. Refrigerate until it gels, then transfer to the freezer until completely solid.
4. Once the stock is frozen, dip the container into a sink filled with warm water. As soon as the edges of the stock melt, tip the frozen block on to a muslin-lined perforated tray and sit this in a larger container. Place in the fridge and let the stock slowly melt over 24 hours (don't try to speed it up). During this time the ice and gelatin will naturally filter the stock and you will be left with a crystal clear consommé in the container underneath the perforated tray. In the muslin on top of the tray will be the remaining filtrate, still icy and filled with gelatin.
5. Pour off the consommé into a clean container and refrigerate or freeze until needed.
6. Reserve the contents of the muslin for poaching the duck meat for the first course.

MAKING THE DUCK CONFIT

1. Place all the spices in a blender and grind to a coarse powder.
2. Mix the spices with the salt and the mandarin zest.
3. Put the duck legs in a container and surround them with the spice-salt mixture. Set aside for 12 hours. Remove them from the salt and wash very thoroughly.

4. Preheat the oven to 65°C/150°F.* Place the duck legs in a roasting pan, cover with duck fat and cook in the oven for 6–8 hours.
5. Cool the cooked duck legs to room temperature, then remove them from the fat. Using your hands, pull off the leg meat and shred it into fine strands. Reserve this for the stir-fry.

MAKING THE PICKLED CUCUMBER
1. Place the water, vinegar and sugar in a small saucepan. Bring to the boil, then turn off the heat. Cool the mixture to room temperature.
2. Use a mandolin to slice thin rounds from either end of the cucumber, where it has fewer seeds. Stop when you get to the thicker part where there are more seeds. Reserve the middle of the cucumber to serve with the crispy pancake portion of the meal.
3. Place the cucumber slices in a small container and fill with the pickling liquid. Cover the container and refrigerate for at least 6 hours (this can be done several days in advance). Use when serving the final course.

FIRST COURSE
Peking duck with pancakes

For the pancake garnish
reserved middle section of cucumber _ 1 bunch of spring onions

For the duck crown
1 cinnamon stick _ 5 whole star anise _ 3 whole cloves _
10 coriander seeds _ 5 black peppercorns _ 60g salt _ 1kg water

For the crispy skin
reserved sheets of duck skin _ 125g malt extract (maltose, available from health food shops) _ 25g rice wine vinegar _ 75g wood chips, ideally cherrywood

* If you don't have a convection oven, set your oven to the lowest it will go. You may need to prop the door open and use an oven thermometer to get the temperature down to 65°C/150°F.

For finishing the duck and skin

reserved unfiltered stock from the muslin, plus sufficient water to make 2kg liquid in total _ 1 reserved brined duck crown _ 2 sheets prepared duck skin _ 2kg grapeseed oil or another vegetable oil

For serving the pancakes

18–20 pancakes (available from supermarkets and oriental grocers) _ reserved sliced duck breast _ reserved crispy skin _ reserved cucumber batons and spring onion ribbons _ Peking duck or hoisin sauce, such as Lee Kum Kee's

PREPARING THE PANCAKE GARNISH

1. Peel the cucumber and cut it in half lengthways. Use a small spoon to scoop out the seeds.
2. Cut the cucumber into batons roughly 5cm long and ½cm square.
3. Trim both ends of the spring onions. Cut the remainder into lengths roughly 5cm long, then cut these lengthways into thin ribbons. Set aside for the pancakes, but reserve 12 strands for the finished consommé.

PREPARING THE DUCK CROWN

1. Put the cinnamon stick, star anise, cloves, coriander seeds and peppercorns in a saucepan with the salt and water and bring to the boil.
2. Remove the pan from the heat and allow the spices to infuse for 10 minutes.
3. Pour the mixture into a container large enough to hold the duck crown.
4. Submerge the duck crown in the brine and cover the container. Refrigerate for 12 hours.
5. Drain off the brine and fill the container with cold water. Soak the duck for 2 hours, changing the water every 15 minutes, to remove any excess salt from the meat.
6. Remove the crown from the water, blot it dry with kitchen paper and refrigerate until needed.

PREPARING THE CRISPY SKIN

1. Take the two sheets of duck skin and spread them out on a cutting board with the external side facing up.
2. Using a sharp knife, trim both sheets into a rectangular shape.
3. Place each sheet of skin, external side up, on a metal cooling rack, and stretch out as far as possible without tearing. Use a barding needle and butcher's string to stitch the skin to the racks around the edges. The skin should be fully stretched out, but not pulled so taut that it will rip away from the string when it contracts during the cooking process.
4. Use a fine needle to prick tiny holes all over the surface of the skin, but be careful – don't push the needle through the skin. The lightly punctured surface will allow moisture and fat to escape.
5. Preheat the oven to 60°C/140°F. Place the racks on foil-lined baking sheets and cook the skin for 3 hours.
6. In the meantime, warm the malt extract in a small pan until it is very liquid, then whisk in the vinegar.
7. Remove the skin sheets from the oven and use kitchen paper to blot away any moisture on the surface of the skin. Increase the oven temperature to 170°C/325°F/Gas 3.
8. Brush the skins with a thin, even coating of the warm malt mixture.
9. While the oven is heating, take the wood chips and wrap them in foil. Heat the package in a sauté pan until the chips begin to smoke, then place in the hot oven. Put the skins in the oven with the smoking chips for approximately 15 minutes.
10. Remove the skins and set aside. Discard the used wood chips.

FINISHING THE DUCK AND SKIN

1. Place the stock in a pan and heat until melted. Skim off any oil on the surface. Add the water and heat to 70°C/160°F, using a digital probe to check the temperature and hold it constant.
2. When the temperature stabilises, insert the probe into the thickest part of the duck crown. (Ideally, use two probes to monitor both the liquid temperature and the meat temperature during cooking.)
3. Submerge the duck in the hot broth and poach the meat until its internal temperature reaches 70°C/160°F.

4. Remove the crown from the liquid and leave to rest in a warm spot for 10 minutes.
5. Reserve 500g of the poaching liquid for the stir-fry.
6. After resting, place the crown on a cutting board and remove each breast from the bone.
7. While the duck breasts are resting, place the racks of skin in a large roasting pan.
8. Heat the oil to 190°C/375°F and use a ladle to pour it over the skin. Hold each rack at a steep angle and let the oil run down the skin and collect in the roasting tray. Continue until the skin becomes puffed and crispy and has taken on a rich colour. (You might need to return the oil to the saucepan and reheat it during this process.)
9. Transfer the racks to a work surface and snip off the butcher's string.
10. Place the crispy sheets of skin on a cutting board and cut into strips. Place on a platter and keep warm.
11. Slice the breasts thinly and fan them out on a serving platter.

SERVING THE PANCAKES
1. Steam the pancakes (allow 4 or 5 per person) in a bamboo steamer. Serve these in their basket along with the platters of skin and meat, the cucumber batons, spring onions and the Peking sauce.

SECOND COURSE
Stir-fried duck confit with shiitake mushrooms and ginger

For the mushrooms and aromatics
140g shiitake mushrooms, sliced 2cm thick _ 15g finely julienned ginger _ 50g finely julienned spring onion _ 25g minced shallot _ 5g minced garlic _ 2g (about 6) seeded and sliced Szechwan chillies _ 2 Szechwan peppercorns, crushed _ 1 small fresh red chilli, thinly sliced

For the glaze
65g white port _ 50g Shao Xing wine or fino sherry _ 500g reserved cooking broth (from the crown poaching liquid) _ 3.5g thinly sliced ginger _ 2g crushed star anise _ sherry vinegar, to taste

For serving the duck confit

grapeseed oil or groundnut oil _ reserved mushrooms and aromatics _ reserved glaze _ reserved shredded duck confit _ soy sauce _ sesame oil _ 1 head of iceberg lettuce, separated into individual leaves

PREPARING THE SHIITAKE MUSHROOMS

1. Prepare all the ingredients as listed and reserve.

MAKING THE GLAZE

1. Pour the port and wine into a saucepan and bring to a simmer. Set the alcohol alight and let the flame burn out while simmering.
2. Add the broth and reduce the liquid to a consistency that coats the back of a spoon.
3. Remove from the heat and add the aromatics for a few minutes, then strain the stock through a fine sieve. Adjust the acidity with the sherry vinegar. Set aside to finish the dish.

SERVING THE DUCK CONFIT

1. Heat a wok or a large sauté pan until very hot.
2. Add a small amount of grapeseed oil, the peppercorns and chillies, and swirl to coat the pan lightly. Add the mushrooms, ginger, spring onion, shallot and garlic. Quickly stir-fry to keep them from burning.
3. When the mushrooms have started to wilt and the pan smells very fragrant, deglaze the pan with about three-quarters of the glaze, then add the shredded confit.
4. Bring the pan to a simmer to warm the meat through. Add more glaze if necessary: it should just coat the meat and vegetables.
5. When everything is hot, remove the pan from the heat and add the soy sauce and sesame oil to taste. It's important not to add the sesame oil until the very last moment or the nutty aroma will be lost.
6. Serve with the lettuce. The stir-fry can be wrapped up in lettuce.

THIRD COURSE
Ice-filtered duck consommé with duck dumplings

For the braised shiitake mushrooms
4 large shiitake mushrooms _ 25g grapeseed or groundnut oil _ 30g
mirin (rice wine) _ 100g reserved duck consommé _ 10g light soy sauce

For the dumplings
200g reserved duck meat (taken from one of the reserved
breasts) _ ½ tsp table salt _ 120g finely minced leek (about ½
a large leek) _ 120g (about ½ head) finely minced Savoy cabbage _
25g unsalted butter _ 1½ tsp skimmed milk powder _ 60g duck
fat _ 50g (1 large) egg _ 14g (1 tbsp) soy sauce _ 25g (1½ tbsp)
sesame oil _ 15g (about 4cm) minced ginger _ 50g (about 5) minced
spring onion _ ½ tsp finely ground and sifted black pepper _
12 very thin, round wonton wrappers (available at Asian grocers)

For serving the consommé with dumplings
800g finished consommé _ 4 reserved braised shiitake mushrooms _
12 reserved dumplings _ 12 slices of reserved pickled cucumber _
12 reserved ribbons of spring onion _ 8 drops of jasmine essential
oil (available at nealsyardremedies.com)

BRAISING THE SHIITAKE MUSHROOMS
1. Remove the stems from the mushrooms. Cut straight across the caps
   to remove the gills and create a smooth surface. Discard the stems.
2. Heat the oil in a small sauté pan over a medium heat, then sear the
   flat side of the mushroom caps until lightly browned.
3. Use kitchen paper to blot up any excess oil in the pan, then deglaze
   with the mirin.
4. Reduce the mirin until it thickens and coats the mushrooms.
5. Add the consommé and simmer for about 3 minutes, until it thickens
   and glazes the mushrooms too.
6. Remove the pan from the heat, add the light soy sauce and transfer
   the mushrooms to a container to cool. Refrigerate until needed.

MAKING THE DUMPLINGS

1. Refrigerate the duck meat and the bowl and blade of a food processor.
2. Process 20g of the meat to a paste and mix it with the salt (this will help to extract the protein from the meat, which is necessary for a good texture). Refrigerate for 1 hour.
3. In the meantime, sweat the leek and cabbage in the butter until very soft. Reserve.
4. After 1 hour, blend the salted meat with 125g of the fresh meat and the skimmed milk powder. Pureé this in the cold food processor. Dice the remaining duck meat into very small pieces.
5. Add the fat, the egg, the soy sauce and the sesame oil. Process with the meat.
6. When the meat is a fine paste remove it from the food processor and fold in the sweated leeks and cabbage, the minced ginger, the spring onions, the black pepper and the diced duck meat.
7. Place the wonton wrappers on a work surface. Roll 15g of the meat into balls and place one in the middle of each wrapper. Wet the outer edge of the wrappers, then gather them around the meat and pinch closed at the top. Place on a tray covered with a damp paper towel and reserve in the refrigerator until needed.

SERVING THE CONSOMMÉ WITH DUMPLINGS

1. Put the consommé in a pan and heat until hot.
2. Meanwhile, cut each mushroom into several thin slices and fan these out in the bottom of 4 warm bowls.
3. Poach the dumplings over the consommé for 8 minutes, then sit three of them on the mushrooms in each bowl.
4. Drain the pickled cucumber and place the slices on a cutting board. Cut a slit from the middle to the edge of each round, cutting through the skin. Roll the rounds into a cone shape and place on the dumplings. Garnish with the ribbons of spring onion.
5. Heat the bowls. Place 2 drops of jasmine essential oil on the rim of each hot bowl and use kitchen paper to wipe the oil around the rim.
6. Pour 200g of hot consommé into each bowl and serve immediately.

Steak

'My favourite animal is steak.'

Fran Lebowitz

History

That's my steak, Valance. Pick it up.
John Wayne in *The Man Who Shot Liberty Valance*

All domestic cattle breeds descend from a single ancestor, the aurochs, a large long-horned beast that once roamed Europe, southwest Asia and Africa, and can be seen depicted in many cave paintings. Its domestication occurred early: in Turkey remains of domesticated cattle have been found that date from 6500 BC. By 55 BC Romans had recorded the existence of red cattle in southwestern England – almost certainly the Red Devon cattle that can still be found in the region and are considered one of the oldest breeds in existence.

Steak itself has a similarly lengthy provenance. The word derives from the Old Norse term *steikjo* – 'to roast on a spit' – a method of cooking that has been around as long as there has been fire to perform it, and that has been a favourite with the English for centuries. The Harleian Manuscripts in the British Library contain a recipe from around 1430 for broiled venison or beefsteaks that wouldn't look particularly out of place on the modern table. By 1748 the Swedish traveller Pehr Kalm could declare: 'Englishmen understand almost better than any other people the art of properly roasting a large cut of meat.' (Though he undercut his praise by pointing out that this was 'because the art of cooking as practised by most Englishmen does not extend much beyond roast beef and plum pudding'!)

The English were noted for their taste for plain food: even in the eighteenth century, the preference of most people (even royalty) was for roasted and boiled meat, puddings and pies. Plain food seems to have encouraged plain speaking: our steak cuts are still named after the part of the animal from which they come – fillet, sirloin and rump. France, not surprisingly, has made a more elaborate affair of it, dividing the fillet (a long muscle below the bones of the sirloin) into chateaubriand, tournedos and filet mignon, cutting between the ribs for entrecôte and removing muscles from the carcass to give other tender cuts.

However, it is in the USA that steak cookery has acquired true cult status (in *The Oxford Companion to Food*, Alan Davidson laconically observes that the American tradition of eating large steaks has 'associations of virility'). Basic cuts include filet, club, rib, shell or strip, sirloin, T-bone and tenderloin, but the need for mythology and romance has given rise to a panoply of more exotic names, often for the same cut. Most of us are probably familiar with the porterhouse steak and the carpetbag steak, stuffed with oysters, but there are also the ambassador steak, Kansas City steak and NY strip steak, not to mention the Delmonico and country club steaks, the Flatiron steak, plus of course names associated with styles of cooking: planked and Swiss, steak Sinatra and steak Jack Daniel's, among others.

Given this vivid steak lore, it's surprising to discover that beef was a relatively late addition to the American diet. Before the Civil War it rarely appeared on the table. Part of the reason for this was that cattle are not indigenous to the Americas: they were brought to the New World by the Spanish in 1540. Even then, the sheer size of the country and its harsh winters prevented cattle-raising from becoming widespread. The railways made the difference. In the 1860s trains made transport feasible, and within fifteen years refrigerated trucks meant the slaughterhouses of the Midwest could send beef east, where a taste for it was developing.

The Quest for the Best

Average American's simplest and commonest form of breakfast consists of coffee and beefsteak.
Mark Twain, *A Tramp Abroad*

UP THE EMPIRE

Given its veneration for steak, America seemed the best place to go in search of the perfect one. I flew to New York.

Although the restaurant scene in New York is one of the most varied, energetic and inventive in the world, and several of its food writers have championed the idea that science plays an important part in cooking, I had never been to the city. So, before we started filming in earnest, I begged the TV crew's indulgence.

I wanted to start my visit with a trip up the Empire State Building.

From the observation platform, the surrounding buildings were all stark light and shadows, reinforcing the impression that I was looking down on an architect's model rather than the real thing. It was in any case a rather unreal experience – so many of the buildings before me had a visual history, and a thousand movie moments crowded inside my head. Above me I could imagine the planes circling an enraged King Kong. To the northeast I could see the silvery geometric patterns of the tip of the Chrysler Building – home to the Kingpin in *Spiderman* cartoons, and highlighted as the pinnacle of architectural perfection in *Hannah and Her Sisters* and *Kramer vs. Kramer*. Further east were the News Building – where the helicopter crashed in *Superman*, leaving Lois Lane dangling in mid-air – and the square bulk of the United Nations, scene of the stabbing in *North by Northwest*. Due north was the green expanse of Central Park, home to hundreds of angsty conversations between New York couples, from Alvy Singer and Annie Hall to Harry and Sally. Downtown there was the impossible thinness of the Flatiron, sharply bisecting Broadway and Fifth like the prow of a ship and, beyond it, the sad absence of the Twin Towers, prey to a destruction that outstripped even the most apocalyptic scenarios thought up by superhero comic-book illustrators.

Even up here you got a sense of the energy and determination in the city, the headstrong craziness, the whole Broadway boogie-woogie of it all. And, though I didn't know it at the time, before I left I'd sample some of that, stumbling across one of my best friends and biggest rivals unexpectedly in a restaurant on the Lower East Side, and ending up in a strip joint near the Hudson …

But that lay in the future. Downtown, to the southeast, I could see the castle-like towers and cat's cradle of suspension wires that marked out the Brooklyn Bridge, reminding me that we had an appointment at the most famous steakhouse in New York.

PORTERHOUSE BROWN

Peter Luger at 178 Broadway in Brooklyn is a phenomenon. It has been going since 1887, and Zagat's, the most influential restaurant guide in New York, has voted it the number one steakhouse fifteen years in a row. Framed certificates attesting to this fact line the wall opposite the bar, along with a photo of Johnny Carson on which is inscribed: 'The best meal of my entire life was at Peter Luger's.'

At first glance, the restaurant seems a rather unlikely place for such adulation. It is brown throughout – the two dining rooms have heavy wooden panelling and timber beams, dark bentwood chairs and battered square wooden tables. The décor is German bierkeller: stamped brass plates and ceramic beer mugs adorn the walls. It is resolutely unfashionable and has a macho, no-frills ambience about it that suits the clientele: in one corner several bulky men in silk suits were talking animatedly in Italian, as though they were auditioning for a mobster movie. The sidewalk outside was littered with fat cigar butts.

It suits what's on the menu too: porterhouse steak, pure and simple – a gargantuan piece of meat cut from the wing-rib end of the sirloin or the tail end of the foreribs, giving you some of the sirloin and some of the filet. It's named after the drinking houses in which it was first served.

Given the macho decoration, I half expected to be greeted by a red-faced man with weightlifter's forearms and mutton-chop sideburns, but Jody Storch was elegantly dressed in blue suede loafers and a light grey suit, and had a fund of tongue-in-cheek stories. As we walked downstairs to the meat-drying room, she told me how she got into this business.

'My grandfather, Sol Forsman, loved this place. He worked across the street and ate here with clients twice a day. So when he heard that Peter Luger was selling up, what else could he do? He bought it, even though he was this simple guy with little education and certainly no experience in the restaurant business.'

It has been in the family ever since. Quality control is one key to their success. Jody's grandfather was determined that all the meat should be dealt with personally. During Jody's childhood, while the other kids were playing, she would be taken by her mother to the meat market to learn the tricks of the trade.

'You need to look for beef that's a rosy pink colour rather than dark purple. It should feel silky to the touch, not gummy. And there's a part of the meat that's known as "the button" – if you look at a steak, it's that thumb-sized chunk of meat out on its own, surrounded by fat. My mom used to tell me to check that bit. She said that if the fat marbling had reached the button, then you knew it had spread well through the animal. And that fat is important. Even though the recent trend for lean meat has hit us hard, in the world of Peter Luger, fat is good. It gives the meat its flavour, makes it much tastier.'

Now Jody, her mother or one of her aunts goes to the meat market. 'They take down the dirty calendars when we're doing the buying.' Each of them has their own stamp with which they mark the cuts they've chosen. Jody's is 4F4. 'It makes sure there are no switcheroos. Though I've had a guy actually cut off the slice of fat with the stamp on and then melt it on to a different flank.' They keep up the rigorous standards of quality control first introduced by Jody's grandfather. 'The US Department of Agriculture grades beef according to quality, from "Prime" and "Choice" at the top end to "Cutter" and "Canner" at the bottom. "Prime" beef accounts for only 2 per cent of the meat available, but I usually still reject about half of that. There's a lot of Prime that should really be called Choice – my grandmother used to call that "Prime Crime". You have to have the best beef. Get second-best and your customers will know. You can't mask low-quality product.'

Jody told me that they generally buy Hereford or Black Angus (the American name for black Aberdeen Angus cattle). At first they graze, but for the last 180 days they're fed mostly on a diet of corn. Although young beef carcasses are more tender, Jody prefers to go for thirty-month-old animals, which give a more complex flavour.

As we talked, Jody led me to the basement of Peter Luger, a warren of interconnecting cellars and alcoves, occasionally interrupted by a staircase or trapdoor leading to the street. We threaded our way past steel tables upon which slabs of steak were piled high, ready for trimming, and came to the drying room.

Dry-ageing gives beef a wonderfully chewy, buttery, nutty taste. As the meat is hung, its natural enzymes (proteins that act as catalysts, building, altering or taking apart other protein molecules) begin their work: generating flavours as a by-product of the catalysis; breaking down largely flavourless proteins, fats and sugars into smaller units that do have flavour; and weakening connective tissue to make the meat more tender and succulent. During ageing the temperature, humidity and air movement must be carefully controlled to avoid bacteria, drying out and spoilage.

This time and effort comes at a price. Only prime cuts can be used because they have sufficient marbling to protect the outer layers while the beef ages. And a large percentage of the meat's original weight is lost because of water evaporation and the necessary trimming of the meat's dried surface. (Jody described this as 'a diamond in the rough: get rid of the outside, and inside is this great solitaire'.) As a result, in the last thirty years dry-ageing has fallen out of popularity to the point where almost no one does it. Peter Luger is one of the few places that do.

The steakhouse buys 10 tons of meat each week, so I shouldn't have been surprised at the size of the dry-ageing room, but I was. Jody swung back the huge metal door of a room 20 feet long. Inside, on four-tier wheeled steel shelving, cuts lay humped in rows as though on bunk beds in a dormitory.

'The drying time's not set in stone,' Jody explained. 'We adapt to the quality of the cut. Beef with fine-flecked marbling takes less time.'

I asked Jody what she thought of wet-ageing, where the meat is vacuum-sealed and stored in a fridge for three weeks. The enzymes still do their job but the result is a wetter product with a less developed flavour. The process was pioneered in the 1970s and quickly became attractive to restaurants ruled by economics rather than taste: wet-aged meat is ready quicker and retains its water, so there's far less wastage; and the vac-pac prevents spoilage and most bacteria, making it easier and cheaper to oversee.

'Meat in a bag sitting in its own juices decomposing? No thanks!' she replied. 'It's soft, sure, but it has little flavour. The only good thing about wet-ageing is it's cheap, and that's not good enough for Peter Luger. We've always done dry-ageing and our customers like it that way.'

They certainly do. The restaurant has a devoted following: it has its own credit card (it accepts no other) and they presented me with one numbered around the 85,000 mark. That's a lot of committed returning customers. Jody pointed out a group on one table that comes in every Monday for steak and a $250 bottle of wine. By resisting change and pursuing an ideal of porterhouse perfection, Peter Luger has carved a unique niche for itself. It's a formula for success they're fiercely proud and protective of. When I asked about minimum and maximum drying times for the meat, Jody replied, 'I'll be fired if I tell you that!'

Although they have their secrets, I was allowed into the inner sanctum of the kitchen, where the broilermen can have as many as a hundred steaks on the go at the same time. Depending on the thickness of the steak, they shoved it in the hotter grill for seven or eight minutes, then removed and sliced it, basting the thick slices with melted butter before putting them under the second grill for three or four minutes, after which a pronged plastic model cow was stuck on top (colour-coded according to doneness: blood-red is of course rare) and the grill-hot plate ferried out to the restaurant.

I was surprised that they didn't rest the meat, and I wasn't sure why the slices were cut up for the second grilling. There was no doubt that it was a great piece of theatre – the meat arrived at the table still sizzling. And it *was* a great steak … but was it the best steak of my entire life? I didn't want to go *mano a mano* with Johnny Carson, but I wasn't convinced it was the last word in steak cookery. I figured I'd hold my judgement until I'd finished the trip.

GETTING A FLAVOUR OF NEW YORK

Because location work is expensive, TV companies try to cram as much filming as they can into the shortest possible time. Most days we'd be up at first light and spend the next fifteen hours filming or barrelling down a motorway to the next location. So it was ironic that, in the city that never sleeps, I suddenly found I had a day off. (Well, almost – I still had cameras tracking my every move.) It was Sunday: the steakhouses and meat markets were either closed or unavailable. I decided to do some sightseeing, but with a culinary bias. Let's call it a cook's tour of New York.

Naturally, the day had to start in a diner. It's such a classic piece of Americana there's even a film named after it: Barry Levinson's 1982 masterpiece, where the diner is the social hub for a bunch of disaffected young men and women in 1950s Baltimore. In midtown New York there's a diner with brass strips on the booths bearing the names of famous people who have eaten there: you can eat at the favourite table of director Busby Berkeley or actor Ed Harris. A few blocks away is another diner where the waitresses belt out show tunes as you chow down on English muffins or eggs over easy. However, I headed for the Empire Diner on 22nd and Tenth, which is so much a part of New York's visual history that it featured in Woody Allen's parade of landmarks in the opening of *Manhattan*.

The Empire is sleek and beautiful. Built during the same wave of industrial optimism that gave rise to the Empire State Building, it's a symphony of chrome and glossy black. We perched on stools by the counter and waited for the waitress to take our order.

Cash-strapped friends of mine who'd come to New York had made a science out of finding the best breakfast deal: for a few dollars you could get the equivalent of a full English several times over, plus unlimited coffee, and then not need to spend a penny on food for the rest of the day. Eggs any style with bacon/ham/sausage; omelette with any of six cheeses or peppers, salsa, apple, walnut; French fries, home fries, sweet potato fries; pigs in a blanket; Belgian waffles the size of dinner plates with a jug of maple syrup and whipped butter on the side – the range and variety were spectacular. Sure, this was in part a hangover from a time when food was an indication of wealth, but what struck me was the harvest-festival abundance of it all. In their own way, Americans celebrate food as much as the Italians, turning it into folklore and surrounding it with a sense of drama. And sitting here, in a lovingly constructed imitation of a railcar, I felt the perfect expression of that.

An hour or so later, walking the streets to work off the waffles, I was in little doubt about where to go next. In *When Harry Met Sally*, Sally memorably fakes an orgasm in a restaurant to persuade Harry that, when it comes to sex, he doesn't know what he's talking about. The film then cuts to an old lady who has observed all this and says to the waiter, 'I'll have what she's having.'

Well, I was going to have what she was having too: the next stop had to be Katz's Deli on East Houston Street.

Katz's has been going almost as long as Peter Luger, and is just as much of a New York institution. Its huge L-shaped room – which resembles a school refectory – is covered with photos of the owner, Fred Austin, standing Zelig-like with a number of famous people: Dan Aykroyd, Elliott Gould, Jerry Lewis, the celebrity lawyer Alan Dershowitz. As in Naples, I found myself face to face with a framed picture of a grinning Bill Clinton, who apparently once held up the traffic on Houston for hours when he spontaneously stopped his motorcade and nipped into Katz's for a bite.

The phrase 'the joint is jumping' could have been invented for this deli: every table was full and many more expectant customers milled around the counter and filled the aisles, so that it was only by shouting out 'Hot soup!' or – waggishly – 'Hot soda!' that the ancient, unimpressed waiters in their sky-blue jackets could carve a way through the crowd and get their trays to the tables. The queue for the till was almost as long as the queue for the counter. I joined the latter and tried to decide what to have.

Chicken noodle soup, chilli dog on a bun, matzo ball or split pea soup, chopped liver sandwich – it was all so evocative, so American. But in the end I chose a true classic: hot pastrami on rye. My server, Eddie Romero, speared a vast steaming slab of pastrami on a carving fork and cut it into thin slices at top speed. 'You want pickle widdat? Some guys say it's the best part of the sandwich.' I did.

It wasn't so much a sandwich as a geological cross-section: a 3-inch-high stratum of pastrami between two slices of bread. Even the pickle was the size of a large pebble. And the texture and flavour were genuinely fantastic – without question this was one of the most memorable sandwiches I had ever had. What impressed me most was the sheer quality of the meat, something I encountered time and again in New York. It didn't matter whether the establishment was highbrow or high-turnover: the meat was better than almost anything you get in the UK. And at Katz's it was cut to order; it didn't sit there, drying out under hot lamps. There was an attitude to meat here, a set of values and expectations, that we could really learn from in Britain.

'Hot soda!' The waiter at Katz's Deli gets himself a bit of elbow room.

Having done the diner and the deli, it was time to go for the dog. The hot dog is an enduring emblem of New York, sold on street corners from one end of the city to the other. No trip would be complete without consuming at least one, and everybody agreed that Gray's was the place to go.

The biggest bargain in Manhattan! blares a placard in the window, quoting the *New York Times*. Gray's likes placards: its mustard-yellow tiled interior has several to entertain you as you work your way through a foil-wrapped dog. *Nobody but nobody deserves a better frankfurter*, they insist, or *The best damn frankfurter you ever ate.* Another simply claimed *Snappy Service!*, which tempted me to go to the counter and order a crocodile sandwich, but I played it safe and asked for a hot dog.

Gray's takes the trouble to keep the bun warm and they serve up a good frankfurter, though probably what I liked best was the way they encourage you to have a fruit juice with your dog. It's an odd combination that works – papaya and pineapple really aid digestion. (Both contain protein-digesting enzymes that will help break down food.)* It's a neat and thoughtful touch that shows the kind of care, even when it's street food, that often typifies American cooking.

What I also liked was the sheer buzz surrounding the place. Gray's has been going for twenty years (another placard behind the till tells you this and punningly finishes *Franks for your business*) and there's a constant stream of customers – kids, businessmen, even a guy in cowboy hat, waistcoat and bootlace tie – through its simple stand-up premises. They grab a dog and go outside to eat and watch the Greenwich Village bustle. Food is fun here, a piece of street theatre, and the placards and puns are part of that. It gives American food a vitality and identity that is somehow missing from our native dishes – and they are all the poorer for it.

---

* Bromelain is the major protein-digesting enzyme in pineapples; papain is the equivalent in papayas. Both are used as meat tenderisers, and bromelain is so powerful that plantation and cannery workers have to wear rubber gloves to avoid their hands being eaten away. (One hundred years ago a group of sailors who got shipwrecked on an island off the coast of Indonesia ended up losing their teeth after living on a diet of pineapples for several weeks.)

Scientists are still undecided as to why various fruits (melon, fig and kiwi are other examples) 'eat' meat. One theory is that the enzymes discourage animals from eating too much of the fruit. So take nature's hint and eat in moderation. In any case, bromelain is destroyed by heating, so cooked and canned pineapple is harmless.

I was keen to finish my cook's tour in an area of the Lower East Side that has, somewhat surprisingly, become known as 'Restaurant Row'. There, amid psychedelic supermarkets and boho bars, is Wylie Dufresne's Michelin-starred establishment, WD-50.

Wylie is one of the most creative chefs in the States, combining technical skill, an enthusiasm for science and technology in the kitchen, and a real sense of fun. I'd wanted to eat at his restaurant for a long time, and I found myself trotting ahead of the film crew towards the kitchen, barely able to contain myself. I knew I'd be stimulated and surprised by his dishes.

'Hey, Heston,' he greeted me. 'There's someone you know here.'

'Who?'

'Guess,' he teased, but I could see him looking over my shoulder and spun round to catch sight of Ferran Adrià, the chef at El Bulli, standing in the kitchen's entrance with a big smile on his face, flanked by another great chef, José Andrés.

It's a small world – when I visited WD-50, the innovative restaurant run by Wylie Dufresne (far left), I bumped into José Andrés (on my right) and Ferran Adrià (on my left).

In many ways, Ferran has revolutionised modern gastronomy and opened the eyes of young chefs all over the world to new culinary possibilities. He and his brother, Albert, had become good friends of mine. So it was a huge pleasure to meet him in New York, but how unlikely a scenario! Four chefs, from different parts of the world, all coming together on the same day at the same time. Once again, New York had performed its movie magic. It was as though we were in the hands of some unseen director, shooting to a script of which we were unaware. Like starstruck kids, we posed for group photos and had a drink together. I'd have loved to talk longer with Ferran but it was late and I knew Wylie was keen to show me his cooking. I didn't want to miss the moment, so I said goodbye and sank into one of WD-50's generous booths.

There's an ocean-liner elegance to the place, with its geometric lines and sumptuous caramel leather banquettes, its orange and blue walls, its artful abstracts. The whole experience is really harmonious and provides the right setting for the menu: modern, minimalist, subtle but not too stuffy, and exuding a certain jazzy excitement. I looked at the menu to see where Wylie's improvisation would take us.

Shrimp cannelloni with chorizo and Thai basil, mussel–olive oil soup, toast ice cream, butternut sorbet – we were treated to lots of marvellous, inventive dishes. At one point we were all given bowls of steaming brown broth accompanied by a small tube marked 'Hair Applicator', the kind of thing you might find in a fancy retro barber's. The soup turned out to be a form of dashi. Squeeze the applicator into it and instant noodles instantly formed. The courses were served up by Dewey, a solidly built man in a denim shirt, with a hangdog expression and a sense of humour so deadpan it was hard to tell whether he was joking or not. Although Dewey's business card drily identifies him as 'chef Wylie's dad', he's a key part of the restaurant's personality, responsible for both the decor and the wine list, which he guided us through with unostentatious expertise.

By the end I had eaten and laughed way too much. It was seriously late and I had to get up early to check out some American pizza joints and see how they compared to Neapolitan pizzerias. I flagged a cab uptown and settled back into my seat. New York cuisine, it seemed to me, was in great shape. From simple steaks to Wylie's innovative creations, I had encountered a spectacular diversity and superb quality.

Clearly the New World could hold its own against the Old World, and the future of creative American cuisine looked very good indeed.

For a day off, it had been a long one. In the Paramount Hotel I plodded to my stark white cube of a room and quickly fell asleep, watched over by Vermeer's *Girl with a Pearl Earring*, a huge reproduction of which served as headboard to my bed.

STRIP STEAK

The next evening, as we drove up Eleventh Avenue, past truck and repair shops and lumber merchants, a vast hoarding caught my eye:

> **Penthouse Executive Club**
> *New York City's newest and most upscale Gentlemen's Club*
> **featuring penthouse pets**

'This is the place,' I told the driver, and he pulled up alongside its floodlit façade.

At this point, you might be forgiven for thinking that I'd stepped out of character – that time on the road had finally had an effect, propelling me towards some rock 'n' roll-style bad behaviour. Whatever next? Maybe when I'd finished here I'd go back to the Paramount, trash the room, turf the TV out of the window and put my boot through the canvas of *Girl with a Pearl Earring* ...

But you'd be wrong. I was here because the club is home to Robert's Steakhouse, which, according to *Vogue*'s Jeffrey Steingarten, offers 'the best steak dinner in town – the meat could not have been more flavourful, tender or juicy, and grilled to that precise point of perfection between rare and medium-rare – while a beautiful young dancer just 8 feet away moved with energy and originality'.

Jeffrey has plenty of energy and originality himself. He is one of the best and most fastidious food writers in the world (he's been known to carry his own salt around with him in a walnut box), so his views are to be taken seriously. He's also one of the funniest, and as such is a bit of a wind-up merchant. Was a strip joint *really* the best place for steak in the city? The only way to find out was to go there and try it.

Robert's Steakhouse is on the mezzanine level of the Penthouse Executive Club and could easily feature in the pages of a design magazine – it is a very contemporary mix of louche lite and borderline kitsch. An enormous glitterball hangs from the ceiling, which seems to be moulded from undulating, coppery-coloured reflective plastic. The lighting is low, the walls mirrored, the colour scheme predominantly red and purple. Down two sides of the room are formally arranged tables for the diners; on the third side is a scattering of high-backed velvet armchairs for barflies. In the corners are small podia for a couple of go-go girls (the main stage is on the floor below), and on the back wall a series of lightboxes illuminate soft-core erotic images: bronzed bare backs silhouetted on the seashore; close-ups of sculpted curves or parted lips. Here was another example of how blurred the line between reality and cinema is in New York: the place looked exactly how you would expect a set designer to style a strip club for a movie.

Robert's head chef, Adam Perry Lang, brought me back to reality by taking me into the subterranean world of kitchen storage. We clattered downstairs to the basement, past industrial-sized mixers and vast stainless-steel Ice-O-Matics, and opened the door of his meat ager.

The room wasn't as generously proportioned as the one at Peter Luger, but gave the same impression of humped figures in bunks. Meat slabs the size of small coal-sacks lay along the shelves, named and dated, and varying in colour from faded red to almost black. The unusual hues and still-life formality made it look like some kind of weird art installation, but it was the smell that made the biggest impression. The air in the room was suffused with a fantastically rich, savoury odour – nutty and grassy, with a strong blue-cheese note, as though someone had just opened a packet of Roquefort.

'That wonderful smell's a sign of the ageing process,' said Adam. 'Meat that has been in here only a week doesn't have that: like a good wine it takes time to mature and develop its characteristic aroma.' He handed me a week-old cut and he was right: it had none of the richness and complexity of smell I'd just been experiencing. 'The oldest we have here at the moment are twelve weeks, but we can age for up to eighteen; we're not afraid to do that. The results are really interesting. As you can imagine, the process gives meat an extraordinary taste and texture. Ageing is nature's flavour enhancer. That's why we do it.'

'Eighteen weeks – that's over a third of a year. It must cost a lot to keep it that long, and it'll shrink a lot.'

'Oh yeah. You can expect 70 per cent loss at a three- to four-week range.'

'What about feeding? Do you prefer grass or grain?'

'The grass-fed in the US – and I'll go on record with this – doesn't have a good flavour because of the moisture in the grass. That has a huge impact on flavour. We choose animals that have been grain-fed for the first twenty-six months, followed by four months on a 99 per cent protein feed.'

The result is meat with incredible marbling, which is crucial to the taste of that steak on your plate. 'You need that fat,' insisted Adam. 'Dry-ageing gets rid of the meat's juices. Fat provides the moisture instead, keeping the steak juicy and giving it lots of flavour as well.'

I've done a lot of work on meat-ageing, so I was eager to see the effects of Adam's ageing process. We decided to take cuts that had been aged for one, four and ten weeks, cook them and taste the results. Adam hauled out three huge chunks and wrapped them in grease-proof paper, and we set off for the cutting room.

The saw kicked into action. Adam snapped on some surgical gloves and ran meat of each age through the machine. The differences between one, four and ten weeks' ageing were clear in the slices he laid out on a tray. At one week the meat was still vivid red: the colour of a knee graze. 'Beautiful,' said Adam. 'Look at the even distribution of fat. There are no chunks of solid white fat. That's a sign of an animal that's been prop-erly fed. If you rush it and try to force-feed the animal just before market, there's no time for the fat to get into the muscles. It simply collects in large clumps, which is no good for your steak: the fat falls out when you cook it and does nothing to flavour and moisten the meat.'

At four weeks, the meat had developed to a cigar brown. It now looked like a rock, and a pretty scuffed, beach-weathered one at that. 'You notice how it's already got a musky smell,' Adam pointed out. By ten weeks the meat was vermilion and looked more like biltong, the sun-dried beef you get in South Africa. It's an extraordinary transform-ation, changing the whole character of the meat.

Back in the kitchen, Adam outlined his cooking technique while he seasoned the steaks and rubbed them with oil. 'I like to char the crust

– beyond even caramelisation. It cuts into the dryish flavour and the gaminess of the fat,' he said as he flipped my trio on to the grill. They were a good 4 inches thick and about a foot long. Each fizzed angrily in the heat.

'To get that charredness they go first on the top grill, which is super-hot – up to 500°C. After ten minutes or so they'll be moved down to the lower grill and a lesser heat for a while.'

'Do you turn them just the once?'

'Nah, I jockey them around a little bit. Look at them now – the meat's already beautifully striped from the grill. They'll be ready soon. You'd better go get your table.'

By now the club was open for the evening. The glitterball revolved, spangling the walls with starlight. On the podia, two girls in white fringed bikinis, knee-high white boots and lots of diamanté were dancing to a heavily discofied version of 'Silly Love Songs'. It was a bizarre experience. Adam and I sat down together to discuss one kind of flesh in the most intimate detail – its firmness and taste; its muscle tone and fat – and all the while another kind of flesh was on intimate display behind our heads, writhing to the music. Out of the corner of my eye I would occasionally catch a glimpse of movement – the white blur of a slow pirouette; the haughty toss of dark hair – as though the twists and turns of our conversation were mirrored by the sinuous moves of the girls on stage.

Quarter-turn, knee bend, hip sway ...

'OK,' said Adam, 'we'll start with the unaged beef. You'll notice it's very juicy and clean-tasting. No funk to it.'

'That's amazing. Even without the ageing, this is fantastic steak with a superb roast-beef quality to it but still exceptionally tender. You simply don't get this kind of meat back in Britain.'

Arm stretch, side-step, booty shake ...

Adam signalled for the next plate to be brought. 'Here's the four-week-old. It's very mild to me but very good. It sets the standard.'

'Yes. There's a slight livery note. And it's got that Stilton-like quality that I really prize.'

'Particularly on the outside,' Adam agreed.

'Though I wonder whether some people back home would find it just too rich ... '

Steak-tasting in a strip club.

Shoulder twist, back arch, high kick …

'Right, this is the ten-week steak. What do you think, Heston?'

'Technically, this is more tender, though now I think you've got a kind of livery texture as well. All three are wonderful. This is how beef should taste. Even with all my experience, this is a revelation for me – above all just how good the meat here is even before you work your ageing magic on it.'

'I know you've done some work on ageing too. What have you come up with?' Adam wanted to know.

Hip twist, pelvic grind, pirouette …

'At the moment, the consensus is that dry-ageing makes no difference to the tenderness of meat after about twenty-one days, but I wonder if it still makes a difference to the flavour. The way I see it, you've got moisture evaporating from the meat as it dries. Eventually this'll mean that there's a disparity between the density of the air and the density of the meat's moisture content. Osmosis will try to balance that disparity, and as it does so, it might transfer some of the flavours on the outside of the meat to the inside.'

Side shuffle, half-squat, two-step …

'You got any evidence for this?'

'That transfer of flavour wouldn't reach the centre of the meat, only the outer parts. Osmotic pressure would probably take it as far as the deco, the strip of meat that lies under the fat of the rib. And it turns out that that's one of the tastiest bits of the meat. I know there has to be a lot more going on than that, and it's a bit of a long shot, but it's an idea I'm pursuing.'

'Oh yeah? Tell me more … '

We talked long into the night, exchanging theories and ideas. I recognised a fellow obsessive when I met one; it was as much of a pleasure talking to Adam as it was tasting his food. And his level of devotion had paid off: his steaks were incredible. It was a great starting point for the steak I'd have to prepare back in the research kitchen.

AGAINST THE GRAIN

Inspired by my experiences in the States, I decided to track down a British steak that could rival New York's finest, and to use the porterhouse cut in my recipe: the combination of ribeye and fillet gave an interesting variation in texture that really appealed to me.

I researched breeds and came up with a shortlist of six: Orkney, Aberdeen Angus, Red Poll, Hereford, South Devon and Longhorn.* Then I sought out the best supplier of each. Although American cattle are grain-fed, which leads to superb marbling and gives the meat a particular richness, I opted mainly for grass-fed animals because I was increasingly convinced that grain-fed meat would actually be too rich for British tastes. (I reckoned in any case that I could still get that wonderful Roquefort character in my steak with a blue-cheese butter, as long as I could get the consistency right, avoiding that gooeyness and mouth-puckering acid note …)

I suffered a setback when the steaks were delivered for tasting, however. Three suppliers had sent porterhouse cuts; the rest had got it wrong. It brought home to me just how unfamiliar a cut the porterhouse is in this country. And if the best butchers in Britain had trouble identifying the cut, it seemed to me vain to try to structure a recipe around it. I portered the porterhouse out of my imagination and decided there and then to opt for a simpler, more familiar cut.

The tasting, then, was no longer like-for-like, but I felt it could still go ahead. Chris and I sniffed around the raw steaks like a couple of stray dogs. The Hereford and Aberdeen Angus (the breeds used by Robert's and Peter Luger) looked and smelt very different from how they had in New York, less characterful somehow, and only the Red Poll gave off an enticing aroma that held some promise.

I cooked and tasted each of them, looking at juiciness, tenderness and flavour. None of the first four – Orkney, Aberdeen Angus, Red Poll and Hereford – had the right balance of the things I was looking for. Even the South Devon, which was the only grain-fed cattle we'd included, lacked the richness and depth of its American counterparts.

So it was a real surprise to find a clear winner right at the end. The Longhorn had it all for me – the nutty, grassy, blue-cheese note I'd hoped to find, plus a marvellous moisture and juiciness alongside a firm but giving texture. The oldest pure breed of cattle in England had come up with the goods.

* A different breed from the American (or Texas) Longhorn.

* **Making the Grade** How British Beef Could Be Better

As I've said before, the single most striking aspect of my trip to America was probably the quality of the meat. Even without ageing, the steak served up by Adam Perry Lang was extraordinary – tender and flavourful to an extent I've rarely found in Britain. And everywhere I went the story was the same. Katz's pastrami and corned beef were equally delicious. It seemed to back up what I'd been told: in terms of eating quality, American and Australian beef is ten to fifteen years ahead of ours.

This shouldn't be the case. Scotch beef is a world-renowned brand name, and we have both abundant supplies of grass and a discerning consumer base. The conditions are perfect, so what's holding us back?

The grading system.

In the UK, carcasses are graded and paid for on yield (the EUROP grid). Only amount counts: there are no controls to ensure that a cut doesn't taste like leather. Nothing is done to ensure the consistency of the product, even though breed alone is no guarantee of quality.

By contrast, both America and Australia have grading systems (the USDA and MSA, respectively) that are consumer-driven: they objectively sort carcasses according to the kind of eating satisfaction they will provide.

In America, the US Department of Agriculture's system has a seventy-year history, and its shield of approval is recognised and respected. It assesses the yield grade of a carcass but allies this to a quality grade, which takes into account the marbling in the ribeye and the physiological maturity of the animal – two of the most effective objective indicators of meat quality. Carcasses are sorted into one of eight grades: Prime, Choice, Select, Standard, Commercial, Utility, Cutter and Canner. In the top grade, Prime, carcasses must have at least 8 per cent intramuscular fat (slightly abundant marbling) and levels of rib ossification that correlate to an animal under thirty months old. Only 2–3 per cent of carcasses meet this specification, and almost all are bought by restaurants such as Robert's and Peter Luger. They buy in the knowledge that they're getting meat that will give their customers exactly what they want: tender, tasty beef. Guaranteed.

In the US, of course, the consumer is king. Americans spend half their food dollars on eating out, and they consume 90 million beefburgers a day. That huge demand no doubt allows consumers to influence how the system is organised. You might think it's a specific set of circumstances – American can-do attitudes backed up by the USDA's long history – which couldn't be reproduced elsewhere. But the situation in Australia contradicts that view.

Australian beef is now widely considered the best in the world, yet twenty years ago consumption and quality had fallen to an all-time low. Meat Standards Australia (MSA) was set up in 1997 and its system prom- ises 'this beef, cooked as labelled, will eat as described, every time'. To do this, taste panels were set up that tested meat for tenderness, juiciness and flavour, and cross-referenced these against production factors such as storage, maturity and marbling to produce overall scores for each muscle. Cuts were then categorised as: Ungraded, 3-star (Tenderness Guaranteed), 4-star (Premium Tenderness) or 5-star (Supreme Tenderness).

Such careful selection has resulted in world-class beef. In Britain, selection generally seems to stop at the breed, which is not enough to ensure consistency. That's probably why many chains here source their striploins from Australia.

We've done so much in the last decade to overturn Britain's bad food reputation that it's disappointing to find we lag so far behind in terms of meat quality. However, there are signs that the situation is changing. The English Beef & Lamb Executive (EBLEX) has set up a Quality Standard scheme to improve product integrity. The approach differs from the American and Australian systems (for example, its criteria don't include marbling content, which is a central part of USDA and MSA grading), so it remains to be seen whether it will have the same influence on stand- ards. Nonetheless, it's a step in the right direction and is the first scheme in the UK to take eating quality into account.

If you want to know more, consult the EBLEX website: eblex.org.uk.

Steak Serves 2–4

Blue-cheese butter captures something of the spectacularly nutty, cheesy character of aged beef. Iceberg lettuce – all too often overlooked in favour of more 'fashionable' salad leaves – provides a crispness that goes perfectly with steak. A marvellous mushroom ketchup adapted from an eighteenth-century recipe boosts all the meaty notes in the recipe, and smoked sea salt accentuates the chargrilled flavours. But, if you've sourced a good breed that has been handled properly, the star of the show will be the meat – blowtorched until browned on the outside, then cooked long and slow for a truly tender inside.

Browning doesn't seal in the juices of the steak (searing at a high heat inevitably leads to the evaporation of water); it kickstarts a complicated process known as the Maillard reactions, which add fantastic depth and complexity to the flavours of meat. To get those flavours without drying out the steak, you need to brown the surface quickly and then take the heat right down.

At the lower temperature muscle proteins contract and squeeze out water far more slowly, which is crucial to keeping the meat moist. But it also needs to be tenderised, which at this temperature is done by enzymes, particularly calpains and cathepsins that weaken or break down collagen and other proteins. Calpains stop working at 40°C/105°F, cathepsins at 50°C/120°F, but below these cut-off points, the higher the temperature, the faster they work. Heating the meat slowly means these enzymes can perform their magic for several hours before denaturing, effectively ageing the meat during cooking. The result is the tenderest, tastiest meat imaginable.

Special equipment

Food processor (optional), oven thermometer, blowtorch (the heavy-duty kind from a DIY store: a *crème brûlée* special won't do the job quickly enough), digital probe

Timing
On the day, a meal for four will take under half an hour, including getting the pan hot enough to fry the steaks. The background prep needs to be staggered over a couple of days: at least 48 hours ahead of time the cheese and butter should be sliced and left in the fridge to infuse. About 30 hours in advance the meat has to go in the oven for a long slow cook on its own. The mushrooms for the ketchup have to sit in the fridge for 24 hours, and then cook for about half an hour. But since the ketchup will keep for a month in the fridge, you can easily prepare this ahead of time – it's a versatile condiment that goes with lots of other stuff anyway.

For the blue-cheese-infused butter
250g unsalted butter _ 250g Stilton

For the mushroom juice
1.5kg button mushrooms _ 75g table salt

For the pickled mushrooms
200g baby button mushrooms _ 100g unrefined caster sugar _ 300ml red wine vinegar

For the mushroom ketchup
reserved pickled mushrooms and juices, plus (per 600ml of mushroom juice): _ 120ml red wine _ 60ml red wine vinegar _ ¼ tsp ground mace _ ½ tsp whole black peppercorns _ 2 whole cloves _ 1 shallot, roughly chopped _ cornflour (to thicken)

For the steak
1 well-aged two-bone forerib of beef (on the bone) _ black peppercorns _ sea salt _ smoked sea salt _ groundnut oil

For the salad
1 iceberg lettuce _ 16 vine-ripened cherry tomatoes _ 2 tbsp white wine vinegar _ 6 tbsp groundnut or light olive oil _ table salt and freshly ground black pepper

INFUSING THE BUTTER WITH BLUE CHEESE

1. Slice both the butter and the cheese lengthways into slabs about 5mm thick.
2. Tear off a large sheet of baking parchment. Place a slice of butter in the centre and top with a slice of cheese. Continue stacking alternate slices of butter and blue cheese until all have been used. Wrap tightly and place in the fridge for at least 2 days. (The flavour will improve the longer you leave it.)

PREPARING THE MUSHROOM JUICE

1. Wipe the mushrooms clean with damp kitchen paper, then chop them finely or blitz briefly in a food processor.
2. Tip the mushrooms into a fine sieve, place over a bowl and stir in the salt. Store in the fridge for 24 hours or until the salt has drawn the juices from the mushrooms.

PICKLING THE MUSHROOMS

1. Wipe the mushrooms clean using damp kitchen paper. Remove the stalks, cut the mushrooms into quarters and place them in a bowl.
2. Tip the sugar and vinegar into a small pan and boil until the sugar has dissolved.
3. Pour the hot pickling liquor over the mushrooms, let it cool, then place in the fridge for 24 hours.

MAKING THE MUSHROOM KETCHUP

1. Weigh the mushroom juice that has collected, and calculate the quantities of wine, vinegar, shallot and spices you will need.
2. Tip the mushroom juice, wine, vinegar, shallot and spices into a pan and bring to the boil. When the liquid has reduced by half, remove it from the heat and strain through a sieve, discarding the spices and shallot.
3. Pour the strained liquid back into the pan. Thicken this by adding cornflour. (To thicken 300ml liquid, mix 20g – approx. 4 tsp – cornflour with 45ml/3 tbsp cold water. Whisk this into the hot liquid. Return the pan to the heat and continue to whisk until the ketchup thickens.) Remove the thickened ketchup base from the heat and set aside.

4. Strain the pickled mushrooms through a sieve, discarding the liquor. To add piquancy to the ketchup, stir pickled mushrooms into the base, to taste.* (Leftover pickled mushrooms are a great accompaniment to cheese and cold meats.) Spoon the ketchup into a clean jar or container, cover and store in the fridge. It will keep for up to 1 month.

COOKING THE STEAK

1. Using an oven thermometer, preheat the oven to 50°C/120°F.
2. Place the forerib in a roasting tin. Brown the outside as quickly as possible using a blowtorch. (It needs to be powerful: if it's not hot enough, it will start to cook the flesh. If your blowtorch isn't up to the job, use a very hot pan to brown instead.) Once the meat is browned, place it in the oven. Use a digital probe to establish when the internal temperature of the meat has reached 50°C/120°F (this should take 4–8 hours, depending on the animal; don't let it go higher than 50°C/120°F – a few extra degrees will ruin the recipe), then let it cook at this temperature for a minimum of 18 hours. Remove from the oven, cover and leave to rest at room temperature for a minimum of 2 hours – 4 hours would be better: it's important that the meat cools down before being subjected to the fierce heat of the pan.
3. To prepare the steaks, hold the forerib upright with the rib bones side on. Run a sharp knife between the meat and the bones and free what should be an L-shaped piece of meat. Trim off any over-charcoaled exterior. Slice the meat in half vertically to give 2 steaks, each about 5cm thick.
4. Place a large cast-iron pan over a high heat for at least 10 minutes. Meanwhile, take the blue-cheese-infused butter out of the fridge and remove the slices of cheese. Crush peppercorns in a pestle and mortar, mix in table salt and a little smoked sea salt and put this seasoning mixture on a plate. Dip both sides of the steaks in the seasoning.

* The ketchup becomes saltier with age, but the pickled mushrooms temper it. So if you're preparing it in advance, it's best to store the base and the pickled mushrooms separately, and put them together just before serving.

5. Add a film of groundnut oil to the pan and, when it's smoking, add the steaks. (The whole surface of each steak needs to be in contact with the pan; otherwise they won't cook properly. If they overlap, fry the steaks one at a time.) Fry for 4 minutes, flipping the steaks every 30 seconds. They should develop a nice 1mm brown crust, while the interior should be uniformly pink.
6. Let the steaks rest. Allow the frying pan to cool slightly, then add the flavoured butter and stir to melt it and collect any bits of meat that remain. Pour into a jug.
7. Cut the steaks into diagonal slices. Add a few grindings of black pepper and a sprinkling of sea salt and smoked sea salt, then drizzle over the butter. Serve with a dollop of mushroom ketchup.

PREPARING THE SALAD

1. Fill a large bowl with cold water. Remove the outer leaves from the lettuce and discard. Pull off the remaining leaves, cut into bite-sized squares (make sure the knife is sharp; otherwise you will bruise the leaves) and place in the bowl of water for 10–15 minutes so that they will rejuvenate.
2. Drain the lettuce and leave to dry for 5 minutes. Meanwhile, cut the tomatoes into quarters and place in a serving bowl. Add the lettuce and dress the salad – first with the vinegar, then with the oil. (The oil will gradually seep into the leaves' interior, displacing air and making the structure of the leaves collapse, so it's best to dress the salad at the last minute.) Season, toss gently and serve.

Spaghetti

Bolognese

'Those who forget the pasta are condemned
to reheat it.'
Anon

History

In his book *Everything on the Table*, Colman Andrews complains that food nomenclature has degenerated into 'a hash of misnomer, a stew of garbled terminology'. The focus of his frustration was fettuccine Alfredo but he might just as easily have been talking about spaghetti bolognese.

In Italy, spaghetti bolognese doesn't exist. If you see it on a menu there, keep walking and keep your eyes open for a restaurant offering *ragù*, which is the Italian word for a meat-based pasta sauce. It won't necessarily be a *ragù alla bolognese* either, especially if you're not in Bologna: each region has its own version of the dish – in Abruzzo the meat will be lamb, in Sardinia wild boar. And it won't be served with spaghetti because meat tends to fall off the thin strands and stay on the plate. The bigger surface area of a ribbon pasta such as pappardelle or fettuccine holds the sauce much better. The people of Bologna traditionally use tagliatelle.

TAGLIATELLE

> *'Tagliatelle is a type of Italian noodle,' the hook-handed man explained ...*
> **Lemony Snicket,** *The Carnivorous Carnival*

Although 'mullet' can refer to a fish or a fourth-division footballer's haircut, food and hair don't generally share a long-standing, inter-twined tradition. Nonetheless, tradition has it that tagliatelle was created in 1487 by a cook called Zafirano on the occasion of the marriage of Lucrezia d'Este to Annibale Bentivoglio, son of Giovanni II, Lord of Bologna, inspired by the beautiful blonde hair of the bride.

However, just as the myth that Marco Polo discovered pasta in China and brought it back to Italy in 1295 turns out to be untrue (there's a reference to pasta in Genoa as early as 1279), so records suggest that tagliatelle pre-dates Lucrezia's locks. In the 1300s there are illustrations of tagliatelle in a health manual, and in the same century there is a list of local Emilian produce that has an entry for fermentini, which sounds a lot like what we now call tagliatelle.

RAGÙ

The word *ragù* comes from the French *ragoût*, meaning 'stew'. It began life as the filling for lasagne and only later became more commonly thought of as a pasta sauce. This was the first of several metamorphoses. The original *ragù* was roughly chopped rather than minced, and contained no tomato. (The addition of tomato was pioneered by Italian-American versions of the dish.) Even now, the true *ragù alla bolognese* is sparing with the tomato.

SPAG BOL

Spag bol is, of course, about as far from a traditional *ragù alla bolognese* as you can get. The name alone suggests something unappetising, and in some areas it's even referred to as 'spag bog', which captures exactly the stodgy, blob-like character of the British version. So how did the dish get so misinterpreted and messed about with? One theory is that when the first Neapolitan immigrants reached America they would often serve meat with pasta as a sign of their newfound prosperity. As their standard of living grew, meat became a commonplace part of many dishes (not least because meat in the States was far less expensive than in Italy); it might well have been added to spaghetti (by far the most popular and readily available pasta abroad) with tomatoes, and given the name of the most famous such sauce: bolognese.

The Quest for the Best

PASTA TESTA

It's easy to dismiss pasta as bulk, a carb-fest that simply provides the base to some tasty sauce, when in fact it's an integral part of the dish and one of the key tastes that will determine its character.

In short, pasta should have flavour. I was determined to track down something suitably delicious for my *ragù*. I also needed to refine my ideas about which shape was the best accompaniment for it. I decided to taste as many types as I could in order to find a top-quality producer, and then go to Italy to talk to them.

Martelli, De Cecco, Barilla, Delverde, Rummo, Pasta dello Scugnizzo, La Molisana, Rustichella d'Abruzzo, Agnesi, Cipriani, Sapori di Casa, Ivana Maroni ... I contacted a number of shops and websites and came away with pasta from many producers in all shapes and sizes: pappardelle, spaghettini, bucatini, bavette, spaghetti, tagliatelle. I'd bought some fresh pasta for comparison, but I was expecting to use dried pasta in the *ragù*: it keeps its al dente texture better, giving the kind of body and 'bite' you need in a meat dish. (At the Fat Duck we make fresh pasta for a lobster lasagne dish, but then dry it to capture that bite.)

Back in the lab I put two large saucepans on hobs and added to each 1 litre of boiling water, 10 grams of salt and 100 grams of pasta. 1:10:100 – the golden ratio of pasta cookery, providing enough water to rehydrate the pasta and dilute the starch that escapes from it, and enough salt to reinforce the 'bite'. Ten or so minutes later, the pasta testing began.

I was almost disappointed that the first two pastas out of the pots were so good. It always makes testing more difficult when the benchmark is set early on. Nevertheless, I felt already that these were the ones to beat. I'd had a hunch before we started that an egg pasta might capture what I had in mind, and these had an eggy note that I really liked (though Chris complained that it reminded him more of a Chinese stir-fry, which just goes to show how subjective perfection is). The texture too was excellent: firm and chewy but not too dense.

None of the next four were likely to knock these off the top spot. The texture was all right, but there was no taste. I could happily have eaten a bowlful of one of the first two on its own. These four, on the other hand, would need to be smothered with sauce to give any kind of interest at all.

The next two were from smaller producers La Pasta di Aldo and Rustichella di Abruzzo. They looked right and, more importantly, they *felt* right.

I mean this literally. Some mass-market producers put out a reasonably tasty pasta, especially given their high levels of output, but they nonetheless have to cut corners – and that shows in the finished product. Using soft flour instead of semi-milled 'semolina'; adding hot water to it rather than cold; quick-drying the strands with hot air – all these practices bulk profit margins but reduce quality. Originally, pasta was dried in the open air and then extruded through bronze dies, which gave it a special texture that held the sauce perfectly. Now major producers tend to use nylon or Teflon dies that create a surface too smooth for sauce. The two pastas I had in front of me had a roughness, a glass-paper texture that suggested care had been taken in their preparation. I expected something special, and I got it: cooking produced pasta with a richness and a big mouthfeel.

Although we sampled many more pastas throughout the afternoon, none approached the quality of these two. La Pasta di Aldo, in particular, captured the opposites that characterise great pasta – good body but with a lightness; a rich flavour that doesn't overpower; substance twinned with a delicacy – and the colour was fantastic: a vivid yolk-yellow that signalled a high egg content and the use of durum wheat semolina, the hard flour that is vital to good pasta. It was clear that my trip to Italy would have to include a visit to Monte San Giusto to see if Luigi Donnari would let me in on how he created it.

HISTORY AND *OSTERIE*

Even though spaghetti bolognese doesn't exist in Italy, and forms of *ragù* can be found throughout the country, Bologna still seemed the best place to start my search for the perfect recipe. Besides, according to Claudia Roden, the people of the region 'eat more, care more and talk more about food than anyone else in Italy'. So much so that Bologna has become known as *la grassa e la dotta* (the fat and the learned) and earned a reputation as the food capital of the country. I was going to the source for my sauce.

Appropriately enough, in the land of the Rinascimento, my trip took shape around the kind of dualities you might find in Renaissance art: old and new; conservative and modern; private and public; traditional and iconoclastic. The journey proved to be a real inspiration – a glimpse into Italy's preservation of its culinary past, and how that might play a part in its future.

That journey began among the medieval and Renaissance splendours of Bologna's expansive main squares, Piazza Maggiore and Piazza del Nettuno, dominated by the imposing bulk of the Palazzo Re Enzo. The palace is a fantasy of battlements and buttresses, galleries and crenellations, as though it has sprung straight out of a fairy tale (though perhaps one by the Brothers Grimm: it is named after a king who was imprisoned there for the last thirty-five years of his life). Each town I visited in Italy had a *centro storico* of similarly breathtaking beauty: it's easy to believe this has an effect on the outlook of the inhabitants, and it's easy to see how the gravitational tug of tradition might be strong in a place where you could take your morning coffee – as Bolognese all around me were doing amid the vaulted roofs and stone porticoes that lined the piazzas – surrounded by some of mankind's finest achievements.

The porticoes seemed to invite a slower pace. Here there was none of the hurried chaos of Naples; instead, well-heeled people strolled, hunched into their overcoats. It felt relaxed and ordered, tranquil – somehow less Mediterranean, more European. It would be interesting to see how this contrast expressed itself in their cuisine.

TRAD *RAGÙ*

The Antica Trattoria della Gigina doesn't nestle among the elegant stone columns of Bologna. It's on a busy intersection on the road to Ferrara and is situated among the usual businesses of suburbs everywhere: sofa showrooms, brightly lit hair salons and anonymous-looking banks. Step inside, however, and you return to old-style grandeur. In the front room there is a framed set of witty and faintly carnal tarot illustrations. Along the pale orange walls are elaborately carved mahogany dressers, upon which I noticed bottles of Ardoino extra virgin olive oil (a good sign: it's used by many of the best chefs in Italy). Beneath extravagant, cascading chandeliers waiters in ankle-length white aprons and natty grey pinstripe waistcoats hurried between tables. Downstairs the wine cellar looked more like the library of a well-to-do bibliophile: hundreds of bottles sat in ordered rows in floor-to-ceiling dark wooden glass-fronted cabinets, with placards to indicate their provenance: *Sardegna, Campania, Sicilia, Calabria*. I could see the labels of some of the great wines of Italy: Barbaresco from Gaja, Ornellaia, Sassicaia, among others.

At the entrance to the restaurant was a heavy marble-topped counter with an ancient, fantastically ornate brass cash register. Above this were two photographs of stocky, serious-faced, dark-haired women in striped shirts and white aprons. One was stirring a large saucepan; the other looked impassively at a big plate of pasta. They were Gigina Bargelesi and her daughter-in-law, Arduina, the founding deities of the trattoria over fifty years ago, and it's their recipe for *ragù* that chef Carlo Cortesi cooks to this day.

In the kitchen one section was devoted to pasta-making. On an L-shaped wooden work surface a woman smoothed and stretched pasta dough with a 4-foot-long rolling pin before hanging it on the slatted bars of a drying rack. She worked with a speed and confidence born of experience, and soon several large, bright yellow ovals of dough hung above her head, looking more like washing hung out to dry than the basis of many of Carlo's dishes. When I asked him what pasta he'd be serving in the restaurant he told me that the choice was dictated by who was at work in the pasta section. 'Some varieties aren't on the menu today because the woman who makes them isn't here.' This shows how seriously pasta is treated in Italy, and how specialised a job it is. Only an expert will do.

As if to confirm this, there was a little window set into one wall of the kitchen, through which customers in the restaurant could see the pasta-maker hard at work in her blue overall and white apron (she could have stepped out of one of the photographs behind the cash till) and appraise the sheets of pasta drying above her. It was as though the pasta was so important that the diners needed the reassurance of seeing it with their own eyes: if the pasta was OK, then the rest of the meal would be too.

That Carlo's *ragù* is traditional is beyond doubt: here was a recipe genuinely handed down the generations. Yet his version contained as many surprises as any other I encountered. It brought home to me again that authenticity and perfection are elusive: even a dish of long provenance, with a city of origin attached to its name, tended to evolve into as many variations as there were imaginative chefs to make them. Carlo made a *soffritto*, as I expected, sautéing onion, celery and carrot to flavour the sauce; then he put beef and cured pork in the pan. But, unlike most Italian recipes I had come across, he added no stock or milk, only a little wine and some tomato purée. The *ragù* was allowed to fry for a couple of hours, by which time the oil was flavoured by the *soffritto*. That was the keynote of Carlo's approach: a long, slow shallow fry rather than a liquid simmer. When the *ragù* was ready, he spooned a small amount on to the tagliatelle but left it unmixed. I'd expected to see the two tossed together so that the pasta could absorb some of the sauce's flavour. I asked him why he kept the two separate, and the reply was: 'That's how it's done.'

I guess there are some parts of tradition that remain sacrosanct.

As Carlo brought the *ragù* to the table, I could see that he had regained his customary ebullience. There had been a period during the afternoon when this had deserted him. I could understand this. Cooking and filming make awkward bedfellows: as a chef you want your creations to be seen at their best. All too often what sits on a plate looking perfect has sagged into something unrecognisable by the time the cameras are trained upon it. The rhythms and energy of the kitchen falter before the demands of the lens – the shots repeated ad infinitum, the slow-paced chess game of manipulating everybody into position. Throughout my series of trips I was amazed at the willingness of people to give up their time for relatively little reward, and at their generosity, even when their patience was stretched to the limit.

'This is going to be my first taste of genuine Italian *ragù*,' I said to camera before digging in. It looked very appetising – the deep yellow of the pasta perfectly offset the rich red of the *ragù* – an almost shameful reminder of how insipid and unappealing the classic Brit bolognese is, with its wan spaghetti and faded brown mince. The fried approach made for quite a dry sauce, taking it in an unusual direction (I'd have to weigh up whether I preferred a wet or dry sauce, and which one would genuinely tap into most people's notion of the essential character of *ragù*), but the oil gave it a deliciously nutty flavour that I really appreciated.

NU *RAGÙ*

We arrived at Osteria Francescana in Modena four hours late, but Massimo Bottura was waiting and ready to go.

Massimo is one of the cleverest and most inventive chefs in Italy. One strand of his cooking might be called 'deconstruction': reducing a dish to the most minimal form of its essential elements. (Later, we'd be treated to an extraordinary example of this.) His cuisine is witty, allusive and playful, demonstrating an iconoclasm that is sometimes ill-received: the flipside of Italy's stalwart adherence to tradition in cooking (which gives it strength and character) is a deep-rooted resistance to radical change. There have been times when Massimo's restaurant has been almost empty (fortunately his well-deserved two-star status has changed that), and there have been fist fights between customers over some of his creations and their provocativeness. If any-one could offer me some eye-popping ideas about *ragù*, Massimo could.

Bouncing along with a barely restrained energy, he led us away from the restaurant through a courtyard, up wide stone steps and across a gallery to his test kitchen. Here, instead of photographs of venerable female chefs hard at work, the walls were covered in modern art. A vast canvas with trowelled smears of oil paint vied for attention with an equally monumental picture of what looked like an apartment block drawn in a kind of crazed pencil scribble. Beyond the Persian rugs and a 1950s Coca-Cola dispenser was an enigmatic photograph of grassland at night, illuminated only by a faint and slightly sinister blue glow.

Art was obviously a central source of inspiration for Massimo: his conversation was peppered with analogies from artists and their ideas or the movements they established. (A first edition of the futurist Filippo Marinetti's *La Cucina Futurista* lay on the table next to the eggs and flour for our session.) Perhaps coming at food from an artistic angle is what fuels his idiosyncratic approach. 'I was born here in Modena. It can be a very blinkered town, thinking only along straight lines,' he said. 'The people are often quite conservative. They just come in and ask for pasta, tortellini. That's why I want to shake it up a little. Do crazy things.' Above Massimo's head an old neon sign flashed out 'Rock 'n' Roll', as though underlining what he was saying.

It seems to me that, in some ways, it's easier to explore culinary innovation in Britain precisely because we have no strong food tradition to enchain us. Massimo agreed: 'In Italy, everybody is a football coach – and a food critic!' At the same time, Massimo knows that to break the rules you first have to understand them. 'Before his blue period and cubism, Picasso learned how to draw and paint like an angel. To arrive at the point where you can change things, you first have to know the tradition. Otherwise you're just a silly boy,' he said. 'But I can show you this better by cooking than talking. Let's get in the kitchen.'

Like any chef with a restless imagination, Massimo is constantly changing and evolving his dishes. Before showing me the *ragù alla bolognese* that he serves now, he showed me his version from three years ago – a version so deconstructed that any innocent customer who ordered it expecting a plateful of tagliatelle and meat sauce would have been seriously nonplussed.

He began by rubbing the surface of a frying pan with fat from a pig's cheek, then popped in two small squares of pasta that he'd pressed together. 'This is just a suggestion of pasta. When I was a kid I used to steal pasta from my grandmother and cook it like this. It's a big memory for me.' He took a hen embryo and blanched it in a mixture of chicken and beef broth before sucking out the yolk with a syringe and replacing it with concentrated essence of *ragù*. 'And that's it! Bolognese,' Massimo finished with a flourish as he placed the embryo on the pasta.

It was a brilliant piece of theatre – the finished dish looked like a child's toy or an architectural model: a flat square plane with a sphere on top – but it was more than that; it had all the elements we associate with bolognese but in a different form. It was the sort of food that makes you think about what you're eating, how it is constructed, how it works, how it might be made different – and that's fascinating. True food for thought. I could see how Massimo's passion for art might have informed this dish because in some ways you had to decode it as you would a painting, thinking about its possibilities and intentions until you'd 'got' it. Of course, you could enjoy the dish without thinking about it at all – it was unquestionably delicious – but if you did think, it could add an extra dimension to the pleasure of the meal (especially if you were an Italian who had maybe pinched pasta and fried it in this way, making the food a kind of keyhole through which to glimpse old memories; food often has such powers of allusion).

Massimo, however, was already moving on. 'That was my *ragù* in 2002, but now I've gone more back to the roots. Sometimes you have to go one step back to go three forwards.' He was still using the hen embryos, this time to make tagliatelle. 'In the Emilia Romagna region people expect a strong-tasting pasta. It has to be rich and crunchy, so you need these.' As he pierced one, the liquid pooled a rich red colour, like cream of tomato soup. I tasted it and the flavour was incredible. Massimo added five embryos and two egg yolks to 500 grams of '00' flour and started to knead 'as my grandmother taught me. Memory is one of the major parts of my cooking. People say I'm an experimentalist when in fact I'm just a romantic. Nostalgia plays a great part in this *ragù*.'

Making pasta requires patience. Massimo worked the dough until smooth, then let it sit for forty-five minutes before flattening it out with a long pasta pin. 'The pasta needs to be rough so that it absorbs the flavour. When I'm eating *ragù* I like to feel the rough edges on my tongue. It shows that the food comes from the heart, that love and care have gone into making it,' he said. The pasta was left again, this time to dry, after which he rolled it into a long loose tubular shape, so that it looked like an oversized enchilada, and made thin slices across it, then unfurled these immediately to make sure the cut strips didn't stick. For cooking, it's best if the tagliatelle is a little bit dry. By the time we'd finished preparing the sauce, it would be ready.

'For me,' said Massimo, 'the most important thing in cooking is the idea. Then pick the ingredients and think about the best way to use them as a route to the idea. And then think about the architecture – the colours, the aesthetic. So, the ingredients … '

He made a *soffritto* with finely chopped celery, onions and garlic. Garlic had turned out to be a source of controversy on this trip. Several chefs, including Carlo at Gigina's, had declared it had no place in a true *ragù*, though they generally couldn't tell me why, or resorted to an adamant 'That's not how it's done.' For Massimo garlic was 'something nice to smell and taste. So why not?' Why not indeed? Once again I was confronted with how personal the idea of perfection is – and how crazy it was to try to pin it down, even though I was picking up lots of ideas in the process. 'The *soffritto* is the major flavour of the *ragù*,' Massimo continued. He added wine to it for a touch of acidity and then combined it with the meat.

'I always look for the best ingredients. The meat is 36-month-old, free-range, grass-fed Chianina, the white Tuscan cow that you see in a lot of Renaissance paintings. I use the *braghetta*, the "skirt" from the belly, which is very, very tasty. I used to use veal but now I've found the Chianina I've switched.'

The meat was mixed in a bowl then put in a vacuum bag along with bay leaves, marrowbone, tomatoes, pork ribs, beef stock and *fleur de sel* before going in the oven. 'I want the *ragù* to be really strong, so I use no milk or cream.'

The choice of a vac bag was encouraging because I'd been contemplating using one myself (it's one of the ways we braise meat at the Hind's Head), but I had wondered whether using shredded rather than minced meat would take a bolognese too far in the wrong direction, giving it an unfamiliar texture that altered appreciation of it.

The bag went in the oven for a long, slow cook. Fortunately, like a *Blue Peter* presenter, Massimo produced one he'd prepared earlier. He removed the bones and chopped the meat up before putting it in a pan and adding some cooked tagliatelle. There was a pause while the pasta absorbed the sauce, and then it was ready.

You could see how good the tagliatelle was even before eating it. There was almost no juice left in the pan – it had all been absorbed by the pasta. If you held up a strand, the meat clung to it, promising a particularly delicious union of the ingredients. It was a promise that was kept: the meat was an enticing, light brown colour and had a grainy, chunky texture. You could still see the bits of tomato in it – there was a roughness that added interest. There was also a richness, a real mixture of flavours that developed and grew as you chewed. As for the tagliatelle, it was silky smooth from the liquid it had absorbed, and it had a taste that stood up to the meat and genuinely complemented it. Although this was in many ways a more traditional *ragù alla bolognese* than Massimo's 2002 version, it was equally fine. He really had taken one step back to go three steps forwards.

Massimo's *ragù* had given me a lot to think about, but I was equally taken with his insistence on the role memory and nostalgia played in food because it reflected something of what I was trying to explore at the Fat Duck, and something that I already felt needed to be incorporated into the sixteen dishes I was going to cook for this project. All of them tapped into a deep well of nostalgia and memory. Most of them were comfort foods, the food of childhood, and everyone's view of them was overlaid by a sense of personal history – perhaps eating pizza for the first time as a kid on a holiday abroad, or digging into a plate of steaming mash and succulent sausages while winter raged outside the windows. I needed not only to cook these as well as I possibly could, but also to capture that nostalgia, to bring to each dish the kind of trigger that would transport people back to their cherished memories of that food.

How to achieve that? I guess you could say I had a lot on my plate …

TAG TEAM

Travelling south, towards Rome, the landscape began to change. The director was playing DJ and, as *Funk & Drive* scudded out of the car's speakers, we whizzed down wide plains, past hills crowned with crumbling *palazzi*. Eventually we left the motorway and began to climb the winding road to Monte San Giusto, home to La Pasta di Aldo – the pasta that had outstripped all the others in our testing.

We pulled in by a nondescript block of flats in front of what looked like a bungalow. This was an area where people worked hard for a living. Small plots of vines and olive trees dotted the valley amid the usual farm paraphernalia: rusting tractors, jagged sheets of corrugated metal. Each property had its guard dog, and barks and birdsong filled the air.

Luigi Donnari was waiting for us on the gravel in front of the bungalow, which turned out to be where he created his extraordinary pasta – a real cottage industry! With his sober shirt and rimless glasses Luigi had the air of a university professor, but his enthusiasm for pasta was anything but academic. Get him talking on his favourite subject and the words tumbled out.

'This is not something I do for money. During the day I work for a shoemaking company so that I have the funds for my passion – the making of pasta. Come and see.'

It's true that Luigi's not in it for the money. He could have expanded his operation but he's determined not to compromise on quality. He has scoured the country for machines that will make perfect pasta. More often than not this means tracking down older models geared towards excellence rather than speed. A bigger output would require more such machinery, and that requires a long-term commitment on the part of the wholesale buyers of his pasta.

We stepped through the row of plastic strips dangling across the doorway and entered Luigi's 'factory'. It was on a completely different scale from anything else I had encountered during my travels: four small rooms contained the entire process, from mixing to boxing-up. It was the workplace of a real artisan. As sun slanted into the preparation room, picking out the vibrant yellow-orange glow of strips of tagliatelle hung up to dry, Luigi explained his methods.

'You need egg whites to help the texture of the dough, egg yolks for the taste and colour.' As we talked, Luigi's wife Maria poured these into a mixer not much larger than a domestic version. 'For every 100 grams of whole eggs, 25 grams of yolks. Then add semolina – 100 per cent durum wheat semolina, not the "00" flour you often use in Britain. One kilogram for every 500 grams of eggs. The semolina helps to give the pasta its golden colour.'

In the mixer, the churning dough had taken on a wonderful bright yellow hue. And the durum wheat would give the pasta that coarser, almost sandy texture that confers character and helps bind the sauce. I had a hunch that the size of the semolina was important, that if it were too small, the starch granules would be damaged and lead to an unresponsive dough. Luigi agreed that the mix of grain was crucial.

'Each type of pasta needs a different mixture of durum wheat to hold its shape. Take the wide flat strips of pappardelle. Their size means they need a longer cooking time, so they have to be strong. For pappardelle I use only 80 per cent Italian durum wheat. The rest comes from abroad, from wheat with a higher gluten content. I read somewhere that the Chinese call gluten "the muscle of flour". Add it to water and the gluten proteins bond together and make a tensile elastic mass.'

By now the dough was ready. It had started off in the mixer looking like a clump of yellow rags, but by the time it was taken out it looked and felt more like a giant lump of Play-Doh. Maria took a big chunk and cut it into squares using a two-handled blade.

'So far we have been trying to keep the pasta light,' Luigi explained. 'We try to do this until it reaches the plate. It should retain an "emptiness" so that it takes up the sauce.' He held up the dough. It had little holes, dents and craters in it. 'If we press out these holes, the pasta won't have that lightness. As we shape and roll it, we have to be extremely careful to keep the air pockets in the dough – just as you would if making puff pastry.'

Maria took a square of dough larger and thicker than a phone directory and fed it repeatedly into the rollers. Each time it emerged longer and more compact than the last. She began to fold the dough between each roll, as though folding a sheet. There was a confident rhythm to her movements – *fold over, feed through, fold over, feed through* – and she narrowed the gap between the rollers as she went, until eventually the dough had transformed from directory to table runner.

Maria folded this in a sort of concertina – over and back on itself, dusting semolina on each time – until she had a fat square once more; she then halved it, flattened out the two pieces and spliced them together. Finally, it was judged to be the right thickness, with enough air trapped in the folds. The dough was ready to be cut into its shape.

The cutting machine was automated but not much bigger than the hand-cranked stainless-steel models people have at home. The long thin sheet of dough was fed into the top and came out of the bottom in a row of flat strips, like the fringes on a cowboy's jacket. Maria put a thin metal rod under the dangling fringe and lifted it up and over to a wheeled, double-rowed, four-tiered metal rack. The rod fitted niftily into grooves in the rack. When the rack was full Maria simply trundled it next door and into the drying chamber, heaved shut the doors, flicked a few switches, and a vigorous turbine hum kicked in.

I wanted to know how much importance Luigi attached to the drying process. 'It's a fundamental part,' he replied. 'If the drying goes wrong, you ruin all the care you've put into making the pasta in the first place.'

The drying process removes moisture from the pasta. I wondered how far this governed its ability to suck up a sauce. Luigi explained that, rather than laying the pasta flat to dry – as others do – he hangs it up. 'This is the most important thing. It keeps it porous. My pasta is so porous that, if you leave it near cheese, it'll absorb the smell!'

'Why is hanging the pasta to dry better than laying it flat?'

'The crucial factor is the air that circulates around the pasta, which allows the moisture to be released *gradually*. It must be not too quick, not too slow. It's a delicate balance.'

'I've heard some people say you should start the drying with a high temperature, to fix the colour and the proteins, and then reduce the heat.'

'Hmm, I'm still experimenting.' Luigi peered at me, a little owlishly, through his spectacles. 'But so far for me the long time, low temp works well.'

It worked well for me too. Luigi made the most textured pasta I'd ever felt: it was speckled with semolina and almost like bark to the touch. That and its superb colour made it really enticing, something you'd want to cook and eat as soon as you caught sight of it, which is surely one benchmark of perfect food.

It was already late afternoon. The road – and the director's head-splitting collection of CDs – awaited. But Luigi was determined that we have lunch with him. It was an offer I couldn't refuse. I knew that, this being Italy, the meal would be turned into an event; and, given Luigi's sympathy and flair, he would make this something special. I wasn't wrong. We sat down with all his family – sons and daughters, aunts and grandmother – to a banquet: prosciutto, olives stuffed with meat, refreshing local white wine and a syrupy warmed red, and of course his unbelievable pasta, simply dressed with lemon and parsley – all prepared by a young chef from the nearby catering school who

Spontaneous hospitality, Italian style. Master pasta-maker Luigi Donnari insisted we stay for lunch, and got a trainee chef to cook it for us.

wore a floppy white chef's hat. The cuts of meat came from Luigi's own animals; the olive oil was home-made. It was hard to believe that he found the time to do all this, and work for a shoemaker, and produce perhaps the finest pasta in Italy. Perfection requires this kind of dedication and devotion, and Luigi was a real inspiration.

DUN ROAMIN

A couple more appointments and then we pushed south to our final destination. We got hopelessly lost on the Rome ring road and drove up and down the darkened boulevards as *Deep Dish Remix* segued into *Trippin' on Sunshine* by Pizzaman. 'You and me are looking for the key that will open the door to the world of love,' cried the singer.

Frankly, right then, I'd have settled for the key to my hotel room.

Eventually we found our hotel, the Mach I. Like Concorde, it had seen better days. The lobby was shrouded in plastic dust sheets and paint spots covered the carpet. We had a last supper in the kind of restaurant found on airport outskirts everywhere: over-lit and with over-fancy dishes that didn't really work. After the marvellous culinary experiences of the last few days it was a sobering and useful reminder of another world, where food is merely functional and fails to live up to expectations. A reminder that it's worth taking the trouble to get it right.

A LOAD OF BOLOGS

A chef spends a large part of each day in a windowless kitchen surrounded by a bunch of equally enthusiastic obsessives. It's a pressure-cooked environment that's not necessarily the best in which to keep a firm grasp on reality. (Indeed, there were those who'd suggested that, with snail porridge and egg and bacon ice cream, I'd already crossed the line.) I'd used what I'd learned in Italy to develop a really vibrant *ragù*, a heady mix of pork skirt, beef and oxtail. I'd tinkered with the taste by adding star anise to accentuate the meat flavours, and with the texture by mincing, hand-chopping and shredding the meat to see what each would bring to the dish. To me, the end results seemed faithful to the Italian tradition while adding a few flavourful twists – but could it still be called spaghetti bolognese? Was it too far from what the British palate expected? I'd reached a point (let's call it spaghetti junction) where I needed to seek out some honest opinion …

Which is why I found myself standing before Allan and Julia, two customers at the Hind's Head, who'd agreed to interrupt their meal and try out three versions of spaghetti bolognese.

Mary-Ellen had cooked my new recipe with hand-chopped and with shredded meat, and had tossed each with spaghetti. She'd also prepared a magnificently faithful bog-standard spag bol: supermarket minced beef cooked with a shop-bought jar of sauce and plopped bang in the middle of a tangle of spaghetti. For a final touch of 1970s authenticity, we even had a cardboard tub of pre-grated Parmesan. As I placed three small white bowls on the table, I felt a bit like an Oxford Street card-sharp about to perform 'Chase the Ace'. Through his spectacles, Allan blinked at me, suggesting perhaps that he thought so too.

I trotted out my patter: 'Hi. Thanks for participating in this. I'm working on a spaghetti bolognese recipe for a TV series, and I'm trying to see how far I can push it. I'd like you to taste these three versions and tell me what you think of them … '

Julia eyed up the spag bol. 'It looks like the sort of thing my daughter used to cook at university. Mmm, it's nice, though. You try it, Allan.' She passed over the bowl and tried the second. I have to admit my heart was in my mouth at this point. All my research and recipe development would look pretty ridiculous if people's preferred pasta topping came out of a jar. 'Oh, that's even nicer. It's got a slight spicing, almost oriental.'

'That's the star anise.'

Allan, meanwhile, had moved on to the version with shredded meat. 'This is good too. It's meatier. I like the way the sauce coats the pasta. I don't know whether you could call it spaghetti bolognese, though. It looks – and feels – different.'

It was beginning to look as though I had some freedom to play around with ingredients as long as the first impression of the dish – both to the eyes and the mouth – retained something of its traditional British character. I left Julia worrying about whether she'd been caught on camera with *ragù* all round her mouth, and collected three new bowls of bol from the kitchen, moved on to Gudrun and Hilary's table, and delivered my spiel once more.

The spag bol took Gudrun on a nostalgia trip, just as it had Julia. 'This looks the most like spaghetti bolognese. It reminds me of home and childhood.' (Since Gudrun was from Austria, this showed that calling spag bol a classic British dish was a misnomer: it had squeezed out its Italian rival on a truly international scale.) 'This is the kind of stuff kids will eat,' she continued. 'Even now we make it like this at home. Whereas this' – she waved a fork at the shredded meat – 'is not what I would normally associate with the dish. That said, it's got a lovely taste. I like the carrots, the big pieces of meat. Yes, it's good.'

Hilary admitted that Gudrun was the foodie of the two, and had railroaded her into taking part. She was formally dressed in a pin-striped brown shirt, and her comments were equally reserved as she tried the hand-chopped version. 'To me this is also quite unconventional. It's nice. The tomatoes are nice.'

'It's a compote,' I offered.

'But … ' She was obviously reluctant to be forthright. It's not easy when you've got not just the chef standing next to you but a camera crew inches from your face. 'It's maybe a little too sweet … '

'That's good to know. That's exactly why I'm doing this – to find out whether it matches expectations. Would all of these be accepted as spaghetti bolognese, do you think? Or are some too far beyond the boundaries?'

'The shredded meat might be a step too far, yes.' Hilary seemed almost relieved to have admitted it.

So far, both tables had chosen hand-chopped *ragù* over traditional spag bol. (Phew!) Both had baulked at shredded meat. Would Chris and Lisa (who were having a drink in the Hind's Head before dining at the Fat Duck in honour of their wedding anniversary) confirm the trend? With practice, my spiel was getting slicker: I'd started to sound like some dodgy fairground barker. 'Spaghetti bolognese is such a part of our culture,' I announced. 'It's bound up in memories – and there's nothing wrong with that. But how far can I play around with people's expectations?'

Chris and Lisa went at all three bowls with enthusiasm and curiosity. They were determined to identify the key ingredients that gave each version its particular personality, as though this were some kind of forensic test. I found myself morphing from fairground barker to game show host. Perhaps I could call it 'Spot the Bol'.

'There's game of some kind in this hand-chopped version,' Chris declared.

'Good guess. There's oxtail in there giving a gamey note.'

'And something spicy. Aniseed? Fennel?'

'Yes. Good spot.'

'I'm not sure about the fennel,' added Lisa. 'It kind of dominates.'

'And what about the third bowl?' I asked.

'Eating it is like being a schoolboy again,' Chris said. 'The white ring of pasta with the blob of meat at the centre. At home we had that every Monday night, with grated Parmesan that smelled like sweaty feet.'

'You think that's bad,' said Lisa. 'We had spaghetti out of a tin, so anything's going to be better than that! I've probably just undermined any credibility my comments might have, but my favourite's the shredded one, even if it is less traditional than the others.'

'I'm very glad you said that,' I told her. 'What about the pasta to go with it? Does it have to be spaghetti? What about tagliatelle?'

'Tagliatelle?!'

I tried several other tables that simply confirmed what I'd learned: I could experiment with the taste of a *ragù* – boosting the flavours; adding new subtleties with unusual ingredients – but the texture had to have a certain homogeneity, a relative smoothness. And, even if it wasn't authentic, even if it held the sauce less well, spaghetti had to be a part of my dish. It might not be an Italian's idea of perfection, but in Britain people's affection for spaghetti with their bolognese was steadfast and unchangeable.

Spaghetti Bolognese **Serves 4–6**

As you might expect from a classic of the Italian kitchen, this involves no special equipment, just a long, slow simmer to allow the flavours to combine. However, I've added a few things to boost those flavours. Caramelising onions with star anise produces vibrant flavour compounds that enhance the meaty notes of the sauce, and the oakiness of the chardonnay complements the sherry vinegar in the tomato compote. Finishing the compote on a high heat captures something of the fried character I enjoyed at Trattoria della Gigina. Using milk might seem strange, but it's a standard part of many Italian *ragù* recipes: as it cooks, the proteins and sugars in milk react to give extra flavour and body.

Timing

Once the meat is browned and the caramelised onions are ready (an hour's work at most), the sauce is left to simmer virtually unattended for 8 hours. Do the prep first thing in the morning and then the day's your own until it's time to serve up dinner (especially if you prepare the tomato compote in advance, though even this involves a fairly simple preparation, followed by a slow, carefree simmer). You can even do all the cooking of the bolognese in advance, then simply warm it through and add the tarragon bouquet garni on the day.

For the sauce base

1 star anise _ 125ml extra virgin olive oil _ 2 large onions (about 450g), finely sliced* _ 2 large cloves of garlic _ 2 large onions (about 450g), finely diced _ 3 large carrots (about 400g), finely diced _ 3 celery stalks (about 125g), finely diced _ 250g pork shoulder, cut into 1cm cubes _ 250g oxtail, boned and minced _ 375ml oaked chardonnay _ 250ml whole milk

* These onions are to be caramelised. The process can be sped up by removing water from the onions beforehand. Place them in a sieve over a bowl, toss with a heaped teaspoon of table salt and leave for 20 minutes.

For the tomato compote

1.1kg vine-ripened tomatoes _ 1 tsp table salt _ 200ml extra virgin olive oil _ 3 large cloves of garlic _ 1 large onion (about 225g), finely diced _ 1 heaped tsp coriander seeds _ 1 star anise _ 3 cloves _ 4–5 drops Tabasco _ 4–5 drops Thai fish sauce _ 2 tsp Worcestershire sauce _ 1 heaped tbsp tomato ketchup _ 30ml sherry vinegar _ 1 bouquet garni (consisting of 7 sprigs of fresh thyme and 1 fresh bay leaf)

For the finished spaghetti bolognese

reserved tomato compote _ 100g good-quality spaghetti per person _ sherry vinegar, to taste _ Parmesan cheese (Parmigiano Reggiano) _ 1 bouquet garni (in a sheet of leek, wrap 6 tarragon leaves, 4 sprigs of parsley and the leaves from the top of a bunch of celery) _ unsalted butter _ extra virgin olive oil _ table salt and freshly ground black pepper

PREPARING THE SAUCE BASE

1. Place a large, heavy-bottomed frying pan over a medium heat for 5 minutes. Crush the star anise and bag it up in a square of muslin. Add this to the pan, along with 25ml oil and the sliced onions. Cook for 20 minutes, or until the onions are soft and caramelised, stirring occasionally. Set aside.
2. Meanwhile, preheat another large, heavy-bottomed frying pan over a low heat for 5 minutes. Mince the garlic. Pour 50ml oil into the pan, then tip in the garlic, onions, carrots and celery and cook this *soffritto* over a medium–low heat for about 20 minutes, or until the raw onion smell has gone. Transfer the *soffritto* to a bowl and wipe clean the pan.
3. Place the pan over a high heat for 10 minutes. Pour in 50ml olive oil and wait until it starts smoking: it must be hot enough so the meat browns rather than stews. Add the cubed pork and the minced oxtail. Stir until browned all over. (To brown properly, all the meat has to touch the surface of the pan. If it doesn't, do it in batches.) Tip the browned meat into a sieve over a bowl (to allow the fat to drain off), then transfer the meat to a large pan or casserole. Deglaze the pan by adding a splash of wine, bringing it to the boil, then

scraping the base of the pan to collect all the tasty bits stuck to the bottom. Once the liquid has reduced by half, pour it into the large pan containing the meat.

4. Remove the bag of star anise from the caramelised onions, then tip the onions into the large pan containing the meat. Add the remaining wine and deglaze the frying pan (as in step 3). When the wine has reduced by half, pour it into the large pan. Add the *soffritto* to the pan as well.

5. Place the pan of bolognese over a very low heat. Pour in the milk and enough water to cover entirely, and simmer very gently without a lid for 6 hours, stirring occasionally. At all times the ingredients should be covered by the liquid, so be prepared to add more water. (Don't worry if the milk becomes slightly granular: it won't affect the end result.)

PREPARING THE TOMATO COMPOTE

1. Bring a large pan of water to the boil. Fill a large bowl with ice-cold water. Remove the cores from the tomatoes with a paring knife. Blanch the tomatoes by dropping them into the boiling water for 10 seconds, then carefully transferring them to the bowl of ice-cold water. Take them out of the water immediately and peel off the split skins. (If the tomatoes are not ripe enough, make a cross with a sharp knife in the underside of each, to encourage the skin to come away. They can be left in the hot water for an extra 10 seconds or so, but it's important that they don't overheat and begin to cook.)

2. Cut the tomatoes in half vertically. Scoop out the seeds and the membrane with a teaspoon over a chopping board. Roughly chop the seeds and membrane, then tip them into a sieve over a bowl. Sprinkle over the salt and leave for 20 minutes to extract their juice, after which you can discard the seeds and membrane, reserving only the juice.

3. Roughly chop the tomato flesh and set aside.

4. Meanwhile, place a large, heavy-bottomed pan over a low heat. Add 100ml of the olive oil. Mince the garlic, then put it into the pan along with the onion. Cook for 10–15 minutes, until soft but not coloured.

5. Crush the coriander and put it in a muslin bag, along with the star anise and the cloves. Add it to the softened onions and garlic.

6. Take the juice drawn from the tomato seeds and membrane and add it to the onions and garlic along with the tomato flesh.

7. Add the Tabasco, fish sauce, Worcestershire sauce, tomato ketchup and sherry vinegar. Drop in the bouquet garni and cook over a low heat for 2 hours.

8. To add a roasted note to the compote, add the remaining oil and turn up the heat to high. Fry the compote for 15–20 minutes, stirring regularly to make sure it doesn't catch, then pour off any olive oil not absorbed by the compote. Set aside a little to coat the cooked pasta. (The rest can be stored in a jar and makes a great base for a salad dressing. The compote itself will keep in the fridge for a week.)

COOKING THE SPAGHETTI BOLOGNESE

1. Stir the tomato compote (including the bag of spices) into the bolognese sauce and cook over a very low heat for a final 2 hours, stirring occasionally.

2. Bring a large pan of salted water to the boil for the pasta. For every 100g of pasta, you'll need 1 litre of water and 10g salt. (If you don't have a large enough pan, it's essential to use two pans rather than overcrowd one.)

3. Put the spaghetti into the pan, give it a stir, then bring back to the boil and cook until the pasta is just tender but with a bite. Check the cooking time on the packet and use that as a guideline, but taste it every few minutes as this is the only way to judge when the pasta is ready.

4. Before taking the bolognese sauce off the heat, check the seasoning and add some sherry vinegar (tasting as you go) to balance the richness of the sauce. Add a generous grating of Parmesan (but not too much, as it can make the sauce overly salty) and remove the sauce from the heat. Take out the original thyme and bay bouquet garni and the bag of spices. Replace these with the parsley and tarragon bouquet garni, stir in 100g unsalted butter and let the sauce stand for 5 minutes.

5. Once the pasta is cooked, drain and rinse it thoroughly. Return to the pan to warm through. (Since the *ragù* is not going to be mixed with the pasta, it needs to be rinsed to prevent it becoming starchy

and sticking together.) Add a generous knob of butter (about 50g per 400g of pasta) and coat with olive oil and the reserved oil from the final frying of the compote. To serve, wind portions of pasta around a carving fork and lay them horizontally in wide, shallow bowls. Top with the bolognese sauce and finish with a grating of Parmesan.

Chilli con Carne

'Anybody that eats chilli can't be all bad.'

Pat Garrett on Billy the Kid

History

The origins of chilli con carne are a stewpot of conjecture.* There are those who claim it was invented in Mexico in the 1840s as a way of turning leftovers into a catch-all stew that was served to tourists who would believe they were eating authentic Mexican food so long as it was spicy and cheap – a kind of Tijuana tapas. Those who nix the Mexican angle tend to quote the famous 1959 Mexican dictionary entry that defines chilli con carne as 'detestable food, passing itself off as Mexican'. And Charles Ramsdell has suggested, in *San Antonio: An Historical and Pictorial Guide*, that chilli con carne is not generally on the menu in Mexico, except in tourist hotspots. If it were a traditional dish, he contends, it would be more widespread in the country: 'For Mexicans, especially those of Indian ancestry, do not change their culinary customs from one generation, or even one century, to another.'

Crossing the border brings different interpretations. There is a cowboy version that has dried beef, suet and dried chilli peppers pounded together and left to dry into bricks that could then be boiled in pots on the trail. Some historians say that Spanish settlers in San Antonio in the 1730s brought with them a spicy Spanish stew not dissimilar to chilli (though they tend to fight shy of actually giving this ancestor a name). Others identify the dish as the traditional food of poor Tejanos (Hispanic Texans), offering a tasty way of turning a few scraps of meat into a filling dish. J.C. Clopper, a visitor to San Antonio in the 1820s, observed this at close quarters: 'When they have to pay for their meat in the market, a very little is made to suffice for the family; it is generally cut into a kind of hash with nearly as many peppers as there are pieces of meat – this is all stewed together.'

This certainly has a ring of authenticity. Poor man's food has always been a stew or hash made up of whatever can bulk it up and

---

* Much as its ingredients are a cookpot of controversy. It has been said that 'in Texas, putting beans in chilli replaced horse thievery as the number one hanging offence'. Tomatoes too, apparently, have no place in a genuine chilli: the red colour should come from the chillies alone, which bind the sauce by acting as a thickener, much as they do in Mexican cuisine.

stave off hunger along with the local produce best able to give the meagre pickings some flavour. And the site of this make-do meatfest, San Antonio, crops up again and again in stories of chilli's origins.* Unquestionably, by the 1880s there existed in this raucous army town and railroad stop a well-documented tradition of chilli queens – colourfully dressed Hispanic women who would gather in the evenings in Military Plaza or, in later years, Market Square to sell chilli from bubbling cauldrons set over mesquite fires. A plate of chilli, beans and tortilla for a dime. It has been suggested that this is where the fabled 'bowl of red' caught on commercially and, as competition between stalls spurred invention, gradually evolved into something resembling its modern form.

As with the hamburger, a public exhibition is credited with bringing chilli to a wider audience. The 1893 Columbian Exposition in Chicago had a San Antonio Chilli Stand that proved popular. The Depression furthered this by foregrounding the dish's benefits for those with an empty stomach and empty pockets, and chilli parlours sprang up throughout the country. Since then, chilli has broken out of its poor-man's-food status to become hankered after by American presidents ('One of the first things I do when I get home to Texas is to have a bowl of red. There is simply nothing better,' said Lyndon B. Johnson) and argued over by American states: in 1993 the Illinois State Senate passed a resolution proclaiming Springfield to be the 'Chilli Capital of the Civilized World'.

* Since the late 1970s, chilli con carne has been the official dish of the state of Texas. This holds some weight in the USA. Although few others have a state dish (Kentucky has fried chicken, of course), various foodstuffs have official recognition, including tubers (Washington: Russet potato), snack foods (Utah: Jell-O; Illinois: popcorn) and jam (Louisiana: Mayhaw jelly and sugar cane jelly).

The Quest for the Best

TEXAS HOLD-UP

Throughout the Lone Star State, bumper stickers proclaim: 'Don't Mess with Texas'. Well, we were messing with it, in scheduling terms at least. We weren't going. It wasn't a question of money, it appeared, but of time. The TV crew and I had to comb Britain and criss-cross three continents in three months. Taking in Texas would play havoc with the timetable. It was impossible to squeeze it in, though it also seemed to me impossible to do a programme on chilli con carne without visiting San Antonio.

The resourceful BBC researchers, however, had a plan. 'You'll be in New York to film burgers. What if we got dozens of chilli cooks from all over the country to come to you, show their best efforts and let you taste them? Maybe let you in on their secrets? How would that be?'

'Huh?' The TV team had worked incredibly hard to set up a series of programmes that accommodated even my most off-the-wall ideas. Now I began to suspect that the process had taken its toll on their sanity.

'We're talking about a chilli cookoff. Like in that *Simpsons* episode where Homer eats Guatemalan Insanity Peppers and hallucinates a talking coyote. That kind of thing. Though obviously without the coyote ... '

A spot on *The Simpsons* is usually evidence of something deeply embedded in American culture. Every year, under the aegis of the International Chili Society (ICS), hundreds of chilli cookoffs take place all over the United States. They're usually a riotous combination of charity fundraiser, barbecue and street-party, but the chilli cooking is a serious business. Under the watchful eyes of a panel of judges, entrants compete in three categories: Best Chilli, Best Chilli Verde and Best Salsa. The rules are stringent: beans and pasta are forbidden; no pre-cooking is allowed; the official 32-ounce ICS Styrofoam judging cup must be filled and labelled in accordance with the stipulated regulations. Whoever best pleases the judges on the criteria of 'good flavour, texture of the meat, consistency, blend of spices, aroma, and colour' gets to compete in the World Championship cookoff held in October.

I'd be too early for the first of New York's three regional cookoffs, in Patchogue, but down in Washington DC the local rock radio station, DC101, was hosting one of the biggest cookoffs on the east coast, or, as *On Tap* magazine put it ...

A BACCHANALIA OF BEER, BANDS AND BEANS

I still had misgivings about trading Texas for the capital. For me, context is such an important factor in the taste of any dish: could I really get an authentic taste of chilli con carne if it weren't spiced not just with chilli, but with the heat and dust of the Deep South?

These fears seemed to be realised when I arrived at the intersection of New York Avenue and 11th and stepped out of the car. The strip of

A stall sign at the Washington chilli cookoff echoes my sentiments exactly.

fake grass leading to the turnstiles couldn't disguise the fact that this was basically a vast parking lot surrounded by blank-faced office blocks and upmarket hotel chains. It seemed an unpromising place for any kind of food experience. At one side of the square a stage had been erected and a band was grinding out a soundcheck loud enough to rip through the internal organs ... *baDOOMbaDOOMbaDOOMbaDOOM*. It was a far cry from the bluegrass of Ferl Dixon and the Second Helping Boys. I crunched across nuggets of green and blue glass towards the opposite corner, where stalls of all shapes and sizes formed the backdrop to a lot of high-speed kitchen prep – chopping and slicing, shredding and dicing. ICS Rule Four states: 'The cooking period will be a minimum of three hours and a maximum of four.' These guys had to get a move on.

The passion for chilli had brought together a fantastically diverse crowd of cooks. Goths chopped meat alongside a team of good ol' boys whose polo shirts, baseball caps and aprons matched the small marquee they were working in. A group of teachers in kilts was laboriously stirring the contents of a cookpot with a large paddle. For every highly organised outfit there was another that behaved more as though they were in their own backyard, stretched out on folding chairs, chugging down Miller Lite. The chief chilli judge, Fred Bell, had told me that the cookoff usually had more entrants than final submissions: already I could see a few who probably wouldn't make it to judging.

Teams tried to outdo each other with names and decoration. Hurricane Chilli, Food Stamp Chilli, Jack's Chilli ('If you haven't eaten Jack's chilli ... You don't know jack!'), Eternal Chilli of Life and Immortality, Chuck Norris Chilli, Rage Against the Cuisine. Chuck's Bucket o' Chilli had a sun-whitened bull's skull on its folding table. Shortbus Chilli ('It's Stoopid Good!') was constructed as a bright yellow bus, while Dr Wally's Magic Elixir was rigged up like the wagon of a Wild West travelling salesman, and they had a pitch to match.

'C'mon, folks. C'mon. Eat some chilli. Drop some change.'

'WHOOOOH, that's got a bite,' hollered a bare-chested, leather-waistcoated man to my left, who'd taken Dr Wally up on his offer. He was right: it was a chilli with real character that I'd revisit once the director had finished his punishing Heston-takes-in-the-scene walkabout.

Dan Bauer had been tipped as one of the hot contenders in Washington (he'd already made the Top Five in chilli, chilli verde and salsa at the Delaware Valley cookoff), so I tracked down his stand, which had all the trappings of a campsite run by a very well-organised holiday-maker: heavy coolboxes, large plastic jerrycans of water, lightweight aluminium folding tables stacked with canned goods and bulk-sized bags of peanuts and Abuelita tortilla chips. Everything was in its place and neatly squared off on either side of a chest-high cooking stove fronted by a placard that gave the team name as 'Cowboy Chilli Too'.

Dan himself was equally neatly turned out, in a blue and white pinstriped apron and a polo shirt on which the team name was embroidered. A nod to the Wild West was provided by the straw cowboy hat perched on top of his silvery hair. Since this was a competition, I was unsure of what etiquette might be involved in asking about ingredients. It seemed best to go to the meat of the matter.

'What's in your chilli, Dan?'

'I use beef in the red, pork in the green. Hand-chopped. Some people go hamburger – mincin' it all up – but not me.'

'And what about the chillies?'

'I'll tell you, Heston, fresh chillies can be a problem. No two are quite the same. It makes it awful difficult to be consistent, and that could cost you the competition. So I only use dried chilli. I tried hundreds of different varieties till I came up with the six that I put in the pot, and they're my secret. I'll tell you what ingredients go in my chilli right down to the last tablespoon, but I won't reveal which chilli powders I use. You'll have to do your own work on that.'

'What about smoked chilli? D'you use any of that?' I wasn't trying to outflank Dan's need for secrecy: I had been toying with the idea of adding a smoked aspect to the dish and thought it best to get the benefit of some gut instincts before I went down that route.

'Smoked is a barbecue thing. It's not a chilli thing.'

'And what about beans? The ICS seems adamant that they're not a chilli thing either. Why is that? What's wrong with beans?'

'I have no idea,' Dan told me. 'I love beans. I'd put in pinto and all that stuff. But in the competition it's against the rules.'

It turned out to be the same with almost every other competitor I met. They all loved beans and had strong opinions about which type

Hot favourites – tasting Washington's top three chillies.

was best for chilli. As soon as the judging was over, they added beans to the pot and served it to hundreds of appreciative customers. It was a telling comment on the quest for authenticity and how it can lead to a form of tunnel vision that prevents any further evolution of the dish. Rules that arise for reasons of taste seem fine to me (Dan wouldn't use kidney beans in his chilli because he felt they dominated the other flavours) but rigid adherence to historical precedence can throttle the character of a dish.

Before moving on, I wanted to know what Dan did to finish off the chilli. Here I was fishing for secret ingredients, for those final little touches that can make such a difference. He leaned in towards me. 'Some brown sugar – just a touch, not enough so that you can taste it. It kinda blends it all together. And then a tablespoon of sour cream to smooth it all out.' It was said conspiratorially, but I think I had been rumbled and Dan was having me on, since more or less every competitor I spoke to afterwards used both these ingredients. But I guess you need to be wily to win a competition like this. I decided that, if I wanted someone to spill the beans on the tricks of the chilli trade, I had better seek out a more casual competitor. Someone without a name tag, perhaps.

I found a stall that not only had no name tags but had no name. The two ragged squares of cardboard taped to tin cans were tight-lipped with their information. *Chicken mole* said one. *Rocket chilli* offered the other. As if to make up for this lack of decoration, the trestle table had at its centre a tub of the key ingredient – Ghirardelli Unsweetened Cocoa. Curious, I took a plastic shot glass of the stuff and downed it in one (there were no spoons, though I never discovered whether this was part of chilli's tough hombre image, or simple disorganisation).

It turned out that the cooks used cocoa powder and chocolate to give a richness to their chilli. It worked, though I'm not sure that a Hershey bar would have been my first choice. Nonetheless, it was an idea worth pursuing. I started mulling over the debate about whether chilli con carne had Mexican roots. If this was indeed the case, then chocolate might be a neat allusion to that country's culinary heritage and the bitter chocolate that is added to *mole poblano* sauce. Drawing inspiration from a dish's birthplace always seemed to me to be a ...

'HONEY, YOU LOOK LIKE YOU COULD USE A SHOT OF TEQUILA!'

Standing before me was my very own chilli queen, with milk-white skin and clad entirely in black – black cowboy hat, black sunglasses, black T-shirt and skirt, black mules. The only touch of colour was her apron – black, but decorated with red and green chillies. It was only 10.00 a.m. but she wouldn't take no for an answer, and, before I knew it, our arms were interlaced in a complicated arrangement that is, I guess, crucial to the tequila-downing ritual, and I endeavoured to knock it back without knocking her in the face with my elbow.

The chilli queen was Monica Parker, who is something of a legend at the DC cookoff, having walked off with the top award for chilli verde for the last two years. She was gunning for a third straight victory.

'Yup. They say three's a charm, don't they?' Her voice had a hoarse edge to it that probably came from the bar-room atmosphere of the

Hard Times cafés, a local chain of chilli parlours owned by her husband, Jim, who was competing both beside and against her. 'But it's a vicious competition. You can get first place one week then last the next.'

'You've got to be good – and then you've got to be lucky,' added Jim, as he rinsed precisely diced pork for the second time. (And he'd do it again after the initial browning.)

Monica eyed Jim's careful preparations sceptically. 'I use chuck shoulder in my chilli, and I grind it. The cubed-meat guys are all snobs. They look down on people like me … '

Jim didn't take the bait, and I took the opportunity to find out more. 'What else goes in there alongside the meat?'

'I use dried chillies and fresh ones from Hatch, New Mexico. Tons of fresh garlic. No beans – nothin' floatin' in my chilli.'

This, however, was simply in response to the rigid guidelines set up by the ICS. At home, Monica told me, she would always add beans, preferably little white navy beans because they've got a sweetness and they're the same size as the meat, which makes for a pleasant texture.

Since we'd already shared a tequila, I figured it was OK to try to sneak some tips from her on extra ingredients and cunning techniques. Monica used sour cream and sugar of course (who didn't?), but she might also swap the sugar for honey. 'And a chef in Connecticut told me he used creamy peanut butter in his red chilli, though I've yet to try that. Said it gave a real nice shine to it. But you wanna know my secret ingredient … ?' I guess the expression on my face gave the answer because she picked up a tin, shading it from the TV camera with her palm, and beckoned me forward. 'White hominy,' she rasped, lifting her hand so I could see the lettering. 'That and the drained juice from a can of kidney beans.'

How did that sit with the judges' 'no beans' rule, I wondered as I moved on. Was it the culinary equivalent of tax evasion or tax avoidance? The ICS seemed like real sticklers on some points, though the whole framework of adjudication was conducted in a charmingly erratic way. In the judges' marquee I'd watched Fred Bell struggle to lay down the rules to his team of volunteer inspectors because his address had been scheduled for exactly the same moment as, across the square, Buckcherry hit the music stage. 'Make your comments instructive,' he advised, over the *kerchugkerchugkerchugkerchugker-chug* grinding in the background. 'Not "Yuck" but "Too thin". Something like that. These folks've come a long way and worked hard. Don't comment on the chilli when you're at the judging table. It might influence the person next to you.' *BabaDABAbabababa-DABAbabababaDABA*. 'Consider the chilli taste, colour and aroma. 'Sgotta be not too hot, not too mild. The meat not tough or mushy. Think about the consistency – thick or thin – and how far the spices have permeated. The balance.' *Zrrrrrrrrrrreeeeeeeeeeeeeeeooooowwww!* Guitar solo time now and Fred was shouting to be heard. 'BASICALLY, IF YOU HAD TO HAVE ONE CHILLI FOR THE REST OF YOUR LIFE, WHICH WOULD IT BE?' *KerCHUGkerCHUGkerCHUGkerCHUG.* ' ... And remember, no double-dipping,' he finally croaked into the mike. 'Use one spoon, one time.'

Before the final judging, there were a few things I wanted to check out. I had been surprised at how few fresh ingredients were on view, and I was curious as to whether they'd bring anything extra to the dish. At Mother Tucker's Chilli (Falls Church, VA) I found Amy Smith diligently trimming green tomatoes and asked what she put in the pot.

'Alongside eight different kindsa powder, our chilli has habañero. And at the end I'll add diced jalapeño and some serrano peppers.'

'I've heard of people adding as many as eight different kinds of fresh chilli. Would a bigger mix mean a better flavour?'

'Nah. That's, like, PR stuff – just for the sake of it.'

'So what does give the chilli its complex flavour?'

'Well, I can't speak for others, but for me cumin is the second most important thing in the chilli. I like to dust some around the bowl so that you get that real spicy thing goin'. Though you don't want to take that too far, of course. If it's too spicy, I cut it with brown sugar, and if it's too tomatoey, I add some fresh lime juice.'

The idea of exploiting cumin's characteristics seemed to me a valuable tip. And I got another when I retasted the elixir of Dr Wally. The good doc was cagey when questioned, but he did let slip that he used a splash of Jack Daniel's in the marinade. JD undoubtedly had an oak aspect that might finish off a chilli really well.

Although I reckoned I had found what I was looking for – a standard for comparison and some useful starting points – I retraced my steps to the marquee for the final tasting. The judges (each of whom was now wearing a tricolour ribbon around his or her neck, bearing a medal upon which was engraved a chef's hat surrounded by red lights that blinked on and off) appeared undecided how best to lay out the numbered legions of official Styrofoam pots, and kept transferring them from one table to another and back again, as though involved in a complicated chess game. Wilting in the heat, people began to wander off in search of water. I chatted to a veteran of the cookoffs who told me his criteria for judging was, simply: 'Check which tubs're the most empty. They're the ones people are diggin'!'

Eventually, though, out of the chaos came the winner. 'First place – pot number seven. Janie Bauer! Congratulations. Come on up and receive your prize.'

After all that, we had got the wrong guy. We had interviewed Dan Bauer but not his wife, Janie, who swept the board. First place for chilli, chilli verde and salsa.

OLD NICK'S DICK

If there was a macho aspect to the chilli cookoff – the raucous rock, the shouting, shaven-headed crowd, the chilli gunned back like shots of hard liquor – it was nothing compared to what I was about to do. Kyle and Chris had gone through hundreds of cookbooks in search of chilli experts who were prepared to reveal their recipes, and had come up with a range of chilli powders for me to taste.

There they sat, in eleven small white porcelain bowls. The textures varied enormously, from the fine, powdery grind of an espresso coffee to the rougher, granulated look of a cafetière blend. The colours also varied, ranging from vivid scarlet to an earthen brown. The names reinforced an impression of wide and exotic variety – El Rey, Durango, Rio Tejas.

And somewhere among them there would no doubt be a hottie that would set my mouth on fire. My money was on the Somalian Extra Hot, which had been put in a smaller bowl than most of the others, as if to say HANDLE WITH CARE, though I was also worried about the Devil's Penis. I was secretly hoping that Kyle had chosen this not for its heat, but for the opportunity to embarrass me on camera.

For a while I managed to delay the inevitable, explaining to the camera that dried chillies are not only a more stable product than fresh, and a more effective thickening agent (making them the preferred choice for most cookoff competitors), but also have a very different flavour profile. Unlike most herbs and spices, chillies benefit from the drying process: the contents of the cells in the fruit wall become more concentrated and begin to react together, producing all kinds of aromas. Eventually I petered out and the TV crew waited, expectant and – it seemed to me – with the satisfied grins of professionals about to capture someone else's discomfort on film. (Kyle and Chris had been smiling like that earlier – until I told them that they'd be tasting alongside me.)

'OK, time to taste some chilli. What's the best way of tasting this – spoons?'

'Nah. Just dip 'n' dab,' Chris advised.

His advice had the nonchalance of someone who had grown up in New Mexico. I pushed the smaller bowls with the hotter chillis to one side, grabbed a spoon and decided to take on the paprikas first because they'd be the mildest. The Smoked Paprika had sweetness and a touch of bitterness at the end. It was exactly the kind of gentle lead-in I needed for this tasting, but I wasn't sure that it had enough character to add something to the flavour of the dish. The Extra Smoked was better, with a greater balance of sweetness and a campfire carbon note. The folks in DC might have frowned on smoked goods, but I felt that, in small doses, a sweetness and chargrilledness would add an extra depth of flavour to the dish.

I moved on, looking for the least-threatening names. Madera seemed harmless enough. We each balanced a pinch on a spoon. 'OK,' I said. 'Like Butch Cassidy and the Sundance Kid. Three – two – one … jump!'

'That's certainly got more heat,' affirmed Chris. (Had his face gone a little red, or was it just the heat of the camera lights?)

'It's a quick heat, though,' Kyle said. 'And quickly gone. A lot faster than some of the others, I bet.'

He was right. Mercifully, it didn't hang around, and it had a slight tobacco note that I found interesting, along with a sun-dried, baked-oven characteristic. Tasting chillies, it seemed, was almost like tasting wine: it was fascinating trying to catch hold of the different traces of flavour at work. I was keen to see how Rio Tejas differed.

'This is sweet,' was Chris's view. 'Almost a candy sweetness.'

I got it too, though to me it summoned up not sweets, but a bell pepper. It had a great depth of flavour coupled to a gentle heat – an extremely useful combination. Eventually I would have to sit down and – like a lab scientist or cocktail barman – compose a blend of ingredients that worked together. If I got to a point where the heat was at the level I wanted but the flavours were still too tame, Rio Tejas might be the perfect way of boosting the latter without upping the former.

'OK. Saddle up, boys ... ' (Chris was getting into this. The chillies seemed to have triggered off some New Mexican nostalgia button.) ' ... for Bull Canyon.'

Despite the evocative name, BC was flat in the mouth. The only change was a bitterness that crept in over time. It had nothing going for it, so it was crossed off the list. Pecos, on the other hand, had a lovely fruitiness to it, a touch of sun-dried tomato that certainly had a place in a chilli con carne. Durango, we all agreed, had a hickory, smoked-barbecue thing going on that we definitely wanted to get into the dish.

Chris was peering at El Rey, which had deep, peaty colour. 'This is a lot darker than any of the others,' he announced solemnly.

'Is that a sign?' I wanted to know.

'I have no idea.'

Perhaps it *was* a sign because El Rey was exactly what I think of in chilli con carne. It was almost chocolatey and redolent of the *mole* spicing in Mexican cuisine. I'd begun thinking of chilli-blending as akin to wine-making, and El Rey would certainly provide a great backbone to a blend. Already a flavour profile was forming in my mind and I'd got some idea of the base notes and top notes I wanted to play around with.

But I still needed some heat. And that's what I had before me. Three bowls were left. The smallest ones: Bird's-eye; Somalian Extra Hot; Devil's Penis. Two of them weren't even ground – just whole chillies shrivelled to the size of a fingernail. Somehow they looked more vicious in that form. 'So what's the best approach to eating these?' I asked.

'Just go for it,' Chris replied, biting into a Penis. There was a pause. Everybody turned in his direction. The camera zoomed in. Had the chilli's fire welded his lips shut?

''Sgotta little heat,' he gasped out, before leaving the room.

'Yuh, that's a creeper heat, all right,' Kyle agreed after taking a bite. His voice sounded tinny, remote.

As for me, I found the heat seemed to build over time. In my head there was the image of a fire taking hold and flaring upwards, a visual counterpart to the scorching inside my mouth. 'I can feel the sweat springing from my face as if someone's turned on a tap,' I mumbled incoherently to camera as Chris returned. He hadn't staggered off to some hidden corner of the premises to collapse; he had gone in search of milk. 'Water just swirls the hot stuff – the capsaicin – around the mouth,' he said. 'But the fat in milk helps dissolve it.'

After this, the Somalian Extra Hot was no challenge. It was another creeper, the heat building slowly to an almost unbearable intensity before levelling out. It had a powerful and distinctive fruitiness to it too. I was looking for chillies that did more than just ignite the head, and this one had potential.

The Bird's-eye, on the other hand, belied its innocuous name and hit me right on the back of the tongue and top of the throat. It was as if someone had lit a Bunsen burner in my mouth. Mopping my face repeatedly with a tea towel, I realised I'd established the upper limit of heat that I wanted, and I'd also now got a question that went right to the heart of cooking a chilli con carne.

How is it that we're so addicted to capsaicin, an alkaloid whose effects – skin irritation, skewed body temperature, increased metabolic rate – are intended to prevent us eating chilli at all? Birds are immune to capsaicin (that's evolution's way of spreading the seed). Mammals in general avoid it. What is it with we humans and spicy food?

* Is it Chilli or is it Just Me?

The Scoop on that Scoville Factor in Capsicums

The heat in chilli is designed to help spread the fruit's seeds by discouraging mammals from chewing and damaging them. (In this case, evolution hadn't bargained for Homo sapiens' culinary contrariness. That heat means it outsells every other spice: we produce and consume twenty times more chilli than black pepper, its nearest rival.)

The ingredient that imparts the heat is the chemical compound capsaicin (8-methyl-N-vanillyl-6-nonenamide), a cytotoxic alkaloid that is synthesised by the surface cells of the placenta (the pale, spongy central core) and collects in droplets below the cuticle of the placenta surface, as well as finding its way into the plant's circulation. Any kind of stress or pressure to the fruit can cause capsaicin to leak on to the seeds and inner fruit wall (which is why cooks advise removing the ribs and seeds to control the heat). The amount of capsaicin present in a chilli depends on many factors – genetic make-up, cultivation, growing conditions – and the molecule itself is found in a number of different forms, which may be what gives chillies their different kinds of heat, from slow-release to full-on flame-thrower. Chuck Norris Chilli anyone?

Although there is still debate about how capsaicin works on the body, current thinking runs along these lines. The capsaicin irritates temperature receptors in the mouth, which cause release of the imaginatively named 'Substance P', which takes the pain message to the brain and triggers that burning sensation. The irritation is self-limiting because the presence of capsaicin will eventually deplete the nerve cells' store of Substance P. Once it has gone, no more signals are sent to the brain and the area is numbed. Shortbus Chilli anyone? It's stoopid good.

Moreover, when the brain is sent a pain signal from some part of the body, it stimulates the release to those nerve endings of endorphins, chemical substances that promote a feeling of pleasure in the body. Eternal Chilli of Life and Immortality anyone?

KIKI AND BOUBA

'So, you see, chilli is "kiki" and sour cream is "bouba" … ' I tailed off, daunted by the glazed, unblinking faces of the chefs gathered before me in the lab. I could see that I'd have to explain this one in more detail. One of the most important ideas underpinning my recipe development at the Fat Duck is that eating is a multisensory experience: it's one of the few activities that simultaneously and intensely engages all the senses. With each dish on the menu I have tried to bring out not just the taste, but also the look, aroma, texture and even sound of the food.* So when I noticed the BBC was going to show a programme on synaesthesia, I made sure to set the DVD recorder.

Although considered largely benign by those who experience it, synaesthesia is a neurological condition in which two or more bodily senses are linked. It can take many different forms (in fact, it can occur between almost any combination of the senses), but among the most common are numbers and letters being perceived in terms of colours; ordered sequences (numbers, letters, days, months) being associated with particular personalities; and words being associated with specific smells or tastes. The TV programme was named *Derek Tastes of Earwax* after the observation of one of programme's synaesthetes, James, who in everyday conversation was 'bombarded with flavours'.

For scientists, the condition offers potential insights into the way the brain processes information – an area of study that had long fascinated me and that I had tentatively explored in cuisine, creating jellies that fooled the eyes, ice cream that fooled the nose and tea that seemed hot and cold at the same time. Moreover, since the synaesthete's interwoven perception of the world echoed the kind of integrated sensory experience I was trying to achieve with my cooking, I had a practical as well as theoretical interest in how synaesthesia

---

* On the menu at the Fat Duck there is a dish called 'Sound of the Sea', which looks like the meeting point between sea and shore. It contains abalone, cockles, mussels and clams plus their salty juices, samphire, seaweed and what appears to be sand. It is served with an iPod that relays the sounds of the ocean. Diners find themselves transported to their favourite beach, especially if – as happened at a demonstration in Las Vegas – I can introduce a fan to the dining room, smear its blades with a special essential oil I have had developed (let's call it *Odeur maritime*) and set the fan going while the course is being eaten.

worked. Bombardment with flavours might be too much, but I had certainly spent a lot of time on flavour encapsulation – developing ways to get flavours to release in powerful bursts that kept the palate stimulated.

Some scientists have suggested that synaesthesia arises in people whose brains allow more sensory feedback than is usual: uninhibited, the information builds to a volume that can trigger and influence several of the brain's processing areas at once (much as, say, switching off the traffic lights on a main road would have a knock-on effect throughout the traffic system). In *Derek Tastes of Earwax* the neurologist V.S. Ramachandran put forward the idea that, in synaesthetes, groups of nerve cells dealing with separate areas of experience had somehow become connected, giving conjunctions of sensation. Their wires had, in effect, got crossed.

Experiments were performed to try to establish how common synaesthesia was, and how far there was an underlying logic to the associations made by synaesthetes. The results suggested that the condition was more widespread than had been thought (one person in a hundred saw coloured letters and numbers), and that some sensory associations (such as matching colours to musical notes) were remarkably consistent among both synaesthetes and non-synaesthetes. Perhaps, the conjecture went, we are all hardwired the same: it's just that synaesthetes are an exaggerated version of this.

Some scientists took this further, arguing that the prevalence of the condition implied some kind of genetic purpose: if we all had it, then natural selection must have found it useful. Perhaps synaesthesia helped us to deal with abstract concepts in concrete terms. Perhaps it was the generator of creativity (since the condition is eight times more common in painters, writers, composers and suchlike than in the general population; and metaphor – seeing one thing in terms of another – is a central source of artistic insight). Perhaps it was part of the mechanism that allowed us to form language.

To explore this, V.S. Ramachandran used a test originally devised by the psychologist Wolfgang Köhler. He constructed two three-dimensional shapes: a spiky one (like the starburst that surrounds *POW!* in comic books) and an amoeba-like one (much like a child's representation of a puddle). Armed with these shapes, he asked passers-by which they thought was a 'kiki' and which a 'bouba'. The results were overwhelmingly (95–98 per cent) in favour of the spiky shape being 'kiki' and the blobby shape 'bouba'. The high percentages pointed to there being a correspondence between shape and sound that wasn't random. Ramachandran felt that a synaesthetic link between the senses of hearing and vision might have provided the crucial step towards the creation of words. Perhaps our ancestors first started to talk by using sounds that actually evoked the objects they wished to describe.

At first this might seem an attractive but fanciful idea, but Ramachandran has begun to search out other links that reinforce this kind of verbal association, such as the way hand and lip/tongue movements mimic one another (for example, the similarity, when saying 'teeny-weeny', of the pushed-forward pout of the lips and the small space indicated by thumb and forefinger). In his opinion, this cascade of links in the brain 'bootstrapped' one another to produce 'the avalanche we call language'.

'I can see what you're thinking,' I said to the chefs' glazed faces. 'What has all this got to do with chilli con carne? Well, it struck me that chilli is as near as you're likely to get to a culinary representation of kiki and bouba. Capsaicin is the spikiness, sour cream the blobby roundedness. I reckon it'd be interesting to use the kiki/bouba idea as the basis for the dish. Explore and emphasise the contrast to see what effect it might have.' The chefs' faces relaxed slightly once I'd mentioned food and a hands-on project they could tackle. 'I know it's a long shot and it sounds a little crazy, but that's often what an experiment is. And, in a way, synaesthetic connections are already part of how we talk about food, describing Cheddar as "sharp" or cream as "soft". It'll be very interesting to see what happens.'

---

* **Head Chef** Investigating the Brain's Response to Chilli

In Cambridge, I had put chicken breasts in an MRI scanner. Now it was the turn of my head chef, Ashley Palmer-Watts. I took him to Nottingham University's School of Physics and Astronomy so that I could put him in a scanner, feed him chilli oil through a tube and observe what went on in his brain as I did so.

This might seem an odd way to reward the man who dedicatedly looked after the Fat Duck in my absence, thereby allowing the 'Perfection' series to happen, but an operation on my back meant I had too much metal clamped to my spine to be allowed inside the MRI apparatus. Part of me was sorry not to be participating in what promised to be an interesting experiment, but another part was glad not to be wedged in the coffin-like confines of the scanner's aperture. Ashley had bravely offered to take my place. As he lay on the wheeled trolley and was manoeuvred into the scanner, I felt almost guilty for having persuaded the lab technician to increase by 50 per cent the strength of the chilli dose Ashley was about to receive. Almost.

'So,' I asked Francis McGlone, the neuroscientist who was guiding me through the experiment, 'what might I learn from Ashley's pain?'

'Neuroscientists have come to understand that the parts of the brain that are activated when you have a pleasant or unpleasant sensory stimulus are emotional systems that form part of the limbic system. By monitoring Ashley's brain, we can see what parts are activated when we feed him chilli oil.' A grin – a mix of sympathy and scientific curiosity – split Francis's face. 'The hope is that the areas that process pain and pleasure stimuli in the limbic system are the ones that light up because of increased activity.'

Ashley remained in the scanner's maw for a heroic 45 minutes – ear-plugged against the brutal noise of the machine, chilli oil pulsing into his mouth at regular intervals – before getting an eyeful and asking to be removed. Meanwhile, I watched as a grid of blue-lit brain cross-sections flickered on a computer screen and acquired clusters of yellow blobs and crescents in various areas.

'What does this tell us, Francis?'

'Well, this is just a first-pass analysis with one person. I'd need to do the same thing on fifteen to twenty people and average out the results before coming to any definitive conclusions. However, if we look at where the cross-sections are lit up yellow we can see – as I'd expect – activation in the brain areas concerned with taste and flavour, but we can also see activity in the areas concerned with emotional response: the frontal cortex, the amygdala and the cingulate cortex. It shows that eating chilli *is not purely a sensory experience. It activates parts of the brain that process emotion.'*

'And what part of my brain is lit up because it's thinking about how to get revenge on Heston for upping the chilli dose?' said Ashley, walking into the room clutching a paper towel to his eye.

HEATBUSTERS

I had taken what I'd picked up in Washington and thrown it into the pot alongside book research and all the stuff I had learned while working on *ragù alla bolognese*. The result was a chilli recipe that, while it still needed work, was good enough that it had me half-fantasising about entering the Fat Duck Chilli in next year's regional cookoffs. ('Fat Duck Chilli – You'll Go Quackers for It.') The dish was coming together; now I had to decide what should accompany this spicy bowl of meaty heat.

By and large, carbs seem to be what people crave with chilli, but what form this takes varies from region to region and country to country. In Britain rice, or perhaps a baked potato, are the sidekicks, and I'd got both sitting in bowls waiting to be tasted with the meat. In America, however, all kinds of other foodstuffs come into play – soft flour tortillas, tortilla chips, cornbread. Stacks of these were laid out too. I had heard that in Cincinnati they teamed chilli with spaghetti, but decided that even I had to draw the line somewhere.

'When I was eating chillies and in considerable pain,' I explained to Chris and Kyle, 'it brought home to me just how crucial it is to build into the dish a contrast – something that combats the heat. So let's look at the traditional garnishes and see which works best.' Each of us grabbed a spoon, dug into the chilli and took a mouthful, then looked about for what might best put out the fire because the latest version didn't mess about: it just got hotter and hotter in the mouth.

'You know,' said Kyle, 'the brain just says "No" to cornchips. They're the wrong feel – you want something smooth. They're even the wrong sound – all spiky, sharp.' (He'd clearly taken on board my kiki and bouba idea.) 'These tortilla wraps are better: at least they're soft.'

'But softness is all they bring,' I realised. 'There's no relief from the heat.'

Nor was there with the potato. It brought back memories of leaving the pub, looking for something to soak up the alcohol and finding the van that served a split baked potato with a lava flow of chilli oozing out of it, and equipped you with a little plastic fork that was virtually useless. Potatoes seemed to me to be more to do with bulk than any particular appropriateness to the dish, as did rice, which, being neither soft nor hard, didn't really complement the meat at all. I wanted a carbohydrate of some sort (I didn't want to stray too far from what people expected with their chilli) but I wanted it to be really soft and really light. Maybe cornbread would be the answer. I'd seen some being cooked in Washington, but I hadn't got the chance to try them.

Chris had prepared three sorts – one with polenta, one with corn velouté and butter, and one with corn velouté and popcorn-infused oil. I tried all three and knew instantly that this was what I was looking for. The oil version in particular had a perfect lightness: it held together in the hand but fell apart in the mouth.

'This is the route to go down,' I declared. 'The lighter and fluffier the better.'

'Yup,' agreed Kyle. 'Cornbread's what we go for in the States.'

'Yes. It's soft but it also adds layers of flavours to the dish. Now, in DC nearly all the chillies were finished off with sour cream. I wonder … What if … '

I was thinking aloud. I left Chris and Kyle waiting for the end of the sentence and stepped out of the lab to raid the pastry section's fridge.

' … we add cream to the cornbread? Eat the two together. Normally, you'd add the sour cream to the chilli. It cuts the heat for maybe a couple of mouthfuls, but that's all. Maybe the sour cream will do its job better if it's kept separate. It'll be more of a counterpoint.'

'Like yoghurt in Indian food,' Kyle said.

'Or the cream in goulash,' added Chris. 'That softening effect it has.'

'Or when you burn yourself and you want to put something on it that's smooth and creamy.'

'Yeah. Sunburn and aftersun.'

The comparisons were getting out of hand and in danger of putting me off eating. I spooned up a couple of mouthfuls of chilli, let the heat spread, then smeared sour cream on to the cornbread and took a bite. It really did have the most amazing cooling effect.

'This is great, but maybe we could go colder still. Make some kind of sour cream sorbet.'

'Sure,' Kyle agreed. 'Bring temperature into play. With chilli it makes complete sense.'

'Ice cream and cornbread.' I was getting excited now, on the trail of a promising idea: the reason why I pursued all these experiments and tests and trials, no matter how banal or crazy they might at first seem. 'Fantastic! It could be a kind of savoury Victoria sponge!'

Chris and Kyle looked at me blankly. 'What's Victoria sponge?'

FINISHING TOUCHES

Almost every dish has a secret ingredient or two – usually added at the last minute in small amounts that nonetheless have a big impact on the final flavour, conferring greater depth and complexity. I was looking for the things that might finish off my chilli, so I had laid out in the lab all the suggestions I'd got from the cookoff conquistadors in Washington. On the black granite work surface stood bottles of tequila and single-barrel Jack Daniel's alongside a cluster of small white bowls containing chocolate, peanut butter, grated cheese and mashed banana. Kyle and Chris eyed it all dubiously.

I was used to that look. (And I have to admit that my research chefs were equally used to entering the lab and finding an unlikely selection of foodstuffs for consideration.) I ignored it, scooped our current chilli recipe into seven bowls and directed them to try out combinations by waving a plastic spoon vaguely threateningly in their direction.

'That is *sooo* wrong,' Kyle declared. Chilli laced with banana had made him speak like a Valley Girl. He was right, though. I couldn't see any merit in adding banana and wondered, once again, whether the cookoff competitors had been deliberately pulling my leg. Perhaps the competitive aspect had become so ingrained that deception was almost involuntary. Perhaps, if I'd hung around long enough, someone would have suggested adding diced red herring to finish the mix.

'I don't know about peanut butter either,' said Chris, stoking my doubts. 'It kinda sticks to the roof of the mouth.'

'There's something unnatural about it,' Kyle agreed.

'Whereas cheese is the reverse,' I decided. 'It's pretty standard, but it doesn't do much for me.' Kyle was busy grating chocolate over a bowl of chilli. Brown on red. 'I tried that in Washington. It was rich, for sure, but it kinda lost focus … ' I seemed to have gone Valley Girl too. Time to try the tequila.

'Now that's weird,' Chris decided. 'Chilli-flavoured margarita. I feel like I need salt and limes.'

It did nothing for the taste of the chilli but it did bring back memories for me. 'By 2.30 at the cookoff, the Budweiser van was really rocking. Every time we tried to film, someone would stalk up to the lens, stick their face in it and yell, "Hell, yeah!"'

'Makes me proud to be American,' Kyle observed, deadpan.

I don't like to discount anything – a lot of my most interesting dishes have come from levering an ingredient out of its pigeon-hole – but I had been fairly certain tequila wasn't going to work. Jack Daniel's, on the other hand, I had high hopes for. In Washington Dr Wally had recommended it, and the single-barrel stuff had an extraordinarily subtle, aromatic flavour that I could see as part of the dish. I popped the stumpy wooden stopper from the long-necked bottle and poured a glug or two into a bowl of chilli.

'Mmm,' said Kyle. 'That comes up in the steam from the bowl real nice. We could develop that as an aspect of the chilli and it'd be really good.'

The taste was fantastic and it triggered another idea. 'In France they finish off lots of sauces with butter. I guess putting peanut butter in chilli is along the same lines. What say we hang on to the butter but ditch the peanut? Put in its place other ingredients that could work in a flavoured butter? Jack Daniel's plus some umami taste: Worcestershire sauce, Tabasco, Marmite … ' We plucked stuff off shelves, flipped open drawers, rounding up unusual suspects, adding a few drops of this, a smear of that to the chilli bowl. I tried a spoonful. It was good.

'This works,' said Chris. 'Add it at the very end.'

It was good. But … 'It needs something else,' I suggested.

'Acidity!' chorused Kyle and Chris. (Not because they're mind-readers, but because they've been working with me long enough to know the bias of my palate.) Chris grabbed some limes, cut and squeezed some juice and grated the zest. We dug in once more.

'All the stuff in it. That bowl's like a cauldron now,' Kyle said. 'The freshness of the lime really livens it up.'

'Yes. The zest is good too, as long as it's kept in check,' I decided.

'Sure thing,' Kyle said. 'Hair-of-the-dog chilli.'

It was a good name. Maybe that was the one for next year's cookoffs.

NOSING AROUND

Some people find the idea of using advanced technology in the kitchen offputting and somehow soulless, but for me the reverse is true. High-tech equipment allows me to pursue my instincts further and faster and better than would otherwise be possible. Far from supplanting the chef's imagination, technology liberates it, opening up the molecular world that is at the heart of cooking, as it is at the heart of all matter.

A good example of this is the gas chromatograph. I have a pretty good nose and a decent bank of flavour memories to draw on. With diligent sniffing, I might well be able to distinguish some of an ingredient's key components, but it would still be a rough and ready approach. The gas chromatograph can act as a kind of booster to that olfactory process, giving me a much higher hit rate on detecting compounds and aromas that are present in a substance. Since whisky had become a key component in the development of my chilli, I wanted to use the technology to explore its spectrum of flavours a little further.

The gas chromatograph at Reading University looks like an over-sized microwave oven – a large metal cube with a door at the front – because that's essentially what it is: an oven (albeit one with a complicated clutter of wires sticking out of the top, and a long black, proboscis-like tube with a clear plastic, nose-sized funnel on its end). The substance under study is injected into the chromatograph and passes into a 50-metre fibre-optic coil, along with helium gas that helps its passage through the system. Volatility and absorption then come into play. The heat of the oven causes compounds in the

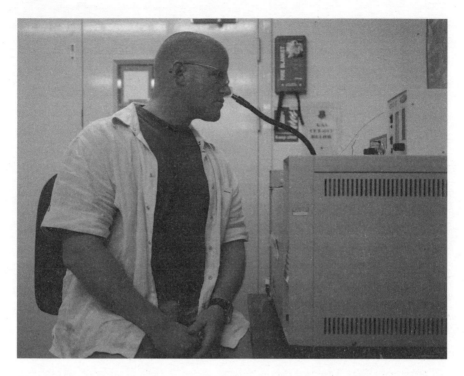

Poking my nose into the flavours of bourbon using a gas chromatograph.

substance to separate, and materials coating the walls of the coil absorb some of the compounds, slowing their rate of progress. Thus, rather like people running in the London marathon, some reach the finishing post (either the nose or the electronic readout of a mass spectrometer; the two can't operate at the same time) early, but others take longer. (The whole procedure takes about thirty minutes.) And just as it's easier to differentiate between runners stretched out over 26.2 miles than huddled together at the starting line, so gas chromatography makes it easier to differentiate between compounds by registering their exit from the coil.

'All right, Heston.' Professor Don Mottram peered at me over the top of his gold-rimmed glasses. His white lab coat had a splurge of black ink on the breast pocket, making him look even more boffin-like. 'If you want to press the start button and lean into the funnel, we'll get going. It should take a couple of minutes for the whisky to pass into the machine.'

I poked my nose into the articulated tube (the BBC researcher later told me I looked like a futuristic aardvark) and waited for the waves of aroma, trying to accustom myself to the background smell of the machine so that it wouldn't interfere with what I was about to encounter.

'You'll just get alcohol at the beginning,' Don advised me.

'It's coming now. Smells like a drunken person's breath at the moment ... Not nice ... Now a mildly fruity note ... Soft fruit, black-currant, a touch of raspberry, Ribena even. There's a backnote of fatty compounds, but it might just be the machine.'

'Mm, could be,' murmured Don. 'I wouldn't be surprised.'

'Boiled sweets ... sugar ... caramel ... now something more like Jack Daniel's. Toasted wood? Toasted oak?'

'Interesting. This is bourbon, so you're getting different aromas from the ones in Scotch.'

I closed my eyes, trying to concentrate, my mouth opening and closing like a fish, sucking up the aromas. 'Not sure if it's just a backnote, but there's something buttery, cakey ... '

'Often what at first seems like a background smell gradually develops and grows until you realise it is indeed another aroma,' Don said, encouraging.

'Something just came but disappeared almost immediately.'

'A very low concentration, then.'

'And now there's something that could be ... malty, biscuity. Butterscotch, toffee. Malt?'

'A bourbon-like note?'

'Yes. Toasty. Oak-like. Ah! Now that is bourbon ... I'm getting something that reminds me of shortbread biscuit or Madeira cake. Spongy ... Blackberry muffin with a toffee sauce.'

'What a lovely description,' said Don.

'And a vanilla note.'

'Vanilla always comes off the chromatograph quite late, as it's not very volatile. And it's present in lots of things.'

'I've got a grain note I didn't get earlier.'

Eventually the smells died away and Don announced, 'That's it.' I always find the gas chromatograph an extraordinary experience – strangely intense and incredibly sharply focused. Some fugitive odours vanished before they could be identified. Some surged more power-fully and mixed with the memory of other odours to produce yet more aromas. It was draining and intoxicating at the same time. Just trying to describe what I was smelling proved difficult: we can differentiate thousands of aromas, but our vocabulary for identifying them is underdeveloped.

'Here we've separated components of bourbons where normally they'd be smelt together, as a mixture,' Don said. 'Flavour chemistry brings together man and machine. A machine can detect compounds, but it still needs a person to say whether those compounds have a flavour or not.'

Well, I'd got four key flavours from this: a blackcurrant cordial, boiled sweet note; that buttery shortbread, Madeira cake aspect; a touch of caramel-toffee-butterscotch; plus the toasted, oaky thing. All four pointed towards comfort foods and they were all quite bouba. The cake tied in nicely with the cornbread. Maybe I could introduce that blackberry note as well. It was an exciting result – the kind I liked, the kind that sparked off all sorts of new ideas.

Chilli con Carne Serves 8

There are beans in my chilli, which means it can't be entered in a cook-off any time soon, but working on the beans turned out to be one of the most interesting areas of the recipe. Beans are difficult to cook well: by the time the centre has reached a lovely creamy consistency, the outside has usually lost its structural integrity and split. Conventional wisdom holds that pulses shouldn't be cooked with acid because it toughens the skin. It seemed to me, however, that, if handled carefully, this could be turned to advantage. I pressure-cooked the beans with tomatoes so that the skins would toughen a little, but the insides would only just have started to soften, then added them to short-ribs for a gentle, five-hour braise. The strengthened skin didn't split and the centre was marvellously soft.

As will have been gathered, finishing a chilli is crucial to the dish's success, and each cook has his or her own 'essential' final ingredients. One of mine was to employ the classic French technique *monter au beurre* – adding richness to a sauce in the form of butter stirred in towards the end. In the lab we gradually developed a compound butter that became known as 'hangover cure butter' because of the Bloody Mary aspect to some of its ingredients – Worcestershire sauce, Tabasco, chilli and lime – and swirled this into the dish at the end. Adding it as a butter let it spread evenly through the sauce and kept the fresh immediacy of the top notes of Tabasco and lime juice.

Special equipment
Spice grinder, pressure cooker, muslin, oven thermometer, silicone muffin mould, food mixer, dry ice

Timing
CHILLI: Preparation takes about 3 hours, plus 18 hours for soaking/brining, etc. Cooking takes about 9 hours.
MUFFINS: Preparation takes 1 hour. Baking takes 20–25 minutes.
ICE CREAM: Preparation takes 10 minutes. Hardening takes 1 hour.

For the short-rib brine
1kg water _ 100g table salt _ 300g Jack Daniel's whiskey _
8 beef short-ribs*

For the kidney beans
1kg water _ 10g table salt _ 300g dried organic kidney beans _
45 (about 1kg) large cherry tomatoes, on the vine

For the chilli powder blend
During my visit to the chilli competition in Washington DC, and
through research on the dish, I learned about how important the chilli
blend is to the success of chilli con carne. The particular blend that
I ended up with, and give below, combines the sweet heat of three
different chillies with the smoky notes from smoked paprika, and the
deep, sun-dried flavours of another five varieties that all bring something different to the table. The chillies that are not available through
thespiceshop.co.uk can be found at pendrys.com.
2–3 dried devil's penis chillies _ 2–3 dried bird's-eye chillies _
1 tsp Somalian extra hot chilli powder _ 10g sweet smoked paprika _
10g Durango ground chilli powder _ 10g El Rey ground chilli
powder _ 10g Madera ground chilli powder _ 20g Pecos Red
ground chilli powder _ 20g Rio Tejas ground chilli powder

For the stock
650g oxtail _ 1kg rib bones (ask your butcher to cut them to fit into
the pressure cooker) _ flour, as needed _ 50g grapeseed or groundnut
oil _ 1½kg lean beef mince _ 25g unsalted butter _ 1 large onion
(about 200g), sliced _ 3 large leeks (about 300g), white and pale
green parts only, sliced _ 2 large carrots (about 250g), sliced _

---

* This recipe, and the one for hamburger, both call for a cut of beef known as the 'short rib'.
During the butchering process, the separation of the rib bones from the rib eye means you
end up with a set of bones with two layers of meat. The first layer – the one you need for
these recipes – lies between and on top of the rib bones. The muscle here hasn't had to work
particularly hard, so is very tender. By contrast, the second layer of meat, between the cap of
fat and the exterior, is very tough and grainy and should be peeled away. Ask your butcher to
cut ribs from the centre portion of the ribcage (this is the meatiest part: as the rib bones extend
out, the meat becomes thinner and thinner), and to cut across the ribs, rather than in between
them, at a thickness of around 7.5cm.

10g (2 tsp) chilli powder blend _ 1 bottle red wine (preferably Syrah) _
5 long peppers (available at thespiceshop.co.uk) _ 10g fresh chives _
10g fresh flatleaf parsley _ 10g fresh tarragon _ 2 fresh bay leaves

For the braised short-ribs
reserved brined short-ribs _ plain flour, for dusting _ 3–4 tbsp
reserved fat from the stock _ 10g (2 tsp) chilli powder blend _
1 large onion (about 200g), sliced _ 4 large leeks (about 400g),
white and pale green parts only, sliced _ 3 large carrots (about
400g), sliced _ 1 bottle red wine (preferably Syrah) _ 5 long
peppers (available at thespiceshop.co.uk) _ approx. 1kg
reserved beef stock _ reserved kidney beans and their liquid

For the cipolline confit
250g peeled cipolline onions _ 10g salt _ extra virgin olive oil

For the roasted peppers
4 red bell peppers _ extra virgin olive oil, as needed

For the finishing butter
120g butter, softened to room temperature _ 20g chilli powder blend
5g cumin _ zest and juice of 2 limes _ 5g Tabasco sauce _
5g Jack Daniel's whiskey _ 5g finely grated Parmesan cheese _
5g (1 tsp) tomato ketchup _ ½ tsp Worcestershire sauce

For the finished chilli con carne
3–4 tbsp (plus extra if needed) reserved fat from the stock _ 1kg
lean beef mince (preferably dry-aged and free of gristle – ask your
butcher) _ 40g reserved chilli powder blend _ 3 whole star anise _
1 large onion (about 200g), finely diced _ 5 large cloves of garlic
(about 50g), minced _ 1 large carrot (about 125g), finely diced _
50g fresh jalapeño chilli, finely diced _ 40g (about 3 tbsp) tomato
purée _ 600g Jack Daniel's whiskey _ reserved short-ribs and
their braising liquid _ reserved kidney beans and their braising
liquid _ table salt _ reserved cipolline confit, drained of oil and cut
into quarters _ reserved roasted peppers _ 1 fresh jalapeño chilli,
finely diced _ reserved finishing butter, as needed

For the muffins

300g butter _ 560g canned sweetcorn _ 50g whole milk _
200g double cream _ 250g plain flour _ 1½ tsp baking powder _
190g caster sugar _ 100g eggs (about 2 large ones) _ pinch of
table salt _ 40g water

For the sour cream ice cream

500g crushed dry ice _ 500g low-fat sour cream (it must be low-fat)

BRINING THE SHORT-RIBS

1. Combine the water and the salt in a storage container and stir from
   time to time to dissolve the salt.
2. Meanwhile, tip the Jack Daniel's into a small pan and bring to the
   boil. As soon as it has reached boiling point, ignite the alcohol with
   a match. (This removes the harsh, raw notes of the alcohol, but take
   care because it will go up with a large flame and will burn for some
   time on the hob.) Reduce it by half, then leave to cool completely
   before adding it to the pan of salted water.
3. Place the short-ribs in the brine. Cover them and refrigerate for
   12 hours.
4. Remove the ribs from the brine and place in a container of cold, fresh
   water. Allow to soak for 6 hours, changing the water regularly.

PREPARING THE KIDNEY BEANS

1. Combine the water and salt in a storage container and stir to
   dissolve the salt.
2. Tip the beans into the container, cover and refrigerate for 12 hours.
   This soaking step will help the finished beans to cook evenly and
   keep the skins from splitting during the cooking process.
3. Meanwhile, bring a large pan of water to the boil. Fill a large bowl
   with iced water (if ice is not available, use the coldest water from
   the tap).
4. Pull the tomatoes off the vine, reserving the vine. Remove the
   cores with a paring knife.
5. Cut the tomatoes into quarters and place in a sieve over a bowl.
   Sprinkle 2 teaspoons of salt over them and leave until about 100g
   tomato juice has collected in the bowl.

6. Place the tomatoes and their juice in a small pressure cooker. Put on the lid and place over a high heat. When it reaches full pressure, cook for 20 minutes.
7. Remove from the heat and leave to cool. Once cool, remove the lid and place the tomatoes back on the hob. Cook over a high heat, stirring frequently, until the liquid has reduced by half, about 15 minutes.
8. Leave the tomatoes to cool again, then tip into a container. Add the reserved vines and cover (this will infuse the fresh, raw aroma of tomatoes on the vine into the liquid). Store this tomato liquid in the fridge until the beans have soaked.
9. Strain the beans and tip into a small pressure cooker. Remove the vines from the tomatoes. Add the tomatoes to the beans. If necessary, add some water so that the beans are covered.
10. Put on the lid and place over a high heat. When it reaches full pressure, cook for 25 minutes. Remove from the heat and leave to cool. Tip the beans and tomato sauce into a large container. Cover and store in the fridge until required.

MAKING THE CHILLI POWDER BLEND
1. Seed the devil's penis and bird's-eye chillies (be warned that these are very hot, so please keep your hands away from your eyes, nose and other extremities when handling, and wash them thoroughly afterwards). Finely grind the chillies with a pestle and mortar or a spice grinder. Measure out ½ teaspoon of each into a container.
2. Add the remaining ingredients and stir to combine. Cover and store until required.

MAKING THE STOCK
1. Preheat the oven to 200°C/400°F/Gas 6. While the oven is heating, toss the oxtails and rib bones in flour to coat lightly. Place in a roasting tray and roast for 40–45 minutes, or until golden brown, turning regularly.
2. Meanwhile, place a large pan over a high heat for at least 5 minutes. Add the oil and wait until it starts smoking: it must be hot enough so that the mince browns rather than stews. Add 1kg of the mince in batches, in a single layer, and stir until browned. You might need

Some of the ingredients we tested for the chilli con carne proved particularly challenging.

to deglaze the pan with water between batches if any crustiness develops in the bottom.

3. Discard the fat left in the pan and add the butter. Melt over a low heat. Add the onion, leeks and carrots and cook for 10 minutes, or until soft. Scatter over the chilli powder, stir to combine and cook for another 5 minutes over a high heat to release the chilli aromas.

4. Turn the heat back to medium and deglaze the pan by adding the wine and scraping up all the tasty bits stuck to the bottom while bringing it to the boil. Once the liquid has reduced by two-thirds, tip it and the vegetables into a small pressure cooker.

5. Add the cooked mince and the reserved raw mince, the roasted bones and the long peppers. Pour in enough water to entirely cover the ingredients. Put on the lid and place over a high heat. When it reaches full pressure, cook for 2 hours.

6. Take the pan off the heat and allow to depressurise. Remove the lid and add the herbs. Allow to infuse for 30 minutes.

7. Strain the stock and cool over ice or in the fridge.
8. When cool, remove all the fat that has come to the top and reserve.
9. Tip the stock into a large pan and place over a high heat. Reduce by half, skimming constantly to remove any remaining fat and impurities. Leave to cool, then store in the fridge until required.

BRAISING THE SHORT-RIBS

1. Dust the ribs on all sides with flour. Melt the reserved fat in a large cast-iron casserole over a high heat. When the fat starts smoking add the ribs in batches. Sear on each side (1–2 minutes) until golden brown. Remove the ribs from the pan and set aside.
2. Lower the heat to medium. Add the chilli powder blend to the pan and fry quickly for around 2 minutes to release the flavour into the oil. Add the onion, leeks and carrots and cook for 15–20 minutes, or until the vegetables are lightly caramelised, stirring occasionally.
3. Pour in the wine and bring to the boil, scraping up all the bits stuck to the bottom of the pan. Meanwhile, line the inside of a storage container or pan with a piece of muslin large enough to hold all the vegetables. Once the wine has reduced by two-thirds, tip the vegetables out of the casserole into the lined container. Add the long peppers to the container. Tie up the muslin and return the 'bag' to the casserole, also returning the liquid that has drained into the container.
4. Preheat the oven to 140°C/275°F/Gas 1.
5. Add the short-ribs, plus the reserved stock and kidney beans in tomato sauce to the casserole. Cover the dish first with clingfilm, then with aluminium foil, and place in the oven for 5 hours.
6. Remove the casserole from the oven and leave to cool. Squeeze the excess juice from the muslin bag. Discard the bag and its contents.
7. Transfer the short-ribs to a large container. Use a slotted spoon to remove the beans and place them in a separate large container.
8. Skim off any fat from the braising liquid and strain through a sieve. Divide the liquid between the two containers, covering the beans and the short-ribs. Store the meat and beans in the fridge until required.
9. After the short-ribs have been stored for a few hours, remove the meat from the gelatinous liquid, brushing off any excess jelly, and place on a chopping board. Remove the meat from the bone and discard both the bones and any heavy connective tissue.

10. Using a fork, shred the meat into long pieces where it wants to separate naturally.
11. Return this shredded meat to the gelatinous liquid, submerging it to keep it from drying out. Store in the fridge until needed.

MAKING THE CIPOLLINE CONFIT

1. Season the onions with the salt and place in a pan in a single layer. Cover with olive oil.
2. Cook over a low heat until the onions are completely tender. Transfer to a storage container and chill in the oil.

PREPARING THE ROASTED PEPPERS

1. Preheat the grill until very hot.
2. Core and halve the peppers, and remove the white pith and the seeds.
3. Put the pepper halves, skin side up, on a grill pan and brush them with olive oil. Place under the hot grill and leave them until they are black.
4. Remove the blackened peppers from the grill and wrap immediately in clingfilm. Set aside for 10 minutes.
5. Unwrap the peppers and peel off the blackened skin.
6. Cut the peeled peppers into 1cm cubes and store in the fridge until needed.

MAKING THE FINISHING BUTTER

1. In a small pan heat 20g of the butter with the chilli powder blend and cumin, and fry lightly. Transfer this mixture to a heatproof bowl and allow to cool to room temperature.
2. Blanch the lime zest briefly in boiling water, refresh in cold water and then mince finely.
3. Add the zest and all the other ingredients to the butter mixture. Fold together until everything is evenly mixed. Transfer to a storage container and keep refrigerated.

ASSEMBLING THE CHILLI CON CARNE

1. Place a large pan over a high heat for at least 5 minutes. Add the reserved fat. When smoking hot, add the mince in batches and cook

until evenly browned. Between batches deglaze with water as needed and save all the bits and liquid that are collected.

2. Using a slotted spoon, transfer the mince to a bowl or plate, leaving the fat in the pan. Deglaze the pan with a little water to remove the bits of meat stuck to the bottom. Add these bits to your browned meat.

3. Turn the heat down to medium and add a bit more of the fat. Add the chilli powder blend and fry briefly, adding more fat if needed.

4. Crush the star anise and bag it in a square of muslin. Add this and the onion to the pan and cook for 10–15 minutes, or until the onion is soft and caramelised.

5. Turn the heat down to low, then add the garlic, carrot and jalapeño chilli. Cook for about 10 minutes, or until soft.

6. Add the tomato purée and cook until it becomes a deep brick-red colour.

7. Deglaze the pan by turning the temperature up to medium and adding the Jack Daniel's. (Be careful as the whiskey will flame.) Bring it to the boil, then scrape up all the tasty bits stuck to the bottom.

8. Add the browned mince plus the short-ribs and their liquid to the pan. Stir in the reserved kidney beans and braising liquid and simmer over a low heat for 40 minutes. Adjust the seasoning to taste with salt. At this point it is best to cool and store the chilli, and finish it later that day or the next. However, you can continue now if you wish.

9. If you have allowed your chilli to cool, reheat it over a low heat. Adjust the seasoning with salt and the chilli powder blend if necessary.

10. Add the cipolline confit, roasted peppers and diced jalapeño. Fold together, being careful not to break the delicate beans.

11. Fold in the finishing butter to give a fresh acidity and glossy sheen to the sauce. The amount that you add depends on your personal preference.

MAKING THE CORN MUFFINS

1. Preheat the oven to 190°C/375°F/Gas 5, using an oven thermometer to check it. Lightly butter and flour a large muffin tin or use a silicone muffin mould.

2. Melt 25g of the butter in a large pan or casserole. Add the corn and fry over a medium heat for 2–3 minutes.

3. Pour in the milk and double cream and simmer over a low heat for 5 minutes.

4. Tip the corn mixture into a food processor and blitz until smooth. Push this mixture through a fine sieve and set aside. Discard what's left in the sieve.

5. With the rest of the butter, make beurre noisette. Put the butter in a pan over a medium heat. When the butter stops sizzling (a sign that all the water has evaporated, after which it will burn) and develops a nutty aroma, remove it from the heat immediately. Strain it into a jug and leave to cool until needed. Discard the blackened solids in the sieve.

6. Sift the flour and baking powder into a bowl. Add the caster sugar.

7. Whisk the eggs and salt together, then pour into the dry mixture, along with the water and 225g of the reserved creamed corn.

8. Pour the beurre noisette into the muffin mixture and stir. (Try to avoid tipping in any sediment that may have collected at the bottom of the jug.)

9. Spoon the muffin mixture into the prepared tin or mould and bake for 20–25 minutes, or until a pale golden brown.

MAKING THE SOUR CREAM ICE CREAM

1. Crush the dry ice either briefly in a food processor or by wrapping in a tea towel and beating with a rolling pin.

2. Tip the sour cream into the bowl of a food mixer. Mix on a medium speed while adding small amounts of crushed dry ice until the sour cream is thick and nearly frozen.

3. Use a spoon to scrape the mixture into a rectangular mould, and place in the freezer to harden for 1 hour.

4. Unmould the ice cream and serve immediately with the chilli and corn muffins.

Hamburger

'Hamburgers. The cornerstone of any nutritious breakfast.'

Jules Winnfield in *Pulp Fiction*

History

The burger is an American icon, summoning up images of the Wild West (that rugged hunk of beef), the romance of the drive-in and of course Elvis, chomping down on several at one sitting. It's the fast food that has taken over the world, a symbol of American energy and entrepreneurial spirit. And, as with any icon, the burger has acquired a colourful history to back it all up.

The burger's story begins in the Wild East, with Genghis Khan's Mongol cavalry. Dinner after a day of destruction was a raw, minced meat patty that had been pressed and tenderised under the saddle while on the move. When Khan's grandson invaded Russia in the thirteenth century, his army brought the saddle patties with them, and steak tartare was born (Tartar being the Russian name for a Mongol).

By 1600 steak tartare had, via burgeoning sea trade, crossed the Baltic to the port of Hamburg, where it gradually changed name and composition: the 'Hamburg steak' was fried and possibly smoked or salted. That cured aspect made it the ideal food for German emigrants to take on their journey from the Old World to the New in the nineteenth century, and thus Hamburg steak made its way across the Atlantic. Alongside this, the busy commerce between Hamburg and America meant that port-side vendors with an eye on the hordes of hungry German sailors fetching up in New York's harbours were busy cooking and advertising 'steak cooked in the Hamburg style'. And so the burger is supposed to have been born.

Food history rarely has this kind of flow-diagram neatness and linearity to it. Linking the minced meat patty to Genghis Khan ignores the fact that chopped meat was already a feature of various European cuisines; and many of the historical 'facts' offered in support of the story fall apart quicker than a badly put-together patty. What is generally accepted is that Hamburg had, by the late eighteenth century, become identified with a style of preparing meat. In 1747 the great English cookery writer Hannah Glasse referred to 'Hamburg sausages' in *The Art of Cookery Made Plain and Easy*, and by the 1830s it is possible that a 'Hamburger steak' was on the menu at Delmonico's restaurant in New York.* The advent of mechanical meat choppers in the first half of the nineteenth century brought the dish to a far wider audience, so from the 1840s the term became increasingly commonplace. Hamburg steak is referred to in a Boston newspaper of 1894, and was served up in a restaurant at the 1904 St Louis World's Fair, where it is supposed to have caused a sensation. It wasn't yet a burger in either name or form, and it had no bun, but it was a recognisable ancestor of what we eat today.

The creation of that first burger is, of course, claimed by a large number of hopefuls, each of them backed up by a good story or good documentation. In 1885 stallholder Charlie Nagreen is said to have invented the burger when he flattened his meatballs so they wouldn't roll off the bun as people strolled around the Outagamie County Fair in Wisconsin. The same year, at a different fair, in Hamburg, NY, Frank and Charles Menches ran out of pork patties and made beef ones instead: when asked what the results were called, Frank took inspiration from the HAMBURG FAIR banner strung across the entrance. Oklahoma says that Oscar Bilby thought up the name in 1891 and the state has published a proclamation to prove it, while Texans insist that Fletch Davis from Athens, Texas, was both inventor and the vendor at that 1904 World's Fair. Louis' Lunch in New Haven, Connecticut, has both a good story – in 1900 a customer rushed in demanding a quick meal to go; the owner put a grilled beef patty between two slices of toast and sent the man on his way – and good documentation from the Library of Congress, stating that it was the first place to serve hamburgers in the USA.

* This may be another bogus historical fact because keen scholars have apparently established that the menu is a facsimile, and the printer credited on it didn't exist in 1834.

The Quest for the Best

FEELING TOASTY

I was in a part of New Haven that seemed an unlikely setting for a burger joint. Yale had given its stamp to this part of town – it was leafy, collegiate, Ivy League.* On wide boulevards imposing, gothic, churchy-looking outposts of the university vied for attention with cosmopolitan arts centres. Against this backdrop, Louis' Lunch, with its heavily bolted front door, cream latticework windows and red barndoor shutters, looked even more as though it had been beamed in from another planet; its minuscule size put me in mind of the Tardis.

It didn't, however, seem that much bigger on the inside. There was just enough room for three tables and a high-sided pew along one wall. The wood was heavy, dark and as scarred with graffiti as a Victorian schoolboy's desk. The place had the solidity of real age. On the black awning outside, knobbly, Western-style writing proclaimed that Louis' was established in 1895.

Back then the business was a lunch wagon parked on Meadow Street, from which Louis Lassen sold steak sandwiches to local factory workers. This was where he served the first burger in 1900, supposedly to a customer in such a hurry that he couldn't sit down to eat it. However, I had also read that the real story was that Lassen didn't want to waste beef left over from the lunchtime rush, so he minced it up, grilled it and slapped it between bread slices. To some this might seem more humdrum but, in a way, I prefer it. Monitoring costs and keeping food waste to a minimum is the bedrock of a restaurant's success: it's vital to use as much of each animal and vegetable as possible. It's highly possible that Lassen's invention of the burger came

---

* In fact, New Haven has several noteworthy claims to culinary fame. In 1892 the confectioner George C. Smith is said to have invented lollipops there. One of the oldest vegetarian restaurants in America opened on the corner of Chapel and College Streets (and should be valued at the very least for the preposterous pun in its name: Claire's Corner Copia). Best of all, the Frisbee is supposed to have originated on Yale campus, where students used to toss around tins from the Frisbie Pie Company.

from his being a thrifty, efficient, professional restaurateur, and I liked that idea. Necessity has invented all kinds of dishes (and it would be the spur for a decidedly upmarket burger that I would encounter later in this trip); why not the burger too?

It was a hugely atmospheric place. The size meant that it was a little like stumbling into someone's living room, in which a lively party was going on. Occasionally, Jeff Lassen could be heard above the hubbub declaring, 'Yeah? Well, they're all fakers' – his habitual term of abuse. A local cop had his arm around Jeff's mother, Lee, sharing a joke. Everyone who came in paid their respects to ninety-year-old Ken Lassen, who sat at the counter like a grandee, keen-eyed, amused at the fuss made of him. Pen and ink portraits of his father and grandfather hung on the walls, either side of a sign that announced:

> **this is not**
> **BURGER KING**
> **you don't get it**
> **your way.**
> **you take it my way,**
> **or you don't get the damn thing.**

Louis' Lunch had the confidence of a place that has done things its own way for a long time. Insiders knew not to ask for ketchup – as the Library of Congress website points out: 'Want ketchup or mustard? Forget it. You will be told "no" in no uncertain terms.'

'Hep yuz?' enquired Jeff. His voice sounded as though he had swallowed a couple of rocks.

'Yes. I'd like one of your burgers and I'd like to see how it's made.'

'Sure. Waddaya want with it?'

Given the fiercely held strictures about accompaniments, it seemed best to bat this question back to Jeff. 'Whatever you'd suggest.'

'OK, so cheese, tomato, onion.'

The patties sat in a steel tray. Without even looking – it was all instinctive, automatic – he fished out two, flattened them, added salt and squashed them together to make one patty. 'To get the salt right in there, y'know?'

'What meat goes in your burgers?'

'We use five different cuts. Only 5 per cent fat. Mom says the recipe is salt, pepper and TLC. She's not had burger from anywhere but Louis' in fifty years.'

'Is the meat aged?'

'Nah. It's ground fresh every day. My brother Kenny does that, downstairs.'

'And what's in the blend?'

'That's one of the few secrets we have here. I'd have a gun put to my head if I told you that.'

'Every kitchen has its secrets. Forget I ever asked.'

'Forget what?' He lopped a thin slice off a Spanish onion and flipped it on top of the patty. It all went in a wire cage with handles, like the fishclamp for a barbecue, which was then closed up and slid – vertically – into an ancient grill.

The grills are another part of Louis' lore. There are three of them: tall metal boxes the size of a couple of phonebooks, with curlicued decoration on the doors and a scalloped roof topped by a stovepipe. Beautiful, practical machines that wouldn't look out of place on *The Antiques Roadshow*. They're stamped 'Bridge Beach & Co. No. 1 Pat. Jan 11, 1898', and they have been cooking Louis' burgers ever since they were made. I wondered how far these grills might actually give Louis' burgers their flavour.

'Those grills mean the meat gets cooked evenly on both sides at once. It's better than flippin' on a griddle. And the fat doesn't drip on to the flames.'

'They're amazing objects. I can see why you're not tempted to change too many things.'

'It's all about history and pride and family. Ya gotta keep the tradition going.'

As he talked, Jeff reached behind for the toast – another part of that tradition. Louis' burgers don't come in a bun: they're served on toast because that's how Louis did it originally. (That's also why no ketchup's allowed: it's all about history and family.) The toaster's not the one Louis originally used, but it's not far off – a Savory Radiant Gas Toaster, as the fancy lettering on the front says, from 1929. It has a fragile web of wires slowly rotating, like a paternoster lift, around the machine. He pulled off a couple of slices, scooped up sharp Cheddar paste from a tub – 'Ya can't put a slice of hard cheese in a vertical grill' – and smeared it on the toast. Slid a burger on top, then a tomato slice and one of the pieces of toast. Cut it diagonally down the middle, wrapped it in waxy paper and served it on a disposable paper plate.

'Try that for size.'

I doubted that I'd serve my own burger without a bun – I didn't have Louis' weight of tradition to back me up – but toast really allowed the quality of the meat to come through. And it had a lovely loose texture. I had already thought that texture would be crucial to a good burger, and this confirmed it. I'd have to look carefully at what grind to use. 'Mmm. This is really superb.'

'It takes a while in one of those old things, but it's worth it,' said an old man in a tweed jacket sitting at the stool next to me. ''Sgreat, Jeff. Medium rare. Just the way I like it.'

'Yeah? Well, every once in a while I get one right.'

WHAT'S SHAKIN'?

I walked between plane trees interspersed with tall shiny metal tree sculptures that caught the light and brought a sense of surreal fun to Madison Square Park. Beneath the dappled shade were wide sandy areas that in France would have been filled with boules players. The French feel was reinforced by a huddle of green slatted folding chairs and small metal tables of the kind that can be found in the Tuileries or Jardin du Luxembourg. This was a sign that I was getting close to the object of my visit – the Shake Shack.

The Shack opened in 2004 as part of the Conservancy's ongoing plans to fashion a park that is an essential part of local life, and it has succeeded spectacularly. Its burgers have been designated The Best by *New York* magazine and described as 'a thing of simple beauty swaddled in a wax paper jacket ... Pretty much burger heaven.' *Time Out* and the *New York Times* both agreed, putting it among their Top Places. With accolades like that, it's not surprising that the queue usually stretches right back to the southwest corner of the park. In fact, the line has become a landmark of its own. (If you think I'm exaggerating, check out the Live Shack Cam for a view of where the line's at right now.)

Although the Shack's website modestly bills it as a 'roadside food stand', the building is a lovely piece of architecture: a corrugated zinc and glass wedge – cleverly echoing the Flatiron – with blocky, foot-high silvery 1950s-style lettering set on a strip that runs along the edge of the roof declaring SHAKES BURGERS HOT DOGS FRIES SUNDAES FROZEN CUSTARD FLOATS CONCRETES CONES. The look is in part a homage to the great foodstands that the team who run the place, Danny Meyer and Richard Coraine, remember from childhood. Before the Shack opened, Richard did a cross-country research tour, stopping at burger joints and custard stands from St Louis to Louisiana, determined to get every detail right. (Meyer and Coraine are famous for this kind of in-depth approach. The restaurants in their Union Square Hospitality Group – Union Square Café, Gramercy Tavern and The Modern at the Museum of Modern Art, among others – have become a benchmark for service in the States. The Union Square Café has won the James Beard Award for Outstanding Service.)

The queue was at least forty deep when I arrived. By now this was such an inevitable consequence of the Shackburger's celebrity that placards had been set up at intervals to keep the snake of people distracted. 'The Shack is not a fast-food joint. We prepare all of your food to order,' explained one, while another answered Shack FAQs like: 'What's with the line?' and 'What is a concrete?'* It was really encouraging to see how long people were prepared to wait for a quality product. I ordered a Shackburger at the side window, then walked around to the front to watch the crowd of cooks in their blue Ts (What's Shakin'? emblazoned across the back) working with intense concentration in the tiny kitchen. After ten minutes my name was called. I picked up the burger in its cardboard carton and strolled to one of the green folding tables to try it out.

Conscious that, with a film crew encircling me, I was providing further entertainment for the queuing Shackfans, I bit in and began talking to the camera. 'This burger's really good. Juicy, chargrilled, nicely caramelised. It's well seasoned too. The flavours are rich, full, complex. The texture firm but melting.' I took another bite, suddenly aware – as people stared – of how difficult it is to eat a burger without

* Three scoops of frozen custard blended at high speed.

spilling the sauce or ending up with a lettuce leaf hanging out of your mouth. A Japanese woman was surreptitiously taking photos – perhaps I had already splodged my shirtfront. 'The bun is great as well. Lightly toasted on the inside and with a slight sweetness. Very nice.'

There was a crunch across the gravel as Richard Coraine joined me to talk burgers. Once the chorus of police sirens had faded (outdoor filming in New York is a constant battle with the bleats of the emergency services and the throaty klaxons of Mack rigs: almost every interview began with the interviewee and me poised to speak but silent, as if frozen in time), I asked Richard about his own search for perfection.

'You've put as much work into developing a burger as anyone I know. How long did it take you?'

'About six months. I racked up 10,000 miles and 30,000 calories!'

'A lot of work.'

'To me it didn't seem like work. The meat is, of course, the key to a great burger. Danny and I really wanted to get a range of flavours in every bite, so we went at it as a wine producer would – searching for a blend that would give the burger character and depth. What we eventually came up with was a mix of sirloin: in effect, the cabernet of our blend – big, structured, full-bodied – along with brisket for a cabernet franc-style softness, plus chuck for bold flavour – the malbec in the blend, I guess you could say.'

'Do you age the meat at all?'

'Nah. To me that seems like overkill. I want the crisp beef flavour to come through, so all we do is sear it. Press it down on the griddle just enough to get those browning flavours, but not so hard you lose the juices. That juiciness has gotta be one of the major aims when you're making a burger.'

'What part does fat play in that?'

'You need about 20 per cent, tops. Any more and it loses flavour. Less and it's just too lean.'

'And what about the grind size?'

'Heston, you gotta let me keep something secret!'

'Well, can you tell me about the rest of the ingredients? Did you put in the same level of research?'

'Lemme start with the bookends – the bun itself. We went through a huge number of white-bread products before finding this potato roll that had the kind of taste and texture we wanted, though it still needed a little something. It lacked depth till we added butter before the griddling.'

'Yes, I really like that sweet note in it.'

'Thanks. The lettuce took a while to get right. The usual choice, iceberg, is to my mind a bit watery and bland. We wanted something with a robust, rustic flavour, something that really held up in the bun. After a lot of searching we found a loose-leaved Boston that fitted the bill.'

'And the tomato?'

'That also went through some changes. The one we originally served was OK but didn't have a real tomato character to it. Then we found this Roma tomato, which is really spectacular, and everything fell into place.'

'What about the sauce?'

'That's really a secret too. It's kinda like a Russian dressing, but with the ketchup taken out and mustard added.'

'But I bet that's not the whole story.' Richard just smiled at me apologetically. 'That's two secrets you've kept, and I wonder how you'll feel about this question. Apart from Shake Shack ...'

'It's the best dining room in the city!'

' ... where else would you go for a burger?'

He looked around, then hunched forward. 'OK, you gotta promise not to tell my employees, but occasionally I sneak off to Burger Joint.'

AT THE JOINT

The Burger Joint had been on my itinerary even before Richard Coraine gave it his whispered approval, but it was encouraging to have the choice vindicated by someone with so much savvy about the New York restaurant scene.

Even so, it wasn't an easy place to find, not least because (as I discovered later) the series producer had gone to great lengths to ensure that no one told me where it was, in the hopes of capturing my bewilderment on film. The candid camera rolled and I walked off 57th Street into the cathedral-like space of Le Parker Meridien hotel, with its arches, high ceilings and vast mirrors on all sides that split me into a million reflected images. Turning left by a curtain, I walked past reception and on to … the revolving doors of the 56th Street exit. Where the burger was this joint?

One of the beauties of film is that you can rewind …

I walked off 57th Street into the cathedral space with its endlessly mirrored reflections, turned left by the curtain and this time spotted a man carrying a brown paper bag. Were there a couple of greasy thumb-stains on it? Beside the curtain was a narrow passageway, illuminated by a single neon light at its far end tracing the outline of a burger, with a red arrow pointing me forwards. I stepped into the dark.

And emerged in another world. A small, square room housed a dozen wood-effect Formica tables and brown vinyl banquettes. Tattered posters crudely taped to the walls advertised *Rocky*, *Wild Hogs* and a *Cheech & Chong* movie. The menu and any other information deemed relevant were written in felt-tip on cardboard offcuts that had been taped to the wood-panelled serving counter. One said: 'We don't spit on your food so please … DON'T WRITE on our walls.' It didn't seem to be working – most of the free space contained scrawled signatures and slogans. This wasn't 1950s retro: it was more the kind of grungy, no-nonsense dive that catered for a blue-collar clientele in one of the rougher parts of a big city. Even the TV picture had an authentic fuzziness to it.

The counter was manned by a Val Kilmer lookalike in khaki T-shirt and forage cap. I ordered what the joint called 'the works': a burger with lettuce, tomato, onion, pickle, mayo, mustard and ketchup. 'OK. No problem,' Val said, smiling as though at some private joke. 'I'll put ya down as "Mr B" and let ya know when it's ready.' I went and squeezed on to one of the banquettes.

'It takes a lot of time and money to make a place look this good,' said a short-haired woman in a blue suit, advancing towards me with her hand outstretched. 'Victoria Barr, director of sales and marketing.'

'This place is extraordinary. What's the story behind Burger Joint?'

'First off, that's not even its name. That's just what customers ended up calling it because it hasn't got one. The Parker Meridien used to have a bar here that was nice enough, but people only came once. It didn't draw them back. So the owners of the hotel, the Parker family, and Steven Pipes, the general manager, began thinking about what they'd like to see in its place. And this is the result. They sourced stuff from all over to make it look and feel authentic. Those old booths came from the Bowery.'

'The attention to detail is really impressive,' I said, gazing up at the ceiling, which had exactly the right pressed white hardboard – that stuff pocked with little irregular holes – held in place by a wide latticework of plastic strips. 'That's what makes it work.'

'Yeah. We expected the ties-and-fries guys, but the place attracts the whole spectrum. Kids, tourists, even women in Chanel suits—'

'Mr B, Mr B,' chanted the counter staff, a cool bunch who operated by their own rules. They were enjoying wrongfooting the camera crew by hamming it up. I wondered if they'd been found down the Bowery too.

'That must be my burger.' I hurried to the counter. (One sign taped to the menu board warned the queue: 'Be ready – or else you go to the back of the line.' I didn't want to find out what punishment awaited those slow to pick up their order.) Grabbing the sizeable waxed-paper parcel, I returned to my seat.

It was big all right. Looked like it could get a bit messy. Another fine opportunity to be caught on camera doing a Heston special – getting more down my shirt than in my mouth. But there was no right way to go about it. I'd just have to get stuck in.

The quality of the meat was apparent at once. It was juicy and nicely textured – loose and falling apart as I bit in. The kind of mouth-feel I wanted. The bun was highly toasted, giving more depth to the savoury flavours. It was a burger that fitted its surroundings: simple and substantial; something you could happily fill your face with. It had a glorious greasy-spooniness to it. 'This is really good,' I told Victoria, reaching for the red and yellow squeezy bottles.

I noticed a man in a tall pleated toque with a small salt-and-pepper moustache hovering politely in the entranceway. 'That's the executive chef, Emile Castillo,' Victoria explained. 'Emile, come on over.'

'It's a very tasty burger,' I said. 'What's your secret?'

'The bun is Arnold's – the classic, old-style. As for the meat, we went through twenty different recipes before we got it the way we wanted. I use chuck. Fresh every day.'

'Otherwise, I guess, the seasoning begins to cure the mix and it emulsifies into something more sausage-like?'

'Exactly.'

'And what kind of grind do you put it through?'

'It's minced at three-sixteenths of an inch.'

'How many of these d'you sell a day?'

'Oh, sometimes as many as eleven hundred. The line's constant.'

On the next table I heard a girl say, 'This might be the best burger I've ever eaten.' And it was true that it was a great burger. But what struck me most was the effort that had gone into creating a context for that burger. It turned the meal into an experience that drew on nostalgia and icons and history and cultural heritage. And even though it wasn't my heritage (except through movies), I enjoyed the romance and the magic of it all.

And that's what made it taste so good.

HANGIN' AT THE MALL

Between 2001 and 2004 a burger war took place in America, as top chefs battled to outdo each other to produce the ultimate luxury patty. The beef became grain-and-beer-fed Kobe, before being dismissed in favour of a generous blob of foie gras (which then morphed into a foie gras milkshake chaser) that was succeeded by beef with shavings of truffles and yet more truffles. The bun and garnish got a similar make-over – focaccia bread, caramelised onion, onion and bacon compote, sautéd porcini, smoked Gouda and even gold leaf were added to the burger. Restaurant-goers and food critics began watching the price hikes with the focused intensity of City analysts. By 2004 it had hit $99.

How far could you go down this route and still retain the burger's integrity, I wondered. I had heard rumours that Thomas Keller's Bouchon Bakery sold a Wagyu beef 'slider'* on a brioche bun, so I decided to go and find out for myself.

As well as being a friend of mine (though it's rare that we get the chance to meet up), Thomas is one of the greatest chefs in America. Two

---

* So called because it's smaller than a normal burger and slides down easily. It's restaurant vocabulary that hasn't really hit the vernacular yet.

of the five restaurants in the country with three Michelin stars belong to him – Per Se in New York and The French Laundry in Napa Valley. He is famous for his precision and his ability to coax the most intense colour and flavour out of each ingredient, and he has taken many familiar foods – ice cream cornets, blinis, agnolotti – and transformed them into something supremely delicate and elegant. These technical skills are allied to two things that are just as valuable: a culinary curiosity that isn't confined to 'fine dining', and a sense of humour. His menu offers many witty and refined versions of humble dishes – fish and chips (red mullet with palette d'ail doux and garlic chips), macaroni and cheese (butter-poached lobster with lobster broth and mascarpone-enriched orzo), coffee and doughnuts (cappuccino semifreddo with cinnamon-sugar doughnuts). Playing a further game with the wordplay, there's even a dish called 'tongue in cheek' (braised beef cheeks and veal tongue with leeks and horseradish cream). If anyone could finesse a luxury burger that still gave a nod to its origins, Thomas could.

After the scuffed-wood solidity of Louis' Lunch, the alfresco retro of Shake Shack, and Burger Joint's hipster grunge, it seemed surreal to be searching for a burger amid the glass, marble and steel of the Time Warner Center. To an ambient soundtrack of tasteful choral warbling, the escalator lifted me up through three floors of shops selling expensive designer accoutrements.

The fountainspray of bright red gladioli bursting from the tall glass vase on the bar counter showed me that the Bouchon Bakery had used this backdrop to its advantage, enlivening it with eye-catching splashes of colour and tactile materials – the small, solid white marble tabletops; the Christine Keeler-style dark wood chairs. The place seemed an accurate reflection of Thomas's personality – uncompromising on quality, elegant, fastidious.

I took my place at one of the tables and waited for the slider to slide on in.

I was brought a trio of baby burgers on a white oblong plate, the curved domes of the brioche buns a shiny lacquered brown with a sprinkle of sea salt grains across them. To the side a scatter of crisp lettuce and a tiny tower of cornichons. It looked fantastic and I knew it would be delicious. I wanted to eat it at once, but I also wanted to delay the moment, savour it.

Greed won out and I took a bite. The meat was superb. Rich and with a long finish. So soft that it melted in the mouth – a really sublime experience. There was rocket and a tangy relish in the bun. They complemented one another perfectly, and their savoury notes mingled with the meat, creating more complex flavours. I had thought the brioche might be a step too far, altogether too bijou, but it worked: the touch of butter added a sweetness and an enticing aroma.

'What do you think? D'you like it?'

Thomas had arrived and, without waiting for an answer, began peppering me with questions about what restaurants I was planning to film and offering suggestions of his own. 'You know, there's a place where they deep-fry everything. Key lime pie, burgers, the lot. It's good. Lovely and crispy on the outside.' He folded his tall, thin frame into the chair beside me.

'You've obviously got a great affection for the burger.'

'I'm from a middle-class family. For us a big night out was at Micky D's. The burger is a big deal for me, one of those comfort foods. I love cheeseburgers too – all that gooeyness.'

'So what meat goes in your burgers?'

'It's 50 per cent sirloin, 50 per cent Wagyu beef.'

'What about the grind?'

'We grind it twice. The second time on medium-small: 4–5 millimetres. You need some texture.'

'I was worried that your burger might be so refined that it lost touch with its roots, but it really retains the spirit of the thing. How has it gone down in Bouchon?'

'Really well. It's not a standard feature at the restaurant. We do it on particular occasions, when it's called an "addition" rather than a "special" because we like to think that everything we serve is special.' He grinned at me.

'How did it come about in the first place?'

'We were serving Wagyu at Per Se upstairs and wanted to find some way of using the offcuts. This is what we came up with.'

I had come full circle. My American trip had begun in New Haven, where the burger was supposed to have been invented by a cook who didn't want to waste beef left over after the lunchtime rush. Now I'd met a chef who had reinvented it because he didn't want to waste the top-quality trimmings from the kitchen. It was a neat way to finish my New York explorations, and it reinforced how everything comes back to the meat. No matter what fancy garnish you put in the bun, the meat is still the key. As soon as I got back to Britain, I decided, I had to get down to the butcher's.

THE BUTCHER WHO LIKES A BIT OF SKIRT

By now it will have become obvious that I harbour a few culinary passions and obsessions that others might consider disproportionate, perhaps even irrational. One of the most enduring is for cuts of meat that are unjustly ignored in this country: bavette (which we call 'flank' or 'skirt'), faux filet, pavé, paleron. One of my absolute favourite cuts of beef is onglet, a strip of meat that sits inside the ribcage close to the kidney and has a gamey character.

In Britain it's fairly rare to find devotees of these cuts, even among chefs, so when I read that a young butcher in Knightsbridge was using Continental techniques and championing unusual cuts, I was keen to find out more. I wasn't disappointed. Jack O'Shea takes the stairs three at a time, and his intellectual curiosity matches his physical impatience. Ask him about a cut or type of meat and in no time you'll have been told not just the best ways to cook it, but also how the heat works on its fibres. He seemed like the ideal person to consult about which meat might make the best burger.

O'Shea's shop stands in a well-heeled street around the corner from Harrods. I walked past white-painted Georgian terraced houses and Bonhams the auctioneers, and stepped in between carefully manicured bay trees and two chalkboards offering 'Sirloin on the bone – 36-day-hung, from southwest Ireland. Well marbled' and 'Black Angus naturally reared grass-fed BEEF – 40 days matured on the bone' to enter not so much a butcher's as an emporium. Above the white-tiled walls, shelves were stacked high with Tracklements condiments, jars of Steenbergs spices, organic eggs, savoury crackers and bottles of single-estate olive oil. One of the glass-fronted serving cabinets had a tumble of delicious-looking cheeses, olives and pies. Hessian carrier bags with the shop's cowhead logo hung from a rail above a window. Beside them hung a double row of pigs' carcasses, as if to remind you that this isn't a deli – the meat is the star of the show. The other glass cabinet had poussin, quail, Cumberland sausage, pork and black pudding sausage, lamb keftas, fat slabs of vivid red onglet, pieces of sirloin that had been aged to a deeper, darker red that was almost black, and knobbly oxtail chunks with their mother-of-pearl swirl of bone at the centre. It all looked fantastic. The TV crew seemed to have forgotten about focal lengths and white balance, and were all gazing intently at what was on offer, deciding what to buy for dinner.

Towards the front of the shop, Jack stood over a well-scarred butcher's block, cutting up chuck. We got down to the business in hand.

'This is the top of the shoulder across the blade,' I explained to camera. 'It has worked hard, so you need to remove the tough bits – all the connective tissue between the muscles – or cook it for a long time.'

'Yes,' agreed Jack. 'As a beast in the field, it's done a lot of work all right.' He gripped a handful of flesh and made a series of small, quick, confident slices, his thumb hard up against the blade's spine. 'But the flavour here is fantastic. People treat chuck as stewing beef, but if it's prepared right, it's a terrific cut. The meat's a bit chewier, perhaps, but I'd choose it over fillet steak any day.' He severed a couple of thin slivers and we did the caveman thing, chewing down on raw meat. It tasted deliciously rich and buttery, with a fine open texture.

'It's important to know that different cuts have different properties in terms of texture and flavour. What cuts d'you reckon would suit a burger, Jack?'

'Well, first it shouldn't be seen as an opportunity for a cheap cut. You put something like that – with lots of connective tissue – in the mincer and all it does is catch in the blades and in your teeth.'

'Yes. It's not going to be cooked long enough to break down.'

'If you've removed all the tricky bits, then one pass through the grinder should be enough. But a lot of butchers'll simply grind the stuff three or four times and end up with an emulsion.'

'Which is what you want in bangers, but not in burgers. In a burger you want the meat to more or less fall apart in the mouth. A nice loose texture.'

'For a burger, I'd choose what the Americans call "under blade", directly below the shoulder. It has worked hard, which gives it that gamey flavour, and it's beautifully marbled, which means there's an even distribution of fat to give juiciness. Here, Heston, put your hand on this.'

He flopped a catcher's mitt of meat on to the block. It felt satisfyingly firm, not at all flabby.

'That's all the intramuscular fat propping it up. And that's the key to your burger. But, once again, the hard work done by that part of the animal means there's lots of connective tissue that has to be got rid of.'

Jack does this by seam-boning, a style of butchery popular on the Continent but not traditionally practised in the UK. It involves identifying the individual muscles and cutting along the seams between them to separate them out. As he talked, Jack eyed up the meat and made short, swift cuts, splitting up muscle groups from which he then removed all the tissue, the blade a flurry of little flicks across the meat's surface.

He made it look easy, but it requires a good knowledge of anatomy to do it efficiently. The British butcher usually concentrates on separating out particular cuts, all of which derive from parts of several different muscles. Tradition and economics play a part in this: there's little history of seam-boning in this country, and things are slow to change, especially since this form of butchery is more difficult to do at speed and produces a surplus of little muscles that are only really good for mincing. However, seam-boning has two huge advantages that offset this: first, since the meat is from a single muscle, it will all respond to cooking in the same way, which allows far greater control in the kitchen. Second, by separating out the muscle and getting rid of the connective tissue, you can get tender pieces of meat from cuts normally considered tough.

By now there was a pile of perfectly prepared meat on the block. It had an attractive, natural shape; it looked as though it had come from an animal. Jack had popped a jar of sea salt and was sprinkling it on small slices that he handed around to the soundman, researcher, producer, book photographer and any customer within range. Justifiably proud of his product, he was keen to convert as many people as possible.

'The marbling means you don't need to add any fat, Heston. At 15 per cent, it's perfectly balanced. Which is good because adding fat stresses the meat. You don't want to pound in artificial flavour. Now that I've cut out all the connective tissue, this'll grind well.'

'What grind size would you use?'

'Eight millimetre, which is pretty standard.'

'I'm also wondering about whether to use aged meat. I know it's unusual in a burger, but in the States I tasted one that included Wagyu beef that had been dry-aged for at least a month. It gave the dish an extra richness and complexity, and a nutty note that I really enjoyed.'

'I've not done it with a burger. I'll have to look into it. That said, we've got a pretty broad spread of clientele, and not everyone likes that gamey taste.'

'Another idea I'm considering is using several cuts of meat rather than just one. That might give a greater complexity of texture and flavour. What do you think?'

'Well, chuck has a firm, steak-like aspect to it. Perhaps brisket would add something. It's a different fat – creamy, nutty. It would have an effect similar to putting butter on a potato. Cut the dryness.'

'What about sirloin?'

'You don't need to spend that kind of money to get the flavour range you want,' Jack advised, ever the thrifty butcher. 'You can get sirloin flavour from the under blade, especially with this kind of marbling.'

'I'd like to include short-ribs. I've been using them at the Fat Duck in a recipe for Beef Royal, a historic British dish that used to be served at royal banquets. Ribs really add something to that recipe, and I think they'd work well in a burger too.'

'Great idea.'

We'd got three cuts to try, so, taking the stairs three at a time, we bounded down to the cramped triangular basement to set about grinding them.

Along one wall were more knife-scarred work surfaces, above which were whiteboards that had recipes for Kentish and Lincolnshire sausages, scrawled reminders – *Wights order for next week* – and the ratios for my burger patties.

	3½kg (1)	3½kg (2)	3½kg (3)
chuck	1.75kg	1.75kg	1.75kg
brisket	0.875kg	0.875kg	0.875kg
short-rib	0.875kg	0.875kg	0.875kg
	no salt	0.5% salt	1% salt

Ultimately, I wanted to explore four key areas: how many cuts to use, how many grinds to put them through and what grind size to use, and how much salt to add.

'There's my grinder: American job.' Jack pointed to a brushed-steel cube sitting on top of a trolley. It had a 120 x 60 cm tray above it, and an L-shaped fat metal pipe jutting out of the front. 'BUTCHER BOY' was stamped on the side. Jack slotted a perforated disc into the pipe's opening, screwed a solid, nubbed metal ring on top to keep it in place, then tightened it with a metal implement shaped like a hand-scythe.

'I want to get an idea of exactly what each one of these meats – brisket, short-rib and chuck – brings to a burger,' I said. 'So how about we start by making a patty of each one on its own, without any salt?'

Again the swift, sure cuts; again the growing pile of beautifully shaped, fist-sized pieces; and then – perhaps because of the lens's aggressive scrutiny, the pressure to perform at your best – a crescent of blood laced Jack's finger. 'That's only the second time I've done that this year. And I had to do it today!' He looked rueful as he snapped on a bright blue disposable glove. Like any true artisan, he wanted everything to be perfect, including the way in which things were pre-pared and presented. Even a cut finger (inevitable in the butcher's trade) represented a falling short of that ideal.

I put the meat on the grinder's tray and pushed it towards the hole with one hand, hitting the motor's switch with the other. There was that slightly sickening squelch (the sound in Hollywood action movies when a body hits an industrial fan) and out came fat red strands, spilling on to a square of clingfilm. Jack hurriedly tried to align them in long rows, as though weaving a hawser, and then rolled the cling-film over them, twisting the ends to form a large sausage shape. Normally the ground meat would be lumped into patties with the strands going in every direction. I was convinced that, if we trained

Jack O'Shea and I align the meat strands to get a really loose burger texture.

all the strands along the same axis, and then cut across the 'sausage' so that the strands in the patties ran vertically, it would have a beneficial effect on the texture of the burger as you bit into it.*

'That's the brisket done,' said Jack. 'Did you see the buttery fat on it?'

'Yes. That should bring a really distinctive flavour and texture to the burger. Now for the short-rib.'

This was minced using a smaller disc. The ribs have so much connective tissue that it's impossible to seam-bone it all out, so the plate has to do some of the work of breaking it down. Jack grabbed a piece of meat and held it to the light. 'D'you want it ground once or twice? I'd say twice.'

We piled chunks, hit the motor, heard the squelch, drew out the strands, tasted the results. 'Not bad,' decided Jack, nipping the end off a strand and chewing. 'Buttery and soft.'

'Yes. That already has a really nice flavour. But I think you were right: let's give it one more grind.'

Eventually we had grinds of each type of meat sitting on a roasting tray side by side. It was easy to see the differences between them. The chuck was a vivid red with subtle flecks of white throughout. It looked, to all intents and purposes, like a piece of red marble. The brisket, on the other hand, had blobs of fat dotted over the surface. In the short-rib the red and white were mixed together to give a paler, stippled effect – speckled granite to chuck's marble. I couldn't wait to see how they responded to cooking.

And I didn't have to. Jack's assistants had set up a portable barbecue outside the shop. Already they had got an audience of passers-by – all men, I noticed, mesmerised by the fire, as though some primitive hunter-gatherer gene had kicked in. Even as I thought this, I felt the lure of the flame and the smell of burnt charcoal urging me forwards.

---

* Later I got the opportunity to test this out at Wageningen University, where they have a machine that measures food's resistance to pressure. Macabrely, it consists of a unit to which you attach a metal rod with a replica of a tooth at the end. (There's even a choice of molar or upper or lower incisor.) The speed at which this lowers is calibrated, the foodstuff is placed underneath and, as the tooth drills in, the computer screen shows on a graph the rate of force and the time taken. A traditionally made burger produced a steep incline on the graph – a pretty chewy piece of meat – while our version with aligned strands had a much gentler curve, evidence of a looser, more open texture.

I too ended up staring at the barbi. I wondered how far that macho, alpha-male, man-make-fire thing was part of the burger's personality. Even men who don't cook tend to be proud and protective of their prowess at the barbecue's grillface, beer in one hand and spatula in the other.

I grabbed my spatula, got three burgers on the grill and began pressing them down and flipping them over to char nicely and heat evenly. I hadn't yet decided how I was going to prepare and cook my own burgers: this was just to see how the meat coloured up.

I flipped a cooked chuck patty on to a plate and we all tore off a piece. It had a great texture and plenty of flavour, even without salt. I had thought all along that this might provide the backbone of my burger, and this tasting confirmed that.

The amount of fat in the brisket and short-rib meant that I had to handle them carefully so they wouldn't fall apart. I edged them off the grill and tried each in turn. The brisket was certainly buttery, which gave it a slightly nutty, grassy note. Also, it was still a bit gristly: it needed a different grind, but it would definitely bring something extra to a burger. The rib was fantastic. 'God, that's really good' was all I managed to say to camera, caught up in the enjoyment of it.

It was great to be reminded of how different cuts from the same animal had such different qualities. And, though I still had plenty of experimenting to do with blends and grinding and salting, I was pretty sure I'd be using all three cuts in the final burger.

Hamburger Serves 8

Getting a burger right is, in many ways, a percentage game: finding the appropriate balance of different cuts of meat, deciding which grind size to use, sorting out the salt content and even finding a bun size that won't crowd the mouth, preventing appreciation of the full range of flavours and textures.

Countless trials and taste tests went into establishing a blend of meats that introduced the gamey richness of aged meat without altering the burger's essential character. Playing around with the grind, I began to see that I could incorporate a textural variety that really added something: putting the short-rib through a coarser disc left it in steak-like pieces.

The salt content was always going to be a crucial feature of the burger's structure because salt not only provides seasoning, but binds the meat's proteins, holding the whole thing together. I wanted the mouthfeel to be very loose, so I had to use as little salt as would allow the burger to keep its shape. At the Fat Duck lab we made patties over and over, increasing the salt content by half per cent increments of the total weight, until we had found the magic number that consistently gave that result.

Bun development was similarly a search for a formula. Oral physiologist Jon Prinz had told me that most people's jaws can open sufficiently to accommodate about two to three fingers. If I wanted the burger-biter to get all the elements of the dish in each mouthful, I had to create a bun that was low and soft enough to fit that space. And it had to be light not just to fit the mouth, but also to counter the richness of the meat. A dough containing a lot of fat would have too tight a crumb structure and make the meal seem heavy. Many store-bought buns get round this by using a very wet dough, but this can only be worked successfully by machine. It took a lot of juggling of every variable in the dough-making process – yeast amount, fat level, fermentation time – to arrive at something that really complemented the burger that would be sandwiched by it.

There had to be ketchup in there too, of course. I wasn't going for the gourmet burger: I wanted to hold on to the traditional elements of the dish, but intensify their flavours if possible. Recently, work that I had done on umami had featured in a scientific paper that explored how far that taste was at its most concentrated in the seeds and pulp at the heart of a tomato (see pages 323–5). Following on from this, it seemed to me a good idea to scoop the centres out of tomatoes and reduce them to get a ketchup that gave a truly intense umami hit – the perfect condiment for a burger.

Special equipment
Food mixer with dough hook, very coarse sieve, meat grinder, large cast-iron pan, digital probe

Timing
Preparation takes 2 hours, plus 24 hours for the pre-ferment and 6 hours for the meat to salt. Cooking takes 1 hour.

For the pre-ferment
400g Canadian very strong bread flour (available at Waitrose) _ 1g fast-action bread yeast _ 400g cold water

For the dough
700g pre-fermented batter _ 200g egg yolks (approximately 10 eggs) _ 60g water at 20°C/70°F _ 400g Canadian very strong bread flour _ 100g unrefined caster sugar _ 70g skimmed milk powder _ 15g table salt _ 14g fast-action yeast (2 sachets) _ 60g browned butter, strained and at room temperature _ 30g grapeseed oil _ 35g Trex, at room temperature (available at supermarkets, Trex is a vegetable fat which is used for pastry and bread)

For the egg wash
50g whole eggs _ 20g egg yolks _ 5g water _ 2g salt _ sesame seeds, as needed

For the burgers
625g chuck _ 25g salt _ 1.2kg short-rib meat, minimum 30-day
dry-aged (for guidance on exactly what cut to ask for at the
butcher's, see footnote in chilli recipe, page 185) _ 625g brisket

For the cheese slices
750g Manzanilla sherry _ 9 cloves of garlic _ 8 black peppercorns
_ 6 sprigs of thyme _ 16g sodium citrate (available from chemists)
_ 850g Comté cheese

For the tomato concentrate
3kg very ripe tomatoes _ salt, as needed _

For the finished burgers
250g butter _ 8 sliced buns _ 16 cheese slices _ grapeseed oil,
as needed _ 8 hamburger patties _ table salt, as needed _ tomato
concentrate, as needed _ mustard, as needed _ mayonnaise, as
needed _ pickles, as needed _ 3 of the reserved tomatoes, each
cut into 8 slices _ ½ onion, sliced thinly and the rings blanched
for 20 seconds in boiling water _ 1 head of crisp lettuce, such
as iceberg, trimmed

PREPARING THE PRE-FERMENT
1. Tip the flour into your mixing bowl and add the yeast.
2. Using a dough hook, begin mixing on low speed and gradually pour
   in the water until it has all been added.
3. Continue mixing on medium speed until a very liquid batter has
   formed.
4. Pour this batter into a clean, dry container (at least four times
   bigger than the volume of the batter). Cover and leave in a cool
   place for 24 hours to ferment.

MAKING THE DOUGH AND EGGWASH
1. After 24 hours, weigh out 700g of pre-ferment and put it in a mixing
   bowl with a dough hook attachment. Add the egg yolks and the
   water and begin mixing on low speed until the dough is homogeneous and very liquid again (approximately 2 minutes).

2. Sift the flour, sugar, skimmed milk powder, salt and yeast into a separate bowl through a very coarse sieve (this will help prevent them forming lumps when added to the dough). Stir to combine. If a suitable sieve isn't available, simply stir the ingredients together.

3. Gradually add the sifted ingredients to the dough while continuing to mix on slow speed. Once all have been added, increase the speed to medium and mix for another 2–3 minutes. The dough will look very sticky and wet.

4. Brown the butter in a pan until it develops a very nutty aroma, then strain it and discard the butter solids.

5. Add the browned butter, grapeseed oil and Trex to the dough and continue to mix for another 3–4 minutes, until well combined.

6. Stop the mixer and let the dough sit for 10 minutes to absorb the water, then continue to mix on medium speed for another 4 minutes.

7. Cover the dough and place in the fridge for 30 minutes to firm up.

8. In the meantime, cut a piece of baking parchment to fit a large baking sheet.

9. Cut eight sheets of aluminium foil 50cm long. Fold each sheet in half in the shorter direction, then continue to fold in half until you have an aluminium strip 1cm tall and 50cm long. Tape one end of the strip to the other with a bit of overlap to form a ring approximately 12cm in diameter. Repeat this process with the other sheets of foil.

10. When the dough has chilled, weigh out eight 85g portions. Any remaining dough can be wrapped up and frozen to use another time.

11. Lightly flour your hands and quickly roll each piece of dough into a small ball using the palm of your hand. Place the balls on the prepared baking sheet and place a foil ring around each one.

12. With wet hands, lightly pat the balls flat, then cover the baking sheet with clingfilm to prevent the dough from drying out.

13. Set the dough aside in a warm place (between 18° and 22°C), for 1½–2 hours to let it prove.

14. When ready to bake, preheat the oven to 225°C/425°F/Gas 7, and mix all the ingredients for the egg wash except the sesame seeds.

15. Using wet hands, lightly flatten the dough balls within the foil rings.

16. Just before baking, pour some water into the oven to make it lightly steamy (this will prevent the buns from cracking on the surface and developing too thick a crust).

17. Bake the buns for 7 minutes, then remove from the oven and brush the tops with the egg wash. Generously cover each one with sesame seeds.
18. Return to the oven for a further 7 minutes, or until the buns are done. Remove and place on a wire rack to cool.

MAKING THE BURGERS

1. Cut the chuck into 3 x 3cm cubes and toss with the salt in a bowl. Cover with clingfilm and store in the fridge for 6 hours. The salt will penetrate the meat during this time and begin to draw out some of the moisture.
2. In the meantime, cut the short-rib and brisket meat into 3 x 3cm cubes and combine the two.
3. Using a meat grinder with a 3mm plate, grind the short-rib and brisket twice. Refrigerate this meat until very cold.
4. Combine the cold ground meat with the cold diced chuck and mix well.
5. Before you begin the final grinding, place two layers of clingfilm across a chopping board or baking sheet and position under the mouth of the grinder.
6. Using a coarser, 8mm plate, pass the meat mixture through the grinder. This will retain some larger pieces of the chuck.
7. As the meat comes out of the grinder, have a second person use their hands to lay out the strands of meat on the clingfilm. Try to keep the grain of the individual strands running lengthwise in the same direction without getting tangled together. To do this, start laying the meat down at the edge of the sheet furthest from the grinder and work across to the closest edge.
8. Wrap the meat up tightly in the clingfilm, twisting the ends in opposite directions to form a log. Prick a few holes in it with a pin to release any air pockets trapped inside, then continue to twist the ends to tighten until the log is about 12cm in diameter.
9. Wrap the log in another layer of clingfilm to keep it from coming apart, and refrigerate until needed.
10. When the meat has chilled thoroughly, place the still-wrapped log on a cutting board and use a very sharp knife to cut slices about 150g in weight. (The clingfilm helps to keep the meat from falling

apart.) Place the finished patties on a baking sheet and refrigerate for later. If you have more patties than you need, they can be individually wrapped at this point and frozen until needed.

11. To finish the patties, take each one between the palms of your hands and gently press into a burger shape the same diameter as the bun and 2cm thick. Take care to keep the grain of the meat running in the same direction.

12. Cover the burgers with clingfilm and refrigerate until you are ready to cook them.

MAKING THE CHEESE SLICES

1. Combine the sherry, garlic, peppercorns and thyme in a saucepan and bring to a simmer.
2. Remove from the heat and allow to infuse for 10 minutes.
3. Strain the infused sherry, then allow it to cool.
4. Pour 500g of the cooled and infused sherry into a pan and whisk in the sodium citrate.
5. Shred the cheese and add to the liquid in small amounts, whisking each addition until it melts and you have a very smooth, fondue-like texture.
6. Pour the liquid cheese on to a large sheet of baking parchment and quickly use a spatula to spread it into a layer about 3mm thick. Cool completely.
7. Using a circular cutter or a knife, cut pieces about 10cm in diameter and refrigerate until needed.

MAKING THE TOMATO CONCENTRATE

1. Cut the tomatoes in half and scoop the pulp and seeds into a bowl. Avoid damaging the central veins so that the sliced tomatoes retain their form. Reserve some of the tomato halves for garnish.
2. Press the pulp through a very coarse sieve to remove any seeds and large pieces of flesh and core.
3. Pour the liquid into a pan and reduce at a simmer until the liquid takes on a thick, ketchup-like consistency. Stir often as the concentrate thickens, and lower the heat to avoid burning it.
4. Season with a little salt. The taste will be intense, but when spread on the buns, it will really enhance the meaty flavours of the burger.

ASSEMBLING THE BURGERS

1. Brown the butter until it develops a very nutty aroma, then strain it and discard the butter solids.

2. Slice the buns in half and brush the cut sides with the browned butter. Place under a hot grill to lightly toast them.

3. When the buns have a nice golden colour, remove them and place a cheese slice on each cut side. Set these aside, but keep the grill on.

4. In the meantime, place a large cast-iron pan over a high heat until very hot – about 5–10 minutes.

5. Drizzle a layer of the oil into the pan, then add the patties, being careful not to overcrowd them.

6. Flip the patties every 30 seconds. This helps create a wonderful crust and even heat gradient, mimicking the action of a rotisserie, which helps to get edge-to-edge, medium-rare meat while still forming a nice seared crust.

7. When a crust has formed on both sides, usually after about 2 minutes,* remove the burgers from the pan one at a time and use a digital probe to check the temperature. If the meat is above 52°C, transfer the burgers to a warm place to rest. Keep the pan hot.

8. Finish the buns by placing them back under the grill until the cheese slices have melted.

9. Remove the buns from the oven and spread with some of the tomato concentrate, mustard, mayonnaise, pickles, sliced tomatoes, blanched onions and lettuce leaves.

10. To finish, brush the burgers with the browned butter and quickly sear both sides of them in the hot pan for about 15 seconds. Remove from the pan and blot any excess juice with kitchen paper. Place the burgers on the prepared buns, sandwich together and serve right away.

* The patties will be rare. If you prefer them more cooked, increase the cooking time.

Bangers & Mash

'These goat sausages sizzling here in the fire –
We packed them with fat and blood to have for supper.
Now, whoever wins this bout and proves the stronger,
Let that man step up and take his pick of the lot!'
Homer, *The Odyssey*

History

SAUSAGES

As the quotation from Homer shows (though I'd not considered goat as an ingredient; maybe it was an idea worth exploring …), sausages have been a part of our culture – and highly prized as such – for a long time. A sausage-seller appears in Aristophanes' satirical play *The Knights* (424 BC), where his skill in mincing meat makes him a suitable candidate for politics, where he can mince words instead. Seneca noted that the sausage-seller's call was part of the cacophony of street cries in ancient Rome, and in Petronius' *Satyricon* the description of Trimalchio's feast includes sizzling sausages on a silver gridiron, with Syrian plums and pomegranate seeds placed beneath it.

The sausage had clearly already become a feature of everyday life – so much so that *Apicius* contains several recipes for sausage. (For example: 'Grind pepper, cumin, savory, rue, parsley, seasoning, bay berries and *liquamen* [salted fish sauce, possibly similar to Thai *nam pla*]. Mix with finely chopped flesh, grinding both together. Mix in *liquamen*, whole peppercorns, plenty of fat and pine nuts, and carefully force into an intestine stretched thinly, and hang up to smoke.') Undoubtedly, its versatility played a part in this ubiquity: a well-spiced sausage could disguise dubious or unusual cuts of meat, and its handy packaging made it good food for soldiers on the march. The sausage may have invaded northwestern Europe alongside conquering armies. Certainly by the third century AD the sausage figured in cuisine in Britain. Excavations of the Roman town of Verulamium (St Albans) have unearthed the remains of what appears to have been a sausage factory.

The sausage's origins reach back beyond Rome and ancient Greece to coincide with mankind's ability to furnish itself with meat on a regular basis: as soon as there was a surplus, people were thinking of ways to preserve it. The pig was domesticated early – about 5000 BC in Egypt and China – and the art of cutting up meat, salting it and putting it in a casing was one of the first methods of preservation. The pork sausage is the brainchild of these two historical facts. (The word actually derives from the Latin for 'salted': *salsus*.) And although the term 'sausage' covers a wide range of objects – there have been fish sausages since antiquity, Glamorgan sausages contain cheese and leeks, and there are seventeenth-century records of mutton-and-oyster sausages – the pork banger has remained the most popular (and accounts for 83 per cent of all sausages eaten in Britain each year).

Despite its wide and long-standing acceptance, the sausage has had a chequered history. Emperors Constantinus I and Leo V both banned sausages because they contained blood (the consumption of which was forbidden by the Bible) and because their shape inevitably associated them with pagan phallic rites. However, the sausage's reputation has probably been harmed more by the very thing that brought it increased popularity in the nineteenth century: mass production. The urge for quantity all too often led to a drop in quality: cheaper cuts of meat, larger percentages of fillers such as rusk or cereals, the parts of the animal that had no other commercial use, artificial flavours and preservatives – all could be hidden beneath the sausage's pink skin.* This downward trend led to the 'economy' sausage, which might contain 30 per cent pork fat, 20 per cent recovered meat (often including skin, rind, gristle and bone), 30 per cent rusk and soya, 15 per cent water and 5 per cent E-numbers. Now there's a sausage worth banning. No wonder Otto von Bismarck observed that 'Laws are like sausages. It's better not to see them being made.'

Of course, the unsung heroes of the sausage industry are the butchers who stayed loyal to a quality product despite falling sales. But the public saviour was an unlikely one: in the mid-1980s the famous society photographer Norman Parkinson created his own Porkinson's banger, and teamed up with Saatchi & Saatchi to persuade the nation back to its senses. (It was served on Concorde and marketed as the world's first supersonic sausage!) By 2005, a hefty 189,000 tonnes of sausages were being eaten in Britain – 17 per cent more than in 2000, and directly attributable to better-quality meat and a wider range of ingredients. This is the way the story ends, not with a whimper but a banger.

* The term 'banger', which is now an affectionate nickname, is in fact a reminder of the sausage's dodgy innards: during the Second World War the high water content of sausages meant they could be a real flash in the pan – exploding as the water turned to vapour and expanded, bursting the casing.

The Quest for the Best

She had a vague impression of ... the hissing and delicious smell of sausages, and more and more and more sausages. And not wretched sausages half full of bread and soya bean either, but real meaty, spicy ones, fat and piping hot, and burst and just the tiniest bit burnt.
C.S. Lewis, *The Silver Chair*

GETTING THE LOWDOWN IN LUDLOW

I wanted to create a bespoke banger, one that really captured the taste, texture and feel of a fine sausage. To do so, I needed first to talk to the experts and get their advice on how it was done. If only there was a way I could meet up with a number of master butchers who were competing to produce the best sausage they possibly could, I thought. If only I could pick their brains, then talk to members of the public about what they thought of the butchers' offerings and of sausages in general ...

As it turned out, I could do exactly that – in Ludlow in Shropshire.

Ludlow is an impressive place. With its tottering, half-timbered Tudor houses and its solidly built red-brick mansions, it must be one of the most picturesque towns in England. And its inhabitants are enthusiastic about their food. The town has several Michelin-starred restaurants, and every autumn it's the backdrop for a spectacular Food & Drink Festival. As well as showing off local produce and suppliers, the festival explores every aspect of food. There were pudding tastings and a pork pie competition, workshops on perry-making and black pudding, demonstrations of Veronese cookery, a fresh herb market and even a waiters' race. It was all very tempting, but I couldn't be distracted. I had come to Ludlow with one aim in mind: to go on the Sausage Trail.

Each year, Ludlow's five butchers create a new sausage for the festival. By the imposing remains of the town's castle (a reminder of a time when, as a border town, Ludlow's skirmishes might centre on more serious matters than sausage manufacture), you can buy a ticket and voting form, which gives you the opportunity to try all five sausages and then vote for which you think is the best. The banger with the most votes is acclaimed the 'People's Choice'.

I paid my £2, received my ticket and a map showing me the whereabouts of the competing butchers, and joined the long queue forming before a small marquee on the High Street.

Mike Wall and his team were neatly turned out in red pinstriped aprons, and they had a long trough of sausages on the go. 'For the competition,' he told me, 'the biggest problem is thinking up new flavours. Last year we came up with a Thai sausage that won us a prize. Usually I'll have an idea, try it out on the lads in the shop. If they like it, we'll ask the opinion of some of our customers – see if they say "That's fantastic" or "Yuck".'

'So what's the idea this year?'

'Pork with beer mustard. It's rare-breed meat – Gloucester Old Spot from local farms – and natural sheep's casing. What do you think of it?'

It was juicy, firm-textured and full-flavoured. The casing broke apart just right as I bit into it. Of course, it was breakfast time, I was hungry and it was the first sausage I'd tasted, all of which probably made me a less than impartial judge, but it seemed excellent. 'That's great. Really tasty. It's nicely peppered.'

'That's the beer mustard doing its job,' Mike said. 'I don't think it's over the top, though. There's only so much you can do with a sausage. Go too far and it ends up being something else.'

He used mainly cuts from the shoulder, along with some from the belly to provide fat. 'We don't do any curing before mincing. And the meat has to be absolutely fresh – there's no ageing involved. Three or four days old and it needs to be used. After which there's probably a week's shelf-life for the housewife.'

One thing that surprised and interested me was that he used 20 per cent filler. I'd been contemplating making a filler-free sausage, assuming that would give a meatier experience, but in Mike's skilful hands the filler appeared to add something important: a more interesting and varied texture, a kind of welcome roughness rather than smooth homogeneity. It would be interesting to see how the other butchers' offerings compared.

Mike Wall had told me he was born and bred a butcher. And he wasn't kidding – he was born in an upstairs room of the family's shop opposite. He knew his stuff, so before I moved on I wanted to cadge his top tips for making a great sausage.

'The quality of the meat is absolutely essential. And the same goes for the seasonings, which have got to be well balanced. On top of that, there's the skin. You've got to use natural casings from an animal of the right age. Older animals are too tough, and nobody likes a rubbery sausage skin.'

With that caution ringing in my ears, I made my way around the other butchers. The differences of opinion and approach made the task of creating my own sausage all the more daunting. Fresh herbs or dried, leg meat or not, rare breed and free-range or not, spiced-up or spice-free – each butcher had a different take. (One even happily admitted to using an E-number as a preservative!) At least I made headway on the question of filler: I tried a 100 per cent meat sausage and it did indeed seem blander in texture, too uniform to really grab the attention of the tastebuds. I'd learned a valuable lesson here and had a hunch disproved.

The final stop on the trail was Andrew Francis's shop, tucked into a corner of Ludlow's market square. It had a very traditional air: two rabbits were hanging up outside, fur and all, and green-framed chalk-boards announced the day's offers – *Pickled Brisket*, *Salted Silverside*, *Ox Tongue*.

The white marquee outside the shop was doing a roaring trade. 'How come you've got the longest queue? What's the secret?' I asked Andrew as he cooked.

'Perhaps they're starting here and working their way down the hill. No – best sausage, that's what it really is! I'm using an old English recipe for pork and mixed herb. The pork's rare-breed Tamworth: all lean prime shoulder which has the fat you need to keep it moist and tasty. And the casing is natural lamb – none of that artificial stuff; it's the real McCoy, that is, a recipe handed on to me by the butcher who had the shop before me.'

'Is the age of the animal part of what makes a good casing?'

'The age is crucial. Spring lambs are small, so you get a small sausage with a skin that tends to split. Mutton, on the other hand, is basically hard and chewy. Animals between four and twelve months old are best.'

By now, the next batch of Andrew's bangers was ready. He handed one over. 'There you are. Fresh off the barbecue. Don't burn yourself. Now, what's the verdict?'

There was a gleam of competition in Andrew's eye as he asked. It was a lovely sausage, with a nice meaty taste. 'It's important that it's not too spicy,' he told me. 'You want the pork flavour to come through. It needs to be a pleasant sausage for everybody, young and old alike.'

Judging by the numbers milling round his marquee, Andrew had achieved that goal. The queue contained all sorts: men in Barbours and green wellingtons, harassed mothers with prams, kids getting a kick out of following a map and having it stamped at each location. It was inspiring to see such enthusiasm for food among such a range of people. Maybe Britain really was shrugging off its past reputation as a culinary no-go area. The ingredients for all the sausages I'd tasted had been sourced locally: a great advert for what was on the doorstep, and how much better it was than its mass-produced counterparts. I came away from the festival full of enthusiasm not just for sausage-making but for the future of food in Britain. At last we were acknowledging and appreciating the quality of our produce – and supporting, encouraging and eating it too.

FROM TASTING TO TESTING

After lining up for the Sausage Trail, it was time to line up the sausages for the Sausage Tasting.

This was not to be a competition. My pastry chef Jocky, Ashley, Chris and I weren't expecting to crown our own 'People's Choice'. We were looking to find out what were the qualities that made the Great British Banger. Even in Ludlow it had become clear that this was a subject of debate: people in the queues agreed that a great sausage must be juicy and densely textured, but they were divided over spicing in their sausages; I also talked to several who insisted that a good banger must be filler-free and yet, as it turned out, their favourite did contain filler. Obviously the sausage's simple, compact shape hid a number of complex considerations. To sort out what went into perfect sausages, we would really have to get under their skin.

In the development kitchen at the Fat Duck, forty sausages rested, plump and pink, on the work surface, as though four fat-fingered pianists were about to embark on a complicated piece of music. We had sourced the sausages from many places. There were several examples from each of the major supermarkets, generally advertised as 'traditional', 'classic' or 'old English' – encouraging evidence of how much we now expect a better bit of banger for our buck. We had included the standard offerings from each of our five butchers in Ludlow, and from other specialists, including Norman Parkinson's supersonic sausage.

This was not the time for a fry-up: browning a banger gives it a lot of meaty flavour and enhances its juiciness. It can disguise a sub-standard sausage, and I wanted the test to be as rigorous as possible. So we vacuum-packed and labelled the lot, and put them in a water bath for one hour at 60°C. After which, like kids at Christmas, we opened our parcels and tried them out.

We chewed on slices and, like forensic specialists, prised open the meat and picked at the casings. Each of us took notes on the texture of the casing and the meat itself, on the juiciness and flavour, on the overall delicacy – whether it burst satisfyingly as you bit into it.

It was a strange experience, but an instructive one. I had spent ten years thinking about and preparing food, and then being judged on it; this was the first time I'd swapped the chef's hat for the critic's pen. What was immediately apparent was what a wide range of product goes under the name 'sausage'. Here, indeed, were the good, the bad and the ugly. There were gutsy little numbers containing offal that tasted delicious but were too far removed from what we thought of as the classic banger. Similarly, some had been seasoned to the point where they tasted positively exotic. The spice was nice, but again not what we were looking for. Only one sausage was so unpleasant and gluey that it was unswallowable, but there were others that had a definite aroma of biscuit tin – as though they'd used Rich Tea as a filler – or that tasted of cheese and onion.

Weeding out the bad and the ugly was easy. Choosing which sausages captured something of the perfect banger and could be used as a template and inspiration for making our own proved much harder. We swapped notes and whittled the choice down to ten, which we then cooked, and tasted, again.

Even at this stage there was disagreement: a couple were too strongly flavoured or herby, and one was so dough-like that we couldn't understand how it had got this far. But eventually we found a sausage that we felt incarnated the qualities of the classic British banger: full of flavour, dense but not overly so, with a nice rough texture that didn't go too far in the direction of charcuterie-like individual chunks of meat.

On camera, while blind-tasting, I'd suggested this might be a mass-produced sausage that nonetheless managed to tick all the boxes, as though a checklist had been involved in its creation. It's possible that there was, for it turned out to be the Porkinson's banger, which had had the might of Saatchi & Saatchi behind it. Had focus groups and ad planning gone into finding out what exactly makes a banger a banger? In the end it didn't really matter: this was the sausage that best captured what I expected in a banger; this was the sausage that gave me the most signposts towards what I wanted to incorporate in my own sausage.

Balance, it turned out, was the key. In making a sausage, there are a lot of variables to be taken into consideration: the texture must be meaty but not too chewy, the seasoning fresh but not overpowering. The meat needs to be tightly packed but not homogeneous or mousse-like. Originally I had thought a good sausage would need 100 per cent meat, yet I'd learned that the filler can add something – a chunkier, more interesting texture (though this depends on your choice of filler: many of the sausages ended up too starchy, too dry). The salting was important – the best examples all had a slightly cured note – and the casing crucial to a sausage's success: anything too tough made you feel as though you were chewing a plastic bag, no matter how delicious the rest of the sausage's contents.

All these things contributed to the rounded flavour and 'natural' taste that seemed to be the keynote of the best sausages we tested, the ones that let the flavour of the meat come out. (That natural aspect is often the downfall of commercially produced sausages. Anything too processed has an artificial character: you can taste the nitrates used for preservation.) And Porkinson's banger was the sausage that best performed that balancing act. Although I had a few ideas of my own (perception of juiciness, it seemed, was all-important in a proper banger; I'd realised I needed to make a sausage dense enough to get the saliva going, which really enhances that juicy sensation), this was my benchmark for the perfect sausage.

PIGGING OUT

> Pigs with character farmed by people with character will tend to produce pork with character.
> **Hugh Fearnley-Whittingstall**, *The River Cottage Meat Book*

Before I even contemplated something approaching perfection, however, I had to find the meat that best suited a banger. I tasted lots of loins, and the one that fitted that bill came from Graham Head's farm in Northumberland: it had exactly the taste and texture I had in mind. I travelled to Lowick to meet him and talk pork.

The weather was doing its best to dampen my enthusiasm. The sky was a theatre curtain of pale grey. Earlier it had bucketed down but now it had settled into a steady drizzle – fine if it's olive oil over salad leaves, not so great when you're tramping across muddy fields and skirting mini-lakes created by the rain. We hurried towards the pig pens.

With his beret, denim shirt, wire-rimmed glasses and close-cropped silvery beard, Graham looked more like a Left Bank painter than a farmer – but then I guess you could call him an artist of the pig world. He led us into a corrugated-metal shed where large, straw-strewn pens gave the pigs plenty of room to run around in.

It was feeding time and the pigs knew it. They reared up out of their pens and placed supplicatory trotters on top of the railings. Their shrieks of excited anticipation were deafening as Graham tipped out the feed. As he moved from pen to pen, the volume would diminish slightly as a set of pigs ceased squealing and started eating. It was like the end of some cacophonous piece of modernist classical music, the discordant crescendo gradually falling off as each section of the orchestra finished, until suddenly there was silence.

Farmer Graham Head and I tramp through Northumberland fields to feed some Middle White pigs.

Well, almost. The pigs now grunted continually and contentedly as they hoovered up what Graham had put before them. His pigs were rare-breed Middle Whites, and I was interested to know why he rated them so highly.

'Middle White used to be regarded as *the* pork pig. Between the wars, this is what British housewives would have bought. The Middle White does produce exceptional pork,' he insisted with pride, 'partly because it's been crossed with Chinese pigs. You can tell that from the snub nose. Chinese pigs laze around and don't burn off much energy, much like Vietnamese pot-bellied pigs.'

'So they'll develop plenty of fat to give flavour to the meat.'

'Exactly. The Middle White also produces a lot of piglets, which is why it was crossed with Chinese pigs back in the mid-nineteenth century. But the problem is that it's a relatively small pig and it doesn't grow fast enough – or big enough – for commercial concerns. The Large White is a much bigger pig.'

It was a familiar story. 'Yes, as commercial pork producers grew, they wanted an animal that yielded more meat.'

'They were also looking for a general-purpose pig – one that would provide not just pork but bacon as well. If you look at rare breeds, the Middle White's a pork pig, Tamworth's bacon: it's got a long back that gives good rashers. Middle Whites went out of favour, to the point where, in the 1970s and 80s, they were really threatened.'

'But you're clearly devoted to them.'

'These guys produce a really good pork experience. Their genetics mean there's a lot of fat on the outside, which is good for basting, and also on the inside, to make the meat very succulent.'

'I can vouch for that. It's why I'm here. The loin tasted fantastic.'

'Thanks. Part of the reason for that is Middle Whites are old-fashioned pigs: they go to slaughter at an older age. Most commercial pigs go off at four months, before they're fully mature. Middle Whites go at seven to eight months – you're getting a more mature pig; the flavour's had a chance to develop.'

'In contrast to the commercial approach, where the whole point is to get pigs as big as possible as quickly as possible and then flog them off.'

'True, but it's not the producers' fault; it's because of the reward system that applies in Britain: no account is taken of the quality of the meat, and we need to replace it with a system that does. I know there's one in Australia for beef ... '

'Yes, MSA.'*

'Well, we need one for pork here.'

'I agree. It's done wonders for the beef industry over there. And pigs like this should be recognised and rewarded for their high quality. What part does diet play in the development of that quality?'

'How the pigs are fed in the last six to eight weeks of their life is extremely important. I give them a mix of wholemeal barley and concentrated protein – soya plus vitamins with lots of lysine in. It finishes them up really well. The pigs are wet-fed, which is a very nice way of doing it: they eat a kind of polenta or porridge. Taking on water and feed at the same time is a very natural way of "growing on" the meat. You can see it: they begin to grow a lot faster and get a lovely sheen of fat on them.'

'And what happens if you speed up the process and feed a pig too quickly?' I wanted to know. 'Do you end up with too much fat?'

'Inside, the intramuscular fat remains pretty much the same. What you will get is a huge piece of fat round the outside. Sometimes this grows so large and fast that it actually depresses the muscles and you get a very thin piece of protein. That's no good. At the same time, people shouldn't be frightened of a bit of fat on the outside. A lot renders off anyway, but it's great while it's cooking: I call it "self-basting". You don't have to eat loads of it.'

'Pigs are one of the most intelligent and sociable farmyard animals. In your experience, Graham, what happens if they get stressed on the way to the abattoir?'

'Stressing an animal's selfish and unforgivable. But even if you discount moral concerns, there are compelling reasons for treating pigs well – and lambs, cattle and poultry, for that matter. Stress affects the taste. You end up with far tougher meat.'

Stress before slaughter can be caused by many things: lack of water or food, bad transportation, exhaustion, overcrowding. Whatever the cause, it results in the animal drawing on its energy source, glycogen (the 'animal starch'). This ruins the quality of the meat because, after

* See 'Making the Grade', pages 123–4.

death, glycogen converts to lactic acid, which then tenderises the meat. If the glycogen's used up, there'll be no lactic acid to soften it up.

This process goes hand in hand with the hanging of the meat. For a short while after death, an animal's muscles are relaxed. After about one to two-and-a-half hours, however, depending on the type of animal, rigor mortis – a clenching of the muscles – sets in. The muscle fibres run out of energy and the protein filaments contract and lock in place. Hanging goes some way towards preventing this via gravity: the muscles are stretched so the filaments can't contract and bunch up, which produces very tough meat. And eventually protein-digesting enzymes from within the muscle fibres begin to break down the meat, softening its texture.

Graham was so interested in his subject that our roles often switched: he ended up asking me about hanging meat. 'Pork requires a lot less hanging than beef. What do you think is the ideal hanging time?'

'For cured products like sausages, fresh is best – a day or so after slaughter. There I'd say a lot of the tenderising happens during the mincing. But for a loin, where you need to develop a certain level of tenderness, I've found a week or so to be good. Any longer and the fatty acids in the meat get oxidised, leading to that slightly sweated, rancid note.'

We continued talking as we headed off towards Graham's farm-house, a beautifully solid brick building with orange tiles and a pointed tower at one end. Large arched windows overlooked a neatly kept garden with flagstone paths, a scatter of small trees and an immaculate lawn glistening in the drizzle.

'Time for breakfast, I think,' he said. 'Fancy a bacon sandwich … ?'

BACK TO THE GRIND

I was in a white room with a blood-red floor. A man approached wearing a lab coat and black and white chequered hat, as though he'd donned a Formula One flag. Below beetle brows, his eyes twinkled with mischievous humour. He advanced towards me, knife in hand. The tinny, scraping sound of the metal blade scything the sharpener rang out – *zing, zing, zing* – faster and louder with each step. 'Halloo Hairrston. It's rrreally grrrreat to meet yoo … '

No, I wasn't having a nightmare brought on by the toxic combination of adrenalin and sleep deprivation that is the chef's lot. The resonant Scottish brogue belonged to Sandy Crombie, owner of Crombie's butcher shop in Edinburgh. I'd eaten sausages in the street and in the lab. Now I'd come to Scotland to see what went into those sausages.

Sandy lifted a slab of meat on to the table. 'We use shoulder and belly of pork. That makes the nicest sausage because it has the right amount of fat to lean – enough fat to give it flavour and a special taste.'

'Yes, you've got to have fat and lean, and in the right amounts. Do you have an ideal fat percentage?' I wanted to know.

'What we really want is a 70/30 split. We make a lot of sausages with a higher lean content, but for me 70/30 is the most flavoursome. There's an old-fashioned way of rearing that makes the pigs incredibly fat, but then you've got to make sure you use all the pig in your sausages so the meat is properly leaned-up.'

I was thinking hard about the number of different processes I'd need to master to make a great sausage. The grind seemed particularly important. 'Do you play around with grind sizes?' I asked Sandy.

'Aye, we do, depending on the kind of sausage. A Toulouse needs a 12.5 millimetre disc and a single grind, but for these traditional sausages I'll use an 8 millimetre disc and the double-mince method – grinding it once, putting it in the mixer, then grinding it again.'

'That'll make for a more even distribution of lean meat and fat.'

'Absolutely,' affirmed Sandy. 'But the main thing to remember while making sausages is that you need to release the proteins inside the meat. Until that happens it won't all stick together.'

Meat contains muscle fibres, which are largely made up of two proteins: myosin and actin. The chopping, grinding and mixing of sausage meat draws these proteins out of the fibres (especially once salt is added) and on to the meat surfaces, where they act as a glue (or emulsifier), binding meat, fat and water together – much as the protein in egg yolk can be used to bind a fish cake.

Mincing was the start of this transformative process. The machine emitted a dull, insistent rumble as Sandy fed in the meat, which soon tumbled out of a long, solid-looking pipe in thick strands. 'The size of the mincer is extremely important,' he explained. 'The bigger it is, and the faster the meat goes through, the less heat is going to be generated. And that's vital because a warm environment encourages the growth of microbes – something you definitely want to avoid.'

Once the white plastic tub was full, Sandy cut the rumble from the mincer and hefted the tub over to the mixer. 'Mixing will help the protein release. But before we do that, we need to add the secret ingredients.'

Fortunately for me, these weren't so secret that they couldn't be divulged. Sandy ripped the lids off several storage boxes and showed me the contents.

'We start by adding the seasonings because, as you'll know yourself, Heston, they should always be added directly to the meat.'

I felt a little like a school pupil being tested. I resisted the urge to put my hand up. 'You'll get a better mix that way,' I offered, 'and the seasoning is absorbed into the meat directly.'

'Absolutely. A lot of our seasonings are just spices, so we add salt separately. As well as tenderising and flavouring the meat and drawing out its proteins, salt will prevent microbial growth.'

'Yes. Just as it draws out proteins, so it'll draw water out of the microbes' cell walls and replace it with salt. The microbes die or slow down to the point of being ineffective.' I was beginning to sound like the class swot. 'How much salt do you add?'

'We usually work to 1.5 grams per kilo,' Sandy said as he weighed and added it. 'Now, here's the rusk. It doesn't really matter what type you use. This is what we normally choose.' He held out a plastic tub containing a coarse yellow powder for me to try. It tasted like dried, hard-baked bread. 'And the final and perhaps most important ingredient is iced water. As I've said, it's vital that you keep down the heat while making sausages. Iced water helps ensure this.'

I saw this in action when the mixing got under way. Sandy periodically stopped the machine to add more of the ingredients, along with iced water to keep everything cool. By now the meat was a lump of pink and ochre, dotted with specks of seasoning. It looked a little like mulched sesame-seed toast. Sandy hauled the tub back to the grinder and ran it through again. Now it emerged looking like tinned spaghetti – fat strands, pale and pink-flecked. 'You can see the mix is more homogeneous. The fat and lean are more integrated,' he said. 'It's ready for filling.'

Once again the tub was carried over to a heavy, silvery machine, this time a square metal tank with a hopper attached.

'After the double-mince, as the meat strands clump together, a lot of air is trapped between them,' Sandy told me. 'One of the things the filling machine does is take out some of that air. You need to get rid of as much as possible; otherwise the sausage will burst during cooking. Obviously people at home wouldn't have a machine so they'd have to work the mix – as you might a dough – to get the same effect.'

At this point the mix did indeed have the appearance of a sluggish, sticky dough, and Sandy kneaded it like a baker to show me what he meant.

I realised I could probably achieve something similar to the filling machine's air expulsion with the vac-packer at the Fat Duck: put the sausages in it, shut the lid and – *schlooop* – all the air would be drawn out. Nifty – a nice piece of insider's knowledge from Sandy that I definitely wanted to try out sometime, even if it was outside the scope of the domestic kitchen.

'It'll make a better end product,' he agreed. 'But perhaps we're getting too fussy … ?'

'No, no,' I contradicted. 'It's impossible to get too fussy. Not if it results in a better end product.'

And I stand by that. Sometimes people have suggested to me that life's too short for the kind of lengths to which I go to create a recipe. But if it results in something delicious, stimulating and surprising, if it turns a meal into an event, a piece of real pleasure, then surely it's worth it? (Julia Child put it another way: 'Non-cooks think it's silly to invest two hours' work in two minutes' enjoyment; but if cooking is evanescent, well, so is the ballet.')

Away from the soapbox and back at the filling machine I watched Sandy feed in the sausage meat. 'If you're doing this by hand,' he advised, 'you've got to get the right amount of meat in the casing. Too much and it'll burst. Too little and you get a flabby sausage – and you don't want that.'

Out of a nozzle at the side spooled an endless pale snake, like the mother of all Cumberland sausages, now sheathed in its casing and twisting into coils on the stainless-steel surface. For the benefit of the cameras, it was being done at quarter the usual speed, but there was still an anaconda's worth in seconds. At full throttle it must be an unnerving sight – like a scene from some venomous horror movie.

'Right,' said Sandy with a certain finality. I felt a lesson coming on. 'Basically we lay one part of the sausage over the other' – he lifted up one end of the snake and turned it back on itself in a loop – 'to roughly the size of sausage we want. Then press and roll with the fingers, using the weight of the sausage to help us. Twist up and through for the next sausage in the link. You've got to be careful not to burst the skin as you're doing it. I use the underhand method … ' He paused. 'Nothing is implied by that, of course.'

Sandy gyrated his hands with skill and assurance, and soon enough he had a bunch of linked sausages dangling from one hand. He reminded me of the magician at kids' parties who effortlessly twists balloons into poodles or aeroplanes. I knew what was coming next.

'Would you like to try?'

I'd never done this before and, as you might imagine, it's the kind of thing that looks easy in the hands of a master but actually turns out to be fiendishly complicated. Perhaps the hardest part was remembering which way to twist and feed the sausage through to get to the next on the link, especially when I already had several hanging from one hand. Sandy ended up calling out, 'That way; the other way', like a driving instructor. Eventually, however, by following his traffic directions, I managed to make a string of sausages that any dog would be proud to steal and run off down the street with, links flying behind him.

'Yeah, they're coming on. That's quite good,' was Sandy's opinion, so I guess the pupil passed.

THE FICKLE FINGER OF PHOSPHATE

There were so many variables involved in sausage-making that it was difficult to narrow down the options. In the development kitchen my team and I weighed up the merits of different casings, of hand-mincing versus machine-mincing, of fresh meat versus aged, of packing methods, of types and amounts of filler, of spicings, seasonings and flavourings. Each change to the recipe seemed to require a re-evaluation of all the other ingredients, as though this were the culinary equivalent of a Rubik's Cube.

Eventually, though, we'd got something that worked. It required a little tweaking, but it was taking shape. Then we hit a bigger problem, which eclipsed all the others we'd had before.

Phosphates.

In animals (including humans), adenosine triphosphate (ATP) is an essential part of the body's energy pack: among other things, it triggers the protein group actomysin to separate into the proteins actin and myosin. This is what allows muscles to flex and move.

After slaughter, ATP soon gets used up. The muscle proteins stay bound as actomysin and, because there's no ATP left to reverse the process, remain in that form (the stiffened-up condition called rigor mortis).

For butchers, actomysin is undesirable: unlike actin and myosin, it's difficult to dissolve it into the meat and it doesn't hold water well. It's not a good banger-binder. On the Continent they get round this by turning meat into sausages before rigor mortis sets in, but in Britain the slaughter set-up means this isn't possible. Instead, commercial producers add polyphosphates to the meat to cause the actomysin to revert to actin and myosin, which can then glue together the meat, fat and water.

However, I was reluctant to use polyphosphates for two reasons. First, because they're an E-number – E452 – and there are under-standable concerns about such food additives. For many people, the perfect sausage would have to be E-free. Second, polyphosphates are almost impossible to get hold of in Britain (we had to order them online from America). If I was going to create a recipe that people could prepare at home, I had to find a way of preparing a sausage without phosphates.

It was a worthwhile aim, but I came to appreciate how far we were falling short of the target when Chris prepared the current recipe with and without phosphates.

It was an unusually domestic scene for the development kitchen – the frying pan on the hob, the rich meaty aromas rising as two sausages steadily and stickily darkened – marred only by the fact that Chris, with his chef's asbestos fingers, was nudging the bangers round the pan with his hand rather than a spatula. He cut thick slices of each and placed them on separate plates for me to try.

In the first, the phosphates had done their job, integrating the meat and fat to give a lovely, juicy sausage. It had a nice dense texture and a full flavour – still a little too salty perhaps, even though we'd cut the salt content right back, but nonetheless this was the best so far, a really encouraging result after all the months of work.

And the phosphate-free sausage? The cameras zoomed in as I took a bite.

'Yeuch! That felt like half a gallon of fat flooding my mouth! The fat hasn't integrated with the meat at all.'

You could see it wasn't working. A sheen of fat filmed the cut surface of the sausage and, if you squeezed it, fat ran out on to the plate – and my hopes along with it. It seemed as though 'phate was against us.

This was doubly problematic because during testing I had come to realise that, for me at least, a proper banger had to have a bready note. We'd worked hard to add that to the sausage, eventually soaking heavily toasted bread in water to give a kind of stock that would then be incorporated in the mix. It worked spectacularly well – except for the fact that bread is far less effective than rusk at holding in moisture and fat, which simply compounded the problems we were having with phosphate. Each route we took seemed to lessen our chances of successfully binding our sausage.

SPUDS-I-LIKE 2

Sausages weren't the only thing offering complications. At MBM's Norfolk distribution centre, Tom Dixon and I had discussed some of the difficulties involved in roasting potatoes. Now we turned our attention to mash. My own experiments had convinced me that choosing the right variety for mashing was only one of many important considerations. Tom agreed.

'The characteristics of a particular variety will give you a guideline as to how it's going to behave in the pot. But dry-matter content's probably more relevant than variety. And how it's been handled, how it's been stored, how it's been managed and grown – all of these also affect what you get on the table.'

'So what happens after a potato is picked is just as influential as the make-up of a particular variety?'

'That's exactly right,' said Tom. 'As always, you have to be very careful about the temperature at which you store potatoes for mashing. You've got a little more leeway than you have with potatoes destined for roasting or chipping because you don't have to worry about fry colour. So instead of 7–8°C, we store potatoes for mashing at about 3°C, which is the best temperature for preventing sprouting and dehydration.'

'So, the million-dollar question is: what would you look for in a perfect potato for mashing?'

'I'd seek out a variety with about 19 per cent dry matter. You can go higher with chips and roast because the fried crust will help the potato keep its shape. But with mash a high dry matter means you run the risk of the potato disintegrating on you during cooking. At the same time, if you choose something with a lower dry-matter content, it's likely to end up bland: a potato with a high water content is going to give a more watery end result.'

'Well, I'd like to pick your brains, Tom. I'm going to try mashing a standard variety such as Maris Piper to set a standard for comparison. But I'd also like to try some new types, preferably exhibiting a wide range of dry-matter content so I can explore how best to manage it and get the most flavourful mash I can. Are there any you can recommend?'

He suggested some varieties that were entirely new to me. I felt excitement rising – I was like a scientist who has been given pieces of moon rock to experiment on – and looked forward to taking them back to my development kitchen.

MONSTER MASH

We'd cooked the potatoes for a long time at a low temperature, then cooled and re-simmered them for another hour before gently crushing them with a masher. Now generous dollops of each potato were laid out before us in eight white china bowls. Chris and I tried the results, looking for the one that best suited bangers.

You could tell from its appearance that Lady Olympia wasn't right: it looked 'wet', and that's just how it tasted. Lady Claire had the same problems – maybe not as wet as Olympia, but still pasty. Claire had a nice chunky texture, but both Chris and I agreed that we expected something drier and fluffier in a mash. We had high hopes for the next on the list, Yukon Gold.

Prospectors might have ended up disappointed during the Klondike gold rush, but with Yukon Gold we hit the jackpot. It had exactly the kind of light texture we were hoping for, and allied this to a fantastic earthy flavour.

Maris Piper got the silver, maintaining its reputation as a great all-rounder, but it just couldn't match Yukon Gold's airiness and lightness of structure.

Despite its name, Desiree had become particularly undesirable: the potato had failed to hold the butter, which now pooled, swamp-like, around the edges of the bowl. This happened only to the Desiree and suggested that something other than dry matter had an effect on mash (since Desiree's dry-matter proportion was almost identical to Yukon Gold's). Testing often throws up as many questions as it answers: although I'd found a great potato for my mash, at some point in the future I'd have to look further into the composition of the starch molecules in a variety of potatoes, and how this might affect their behaviour when cooked.

Lady Rosetta, meanwhile, demonstrated that there's a limit to how much dry matter you can put in a mash. It was visibly drier than any of the rest and far too chewy in the mouth. It was altogether the wrong potato. As were Melody and Juliette, but for different reasons. I'd included them as examples of potatoes with a dry-matter content lower than Tom's recommendation of 19 per cent, just in case they produced an interesting result. But in the end they both had the wrong texture – a silkiness that was perfect for a real French-style *pommes purée* but hardly right for mash.

It had proved harder than expected to get the right proportion of dry matter for a mash that was neither too wet nor too dry. So it was very satisfying to have one potato really stand out as the winner. We were going for Gold. It had the fluffiness and flavour that would provide the gutsy comfort food to complement our sausages.

Bangers & Mash Serves 4

Toasted-bread stock really turned a sausage into a banger, especially once I'd come up with the idea of smoking the back fat to get that chargrilled, campfire note. (I could have achieved a similar effect by putting the finished sausages on the barbecue, but the aggressive heat might have caused them to burst, losing all those precious juices.) By using pork leg I was able to boost juiciness because the muscle structure there is better at retaining moisture than other parts of the animal. And putting golden syrup in the mix added a colour and sweetness that balanced the spices really well, and helped develop those all-important browning flavours.

However, the key to sausage success is keeping the meat cold as you prepare it. If it warms up too much (the rapidly spinning food-processor blade soon heats up to 65°C/150°F – hot enough to begin cooking the meat!), the heat causes the fat to split, which wrecks emulsification (just as heating butter causes it to melt and split, losing the emulsion of fat and water). So work in batches, probing continually, and whenever it seems as though the meat is getting too warm, put it in the fridge or freezer to let it chill back down.

There can't be many things as stylish as serving up a batch of handmade sausages, but if you don't want to wrestle with hog casings and a stuffer, you can still prepare the sausage meat and use it in sausage rolls and pork pies, or form it into patties or skinless sausages (roll the meat in clingfilm and form into a tight sausage shape, then leave in the fridge to firm up). You don't even have to smoke the back fat: the sausages will still taste great, especially if fried in smoked oil. But it won't be the classic banger experience. I say get out the barbie and get hold of some casings – go the whole hog!

That campfire note also took the mash in a particular direction. A wood fire and a baked potato go together so well – there's something so right about them – that, in the end, nostalgia pushed science aside: these bangers had to have a mash with the flavours and fluffiness of a baked potato. So that's what you've got here.

Special equipment

Oak chips (approx. 500g), barbecue, charcoal, firelighters, safety or barbecue gloves, large tongs, food processor, digital probe, sausage stuffer, pressure cooker, stick blender and beaker (optional)

Timing

With practice, making sausage meat becomes straightforward – a matter of getting the ingredients to hand and gradually processing them together while keeping an eye on the temperature. And since sausages can be stored in the freezer for three months, there's a lot of freedom as to how far in advance they're prepared, leaving plenty of time on the day to cook the gravy. The mash, meanwhile, is simplicity itself: no prep, just put the potatoes in the oven and forget about them for an hour so.

For the sausages and the base of the gravy

(if you're not making gravy, halve the quantities)
1 x 800g loaf of medium-sliced white bread _ 500g pork back fat (a single piece rather than slices), rind removed _ 50g rusk _ 1 tsp ground black pepper (it's best to grind all these spices yourself, just before using) _ 1 tsp ground white pepper _ ½ tsp ground nutmeg _ 1 tsp ground mace _ ½ tsp ground ginger _ 20g (2 tbsp) golden syrup _ 1kg minced pork (preferably from the thigh), chilled _ 2 tsp table salt _ 2.5m of hog casings (32–45mm in diameter) _ groundnut oil

For the onion gravy

2 star anise _ 75ml light olive oil _ 6 large onions (about 1.2kg), finely sliced* _ 100–150g pork skin (it should be possible to obtain this from a good local butcher), chopped _ 250g pork leg or shoulder, roughly chopped _ 400g reserved sausage meat _ 3 fresh sage leaves _ sherry vinegar, to taste

* These onions are to be caramelised: the process can be sped up by removing water from the onions beforehand. Place them in a sieve over a bowl, toss with a tablespoon of salt and leave for 20 minutes.

For the mash

6 large Yukon Gold or Maris Piper potatoes (about 1.5kg) _
150ml whole milk (or to taste) _ 150g unsalted butter (or to taste) _
table salt and freshly ground black pepper

For the gelled butter

125g butter (I'd use Anchor for the full nostalgia trip) _ 60g water _
2g (approx. ½ tsp) powdered agar agar

MAKING AND COOKING THE SAUSAGES

1. Preheat the oven to 180°C/350°F/Gas 4. Leave the oak chips to soak in a bucket of water. Light the barbecue and leave for 20–30 minutes, until the coals are white flecked with glowing red spots.
2. Meanwhile, lay 16 slices of bread on baking sheets. Place them in the oven and leave for 30–40 minutes, until the bread is an even dark brown colour throughout. Break up the bread and put it into a large bowl. Fill the bowl with cold water and set aside for at least 1 hour.
3. Drain the oak chips and throw them on the barbecue. Once these begin to smoke, place the back fat in the centre of the grill and barbecue until it is blistered and charred on the outside and giving off that flame-cooked sausage smell. (The fat will catch fire: that's what reinforces the charred, smoked flavour. It's dramatic and needs to be handled with care. Wear safety gloves and use a large pair of tongs.)
4. Remove the fat from the barbecue, allow to cool and then chill in the fridge. Once chilled, cut it into small cubes. Blitz the cubes, in 2–3 batches, in a food processor until smooth and paste-like. (It will have an ashen grey appearance.) Scrape the fat into a bowl and set aside (not in the fridge) until required. Wash the food processor's blade and mixing bowl, ready for the next step.
5. Tip the rusk into the clean mixing bowl of the food processor and blitz until it is as fine as possible. Pass it through a fine sieve into a large measuring jug. (The rusk should now resemble fine flour.) Rinse the blade and bowl of the food processor and place them in the freezer to chill.
6. Pass the spices through a fine sieve into the measuring jug containing the rusk. Add the golden syrup. Drain the oven-baked bread

pieces into a colander set over a bowl, then squeeze the bread to extract as much water as possible. Pour 400ml of the toast-flavoured water into the jug containing the spice mix, stir and place in the fridge to chill.

7. Remove the food-processor bowl and blade from the freezer, along with the chilled minced pork. Put batches of the pork and salt in the food processor and blitz until smooth and paste-like. Blitz no more than 200g of meat at a time, to help prevent it overheating. Use a digital probe to check the temperature of the meat every 30 seconds or so, to make sure it doesn't exceed 10°C/50°F. If it is in danger of doing so, put the meat, bowl and blade in the freezer. Once all the pork is ready, put the meat, bowl and blade in the freezer once more.

8. Once the pork has chilled back down to near freezing, add the fat, the chilled spice mix and 1 slice of white bread. Blitz in the food processor until the bread has broken down and the mix is a smooth emulsion. (Again, this needs to be done in small batches to ensure the temperature of the mixture does not exceed 10°C/50°F.) Scrape this mix into a large bowl, cover and store in the fridge while preparing the hog casings.

9. Untangle the casings, put them in a bowl and soak in warm water for a few minutes. Flush the salt out of the interior by holding the casings up to the tap and letting warm water flow through. (The water usually collects in the form of a bubble at the top of the casing, which can then be eased down the length of the casing with finger and thumb.) Leave the casings to soak in a bowl of warm water for 15 minutes, or until soft and pliable. (If the casings aren't soaked enough, there is a risk of them bursting during stuffing.)

10. Set aside 400g of the sausage mix for the onion gravy. Scrape the rest into the barrel of the sausage stuffer, packing it as firmly as possible and knocking out air pockets as you go. Push the casing on to the nozzle of the stuffer so that it bunches up, concertina-style. Extrude a little of the sausage meat and tie a knot in the casing as close up to this meat as possible, leaving at least 10cm of casing dangling.

11. Feed the sausage meat into the casing, applying uniform pressure. (Be careful: too fast and the skin will rupture; too slow and air

pockets will form, causing the sausages to explode when cooked.) When finished, tie a knot in the other end of the casing.

12. To form the sausages into a chain, pinch and twist the stuffed casings at 12–15cm intervals. (Turn the first clockwise, the second anti-clockwise, and so on, to prevent them unravelling.) Store the sausages until you're ready to cook them. They will keep in the fridge for up to 3 days, and in the freezer for up to 3 months.

13. To cook the sausages, heat a large pan of water to 65°C/150°F. Add the sausages and poach for 20 minutes. (This gentle cooking helps keep in the meat's juices.) Lift the sausages from the water and pat dry with kitchen paper.

14. Put a splash of oil in a large frying pan, add the sausages and fry them until brown all over. (This needs a medium heat: if it's done too quickly, the sausages will split. Too slowly and the outside will overcook.) Remove the sausages from the pan. Serve with onion gravy and baked-potato mash.

MAKING THE ONION GRAVY

1. Place a small pressure cooker over a medium heat for 5 minutes. Crush the star anise and bag it up in a square of muslin. Add this to the pressure cooker, along with 45ml olive oil and the sliced onions. Cook for 20 minutes, or until the onions are soft and nicely browned, stirring occasionally.

2. Meanwhile, place a large, heavy-bottomed frying pan over a high heat for 10 minutes. Add the remaining oil and, when it starts smoking, the chopped pork skin, chopped pork and reserved sausage meat. Stir occasionally until browned all over. (To brown properly, all the meat has to be in contact with the surface of the pan. If need be, fry it in batches.)

3. Remove half the caramelised onions and set aside. Tip the browned meat into the pressure cooker containing the rest of the onions. Return the frying pan to a high heat and deglaze it by adding 100ml water and bringing it to the boil, then scraping the pan to collect the bits stuck to the bottom. When the liquid has reduced by half, pour it into the pressure cooker.

4. Add enough cold water to cover, attach the lid, bring up to a high pressure and cook for 45 minutes.

5. Remove the pressure cooker from the heat and let the pressure reduce slowly. Leave to cool, then take off the lid and strain the mixture into a clean pan. Discard the onions, meat and skin.

6. Tip the reserved caramelised onions into the pan. Place over a high heat and reduce the liquid by half. Remove from the heat. Rub the sage leaves between your palms, then add them to the pan. Taste the gravy and add a drop or two of sherry vinegar to cut through the richness.

MAKING THE MASH

1. Preheat the oven to 180°C/350°F/Gas 4. Place the potatoes in a baking tray and bake for 1–1½ hours, depending on their size.

2. Cut the potatoes in half and scoop the flesh into a bowl. Gently warm the milk, then pour on to the potatoes. Add the butter and mash with the potatoes until well combined. Season with salt and plenty of pepper. Serve with gelled butter.

MAKING THE GELLED BUTTER

1. Melt the butter and water in a small pan, then whisk until combined. Add the agar agar and boil for 1 minute, whisking continuously until the agar has dissolved. Pour through a fine sieve into a small container and leave to set in the freezer. (It needs to chill as fast as possible so that the emulsion doesn't split.) To serve, remove from the container, cut into cubes and dot over the mash.

Fish & Chips

'… fried fish and chips served by S. Gamgee.
You couldn't say no to that.'

J.R.R. Tolkien, *The Lord of the Rings: The Two Towers*

History

FISH

Confined as the limits of Field Lane are, it has its barber,
its coffee-shop, its beer-shop, and its fried fish warehouse.
Charles Dickens, *Oliver Twist*

For a meal that has virtually become Britain's national dish, fish and chips has a surprisingly short history – barely 150 years. And, despite its recent appearance, its birthplace is unidentifiable. Lancashire, London and Dundee have all put forward a claim. The combination of fresh fish and a working class hungry to consume makes it likely that a tradition developed in the northern ports. In the south, the alliance of fish and potato could well have been forged in the crucible of the East End of London, where the close confines of the tenements meant the fried-fish tradition of Jewish immigrants would have come into contact with the Irish immigrants' diet of potato. Food history is rarely neat and tidy: it's entirely possible that both claims are true.

What we do know is that fish and chips came out of a tradition of street food that was already growing in the nineteenth century: the hot-pie shops of Victorian England satisfied an increasing need for fast food on the go. Certainly fried fish was a feature of street life by 1837, when Dickens began publishing instalments of *Oliver Twist*, though it was then sold with a hunk of bread or a baked potato. It's not clear when divorce from the baked spud and the happy marriage of fish and the chipped potato took place, but it's a union that has prospered.

The rapid growth of industrialisation in Britain provided a market for quick and thrifty meals such as fish and chips. It also provided the means to expand that market. Three factors in particular furthered the dish's popularity: manufactured ice meant fishermen could travel further and catch more, preserving what they caught in ice in the hold; steam trawlers also greatly increased the range of fishing opportunity; and railways meant distribution could reach inland areas. Cod became commonplace, and so too did the fish and chip shop.

CHIPS WITH EVERYTHING

The main reason potatoes are up there among the top crops boils down to one thing: chips. The fast-food industry is in many ways the potato's saviour. Although potato consumption in parts of Europe has declined drastically over the last forty years (as we have switched to a more Mediterranean-type diet with an emphasis on pasta and rice, and gained access to more fruit and vegetables), American production has more than doubled, with most of it turned into crisps and frozen chips.

Although the potato has a long history, the story of chips – or fries – is comparatively short and obscure. Both the French and the Belgians say they invented them in the nineteenth century. Fries were certainly popular in both countries by the 1830s, and had reached Britain before the turn of the century. Like pizza, the chip's status as an international food is the result of the cultural shake-up of a world war, in this case the first rather than the second. American soldiers stationed in France (or Belgium) developed a taste for chips and took them back to the States on their return. For the chip, it was then a short skip to world domination.

The Quest for the Best

UNDERNEATH THE ARCHES

The railway arches off Black Prince Road in Lambeth have a Dickensian air about them. Most have been colonised by car-repair and body-part shops, where every surface is coated in a thick patina of sticky, sooty blackness and the tart tang of engine oil hangs heavy in the air. The street seems almost deserted, and dog-legs abruptly into a dark tunnel that stretches off under the tracks.

What was I doing, walking around here at six in the morning?

You might think it all seems a bit fishy – and you'd be right. For somewhere hereabouts, unlikely as it might seem amid the grime and garage grease, are the premises of James Knight of Mayfair, fishmongers by appointment to Her Majesty the Queen. I hurried past the gloomy tunnel and came upon a courtyard of scrubbed yellow brickwork, a sharp contrast to the surrounding premises. I could see men and women in heavy blue plastic aprons carrying polystyrene cartons of fish and sacks of crushed ice. Memories of bad puns on the signs of a thousand chippies filled my mind. *This must be the plaice*, I thought.

I was here to buy some fish from David Blagden, a big cheery man with a nice turn of phrase – just what you'd want in a fishmonger. He has had many years' experience – first in his own shop on Marylebone High Street and now with James Knight – and he seemed like the ideal person to advise me on how to finesse my fish dish. I had a lot of questions that needed answers.

Cod, haddock and plaice have long been the most popular options for a fish and chip supper. But are they the best? I didn't know whether these three had become the chippie's choice because they were – at least at one time – plentiful, local and cheap, or because they were indeed the top fish for the job. Their mild flavour certainly goes well with frying, and cod and haddock also have firm, large-flaked flesh that seems the perfect contrast to a crunchy textured batter, but I still wondered whether other fish might have these qualities and be able to add something extra to the experience. Might not a fish with a pleasant texture and a fuller flavour produce a more complex and delicious dinner? My own candidate for this role was turbot, followed by John Dory and brill. I wanted to see what David thought of these, and whether he could suggest any other interesting alternatives.

He led me through a curtain of heavy plastic strips into a high arched room: the Goods Out Fridge. Large sinks with hose-taps lined the walls, and a worker was bent over each one of these, briskly gutting and cleaning the deliveries. Down the centre ran a long stainless-steel table piled high with polystyrene boxes; a slew of monkfish tails filled one of them, another was stamped *Wild pacific halibut*. David hoisted two cartons on to a worktop and took me through their contents.

We'd decided I would take a cod away with me as the benchmark fish. David also suggested haddock, plaice, lemon sole, red mullet and Dover sole. 'I'm a haddock man myself,' he said, 'but all of these might give you the combination of texture and flavour you're looking for.' He explained that, as with meat, the cut you choose is important. 'Plaice, brill, turbot and sole are flat fish, perfectly adapted to feeding on the bottom of the sea. Their belly keeps its creamy white colour, but the back darkens so that, from above, predators can't distinguish it from the ocean floor. It's the back that does all the work – fighting the fish's natural buoyancy to keep it on the bottom – and so the back has most of the muscle. For my money, that makes for a fleshier, tastier fillet.'

The question of muscle appeared to be crucial to the flavour, whether you chose a flat fish, a flaky fish like cod or haddock, or a round fish like red mullet or John Dory. David advised me to use male fish, if possible: they develop more muscle while swimming around trying to impress females, and they don't waste energy on reproduction. And what did he think of my turbot-charged option? 'Ah, turbot. Well, if salmon is the king of fish, then turbot is the queen. It's very expensive, which means it's unlikely to be in danger of overfishing. And it's likely to stay expensive because they've had little success with farming it.' He showed me an example of farmed turbot. The skin was unpleasantly waxy and the flesh drumskin taut. 'Turbot's undoubedly tasty, but I wonder whether it'd be too gelatinous when deep-fried. I prefer my fish a little drier.'

David went on to tell me how much geography affects the look and taste of a fish. 'Most of the lemon sole we sell come from Scotland, but I'd say those from the south coast are better. Lemon sole prefer warmer water. And the southern ones look completely different. Instead of a green colour, they're more pale caramel.'

If I wanted the best, he explained, I needed to consider where exactly in the world I got my fish from. 'Brill like the sandy warm waters of the southwest coast. Turbot like a similar environment, but the best generally come from the south coast. Plaice also like a sandy situation, but prefer the colder water around Denmark. Dover sole like the fast flow and purity of the waters around Fastnet, while cod and haddock like it cold. Iceland is a good source (and currently sustainable). For red mullet, on the other hand, it's got to be the Gulf Stream.' The list of compass points was becoming bewilderingly diverse. I was glad to hear that John Dory is equally tasty wherever it's fished.

'Thanks,' I said. 'You've given me a lot to think about. I'll have to mullet over.'

David's expression suggested he might have heard that joke before.

In the end, he loaded me up with six fish: cod, plaice, Dover sole, John Dory, turbot and brill. And I drove back to Bray to batter them.

Peking duck served, in accordance with tradition, in three courses

Blue-cheese-infused butter

Steak with mushroom ketchup

Spaghetti bolognese

Chilli con carne and corn muffin

Bangers and mash

Fish and chips

Fish pie, accompanied by the sounds of the sea

Pizza Margherita

Risotto with saffron butter
and pandanus crème fraîche

Mushroom velouté, Horlicks and
coffee salt cubes, toasted rice tuiles

Kirsch mist

Black Forest gateau

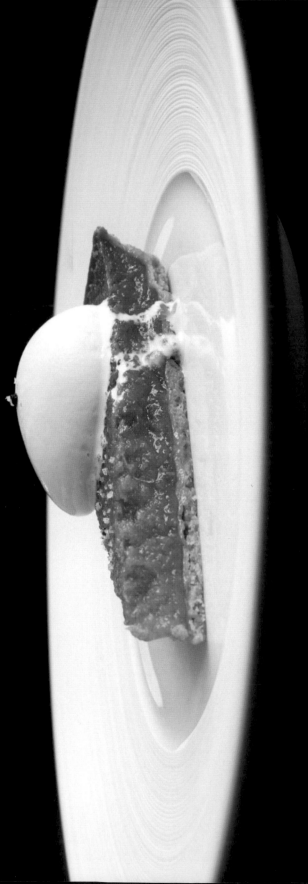

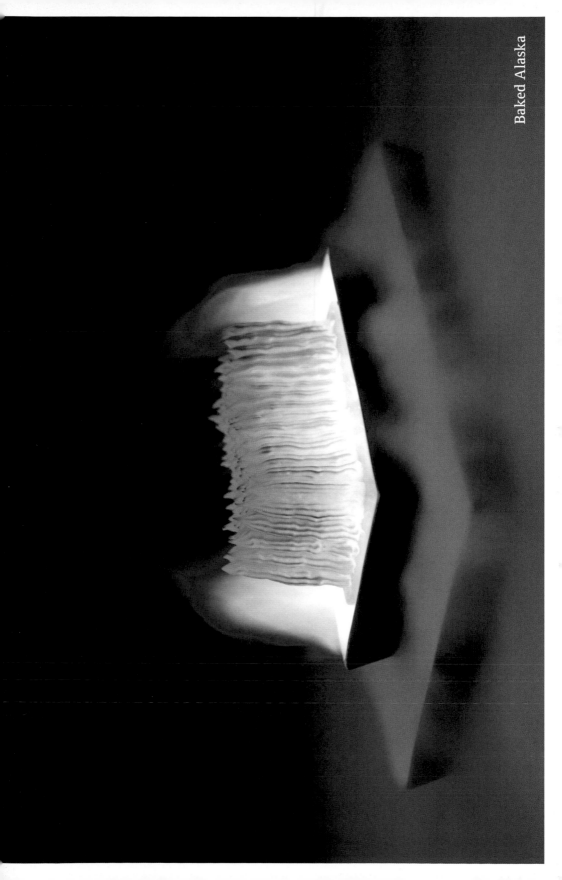

* Overfishing

Fish are one of our most ancient food sources. Geologists have found huge piles of oyster and mussel shells – evidence of fish feasts – dating back 300,000 years. This lengthy and relentless plundering of the oceans' abundance has come at a cost. Many once-common fish are now rare. Others suffer a kind of boom–bust economy, appearing on market stalls only to vanish suddenly as stocks deplete. The productivity of our seas and rivers is all but exhausted, and if we don't adopt a responsible attitude and change how we eat, we're going to run out of fish. It's as simple as that. The consequences are unthinkable: it would certainly be a disaster for our diet and health, and a catastrophe for the world's eco-system and biodiversity.

We're not powerless to prevent this. First, check accreditation. The Marine Stewardship Council (msc.org) is an independent charity that inspects fisheries and certifies those that comply with sustainable fishing practices. Find out if what you buy is from MSC-approved sources. And if the fish is farmed rather than caught, make sure it's organic and, preferably, Soil Association-accredited. (Fish farms exact their own damage on the environment, so it's important that these too are run in a responsible manner.)

Second, find a good local fishmonger and make friends with him. He should be able to tell you which fish to choose and where they come from. His advice will, in any case, be invaluable. You'll learn a lot about fish that will be useful in the kitchen, and gain a better understanding of the ecological concerns involved. It's certainly worth finding out which fish are abundant in British waters and trying them out as an alternative to fish that have been air-freighted thousands of miles.

There are other sources of information on what to fry and what not to buy. The Marine Conservation Society's 'Good Fish Guide' is a great starting point (obtainable from their online shop at mcsuk.org), as is the website fishonline.org, which has a search facility so that you can check instantly whether the fish you're after is on the endangered list.

FRYING TONIGHT!

That fish is a riddle!
It's broke in the middle,
A turbot! a fiddle!
It's only a brill!
Thomas Hood

I deep-fried my top six fish one at a time at 190°C/375°F. The perfect batter would have to wait until I'd found the perfect fish (as the size of that fish would determine how long it would take to cook, and I'd have to prepare a batter that suited that timescale), so for the purposes of testing, I used a fairly standard beer and flour mix. I kept the skin on the fillets because I wanted to explore whether, contrary to what *Star Wars* tells us, the dark side really *is* better.

Even while the fillets rested on plain white plates, waiting their turn in the fryer, great variety could be seen, especially in the dark skin – the wide-weaved pattern of the brill's skin resembled a snake's, whereas the turbot was almost crocodile-like: seaweed-green and knobbled. Plaice and Dover sole were finer patterned, as though cross-hatched. I wondered how far this variety would be reflected in the tasting.

To make this test objective, I'd asked Ashley and Chris to try the fish with me. First up was Dover sole. It had a good taste and texture, but what was most noticeable was the difference between the light and dark sides of the fish. And it was the latter that was disappointing: it was denser and drier. In plaice too this turned out to be the case. (These were the most exaggerated examples. For the rest there seemed to be little difference between light and dark. I made a note to investigate this some time in the future: it would be interesting to discover what it was about Dover sole and plaice that caused the variation.) And the flavour of plaice was altogether too delicate – less tasty than the sole. Neither was the right fish.

John Dory was much more promising – an altogether heftier chunk with a dense texture and a distinctive rich flavour. But, just as in our mammoth sausage-testing we had tasted superb examples that were nonetheless too far from the ideal of the British banger, so here John

Dory was perhaps too dense in texture and thus too far from what we expect to find inside our batter. JD has a lovely flavour, but it felt all wrong in the mouth. Perhaps we really did need a fish with big flakes of flesh.

As if to bear this out, the turbot was terrific. The combination of large flakes, moist, succulent flesh and good flavour instantly made it the front-runner. Texture did indeed seem to be the key, for although brill also had a wonderful flavour, its smaller flakes made it less attractive overall. So we had a clear winner – unless the chippie's choice could come up with something special.

Our final fillet was a block of cod so encrusted in batter that it looked like a ship salvaged from the ocean floor. (Frying oil improves with use; coming last, cod probably had the advantage of the best batter.) It had good texture, and a good flavour, though the turbot's was better. The cod was moist too, but its juices were far thinner than those of the turbot. Despite David Blagden's fears about it being too gelatinous, the gelatin* in the turbot seemed to be the X factor that worked in its favour, thickening up the fish's juices and really adding to its succulence and flavour. This was clearly going to be an important consideration for my recipe: how to make sure the gelatin didn't leak out during cooking. The batter would help lock it in, of course, but perhaps there were other things I could do to reinforce that.

We fried another piece of turbot to make sure we hadn't somehow got a freak fillet. It was still delicious. We had found our fish. Now all we had to do was marry it to a batter worthy of it, and a plateful of lovely crunchy chips.

---

* Gelatin is a protein. When three of these proteins are twisted into a helix, they form another protein, collagen, which coats bundles of muscle fibres and is a key component of skin and of the sinews that connect muscles to bones.

Meat collagen is tough because it contains a lot of amino acids that bolster its structure, and it gets reinforced with age. Fish collagen contains fewer such amino acids and, because it provides part of the fish's energy store, is continually built up and broken down. Thus even a low temperature quickly denatures the collagen present in fish muscle-tissue, turning it back into strands of juicy gelatin, which contribute to a fish's moistness. That's why fish with little collagen, such as trout or bass, often seem drier when cooked than those with more, such as shark or halibut.

SPUDS-I-LIKE 3

Recipes are not set in stone. Occasionally, at home, you get lucky and find a recipe that captures exactly what you had in mind. More often than not, though, a good recipe evolves through trial and error, the product of ideas pinched from several sources and combined to achieve the right effect.

Unsurprisingly, professional cooking follows the same process. I'd researched hundreds of varieties of potato and forced them through all kinds of experimentation in order to create a great chip. At one point I was even pinpricking chips between stages in the frying, as though acupuncturing them into shape (I was trying to get rid of the excess moisture that would make the crust soggy). The result had garnered many column inches in the papers – sometimes satirising the lengthiness of the process, sometimes focusing on the price, but more often declaring how tasty they were. But a good recipe doesn't stand still either: that's part of the fascination of cooking. I was forever changing the recipe and looking for ways to make it even better. My trip to MBM offered a valuable opportunity to talk about chips and exchange ideas.

It's hard to convey the overwhelming impression that the storage chambers at MBM make when you first encounter them. When I was a kid and heard talk of EU wine lakes and butter mountains, I imagined them literally: a huge pool of red in some spacious part of France perhaps, or a vast peak made up of brick-shaped butter pats. Here these childhood misunderstandings seemed suddenly to be made real. In the hangar I was confronted with a 10-foot-high surfers' wave of potatoes. I clambered up a metal ladder on to a gantry and saw that it extended back 60 feet or so, like some phenomenal groundswell. Against this strange backdrop, Claire Harrison and I discussed which potato makes the perfect chip.

'I'm looking for a potato that, when fried, will be light and fluffy on the inside, with a wonderful glass-like crunch to it. It needs to break up a little on cooking too so that those rough edges will absorb some fat.'

'Of course, you all know about Maris Piper,' said Claire, 'but have you tried Lady Rosetta? It's used by a lot of commercial chip companies because it's got the high dry-matter content that's the key to good flavour and texture.'

'I want to try whatever potato you've got that has the highest dry matter of all.'

'Yes, it'll be fascinating to find out at exactly what point dry matter stops improving a chip. Certainly you'll want to avoid waxy potatoes with low dry matter. They fry too dark and the inside is almost wet. It sticks to your tongue, like eating wallpaper paste … not that I've ever tried it,' Claire added. 'But you also need to consider how well your chipping potatoes are stored; if they're kept badly, they'll be ruined. They need to be stored at the same temperature as those for roasting, 7–9°C, and for the same reason: you want to avoid the starch turning to sugar and giving the potato a dark fry-colour.'

'So, in addition to Lady Rosetta, what would make your top three?'

'Daisy will give a crisp outside and a lovely flavour – very different from Maris Piper. And I'd go for Pentland Dell, which is a lovely potato. Are there any others you want to try, Heston?'

Greedily, I seized my chance. 'I'd like some Arran Victory, Bruise and Yukon Gold. I'd like to take a look at another lady – Lady Claire. And I'd also like some Russet Burbank, since that's popular with the American fast-food industry.'

'With the Russet, you can take your pick,' said Claire. 'That's what you're standing on.'

WHEN THE CHIPS ARE DOWN

Like a gambler finishing a spree at Vegas, I was ready to tally the chips. My haul from MBM looked like this:

	% dry matter
Russet Burbank	22.3
Daisy	21.1
Pentland Dell	21.2
Maris Piper	21.9
Lady Rosetta	23.4
Yukon Gold	20.3
Lady Claire	21.8
Bruise	24.7
Arran Victory	21.8

Each was cut into chunky rectangles, like miniature two-by-four planks, then cooked by the method I'd developed: simmered until barely holding their shape (a tricky business this, requiring constant vigilance as the transition from softened strip to potato soup can be surprisingly swift), then dried and fried twice at different temperatures. This was how chips were prepared at the Hind's Head, using Maris Pipers. It might seem laborious, but the end result was delicious. I was very keen to see how my new potatoes would respond to the process.

First out of the pot was Russet Burbank. I'd been curious about this potato for a while because it's so ubiquitous in the States and so difficult to get over here. I had high hopes for it, but they didn't pay off: it was tough-crusted, slightly leathery. Not at all what I was after.

Daisy and Pentland Dell also went in the discard pile: they both had a crust and centre that was OK, but that was all you could really say about them.

Maris Piper, of course, turned out to be a much better bet: it had a far more delicate crust, which is one of the key attributes I look for in a chip. This was the one to beat. And neither Lady Rosetta nor Yukon could raise the stakes. With its slightly dry, tough crust, Lady R resembled Russet Burbank. Yukon Gold looked fabulous on the outside – living up to its name by presenting a lovely golden colour – but soon slackened to sogginess.

And Lady Claire didn't fare much better. Dense and chewy on the outside, waxy-looking inside, it too dropped out. Only two potatoes were left to trump Maris Piper. I was gambling on Bruise – with its extra-high dry matter – scoring big-time, but it didn't come up with the goods. The skin was way too tough.

Arran Victory, on the other hand, lived up to its name as much as Yukon Gold had – a clear winner. It had the perfect balance of flavour and texture: the glass-like exterior crunching apart readily, the interior soft and delicately fluffy. It's the contrast of the two that makes a great chip – the mix of two very different textures giving the mouth a sublime surprise – and Arran Victory really delivered that.

It was exciting to find a potato that outplayed Maris Piper. But equally exciting to learn something about the limits of dry matter: all the high-percentage potatoes (Russet Burbank, Lady Rosetta and Bruise) had turned out too tough, and it seemed that as little as 0.5 per cent could make a huge difference to the end result. It was an area that clearly deserved more exploration in the long term.

FRYER TUCK

These programmes had thrown up some odd combinations. In a strip club I'd had one of the best steaks I'd ever eaten, and I was expecting to put French or Italian chocolate on a very German dessert. Now I was visiting a fish and chip shop in New York, of all places.

In part this was – as the mountaineer George Mallory replied when asked why he wanted to climb Mount Everest – because it was there: the TV team and I were in New York researching steak and it seemed too good an opportunity to miss. In part too it offered insights into the roles memory and nostalgia play in food. The chippie – A Salt and Battery – is part of a little enclave of British shops on the edge of Greenwich Village, a kind of expatriate paradise where you can indulge in a romanticised celebration of British culture. At Tea & Sympathy you can pig out on roast beef and Yorkshire pudding or scones with clotted cream before visiting Carry On Tea & Sympathy to buy Weetabix, tea cosies and, of course, *Carry On* DVDs. As I arrived, a stream of kids left the shop clutching brown paper bags filled with butterscotch and sherbet lemons. Parked in front of the store was a pillar-box red Mini Cooper with a Union Jack painted on the roof, as though I'd stumbled on to the set for the next *Austin Powers* movie. (It belonged to Nicky, of course, the owner of all three stores. How else would an expatriate Anglophile get around town?)

A Salt and Battery was almost too perfect: it was as though a magazine stylist had isolated all the elements that give a chippie its character and set about faithfully reproducing them for a shoot. Everything was gratifyingly familiar, everything triggered off fond memories, but you'd never find all of these features in one place in Britain. It was uncanny. The steel and glass partitions where the fish were kept warm were disobligingly high, just as I remembered as a child, when I'd have to stand on tiptoe to see the fabulously crusty, golden-brown battered fish. Above these was a row of available drinks:

R. White's Lemonade, bitter shandy, Irn-Bru, Newcastle Brown Ale and Dandelion & Burdock. (D&B was proving a disappointment to one American customer, who suggested it was one export we could take back.) In suitably haphazard lettering the menu board offered cod, mushy peas, steak and kidney pie and even deep-fried Mars bars. It was all there, right down to the terrible puns that a good chippie revels in. You could join the Frequent Fryers' Club (ten meals and you got the eleventh free) or show your appreciation for the service in a jar on the counter marked 'Fish 'n' Tips'.

Of course, this could all be a cynical cash-in, a bit of marketing genius to mask an inferior product. After all, the shop has a captive audience of hungry Brits. But I discovered that fryer Matt's attention to detail matched his surroundings. He was as dedicated to his craft as any other artisan I had met on my travels, and had encountered difficulties just as great. He showed, once again, the lengths you have to go to to achieve perfection.

Matt was tall and skinny, and his head was as close-shaven as mine. I could imagine that New Yorkers had trouble deciphering his northern accent. 'I come from a family of fryers,' he told me. 'My mum and dad have a fish and chip shop in Accrington. But here in America things are different. For a start, potatoes are a problem. I can't get hold of Maris Pipers and have to use Russet Burbanks, which behave differently during cooking. And, unlike Britain, America has only one potato harvest a year, in September. This means that the potatoes I'm cooking the following August are fairly old and tend to scorch because some of the starch has broken down. That said, a lot of Americans seem to like their chips really well done – what I'd call burnt. So I guess they've got used to it.'

It was another reminder of how impossible it is to pin down perfection. For me a scorched chip was an inedible one, yet others were clearly devotees. One man's meat really is another man's poison. After all, there are even people who don't like Dandelion & Burdock.

Matt had had problems with oil too. 'I blend my own, using mainly corn oil, but it's taken a long time to get it right. I had to get used to the different starch content in the potatoes here and find a mix that suited it. Plus a lot of our business comes from deliveries, so I needed an oil that didn't harden the chips as it cooled.'

Some of Matt's difficulties arose from the fact that no market for fish and chips existed on the east coast: A Salt and Battery was pretty much the first and had to build up its custom. 'Sourcing the ingredients was a nightmare – probably the hardest part of the whole business. As you might expect, I couldn't easily buy mushy peas or Cumberland sausages. And as for pickled onions … I had to ring up my grandma for a pickling recipe.'

Gradually the determination has paid off. The chippie is *Zagat*-rated and won 'Best Takeout' in the latest AOL CityGuide. 'At first all our customers were expats, but now about half our customers are Americans,' Matt told me.

'Don't they expect fries rather than chips with their fish?' I wondered.

He grinned. 'If someone comes in and asks, "Can we get French fries with that?" we tell them, "Here we don't use the F word – only the C word."'

A simple but invaluable part of the multisensory chef's arsenal – an atomiser.

Fish & Chips **Serves 4**

No matter how good your fish, it can be ruined by bad batter. Batter has to insulate the fish from the high heat of the fryer, and also turn a crunchy crusty brown in the time it takes for the fish to cook, so for this recipe it was vital to develop a batter that suited the thickness of an average turbot fillet.

A water-based batter takes a long time to go brown because you have to make all the water evaporate before it will cook, and that's a slow process (think how long it takes to boil a pan dry). Vodka, on the other hand, is much more volatile, so it disappears much more quickly. And it has the added benefit of not developing the flour's gluten the way water does, which means you get a crisper crust. Lager and the soda siphon enhance the crispness and crunchiness by introducing lots of bubbles to the batter and giving it a marvellous lightness.

Good chips also depend on the removal of liquid. Allowing the chips to cool right down between each stage of cooking gets rid of much of the moisture that would otherwise escape from the chip as steam during frying, causing a soggy exterior. Instead, you'll have a crisp crust and a fluffy centre – the perfect chip, especially if you use an atomiser to spray it with the juice from a jar of pickled onions. The smell will be a fantastic nostalgia trigger, conjuring up memories of your favourite fish and chip shop and tasty fried suppers.

Special equipment
Soda siphon + CO_2 charges, digital probe, deep-fat fryer, atomiser (optional)

Timing
Making the batter is easy, but it needs to chill for half an hour in the fridge, after which speed is the name of the game in order to keep the bubbles in the batter – a matter of a few minutes' frying. Cooking the chips is a three-stage process; it's not complicated but it takes a little longer because the chips have to cool down before and after the first

frying. Preparing the chips to this point and then leaving them over-night in the fridge makes a fish and chip supper a very quick and simple affair.

For the batter and fish
200g plain flour _ 200g white rice flour, plus extra for dusting _ 1 tsp baking powder _ 1 tbsp honey _ 300ml vodka _ 300ml lager (Kronenbourg 1664 works well) _ 2–3 litres groundnut oil _ 4 large turbot fillets, 2–3cm thick (ideally, get 1 whole turbot weighing 2.5kg and either fillet it yourself, or get the fishmonger to do it) _ table salt and freshly ground black pepper

For the chips
1.2kg Arran Victory or Maris Piper potatoes _ 2–3 litres groundnut oil _ table salt and sea salt

To serve
1 jar of onions pickled in malt or white wine vinegar (whichever is the more evocative)

PREPARING THE BATTER AND FRYING THE FISH
1. Tip the plain flour, rice flour and baking powder into a bowl. Put the honey and vodka into a jug, stir and then add to the flour to create a batter mix. Open the lager and stir it into the batter until just com-bined. It doesn't matter if the consistency is a little lumpy. The most important thing is to open the lager just before stirring and transfer-ring the batter to the siphon, to retain as many bubbles as possible.
2. Transfer the batter to a jug, then pour it into a soda siphon. Charge the siphon with three CO_2 charges and put it in the fridge for a minimum of 30 minutes to chill.
3. In a large pan or casserole, put enough groundnut oil to cover the fish. Heat it to 220°C/425°F, using a digital probe to check the temp-erature. (It's best not to use a deep-fat fryer here as the temperature fluctuates too much and has trouble reaching 220°C/425°F.)
4. Rinse the turbot fillets and dry them with kitchen paper. Season well, then dust with rice flour. (This ensures the batter sticks to the fillets.) Shake off any extra flour.

Using a soda siphon produces a batter that has an amazing lightness, crispness and crunchiness.

5. Remove the siphon from the fridge. Shake it vigorously, then squirt enough batter into a medium-sized bowl to cover a fillet. (Don't squirt out too much: the batter begins to lose its bubbles as soon as it leaves the siphon.) Dip the fillet into the foamy batter. When it is completely coated, lower the fillet into the hot oil.*

6. As the fish fries, drizzle a little extra batter over it, to give a lovely crusty exterior. When it has turned a light golden brown (which will take about 1–2 minutes), turn the fillet over and drizzle more batter on top.

7. Let the fish cook for another minute or so, until it has coloured to a deeper golden brown, then remove it from the oil. Use a digital thermometer to check it is cooked: insert the probe into the thickest part of the fish. Once it reads 40°C/105°F set aside the fillet so that the residual heat will cook it to a temperature of 45°C/113°F.

8. Repeat the above process with the remaining fillets.

MAKING THE CHIPS

1. Wash and peel the potatoes, then cut them into chips about 1.5cm thick. (Don't worry too much about making them all the same size: the variation will give a greater range of textures.) As soon as the chips are cut, place them in a bowl under cold running water for 2–3 minutes to rinse off some of the starch, then drain.

2. Bring a large pan or casserole of salted water to the boil (10g salt per litre of water), add the chips, bring back to the boil, then simmer until the chips have almost broken up (it's the fissures that form as the potato breaks up that trap the fat, creating a crunchy crust). It is important to make sure the simmer is gentle so that the potatoes don't start to full apart before they have cooked through.

3. Using a slotted spoon, carefully lift the potatoes out of the water and place on a cake rack. Leave to cool, then put in the fridge until cold. (The dry air of the fridge makes a good environment in which to remove excess moisture from the chips via evaporation.)

4. Pour enough groundnut oil to cover the chips in a deep-fat fryer and heat it to 130°C/250°F. Plunge in the chips and allow them

---

* To avoid hot oil splashes as the fillet goes in, hold it by the narrower, tail end and lower it head first into the pan and away from your body so that the tail is the last part to reach the oil and points towards the outer edge of the pan.

to cook until they take on a dry appearance and have become slightly coloured.

5. Remove the chips and drain off the excess fat. Place them on a cake rack and allow to cool, then return to the fridge until cold.

6. Reheat the groundnut oil to 190°C/375°F. Plunge in the chips and cook until golden brown. This may take 8–10 minutes.

7. Drain the chips, season well with a mixture of table salt and sea salt, and pile by the fish fillets. Decant the pickling juice from the jar of pickled onions into the atomiser, and squirt it around the room or on the fish and chips.

Fish Pie

'What'll you have?'
'Fish pie,' said she, with a glance at the menu.
'Fish pie! Fancy coming for fish pie to Simpson's.
It's not a bit the thing to go for here.'

E.M. Forster, *Howards End*

History

It's difficult now to visualise the immense scale and effect of the Catholic Church's one-time insistence on meatless days (it originated in a view that red meat encouraged lechery and should therefore be eaten sparingly, coupled with the belief that personal privation was good for the soul). A passage from a fifteenth-century schoolbook puts it bluntly: 'Thou will not believe how weary I am of fish, and how much I desire that flesh were come in again, for I have ate none other than salt fish this Lent, and it hath engendered so much phlegm within me that it stoppeth my pipes that I can neither speak nor breathe.'

Fasting days in which 'the meat of quadrupeds' could not be consumed were firmly in place before the Norman invasion, and took up two-thirds of the calendar. They continued after the Reformation (1529–33) had swept away many other practices (though this continuation probably owed as much to government's need to preserve the country's maritime industry as to any religious conviction). Even in 1563 the penalty for non-observance was £3 or three months' imprisonment, unless you had obtained a special licence to eat meat; and it was still legally possible for an Englishman to be hanged for eating meat on a Friday, the Christian day of abstinence.

Perhaps that's why, despite being an island nation in which no one is more than 70 miles from the coast, we have such a slim tradition of fish cookery, and much of our wonderful produce is sold elsewhere: we became weary of fish and it has taken time to recover from that. In the past, however, one positive result of the fast-day strictures was that they encouraged great culinary ingenuity. If we had to eat fish for half the year, it needed to be palatable.

Originally, this enforced fish cookery took its cue from the ingredient it was designed to replace, resulting in a number of fishy stews and baked pies. In the twelfth century the Abbot of Cirencester, Alexander Neckam, advised boiling fish in a mixture of wine and water, and was already recommending pairing fish with some form of green sauce containing herbs such as parsley, sage, thyme and mint.

Fish was also added to the spicy soup (or pottage) that was a staple part of the Anglo-Norman diet, and gradually, of course, this evolved to produce pottage that specifically suited fish, such as 'balloc' or 'ballourgly' broth, in which pike and eels were cooked in wine and water that were strained off, spiced and then poured over the fish as a sauce.

Fish pies were eaten both hot and cold. Before the introduction and acceptance of the potato in Britain (a very gradual process from the late 1500s to the 1940s) the topping would generally be a pastry shell, used either as a means of insulation during cooking (in the same way that batter protects fish) and then discarded, or as a form of preservation: covering the cooled pie's crust with clarified butter formed an effective seal once it set, preventing spoilage through oxidation.

This protective layer of pastry also went through evolutions – first it became a richer, shorter pastry that could form part of the dish itself, and then it was simplified to a topping of breadcrumbs. Replacing this with potato was a logical next step: it was more substantial than breadcrumbs, simpler to prepare than pastry, and plentiful and cheap. It has been suggested that the Scots first did it, using potato to balance the flavour of the salted and smoked fish that were the mainstay of their pie.

As with any dish created by working people for whom time, money and choice were in short supply, fish pie adapted to the ingredients at hand. In the past, London versions often contained eels from the Thames. Cornish stargazy pie has a pastry crust through which pilchards or herrings poke their heads, as though to make a last-gasp escape. Although many recipes will claim to be a 'traditional' fish pie, as though the ingredients were fixed, this is misleading because part of the dish's virtue is its versatility. There is no single, definitive recipe. Many very different versions of fish pie have developed over time, each one a reflection of its region's coastal produce.

The Quest for the Best

PRAWN STAR

Nephrops norvegicus, aka Norway lobster, scampi, langoustine or Dublin Bay prawn, is an unlikely saviour of the Scottish fishing industry. Bigger than the common prawn, pink even before cooking, and wielding a pair of vicious claws, it looks like the result of some monstrous cross-breeding experiment – a fugitive from the waters around Dr Moreau's island.

Nonetheless, as stocks of haddock, whiting and sole have depleted catastrophically in Scotland, langoustine have thrived, partly because they now have fewer predators, and partly because the muddy Scottish sea-floor, with its clay-and-silt sediment, provides the perfect habitat for their burrows. The population is estimated at 10 billion and has become big business, providing an annual catch worth £200 million.

Bizarrely, most of that catch isn't destined for British tables, but goes instead to France, Italy, Portugal and Spain in water-filled Vivier trucks. I can't understand why this superb crustacean is so under-valued in the UK. At the Fat Duck we serve several dishes containing langoustine: lasagne of langoustine with truffles and pig's trotter, for example; and the garnish for our turbot dish is a mushroom velouté with a royale of mushrooms and langoustine. The heads and tails help make a langoustine cream to accompany quail jelly.

Langoustine have a fantastic sweetness, and because they contain compounds called glutamates, they also pack a punch of umami: the brothy, meaty taste that can be found in tomatoes, Parmesan, soy sauce and ketchup. My big problem with fish pie is that the fish is usually overcooked, and it often turns out to be disappointingly bland. I was certain that langoustine would bring to the dish a much-needed extra flavour dimension. And maybe I could also do my bit to encourage home consumption of the neglected *Nephrops*.

First, though, I wanted to make sure the seafood in my pie was sustainable. It's easy to forget the dangers of overfishing when faced with the langoustine's spectacular abundance, but stocks are already low around the coasts of Spain and Portugal. Fishing needs to be managed carefully if we are to avoid adding langoustine to the long list of endangered species, which is why I found myself on a trawler at dawn, chugging towards the mouth of the Firth of Clyde.

At first glance, it seemed like any other fishing boat, with men in blue overalls paying out metre after metre of green nylon net. Below decks, however, was a bank of keyboards and computer screens. It looked more like a university department than a seagoing vessel – mainly because that's what it was. The boat belonged to Glasgow University, which is conducting a six-year study into the crustacean's behaviour and habitat in conjunction with Britain's biggest seafood supplier, Young's.

'This is what we call the dry lab,' explained Professor Douglas Neil. 'There are cameras beneath the boat recording what's happening and relaying it to us up here. You need a trained eye to spot them, but … there's a *Nephrops* entrance … there's another … '

He wasn't kidding about the trained eye. It was difficult to make out more than shadows on the murky blue screen.

'This form of monitoring has become the accepted method of estimating the population size. Look – there's one swimming. They do it by flicking their tale like a jack-knife. The muscle that we eat is their method of propulsion.'

'I know what you mean. At the Fat Duck they're delivered live, and that tail really starts flipping when you handle them.' I was getting used to the screen now, and could see the langoustine jetting backwards. 'Is this the best time of day to see them?'

'They respond to the level of light, so at this depth they tend to come out first thing in the morning, then return to their burrows until the light drops near dusk. Those are the times to catch them.'

Douglas showed me a resin cast of a burrow. Three fat tubes formed a Y-shape, each branch of which curved upwards, flaring out towards the lip. It looked like a scale model from an SFX studio – a prototype Star Wars fighter perhaps. I had read that these burrows are one of the keys to the langoustine's survival. Long periods are spent in the burrows, particularly when the females are bearing eggs and while the young are growing up. This protects them from fishing nets during the period critical for continuation of the species.

Fresh from the sea – eating raw langoustine on board a Scottish trawler.

A drum-shudder and chain-clank above my head heralded the reeling in of the catch. We made our way on deck to inspect the haul. Men in orange raingear manoeuvred the net over the guardrail and let the contents cascade on to the deck. It was a real wriggling seafood salad of langoustine, clams, sole and a stumpy cod. Douglas plucked a couple of langoustine from the skittering pile and held them gently between thumbs and forefingers. 'You can see there's a marked colour difference between these two. The tailfin of one is much redder than the other. That colour change is a sign of stress.'

'As I understand it, high levels of anxiety make the langoustine burn up their sugar reserves, making them less sweet.'

'We have found that there are definite stress-related changes to the quality of the meat, which then takes on a whiter appearance.'

'And the texture becomes pappier.'

'Exactly. The flesh begins to break down, so it's not as firm. Careful handling of the catch can prevent this. Above all, it's vital that the langoustine don't increase in temperature. Get them chilled as soon as possible.' As if to illustrate his point, Douglas began lifting langoustine into a polystyrene box filled with crushed ice. 'If they're allowed to stay above 12°C for any length of time, it accelerates the breakdown, and it's impossible to reverse that.'

Here was another example of food ethics and aesthetics comfortably and conveniently dovetailing. During my search for the perfect banger, pork farmer Graham Head insisted that the better pigs are handled, the better their flesh tastes. The same seemed to be true for langoustine. We eat well if they are treated well. By insisting on a top-quality product, we ensure the langoustine has a decent quality of life.

Until, of course, something larger comes along and eats it. I picked one up and twisted off its head, then slit the shell with my thumb and sucked out the mid-gut. It was wonderfully sweet.

CLAMMING UP

'In the USA ... clam chowder!' By now I had said it so often to the camera, trying to get the intonation right and ending up sounding like a game-show host, that the sentence no longer made any sense and with each take I'd end up fluffing it earlier and earlier. The TV crew had placed me at a table on the decking outside Sono Seaport Seafood, a homely, unpretentious fish restaurant situated by a squat octagonal red and white clapboard lighthouse near the mouth of the Norwalk River in Connecticut. They had already filmed me in Elie gurning, 'In Scotland … cullen skink', and saw no reason not to turn this into an international montage. En route from New Haven to New York they had spotted the opportunity for a film sequence and taken it.

I took a spoonful of New England Clam Chowder (Cup $4.00; Bowl $5.00) and looked out over the river at a dun-coloured seagull wheeling in lazy arcs, then cresting a thermal before dropping abruptly on to a piling and standing stock-still, as though carved in the wood. I took a second spoonful. It was all I wanted right then, and it tasted as good as any clam chowder I'd ever had. I wondered how much of that taste was down to what was going on around me – the faint play of salt on the air, the pungent, resinous aroma of marine varnish, the feel of weatherbeaten wood beneath the fingers, and the mournful hoot of boat horns from Long Island Sound. How could it ever taste that good when removed from sea and sky and breeze? In cooking, context is everything.

THE COOK, THE CAGE, THE FISH AND THE SMOKER

In the Fat Duck's research kitchen, I had laid out the ingredients and equipment I'd be using.

> **2 cured haddock fillets**
> **1 plastic bag of 'Sweet-Scented & Meadow Fresh' hay**
> **1 B&Q (humane) squirrel cage trap**

On the side of the box the cage came in it advised that it shouldn't be used in red squirrel areas, and warned against releasing greys back into the wild. Nowhere did it say that it was unsuitable for haddock or other North Atlantic seafood. Which was just as well because I was going smoking.

I had thought about using Arbroath smokies in the pie, but decided that their flavour would be too strong. They would muscle all the other more delicate fish out of the way, giving the dish a one-sided character that would soon pall. I was looking for a much subtler smoked flavour, and I believed I could get it by smoking in hay.

I'm a big fan of using hay in cookery. Some people might assume this is my way of playing the mad scientist but, as with many of the techniques I use and for which I'm notorious, it has a long culinary history. In Lyonnais and Burgundy whole legs of ham used to be cooked in hay to give a magnificent farmyard flavour to the meat. I've put hay in the cooking water of potatoes destined for triple-cooked chips and I've used it at the Fat Duck to cook sweetbreads wrapped in a salt-crust pastry. Alan Davidson's *North Atlantic Seafood* suggests that smoking fish in hay gives a very gentle result because the hay burns up in seconds: it doesn't have time to impart the aromas that a long, slow smoke over wood can. And that's just what I wanted – a suggestion of smoke, no more than that.

As far as I knew, the squirrel cage didn't have a long culinary history. I hadn't unearthed a fifteenth-century recipe in *The Vivendier* for halibut-stuffed red squirrel. Having found that a fishclamp compacted the hay too tightly, preventing it from catching fire properly, I needed something that held it loosely enough to allow air to circulate through it.

I fashioned a large nest of hay, picked up the fillets and laid them one on top of the other, nose-to-tail, skin side out, on top of the hay. They had been cured for twelve hours in ground kelp with three parts salt to one part sugar. The kelp gave the fish a speckled green appearance, and the flesh was tacky to the touch – this sticky layer conferred by the curing is known as the 'pellicle'. It would ensure that the smoky flavours adhered to the fish. I covered it all with another clump of hay (the lab now looked like a farmyard, with haystalks scattered across the work surfaces and floor) and shoved the lot into the cage.

In the Hind's Head car park a Weber barbecue was already white-hot. I placed the cage on top and smoke billowed out immediately followed by flames snaking their way along the hay and reaching out in long fingers beyond the cage to be followed in turn by the swift switch from straw colour to black as the hay burnt up and reduced in bulk to settle finally as a small clump of ashes on the cage's floor revealing two richly yellowed fillets of fish. It had taken a minute.

I flicked open the cage, tore off a chunk of fillet and tasted. There was the occasional hay stub to spit out, but it was delicious. Delicately smoked on the outside but still raw in the middle, which was important because I intended to trim the fish, cube it and include it in the pie. I didn't want something that was in danger of overcooking and becoming rubbery. This had the taste and texture I was looking for.

---

* **Smoking Jacket**

Salting fish for a while before smoking brings a little welcome seasoning to it, but it also has other advantages. The salt draws to the surface some of the proteins in the muscle fibres, especially myosin. Hang the fish on a line to drip-dry it and the myosin dissolves to form a shiny gel, or pellicle, that allows the outside of the fish to develop an attractive golden-yellow colour (as opposed to the in-your-face yolk yellow induced by artificial colouring) during smoking. The colour comes from dark resins in the smoke vapour sticking to the fish's surface, and browning reactions that occur between aldehydes (a group of highly reactive chemical compounds) in the smoke and amino acids (the small molecular units that combine to create proteins) in the pellicle.

SOUNDS FISHY

Everybody would, of course, agree that taste and texture are essential features of any dish, but what about sound? At Oxford's Department of Experimental Psychology, Professor Charles Spence once conducted an experiment in which I ate Pringles in front of a microphone while wearing headphones. Charles gradually adjusted the amplifier, boosting the higher frequencies of my munching noises. The crisps immediately seemed unbelievably crunchier. I had tried the test several times since and it never ceased to amaze me how dramatically sound can alter the eating experience. It is said that we taste with our eyes but, clearly, we also taste with our ears.

I had returned to Oxford to explore this idea in the context of fish pie because seafood seemed to me to be associated with a particularly evocative set of sounds. I had brought to Charles's cluttered lab a

Professor Charles Spence and I discuss how the senses affect our appreciation of food.

consignment of oysters and I was looking for a person who would be willing to eat them.

'Guinea pig? Yuh, I'll be your guinea pig.' Charles had asked around the department and found Carmel from California. She was wearing a very psychedelic shirt, so I figured she'd probably be broadminded enough to deal with what we were about to do, even though she had never eaten an oyster before. 'Not rilly in my budget, y'know?'

While Kyle shucked the oysters and sliced each one in two, I ushered Carmel towards a gold-coloured booth about the size and shape of a phone-box and invited her to sit on a stool facing the two small white speakers gaffer-taped to its walls. 'Thanks for being our willing victim, Carmel. I'm going to feed you two halves of an oyster, each of which will be accompanied by a sound. All I'd like you to do is mark on the sheet I've given you how pleasant or unpleasant each experience is, and how intense or otherwise each oyster's flavour is. There'll be four tastings in all.'

'OK. Go for it.' She sat back, ready, relaxed.

Kyle methodically laid one half of each oyster in a plastic Petri dish and put the other back in its shell. (They had been cut in two so that, as far as possible, the flavour was objectively identical.) Visually, it seemed to me there was already a huge difference between them that impinged on my appreciation. The Petri dish emphasised the oyster's weird, organ-like appearance. It looked unappealingly like a lab specimen. In its shell, on the other hand, it looked natural, even beautiful.

'What do you think, Charles? Will the two sounds we're using – the surf's roar and the farm's cacophony – further accentuate the differences between the oysters' settings and so influence Carmel's enjoyment?'

'Research we've done suggests that, yes, they should have a marked effect. Context is hugely important to how we perceive our food. Changing any kind of environmental cue – the wall colour, the smell – affects the brain and hence our perception of what we're eating.'

'Much as, say, I've tasted Muscadet on the banks of the Loire and it has been fantastic, but I've never managed to recreate that experience at home. People put that down to the wine "not travelling well", but in fact it's more to do with what's going on in our brain.'

'Yes. All the congruent factors – the sights, sounds, smells – are part of the taste. In a way, you're tasting France. Remove that, and it's not going to be the same.'

The oysters were ready. I handed Carmel a Petri dish and plastic spoon, and signalled to Charles to play the first track. The frenzied clucking of chickens was cut off by the closing door. Looking through the booth's side window, I found it difficult to read her face. She looked a little nervous; keen to get it right.

'OK. Now the next. Track two.' I offered up the second oyster. The sounds of tide and gulls crescendoed from the speakers.

'All right. Now we're talking,' she called out as the door closed once more. California surfer girl.

We went through the whole thing a second time, then released Carmel from the booth. 'What difference did the sounds make to your enjoyment?' I wanted to know.

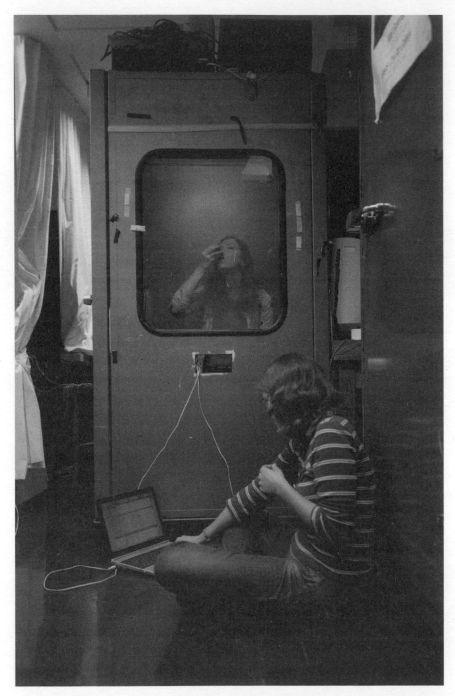

In a sound booth in Oxford, Carmel tests whether an oyster tastes better when accompanied by the sounds of the sea.

'Oh, the oyster was so much better with the sounds of the sea. It felt much more ... I don't know ... authentic with the shell. That was a lot of it, actually, the shell.'

'And what about when you tried each for a second time?'

'Yeah, going back to the farm was the worst. Because, I guess, I'd got a comparison. It was so nice with the sounds of the sea and the other sound just took away from that. Spoiled it.'

'Thanks.'

'Thanks for the oysters. I've developed another expensive habit. Call me any time you want more testing done ... '

What Carmel had marked on the sheet backed up her observations. On a scale of one to ten, the ocean oysters had scored ten for both intensity of flavour and pleasantness. The first farmyard oyster, by comparison, got seven for flavour and five for pleasantness; and these figures dropped further with the second, to five and two respectively. The message was clear: the right context and the right sound could make a big difference to the taste of a fish pie. I would somehow have to weave them into my recipe.

Fish Pie Serves 8

In my experience, fish pie often ends up bland and overcooked. I wanted to create a fish dish with strong, distinct flavours that nonetheless kept faith with the ideas behind the tradition. The development of a fortified stock went a long way to meeting both requirements: making a classic stock of the haddock's head and bones, then roasting the langoustine shells and adding them produced a fabulous intensity of flavour and, equally importantly, meant that absolutely nothing was wasted. The original dish was as much about thrift as ocean drift, so it seemed appropriate – especially as the question of sustainability becomes ever more pressing – to produce a recipe that didn't call for just the best bits of the fish and have no use for the rest.

To add a further nod to the dish's maritime connections, the stock is foamed up to give a suggestion of the sea's spume, and delicately laid on top of the dish, alongside fried breadcrumbs that represent sand.

Special equipment
Heavy kitchen shears, barbecue, lumpwood charcoal, sweet meadow hay and metal squirrel, rabbit or hamster cage (available from B&Q, pet shops or petplanet.co.uk), pressure cooker, hand-held blender, food processor, digital probe, drum sieve (available through Continental Chef Supplies), piping bag, 8 individual cast-iron cocotte dishes (11cm in diameter and 5cm deep)

Timing
Preparation takes 6½ hours. Cooking takes about 14 hours.

For the haddock
1 whole haddock (about 5kg)
The most efficient way to approach this recipe is to ask your fishmonger to clean and fillet a whole haddock and to give you a separate bag with all the bones and the cleaned head to make your stock. If a whole

haddock is not available, you can use two sides of haddock with the skin on, and then supplement the recipe with white fish bones in the amount required (ask your fishmonger). If you do go down this route, be sure to ask for meaty fish bones (free of blood) from haddock, sole, turbot, flounder or halibut. With both these approaches, start the recipe at step 11 of the filleting process.

If you decide to have a go at filleting the fish yourself, see the instructions on page 289.

For the haddock and salmon cure

2 reserved haddock fillets (combined weight approximately 800g) _ 400g salmon fillets, preferably cut from the centre, skin on, pin bones removed _ 3 parts by weight table salt (approximately 200–225g) _ 1 part by weight caster sugar (approximately 60–80g) _ 0.25 part by weight kombu (kelp – available in packets from oriental grocery shops), finely ground in a coffee grinder or food processor _ 20g vermouth

For the stock

It is possible to combine this stage and the next by adding all the ingredients from both to create one final stock. I have broken it into two stages in my recipe because I want to extract as much flavour as possible and also because of the capacity of a home pressure cooker. If you have a pressure cooker large enough and want to save a bit of time, combine both recipes to create one master stock.

100g grapeseed or groundnut oil _ 200g thinly sliced onion (about 1 large onion) _ 150g thinly sliced button mushrooms (about 15), cleaned _ 100g thinly sliced leek (about 1 large one), white and pale green parts only _ 100g thinly sliced fennel (about ½ a large bulb) _ 250g thinly sliced carrots (about 2 large ones) _ reserved haddock tail flesh _ 1kg cleaned bones and head from haddock or other white fish _ 50g vermouth _ 100g dry white wine _ 4 cloves of garlic _ 6 allspice berries _ 1 star anise _ 15g coriander seeds _ 10g kombu _ ¼ bunch of parsley

For the stock fortification

16 whole langoustine, preferably live* _ 25g grapeseed or groundnut
oil _ 100g thinly sliced leek (about 1 large one) _ 100g thinly sliced
carrot (about 1 medium carrot) _ 100g thinly sliced onion (about ½
a large one) _ 25g thinly sliced garlic (about 3 large cloves) _
50g vermouth _ 100g dry white wine _ reserved stock

For the hay-smoked haddock

2 reserved cured haddock pieces

For the smoked haddock sauce base

25g grapeseed or groundnut oil _ 400g thinly sliced onions (about
2 large ones) _ 3 cloves of garlic, crushed _ 40g vermouth _ 100g
dry white wine _ 100g reserved hay-smoked haddock _ 400g
reserved stock _ 500g double cream _ 35–45g agar agar powder
(available through japanesekitchen.co.uk)

For the foaming seawater sauce

20g thinly sliced shallot (about ½ a shallot) _ 2g thinly sliced garlic
(about 1 clove) _ 10g vermouth _ 20g dry white wine _ 200g water
300g reserved stock, skimmed of any surface fat _ 5g kombu _
100g oyster juice (reserved from the final assembly – see page 289) _
5g soy lecithin powder (from health food shops) _ 5g skimmed milk
powder _ table salt

For the onion confit

300g (about 12) cipolline or pearl onions _ 10g (2 tsp) salt _ extra
virgin olive oil

For the 'sand'

The exotic ingredients needed for this can be bought from oriental and
Asian grocers.
100–200g grapeseed or groundnut oil _ 40g panko breadcrumbs _
10g frozen shirasu (raw/frozen baby anchovies) _ 1g lightly roasted
kombu, ground to a powder (weigh the powder itself) _ 1g salt

* If live langoustine are not available, use best-quality frozen ones, such as Young's, with the
shell and head on.

For the potato purée
500g peeled Belle de Fontenay or Charlotte potatoes _ table salt

For finishing the potato purée
150g unsalted butter, cubed and chilled _ reserved hot cooked potatoes _ 100g whole milk _ 3 egg yolks _ 75g Comté cheese, grated (a 100g piece will yield this amount) _ 20g wholegrain mustard _ 15g Worcestershire sauce _ 10g creamed horseradish _ table salt

For finishing the smoked haddock sauce
800g reserved smoked haddock sauce base _ 10 egg yolks _ 2 tsp chervil, finely chopped at the last minute _ 2 tsp chives, finely chopped at the last minute _ 1 tsp tarragon, finely chopped at the last minute _ 2 tsp parsley, finely chopped at the last minute

For finishing the fish pie
reserved cured salmon, cut into 2 x 2cm cubes (3 cubes per portion) _ reserved cured haddock cut into 2 x 2cm cubes (4 cubes per portion) _ 16 langoustine tail portions, cut in half widthways _ 8 oysters, opened and the juice strained through a fine mesh and reserved _ reserved onion confit, drained and cut into quarters _ 80g Bird's Eye frozen peas _ reserved smoked haddock sauce _ reserved potato purée, gently reheated and placed in a piping bag _ reserved 'sand' _ reserved seawater sauce

FILLETING THE HADDOCK
1. Using a pair of heavy kitchen shears, remove the fins from the fish.
2. With a scaling tool or the back of a heavy knife, scrape off all the fish scales. Rinse the fish thoroughly.
3. Inside the belly flaps, cut open the length of the membrane that covers the central bloodline. Holding the fish in both hands under running cold water, rinse it well to flush out all the blood.
4. Return the haddock to your cutting board and cut horizontally along each side of the fish to remove both fillets. Refrigerate until needed.
5. Remove the head from the bones and set aside. Cut off the tail and discard.

6. Cut the bones into manageable pieces and reserve for your stock.
7. Using a heavy chef's knife or cleaver, cut the fish head in half from top to bottom, then from side to side.
8. Use your heavy kitchen shears to remove the gills, lips and eyes.
9. Rinse the head, then soak it for 30 minutes in several changes of cold water. Drain and reserve for the stock.
10. Clean your work surface thoroughly and return the two fillets to your cutting board.
11. Divide both the fillets in half widthways and reserve the two thicker pieces from the head end for the cure. Take the two pieces from the tail end and remove the skin. Reserve these pieces for stock.

MAKING THE CURE
1. Weigh the haddock and salmon pieces and add the two amounts together. Divide that figure by four to give you the amount of cure mixture you need to make. In a bowl combine the correct proportions of salt, sugar and kombu.
2. Line your work surface with a large piece of clingfilm. Place the pieces of fish on it skin side down. Brush the flesh evenly with the vermouth. Calculate a quarter of the weight of each piece of fish and apply that weight of cure mixture to the flesh side. Wrap each piece of fish separately in clingfilm.
3. Refrigerate the haddock for 4 hours and the salmon for 6 hours. When you remove the fish from the fridge, unwrap immediately and brush off the cure mixture. Rinse the fish under cold water to remove any remnants of the cure.
4. Dry the haddock with kitchen paper and return to the fridge on a rack, uncovered, for 1 hour to form a tacky surface (pellicle) that the smoke flavour will adhere to later in the process. After the hour, wrap in clingfilm and refrigerate until needed later. This step is not necessary for the salmon as it will not be smoked. Simply rinse and blot dry, cover with clingfilm and return to the fridge until needed. Note: You can use these simple steps to cure any fish.

MAKING THE STOCK
1. Pour the oil into a small (8-litre) pressure cooker and place over a medium heat.

2. Add the onion, mushrooms, leek, fennel and carrots and cook for 10–15 minutes, until soft, stirring occasionally. Meanwhile, place the haddock flesh in a food processor and blitz to a rough paste.
3. When the vegetables are softened and translucent, but not brown, add the fish, the head and the bones.
4. Immediately add the vermouth and the white wine and bring to the boil, stirring in the garlic, allspice, star anise and coriander seeds.
5. Add enough water to make about 4kg of liquid. (The pan should be about two-thirds full.) Cover with the lid and bring up to full pressure for 30 minutes.
6. Remove from the heat. Allow to depressurise before removing the lid.
7. Add the kombu and parsley and allow to infuse for 30 minutes.
8. Strain the stock and reserve.

FORTIFYING THE STOCK
1. Twist the heads off the langoustine. Return the tails to the fridge.
2. Cut the antennae and eyes from the heads with scissors. Discard the lungs and gills, but reserve the rest of the heads and the claws. Reserve the liver and entrails separately for finishing the stock.
3. To prepare the tails, grasp the centre flap (teslon) between your thumb and index finger, then gently twist and pull to remove the intestines. (This works only with live langoustine; if using frozen ones, simply remove the intestines with a paring knife.) Using a pair of kitchen scissors, cut along the shell lengthwise, taking care not to cut into the flesh, and separate the flesh from the shell.
4. Wrap all the tail meat in clingfilm and refrigerate until required.
5. Preheat the oven to 200°C/400°F/Gas 6. Combine all the shells with the heads and place in a single layer in a roasting pan. Place in the oven to dry roast, tossing them every 5 minutes until the moisture has evaporated and the shells have a light roasted aroma. Remove and set aside.
6. Meanwhile, pour the oil into a small pressure cooker over a medium heat. Add all the vegetables and cook for 10 minutes.
7. When the vegetables are softened and translucent (but not brown) add the vermouth and white wine and bring to the boil.
8. Tip in all the roasted shells, then pour in the reserved stock. Cover and bring to full pressure for 30 minutes.

9. Remove from the heat and allow to depressurise before removing the lid. Add the reserved livers and entrails and infuse for 30 minutes. Strain the fortified stock and allow to cool.

SMOKING THE HADDOCK

1. Light the barbecue and leave for 10–15 minutes, or until the coals are glowing and there are small flames.
2. Meanwhile, take the two pieces of haddock and place one on top of the other, flesh sides together.
3. Cover the inside of the squirrel cage with a layer of hay 10cm thick. Place the sandwiched haddock in the centre and cover with another layer of hay 10cm thick.
4. Place the cage on the barbecue: the hay will ignite and smoke the haddock inside. Leave for 4–5 minutes, or until most of the hay has burnt away. Lift the cage off the barbecue and leave to cool before removing the haddock.
5. Brush away the burnt hay, then peel off the skin and discard. The outside edges of the haddock will be cooked through, while the centre will remain raw.
6. Trim off all the cooked edges and set aside for the smoked haddock sauce. You will be left with a raw portion from the middle weighing about 100g. Wrap in clingfilm and refrigerate until required.

MAKING THE SMOKED HADDOCK SAUCE BASE

1. Place a large pan over a medium heat and pour in the oil.
2. Add the onions and garlic and cook for 10 minutes, or until soft and translucent.
3. Deglaze the pan with the vermouth and wine, bringing the mixture to the boil.
4. Add the pieces of cooked smoked haddock, the stock and the cream and bring to a simmer. Cook very gently for 20 minutes.
5. Remove the pan from the hob and leave to infuse for 20 minutes.
6. Strain the sauce, allowing the liquid to run through freely without helping it along. Leave to cool, then transfer to the fridge to chill.
7. Weigh the sauce and calculate 0.5 per cent of that figure. Measure this weight of agar agar into the sauce and mix with a hand-held blender.
8. Tip the sauce into a pan and place over a medium heat. Bring to a

simmer (around 95°C/200°F), stirring constantly until the agar agar has dissolved (approximately 1 minute).

9. Pour the sauce through a sieve into a container. Leave to cool, then store in the fridge until required.

MAKING THE FOAMING SEAWATER SAUCE

1. Put the shallot, garlic, vermouth and white wine in a pan over a medium heat. Bring to the boil and cook for 2–3 minutes.
2. Add the water and the stock and bring it to just below a simmer.
3. Remove the pan from the heat and add the kombu. Cover and infuse for 20 minutes, then strain through a sieve. Cool completely before proceeding.
4. Add the oyster juice, the soy lecithin and skimmed milk powder and mix thoroughly with a hand-held blender. Taste and adjust the seasoning with salt, then cover and place in the fridge.

MAKING THE ONION CONFIT

1. Place the onions in a small pan and season with salt.
2. Pour over enough olive oil just to cover. Place over a medium heat and cook for 15–20 minutes, until soft.
3. Tip the onions and the oil into a container and leave to cool. Store in the fridge until required.

MAKING THE 'SAND'

1. Pour the oil into a small pan and heat to a temperature of 170°C/325°F.
2. Add the panko and fry for 1–2 minutes, until golden brown.
3. Using a slotted spoon, transfer the breadcrumbs to kitchen paper and blot dry.
4. Add a thin layer of the grapeseed oil to a small pan and place over a medium heat. Add the shirasu and fry until golden brown, stirring constantly with a rubber spatula. Transfer to kitchen paper and blot dry.
5. Place the fried panko and shirasu with the kombu powder and salt in a mortar and pestle or a food processor and combine until the mixture has the consistency and texture of wet sand. Set aside to finish the fish pie.

MAKING THE POTATO PURÉE

1. Cut the potatoes widthways into 5mm slices, taking care that they are all the same thickness so they will cook evenly.
2. Run the slices under cold water to rinse off the excess starch.
3. Fill a large pan with enough water to cover the potatoes completely and heat to 80°C/175°F* (for this recipe using Fahrenheit gives greater accuracy). Add the potatoes and maintain the temperature at 70°C/160°F for 30 minutes.
4. Cool the slices under cold running water.
5. Meanwhile, rinse the pan they were cooked in and fill it with the same amount of water as before. Add the potatoes and salt (for the taste of seawater) and bring to the boil. Simmer for 15–20 minutes until soft. It is important that the potatoes are completely cooked or the purée will be grainy.
6. Drain the potatoes again, then return to the pan and dry them by shaking over a low heat.

FINISHING THE POTATO PURÉE

1. Place the butter in a large bowl. Push the potatoes through a potato ricer or vegetable mill over the butter.
2. Fold the potatoes and butter together, then pass the mixture through a fine sieve (a drum sieve is ideal).
3. Heat the milk in a medium pan and bring to a gentle simmer. Add the potatoes to the milk and fold together to obtain a loose consistency that can be piped. (You can add more milk if necessary to achieve this. If the mixture becomes too loose, heat gently to tighten.) The purée can be kept in the pan until needed; simply place clingfilm directly on top of it.
4. When you are ready for the final assembly gently rewarm the potato purée and remove from the heat. Fold in the egg yolks, along with the cheese, mustard, Worcestershire sauce and horseradish. Taste and season with salt. Pack the purée into a plastic piping bag and keep warm until needed.

---

* Use a digital probe to check low temperatures on the hob. You may need to temporarily remove the pan from the heat to maintain the temperature if it gets too hot.

FINISHING THE SMOKED HADDOCK SAUCE

1. Tip the sauce into a medium pan, place over a low heat and bring gradually to just below a simmer. Lower the heat, stirring constantly, until the temperature is 55–60°C/130–140°F.
2. Whisking constantly, add the egg yolks to the sauce, keeping the temperature below 65°C/150°F. Continue to stir in this manner for 2–3 minutes, until the sauce begins to thicken. Take care not to overcook and scramble the yolks.
3. Fold in the herbs and check the seasoning, keeping in mind that the seafood is cured and will further season the liquid.
4. Have your sauce at 60–65°C/140–150°F when you assemble the final dish.

FINISHING THE FISH PIE

1. Preheat your grill until very hot.
2. Arrange 8 cast-iron cocotte dishes in a tray that will fit under the grill. Divide the four different types of seafood among the dishes so that they all fit tightly in a single layer.
3. Add equal amounts of the onion confit and the peas to the dishes.
4. Spoon the warm smoked haddock sauce over the seafood so that the dishes are two-thirds full.
5. Cut a 1cm hole in the piping bag tip and pipe the warm potato purée on top of the seafood, working back and forth widthways. Use the back of a spoon to spread the potato out evenly, taking care that there are no holes where the sauce can bubble through. The level of the potatoes should be 2mm below the surface of the pot.
6. Place the tray under the grill, making sure it is 15–20cm below the heat source. Lightly and evenly gratinée the top of the potatoes, taking care not to overheat and therefore overcook the seafood underneath. (The seafood will continue to cook after being removed from the grill.)
7. Place the tray on a work surface and spoon some 'sand' on to each portion, covering only half the surface of the potato.
8. Heat and froth the seawater sauce with a hand-held blender and spoon the foam on to the plain side of the potato so that it 'laps' on to the sand like waves crashing on to a beach. Serve while listening to sounds of the sea.

Pizza

'The Neapolitan pizza is a beautiful thing
to look at, and extremely substantial to eat;
coarse food, to accompany copious glasses
of rough wine.'

Elizabeth David, *Italian Food*

History

The origins of pizza are fiercely fought over: the Koreans claim its invention, as do the Chinese, whose Historical Society put forward the thesis that *ping tse* – a flat bread made from sweet rice-flour and spices – is the true precursor of the pizza.

However, the word 'pizza' has the same roots as 'pitta', a flat disc of bread that has been baked since at least 2000 BC. The Egyptians invented both leavened bread and the oven, so it's a safe bet that the unacknowledged inventor of the pizza was the first Egyptian who got bored of a diet of pitta and chucked a topping on top.

Over time, of course, pizza has become identified with Italy. The word itself was used as early as AD 997 at Gaeta, a port between Naples and Rome, and by the twelfth century there were varieties from Apulia to Calabria. In the last hundred years, the pizzas of Naples – the marinara (or Napoletana) and the Margherita – have come to be seen as the archetypes. Certainly it is the Neapolitans who, in the late seventeenth century, combined the pizza base with tomato (then generally still viewed with some suspicion, despite being introduced from Peru some two hundred years earlier) to produce what is undoubtedly thought of today as the standard pizza.

Pizza began life in Naples as fast food. Pizzerias were originally simply workshops where the pizzas were prepared and cooked. Salesmen would then wander through the town carrying the pizzas on their heads in a *stufa*, a round metal container with shelves. They also carried a *lanzuno*, a small foldable table. If they made a sale, the *lanzuno* would be whipped out and the *stufa* set upon it while negotiations took place. The last – and therefore coldest – pizza was usually sold at a knock-down price. (In a region as poor as Naples, such financial compromises were commonplace: you could even buy a pizza on credit, giving you seven days to find the money somehow, anyhow.)

The purchased pizza would be folded in half, then half again, and eaten from the point outwards. Here was a perfect food for the busy working man: no knife and fork needed, and the dough doubled as a plate. The Neapolitan fishermen sought it out when they returned from work and needed something quick and light to eat straight away, and so they gave their name to the first classic Naples pizza, the marinara.

From here to a pizza named after a queen seems quite a leap. And it's true that pizza was considered a platter for the poor until 11 June 1889, when King Umberto I and his wife, Queen Margherita, requested to taste the local speciality. Raffaele Esposito of the pizzeria 'Pietro … e basta così' was summoned to the Capodimonte Palace, where he offered up three types of pizza: one with small fish (*cecinielli*), one with olive oil and cheese, and one with tomato, mozzarella and basil.

Pizzeria Pietro has since changed its name to Brandi, but it still proudly displays the queen's response to her first taste of pizza. On headed notepaper, the head of the Servizi da Tavola della Real Casa (the Royal Household Culinary Service) declares that the pizzas 'were found to be very good'. From that point on, the pizza with tomato, mozzarella and basil became known as the Margherita – the queen of pizzas – patriotically decked out in the green, white and red of the Italian flag. And with royal blessing, of course, the pizza was finally accepted by the local bourgeoisie.

PIZZA AMERICANA

Pizza remained a Neapolitan speciality, however. As late as the 1970s it was still largely unknown in the north of Italy. For its current status as a truly international food, we have to thank American fast-food franchises.

Italian immigrants and American soldiers stationed in Naples during the Second World War had taken the pizza to the States, at about the same time as the McDonald brothers began introducing assembly-line production methods into the restaurant business. Several chains hit upon the idea of marketing 'ethnic' food in the same way, and suddenly Tex-Mex and pizza joints sprang up all over the place. By 1970 Americans were eating two billion pizzas annually, and exporting their version of the Neapolitan pizza throughout the world.

Of course, the American pizza bears only a passing resemblance to its Italian cousin. With its light, elastic crust and deliberately sparse ingredients, the Neapolitan pizza can come as a surprise. President Eisenhower certainly thought so, and caused a diplomatic incident when he said he'd tasted better pizza in New York than Naples.

I had no intention of causing another diplomatic stand-off. Most great chefs, food critics and cookbook writers still insist that Naples is the place for pizza. If I was to have any chance of creating a decent pizza, I had to go there and see for myself.

The Quest for the Best

THE SECRET OF SAN MARZANO

In *Treasures of the Italian Table*, Burton Anderson notes, 'It has been said that if Naples had managed to patent the pizza it would now be among Italy's wealthiest cities instead of one of its poorest.' Perhaps that is why, a little late in the day, the Neapolitans are trying to protect their product against pale imitations (to say nothing of the viler variants that have been foisted upon us, such as Pizza Hawaii with its chunks of tepid pineapple). The Associazione Vera Pizza Napoletana has drawn up a code that regulates every aspect of preparing the proper pizza, from the exact heat of the oven to the techniques employed to knead the dough. The grade of flour, the types of cheese, the kinds of tomato – each part of the process is specified in minute detail. And there are now moves to get the Neapolitan pizza included in the list of products recognised by the EU as traditional specialities, and effectively copyrighted as such. This might seem heavily tradition-alist, and counter to a spirit of adventure, but to me it was very encouraging. Although I could never hope to emulate the lengthy apprenticeship of the *pizzaiolo* (pizza-maker), here at least was a blue-print for the perfect Margherita and marinara. Surely this was a short cut to success. I flew to Italy full of confidence.

The Italians are passionate about their food. This was borne out almost as soon as I touched down in Naples. In the bus from the airport the driver began arguing about the best pizza, insisting that the

Neapolitan product was superior. 'It's the way the *pizzaiolo* works the dough,' he declared, 'and the silkiness of the mozzarella, the juiciness of the San Marzano tomato.' For Italians, food is not just the stuff of life but an everyday drama, a ritual to be enacted and enjoyed, a communal celebration. This is part of what makes their cuisine great, but the mythical status accorded to much of their food makes it almost impossible to separate fact from fiction. Marco Polo, for example, is credited with the discovery of many foodstuffs, even though the dates often deny this. Similarly, people claim the Margherita was invented for the queen, yet it pre-dates Raffaele Esposito's excursion to Capodimonte. In Italy, it seems, the bigger and better the story, the more it has to be taken with a large pinch of salt (any kind: the Associazione offers no stipulations here).

So it was with a mixture of excitement and uncertainty that I set out from the headquarters of Solania, one of the top producers of canned San Marzano tomatoes in Italy. My bus driver wasn't alone in his esteem for the San Marzano: almost every Neapolitan I met said it was the best tomato for pizza, and I'd come across several Italian chefs who were gripped by nostalgia at the mere mention of its name. The celebrated Marcella Hazan says that the authentic flavour of Naples pizza owes much to the San Marzano. Could it possibly live up to the hype – or would it turn out to be just another story?

Our simple trip to the tomato fields was, of course, turned into ritual and drama. By the time we had bumped our way down the rutted track at the end of our journey, we were part of a motorcade that included members of the Italian press (Solania's general manager had a keen eye for any publicity opportunity) and a local government dignitary. The pomp and circumstance seemed at odds with the rustic setting: the fields spreading out haphazardly, like allotments, with tumbledown huts and sagging netting attached to staves.

If you could bottle romance alongside the product, the San Marzano tomato would undoubtedly be the most delicious in the world. The fields lay in a wide valley between the steep green ridges of the Picentini and Lattari mountains. In the background loomed the stubby peak of Vesuvius, familiar from hundreds of photographs, paintings and engravings – the inescapable, brooding symbol of Naples. Occasionally a tiny Piaggio van trundled past, its flatbed stacked with sheaves of freshly washed rocket, but most of the time the only sound was the low moan of wind. At midday the church bells rang out the *mezzogiorno*, as they have for centuries.

The fieldworkers too looked as though they had stepped out of an old photograph – especially the women, who wore brightly patterned aprons over shapeless dark skirts. Both sexes had close-cropped hair and weather-beaten brown faces that signalled a lifetime spent working out of doors. They were all old: the San Marzano is a notoriously delicate tomato – it needs constant, careful tending (*com' un bambino* – like a child) and the harvesting has to take place by hand; it's back-breaking work, and the young simply aren't interested.

This isn't the only factor jeopardising the tomato's future: over time the soil has lost much of its ability to hold water and now needs an elaborate system of pipes and irrigation to support it. This worsens the fragile economics of a fruit that's difficult to grow, and already there is strong competition in the area from hardier varieties. A hybrid has been developed from Chinese seeds: the tomatoes give a higher yield but they're not the pure San Marzano. Locals contemptuously dismiss them as 'Chinese balls', but you can see that the bravado hides a certain anxiety.

Despite their hardships, the workers were incredibly welcoming, and eager for us to try their tomato. From somewhere they conjured up rough chunks of fennel bread, a bottle of extra virgin olive oil and a jar of salt. Stemfuls of *peperoncini* – small round chillis with a purplish tinge – were wrenched from the ground. There was even a bottle of rough red wine that had to be levered open with a hammer and screwdriver. A plastic crate was up-ended to serve as a table. Someone cut open a tomato and held it out to me. *'Vai, vai. Mangia.'*

I was about to get my first taste of the fabled San Marzano.

What can I say? The tomato's elongated shape – like a fat teardrop – sat satisfyingly snugly in the hand; it filled the palm and it felt good, firm but fleshy.* It looked good, too, with its instantly recognisable *pizzetto*, or small pointed pimple, at one end. But the taste? It wasn't

---

* Some people had told me that the secret of the San Marzano depended on that shape: that the key to its success was not gastronomy but economy. Increased use of the San Marzano coincided with the growth of the canning industry, and its shape meant you could fit more in a tin. In Italy, no one could confirm this. It was a secret that stayed secret.

what I'd hoped for – it was fresh-tasting, sure, but I've had more sweetness and flavour complexity from a cherry tomato. (And before you start thinking that I'm just a fussy chef who's spoilt for choice, this wasn't only my opinion. I took a bunch of San Marzano back to my restaurant and everybody felt the same. During my time in Italy I bought bags from several greengrocers, hoping for an epiphany, hoping to have my verdict overturned. It never was.)

Masking my disappointment from my generous hosts, I chatted with the government representative, Francesco di Pace, and Laura, Solania's PR, trying to discover the secret of the San Marzano tomato. Italians are fiercely protective of their local produce but they're also intolerant of anything but the best. There had to be a reason why they prized this tomato above all others.

They told me that the San Marzano is a 'dry' tomato: the low water content means it doesn't over-dampen the dough, causing the base to go soggy. (In fact, in Naples the ovens are so hot that a pizza is only in there for a couple of minutes at most. That's nowhere near enough time to dry out the tomatoes.) And it turned out that Vesuvius isn't just a picturesque backdrop to the fields: its volcanic content feeds the soil, producing a fruit that is low in acid and low in pectin (the jelly-like substance that helps reinforce plant cell walls, much as cement surrounds the iron rods that run through the walls of a building).

Finally, I thought, we're getting somewhere. Acid and pectin play a significant part in the canning process: a high concentration of both can lead to a toughened tomato, as the acid binds to the pectin and hardens it. (A similar process happens in jam-making: we add acid to the fruit so that it reacts with the pectin to give a denser, drier structure.) Maybe this was the secret of the San Marzano – maybe the balance of pectin and acidity meant its perfection manifested itself only after canning, producing a soft, moist tomato that broke down particularly easily. I'd have to go to some pizzerias and find out.

A PIZZA THE ACTION

Where better to start than the most historic pizzeria of all? Pizzeria Brandi is in a narrow cobbled alley in the Chiaia district. A stone plaque on the wall declares that pizza Margherita was born here:

QUI 100 ANNI FA
NACQUE LA PIZZA MARGHERITA
1889–1989
BRANDI

The place is steeped in history. In the small front room, open to the street, old wine bottles line the shelves and every inch of wall space is covered with photographs. There are kings and queens, government ministers and even Chelsea Clinton, though the real royalty seems to be Luciano Pavarotti, who smiles stiffly at you from all sides.

In the kitchen, copper pots hang on hooks, and there are several examples of old *stufe* proudly emblazoned with the pizzeria's name. The huge dome of the oven is tiled in blue and white, like the onion dome of a Russian Orthodox church. Before it, clad in white like priestly acolytes, the chefs went about their business. A dusting of flour had settled on all of them, making them look older than they really were.

On fact-finding trips like this, it's best not to build up your expectations too much because they are often overturned. It's frustrating and exciting in equal measure – going back to the drawing board is often the springboard to a better idea. I'd been wrong-footed by the fact that the San Marzano, although delicious, didn't live up to its reputation. And at Brandi I was disappointed to discover that they sieved the tomatoes before putting them on the pizza base. Suddenly my image of the *pizzaiolo* appreciating this tomato because it could be easily squeezed and crushed by hand seemed utterly fanciful.

Even the pizza wasn't quite what I'd hoped for. I liked the use of provola cheese, which gave it a smoked character that is often absent from the Naples pizza because of its short cooking time, but in general the dough was thick and the taste nothing special. I'd flown across Europe for this, so perhaps my expectations were unreasonably high, but I couldn't honestly claim it as the perfect pizza. I asked our driver, Dario, what he thought, and got cautious approval, so I pressed further.

'You live in Rome. How does this compare with the Roman pizza?'

'Oh, the pizza there is disgusting. Too crispy – a nothing! Naples is the only one ... '

Great! I thought. Here was the opportunity for some inside information from someone I knew would be straight with me. Now I'd get to the bottom of what made Naples pizza the best.

'... But I don't really eat pizza. I don't much like it,' he finished abruptly. It put my quest for perfection in perspective. There were as many pizza points of view as there were people to eat it (or not eat it).

The taste at Brandi might have been a bit of a let-down, but it was still an instructive experience. The pizzas were certainly authentic: the marinara relying for its flavour on tomato, garlic and oregano; the Margherita swapping garlic for basil and mozzarella. Nothing else. I was reminded of pizza's origins in pitta, and reflected that not much had changed. With so few ingredients, pizza was still basically a flavoured bread. There was so little to disguise it that the quality of the dough was paramount. I had begun my Italian journey of exploration with the San Marzano tomato because it was the very last day of the harvest. Now, I decided as I walked away from Brandi, I had to investigate the start of the pizza process. I needed to visit a flour mill.

FLOUR POWER

The next morning, when I arrived at the Caputo mill on Corso San Giovanni, the first delivery of wheat was thundering in on a huge Fiat truck covered by a tent of blue canvas. It pulled up on the parking plate and the driver jumped down. With a long pole he knocked out the bolts holding the flaps on one side of the truck. The resounding clang of metal on metal was drowned by the sound of hundreds of kilos of wheat avalanching through a metal grid in the floor. As the deluge slowed, the parking plate tilted upwards through 45°, like something out of *Thunderbirds*, to pour the remaining wheat into its underground silo. This is the raw product from which the Caputo brothers make what is reputedly one of the best pizza flours in Italy. I wanted to find out how they did it.

Antimo Caputo Srl has been on the same street, and in the same family, since 1925. It was established by Carmine Caputo, the grandfather of Carmine and Eugenio, who now run the company along with Carmine's son, Antimo. This continuity might seem unusual to us in Britain, where relocation and high turnover are the norm, but it's part of what ensures the quality of Italian food. Italian businesses are often handed from father to son, and they take their legacy very seriously.

Eugenio escorted me from the delivery bay across the hacienda-style courtyard, dodging busy fork-lifts, and led me up three flights of stairs to the top of the mill. The din outside was nothing compared to the roar of the sieving room. Here, what looked like gigantic school lockers suspended on rods shook back and forth with a relentless, dizzying energy. These were the sieves. Even before reaching these, Eugenio explained, the wheat underwent several processes: it was tested for quality and cleaned of impurities before being passed through break rolls that split it open ready for separation.

Wheat consists of bran (the outer skin) enclosing the germ (the embryo which, in the right conditions, will grow into another plant) and the endosperm, which is mainly starch and acts as a food store for the embryo. The huge sieves before me were vigorously separating wheat into these three constituent parts. It's the sieved endosperm particles – known as 'granita' or 'semolina'* – that produce white flour. Sieving takes place after each rolling, and each time the granita is removed, leaving the rest to go through the whole process again.

After a while the noise and motion became hypnotic, disorientating. Even the floor tremored constantly. I was beginning to imagine what it would be like if one of the machines broke free of its slender rods and catapulted forwards, so it was a relief to leave the sieving room behind and go down one flight to the milling room.

The smell hit me as soon as the doors opened. The pleasant, creamy smell of a freshly opened bag of flour. It took me back to childhood memories of home-baking – so much so that I almost expected the workers here to be dressed in a black suit and bowler hat, like the Homepride man, rather than their usual brown overalls and jaunty white cap. Above me was a forest of pipes, branching and criss-crossing, feeding into the square grey Buehler reduction rolls that grind the endosperm to a fine powder. 'We mill up to twenty-two times,' Eugenio told me. 'The first and second millings are the finest and these are for pizza flour. Later millings have more bran particles, and are used for other types of flour. And we can add in some of the

---

* Not to be confused with durum wheat semolina, which is entirely different.

The forest of pipes feeding flour into rollers at the Caputo mill.

bran or wheatgerm to produce brown or wholemeal flour. It's a little like the pressings of olive oil. The quality and character changes each time you put it through the machines.'

We walked down one more flight to the packing room – a W. Heath Robinson tangle of pipes, cogs and conveyor belts. Paper sacks stamped 'Caputo' and striped with different colours according to flour type were stacked in tall towers around the room. When these were fed into the machines I was pleased to see that their filling echoed the rising process itself: mechanical guiders up-ended the flattened sack in front of a chrome nozzle, whereupon it ballooned into a rounded shape before travelling on, now full of flour, to a chute through which it would abruptly disappear into the warehouses below – eagerly awaited by those busy fork-lifts.

My last stop was Caputo's laboratory. I wanted to know what was so special about Caputo flour. 'Making the flour for pizza is a very complex business,' said Eugenio. 'It has to have good water absorption so that the dough rises evenly and has a good texture. It must not be too high or low in protein because that will affect the elasticity of the dough. Ideally the flour should have 55 per cent absorption and 13 per cent protein. We do tests on our wheat and flour every day to make sure that they do all these things. And we source our wheat from many different places – Manitoba, Lithuania, Kazakhstan – and monitor and test and mix it together because the quality changes all the time. Bad weather has meant that Manitoba wheat is not so good this year, and we have had to replace it with another. It's important, too, that care is taken not to crush the wheat too much during milling, as this harms the protein, which then affects not only the elasticity but also the lightness and flavour of the dough. Not so good for pizza!'

This care and consideration is perhaps the key to the Caputos' success and reputation. They even arrange for their flour to be tried out regularly by pizza-makers to ensure consistent quality. 'Most of the pizza is dough,' observed Eugenio. 'Only that. It has to have that special flavour, that strong taste. The flour must be soft … but with a texture, a roughness to it. You in Britain mill your flour much softer than we do, so you don't get that flavour.'

Well, I wanted to get that flavour. And it seemed that the most likely way to achieve that was to use not just '00' flour (which the

Associazione considers essential for a good pizza) but Caputo '00'. As I packed flour sacks into the car, I asked Eugenio whether he had any advice on how to make the perfect pizza.

'The only way is to go to a pizzeria, watch the *pizzaiolo*, watch what he does. And then have a go yourself. And if you're still having trouble after that, you can always give me a call.'

I thanked him and said goodbye, tucking the business card bearing his phone number into a safe place in my wallet. I reckoned I might need it.

PRESIDENTIAL PIZZA

'The only way is to go to a pizzeria ... ' It seemed like good advice and, besides, it was lunchtime. I went to Il Pizzaiolo del Presidente on Via dei Tribunali in the Duomo district.

I had visited Brandi because of its history, but I visited Il Presidente because of its gastronomy: one of Italy's top food critics had told me that if I wanted to eat perfect pizza, this was the place.

I liked Il Presidente immediately. It has a brisk, business-like air. The kitchen is right at the front of the restaurant, with a glass counter looking on to the street from which you can buy pizza without setting foot inside – a reminder of pizza's origins as fast food for the working man. I squeezed past the kitchen and went downstairs to a bright room with exposed brickwork and a vaulted ceiling. Once again, the walls were covered with photographs, though this time most featured the pizzeria's charismatic owner, Ernesto Cacialli, at various pizza festivals around the country, wearing the red neckerchief of the *pizzaiolo*. There were no pics of Chelsea Clinton; instead her dad grinned down at me. He ate pizza here during the 1994 G7 summit and the pizzeria was promptly renamed in honour of his visit.

From the photos it was evident that Ernesto is a great roving ambassador for pizza, and his spirit spills over into the atmosphere of the restaurant: lively, noisy, energetic. There's no menu, you simply negotiate with the waiter for what you want on your pizza. My request was simple: I wanted the two classics, marinara and Margherita; then, if possible, I wanted to have the opportunity to watch a *pizzaiolo* at work and maybe have a go myself ...

When they arrived, the pizzas looked promising. The *cornicione* – the unadorned dough around the edge of the pizza – was narrow and attractively charred in places. Given the brief oven time, I wasn't sure how Ernesto had managed this, but it added an extra flavour dimension to a terrific pizza. The tomatoes had both fresh and cooked notes (I was pleased to notice later that they weren't sieved but lightly crushed, so there was still hope for my canning theory). I was sure I could also taste some provola in there – that deliciously smoky, almost meaty flavour – although when I asked the waiter about this, he got a rabbit-in-the-headlights look and started to edge away from me. Was it a trade secret? Was provola banned by the Associazione? Or was there some other reason for such behaviour? Maybe I'd mangled the Italian language so much that, instead of asking about cheese, I'd said something that could frighten and repulse waiters? It was impossible to tell, although I was to discover that a shroud of secrecy often surrounds unexpected areas of Italian cuisine: whenever I stumbled across one I was given the verbal runaround until the cameras were turned off and I gave up. Perhaps it's a way of keeping the myth and romance going.

Provola may or may not have been a secret, but Ernesto didn't hold back in sharing his expertise. Although we'd arrived in the middle of service, he took the time to show me how he made a pizza base. The dough was flattened by hand into a rough disc and then turned and worked with the fingertips. Once it had the right shape, Ernesto held the base in his right hand and, with his left, flapped and turned it until the disc had stretched, elongated and thinned to just the right size and thickness. He made it look easy, but as soon as I had a go I began to understand how a losing contestant must have felt during one of those impossible tasks on *The Generation Game*. I couldn't get it to work, couldn't get the rhythm going. No *pizzaiolo* was going to lose sleep over my performance.

Using the long-handled paddle – known as a 'peel' – to move the pizza in the oven proved no easier. The aim is to cook the pizza evenly. To this end, Ernesto wielded the peel with the dexterity of a test-match batsman, giving the pizza a number of quarter-turns without shifting its place in the oven (which is vitally important because the stone floor will be hotter around the pizza than under it; shift the pizza to the left or right and you burn the base). His pizza came out looking as it should; mine came out looking like an unmade bed, the dough gathered and ruckled in places, the topping erratically scattered. Clearly, I was going to have to work on these skills.

A WATER FOUNTAIN IN THE VILLA COMMUNALE

After lunch I had a rendezvous in the Piazza Vittoria. So I returned to the car to sample another unforgettable Naples experience: driving through the city.

Braking distance and lane discipline are mere memories. Drivers switch lanes abruptly whenever there's an opening, and hit full throttle as soon as they can see 3 feet ahead of them. Each car stutters along the tarmac in a stop–start–swerve pattern, veering past the swarm of Vespas that weave in and out at breakneck pace, and accelerating past any pedestrian unwise enough to try their luck at crossing. It's survival of the fittest – or at least the fastest. Several times we left the road altogether and hurtled down the tramtracks instead. 'Is this legal?' I wondered aloud as a tram loomed increasingly large in the rear-view mirror. But the bored look on the faces of policemen we passed suggested this was normal.

This time my destination was the Villa Communale, a large park by the coast with broad avenues bordered by scraggy palm trees. I'd come to visit a drinking water fountain. And I'd come armed with two nifty pieces of technological hardware: a pH meter to test the acidity of the water, and a conductivity meter to establish how hard or soft it was.

Heston the mad scientist going too far? Certainly some of the locals seemed to think so, eyeing me dubiously as they bent to take a drink while I dunked what looked like a TV remote control into a plastic beaker of water. However, scientists have determined that the chemical composition of the water used when making dough will affect its behaviour. And, although they use different words, Neapolitans agree with them. They declare that water is what makes their pizza so perfect – the water of the Serino aqueduct, which is so soft and light that it makes for superior dough. Since the Serino aqueduct supplies only a small part of the city, there's a certain amount of myth-making involved. I wanted to strip away the myth and find out whether Naples water really was perfect for pizza.

Making dough relies above all on one thing: the formation of gluten, a kind of super-protein with the characteristics we recognise in dough – plasticity and elasticity. Gluten is made up of two proteins in flour: gliadin and glutenin. When water is added to them and the mixture kneaded, the proteins stretch and spread out, like tentacles, gradually intertwining to form a complex, tensile network.

Water's constituents affect the strength of this network. First, high acidity interferes with the proteins' ability to form bonds, resulting in a dough that's not stretchy and that snaps when pulled apart. (Conversely, too alkaline an environment encourages the bonds, creating a dense, brick-like dough that's impossible to work with.)

Second, harder water produces a firmer dough. Water is very good at dissolving other substances, the two most common of which – depending on where your tap water originally comes from – are salts of calcium and magnesium, which crust up in your kettle to form a fur and dull the vibrant green colour of vegetables during cooking. They also have a cross-linking effect in dough formation, helping to chemically join the molecules in strong bonds. So too much calcium and magnesium has the same effect as too much alkali, producing a tough, inelastic dough. I was curious to see how the fabled Naples water measured up on the meters.

The pH scale runs from 0 to 14. The pH of neutral water is 7. Anything above this is increasingly alkaline (ammonia measures 11.9); anything below is increasingly acidic (lemon juice is 2.1). Trying to look nonchalant before the suspicious gaze of several old men on the bench opposite, I lifted the pH meter out of the beaker of water. The read-out was 7.2, which seemed to me pretty perfect for pizza dough: near neutral but with just enough alkaline content to strengthen the gluten network a little.

I put the pH meter away, plucked the conductivity meter out of my pocket and popped it into the beaker. (By now the look on the faces of the men opposite had shifted from suspicion to downright hostility.) The digital screen flashed out 0.9 and I multiplied this by 1,000 to get a reading in microsiemens of 900. Since the maximum was 2,500, this showed that Naples water had the suitable softness for pizza dough. The Neapolitans were right: their water was indeed soft and light.

DA MICHELE

It was fast getting dark but there was another pizzeria in Naples that intrigued me because its minimalist menu – it serves only the marinara and Margherita – seemed to reflect the purity and simplicity of the original Neapolitan pizzas. So we drove (and swerved and slalomed) over to Via Cesare Sersale, where the Pizzeria da Michele has been serving up its twin attractions since 1870.

By the time we arrived, night had fallen. Already a crowd had gathered outside. They had all taken a numbered ticket from the dispenser and awaited their turn at the tables. Few talked; most gazed expectantly through the narrow doorway, as though mesmerised by the glow of the brick oven – or faithfully anticipating that they were about to eat the perfect pizza.

Where Brandi is stately and Il Pizzaiolo del Presidente is no-nonsense modern, Da Michele has more of a 1930s feel. Its two small, high-ceilinged rooms have green and white tiles from floor to dado rail. The customers sit at marble-topped tables while sepia portraits in dark wood frames gaze down upon them. High in an alcove sits a statuette of St Anthony.

While talking to Eugenio Caputo in his flour mill, I had become increasingly convinced that good dough was the key to pizza, so although I would enjoy tasting the toppings, it was Da Michele's dough that I really wanted to try out.

It didn't disappoint. It was delicate and light, with a nice slightly charred character. And the flour really did seem to give it a special taste. Before coming to Naples I'd have dismissed such a claim as fanciful romanticism, but it turned out to be true. The dough had a particular flavour, and I'd have to try to capture that back at the Fat Duck.

That was going to be a big challenge, bigger maybe than what went on top. Already I had a few ideas about that – perhaps using a combination of provola and buffalo mozzarella to get both a stretchy cheese and that wonderful smoky note. By exploring the city and eating in places with very different styles, I'd picked up a lot of tips. But what I'd learned above all was how complicated the process was that shaped something as apparently simple as pizza. I'd encountered obsession and sleights of hand, myths that turned out to be true, vital techniques and subtle nuances. It had become much more than just a few ingredients, and it was going to be tricky translating that into what I wanted. The possibilities kept multiplying before me, like a funfair's hall of mirrors. I hoped the joke wouldn't be on me.

PIZZA SCHOOL

Drive up and away from the Bay of Naples and it's another world. For centuries the rich have chosen to live high up here in the hills, rising above the ravages of plague and the harsh heat of summer, and with spectacular views across the azure bay and moody Vesuvius to boot. The wealth shows: the streets widen into generous boulevards, beyond which I caught glimpses of vast apartment blocks, painted in hectic lemons and pinks that offset the deep greens of the roof gardens with their elegant furniture.

Enzo Coccia's Pizzeria La Notizia, however, is a simple place – a small, brightly lit room with space for perhaps thirty customers and a TV in one corner. The walls are dotted with reproductions of antique prints: the Teatro San Carlo; fishermen by the Gulf of Naples. It's a welcoming, practical place, and I could imagine it was a favourite with local families, eager to catch an early dinner together. However, I wasn't here to eat but to learn, because Enzo also runs a small pizza-making school.

Pizza-making is in Enzo's blood. His father, Antonio, owned Pizzeria Fortuna near the Piazza Garibaldi and handed on his passion to his son, for Enzo is an apostle of pizza. In addition to revealing the secrets of the *pizzaiolo* (I could see young men of various nationalities in his kitchen, effortfully twisting and flipping dough on their forearms to stretch it into a workable pizza base), he has invented cartoon characters for wheat, tomatoes and mozzarella, in an effort to educate kids about their food. When he realised I was interested in more than just the basics, his eyes lit up. As I asked questions about temperature and protein content and rising times, he sprang into action, scribbling diagrams and grabbing scales, shaving slivers off a block of yeast, filling the air with its malty aroma. He was so excited that he would often cut in before the translator had finished the previous sentence. Here was someone as fired up by the technicalities of his trade as I was. Enzo was *simpatico*. If anyone could help me master the intricacies of the perfect pizza, it was him.

As if to confirm my impression, Enzo asked to change before the filming started. He returned in full *pizzaiolo* regalia: beautifully laundered whites and the traditional red neckerchief. This was clearly going to be the full monty – or perhaps, since we were in Naples, the full Capodimonte.

Enzo hauled out a small square wooden trough with handles at the four corners. Into this traditional mixing bowl went the best part of 3 litres of ordinary tap water at room temperature, plus about 150 grams of salt.

'How important is salt for the taste of the dough?' I wanted to know.

'It improves the taste, but you've got to be careful because it slows the rising and too much will make the dough too compact and difficult to work with.'

He sliced off 8 grams of yeast and told me to dip it in the water and rub it between finger and thumb until it dissolved. Then I added flour – Caputo flour, I was pleased to notice – in great scoopfuls while Enzo stirred it with his hand. *'Vai, vai. Mette farina.'* Another scoopful. *'Vai, vai.'* And another, until the mixture became less liquid and Enzo began advising just a sprinkle of flour each time, aiming for exactly the right consistency.

'OK, it's ready,' he declared eventually. 'Take off your watch, roll up your sleeves. Work with me.'

Normally, kneading is now done by machine: it makes no difference to the outcome (it's even sanctioned by the Associazione) and cuts kneading time from forty to twenty minutes, though you still have to oversee the whole process rigorously in case more flour is needed. We, however, were going to do things the traditional way. Enzo and I stood either end of the mixing bowl and went at it.

Enzo demonstrated a kind of up-and-down rhythm. 'This is to make sure that the dough is soft, elastic, uniform and – most important of all – that it has plenty of air in it. All of this activity is to get air into the dough,' he said. 'Like this: *uno, due, uno, due.*' I thought he was suggesting giving it the old one-two, like a boxer, and started pummelling, but he reined me in. 'Strong but slow. You don't have to fight it.'

We walked our fists along the dough towards the centre, then folded it and began again. At intervals, Enzo would pick up the dough and hold it out, as though showing off a baby – testing the feel and consistency, how loose a shape it made as it hung. Then he'd flip it over on itself and return it to the bowl. *'Un poco di farina,'* he'd announce, and off we'd go again.

'Enzo, how come on my side the dough's all sticking to the bowl but on your side it's not doing that at all?'

He laughed. 'Maybe you're not working hard enough … '

Despite this, the dough gradually became softer, whiter and more resistant to our fists. It must have been exhausting work in the old days before machines, especially if you had to do it every day. Although I train in a gym, by the time Enzo judged the dough ready for the next stage I'd really broken out in a sweat. I decided that if a kneading machine was OK with the Associazione, then it was OK with me. That's what I'd use in Bray.

All the hard work had been to good purpose. The dough sat on the table, dense and plump, like a small pillow. Enzo grabbed a scraper and severed it neatly in two. The cut face looked like the moon's surface, cratered and pock-marked, evidence that there was plenty of air in there. (This would give the pizza base its lightness: in the heat of the oven the air would try to escape, rising up and giving the base that characteristic bubbled texture.) He looked happy with the result, which meant I was too, though I knew that the next job was another of those that looks easy when done by an expert but is in fact very tricky indeed.

In one swift movement Enzo cut a long thin strip from the dough, grabbed it between thumb and forefinger as though holding a snake, and worked the dough with his other hand until, magically, a small white globe of dough seemed to grow out of the top of his fist. A firm final squeeze and he separated it from the rest of the dough and placed it – by now about the size of a large bread roll – on a tray. A minute later there were fifteen of them, tidily ranked in three rows.

My first attempt spoiled this symmetry – it was smooth and round all right but barely larger than my palm – but gradually, under Enzo's patient guidance, I got a feel for the character of the dough and produced my own neat row of balls, though I was never going to match his speed.

The trays would be left to rise for anything between four and eight hours. (Before even mixing the dough Enzo had checked the weather for humidity, assessed how much moisture the dough might take up, and adjusted the amount of yeast accordingly. This is part of the art of the *pizzaiolo* that can't be learned. Over time Enzo has developed an instinct for how much is needed, and knows exactly how long it will take to perform its task.) Eventually, the dough balls should have increased in size by about 50 per cent, spreading outwards rather than up, until each ball is just touching its neighbour. The dough will be much softer than at the start of the rise, as carbon dioxide does its work, moving from the yeast cells into air pockets in the dough and inflating them. It's then ready to make pizza.

With all this care and attention, Enzo's pizzas rivalled anything dished up by more famous places: the dough was deliciously savoury, the tomato moist and characterful. Long after I should have left to catch the flight home, Enzo was expertly presenting pizza after pizza for me to taste. Eventually I had to insist, regretfully, that it was time to go. His parting words were, 'For the perfect pizza you need water, flour, yeast, salt – and a little love.' Well, I loved cooking and I'd just received a masterclass in handling the ingredients. I hoped it would be enough.

The film crew and I got to the airport just in time. But Naples had one last surprise, one last reminder of the theatre, spectacle and generosity that surrounds food here. It was my daughter's birthday that night, so I had asked my friend Enzo Caldarelli if he could get me a cake to take back to Britain. As we queued at the check-in, he arrived, breathless, in a dark suit, white shirt and wraparound shades. 'Heston, *aspetta*! Wait!'

Wait we did, nervously eyeing the clock ticking towards the time when the gate would close. At last two men arrived pushing trolleys piled high with handmade biscuits, cellophane-wrapped lemon desserts and cartons of mozzarella. They were followed by Pasquale Marigliano, one of the best pastry chefs in Italy. His whites still had a dusting of sugar on them and he was carrying an impressively large cake box.

We set aside what we could carry on to the plane, but that still left an awful lot of food on the trolley. And so, as onlookers stared, we ripped open cellophane and polystyrene and had a final taste of the best Italy has to offer. It was a fitting end to the trip.

And my daughter loved the cake.

OFF THE SCALE

While I was in Italy, in addition to my pH and conductivity meters I'd carried another neat bit of kit: a thermometer that went up to 500°C. It hadn't been easy to come by: conventional oven thermometers don't go anywhere near this high because there's nothing in the kitchen that requires that temperature. But the Naples pizzeria is an entirely different ball game. The oven takes little more than a minute to cook a pizza, which gives you some idea of the tremendous temperature involved. The Neapolitans may not have experienced the volcanic heat of Vesuvius since 1944, but their ovens are real furnaces!

Of course, this has a dramatic effect on the taste and consistency of the pizza itself. For one thing, the brief cooking time means the tomatoes remain moist and runny, retaining an intense tomatoey flavour rather than acquiring the thicker, jammy character of their British counterparts. In order to produce a truly authentic pizza, I'd have to replicate that kind of heat, so I wanted to know what temperature I was aiming for.

When I'd first tried out the thermometer in Da Michele, I thought the equipment was on the blink. The digital read-out raced through the 300s and 400s before feebly flashing out 'error'. But at La Notizia the same thing happened and I realised it wasn't the machine that was at fault: the oven was simply too hot to handle. It topped 500°C.

The thermometer may not have given me an accurate read-out, but it did tell me one thing: I would have to either make my own pizza oven or do something fairly unconventional to a conventional oven.

DOUGH BOYS

Naples had shown me that dough was the key to pizza. Just as a good pasta provides fundamental flavour to the dish it graces, so the pizza base is more than a backdrop to the toppings, or the ultimate bio-degradable plate. It provides the underlying taste of any pizza, so I had to come up with a dough delicious enough that you could eat it on its own.

Neapolitans would say that achieving this was simple – just use Caputo flour! I suspected they were right but I wanted to see for myself; besides, Enzo's dough-making techniques were all about feel and touch, and I wanted to get in some practice. I enrolled the help of Chris and we each made a batch of pizza dough – me using Caputo while he used standard, superfine plain flour. We'd check out how they responded to kneading, then cook them and taste the results. At the very least we'd gain some idea of how much flour type influenced dough behaviour.

I had a vague fear that, back in Bray, I wouldn't be able to summon up what Enzo had taught me. But it turned out that, like riding a bike, it was knowledge that didn't really leave you. As I placed the dough on the table, marched my fists up and down it, then folded it over and started again, my muscles seemed to relax into a familiar rhythm. The manual-labour pleasure that is part of working in a kitchen took over.

Although the rhythm was familiar and I was no longer a new-comer to the process, I still found the thirty-minute push 'n' pummel a real workout. I'd been wondering if I would recognise the precise moment when the dough was ready. As perspiration began to bead on my forehead, I decided I should probably patent a Sweatometer: clap the electrodes to your forehead and start kneading; a red light would tell you the dough was ready once you'd worked up enough of a sweat.

Chris, I was happy to notice, was finding it no easier. We stood side by side, hunched over the polished black granite work surface, silently rucking and knuckling the dough. Chefs are, by nature, a competitive bunch. We both affected a nonchalance that was hardly backed up by our reddening faces and ragged breathing, and then redoubled our efforts. I tried to remember the texture of Enzo's dough. Mine was still too soft, too flaccid. It needed to gain more body and acquire that cratered, aerated texture. Gradually it became springier. I held it at arm's length and let it hang there, to check elasticity.

'I've got bubbles,' I called out like a boastful schoolboy, even though I'd started fifteen minutes before Chris. The dough was now white, smooth, tensile. I sliced it in two with a knife and examined the cut face. It was riddled with bubbles – real Enzodough. 'Are you ready, Chris?'

'I'm almost done.'

From the look on his face, he was almost as done in as I was. But we had two pillows of dough to show for it. They had to rise for about eight hours, but we twisted pieces off to taste right away. Already there was a marked difference: the Caputo flour had a strong toasted bread-crust flavour that the other couldn't really match.

'The insipid one's yours, Chris,' I said. 'Enzo told me that for dough you need five ingredients: water, flour, yeast, salt and a little love. Maybe you didn't put enough love in … '

Professional that he is, Chris didn't rise to the bait. 'I'm amazed at how noticeable the difference is between the two, even now. It'll be exciting to see how they bake off and taste after that.'

But before that happened we had one other test: we wanted to compare hand-kneaded dough with machine-kneaded. We used one type of flour, one recipe, one rising time, and the results were as unexpected as they were extraordinary. After rising, the machine-kneaded dough balls had spread and softened on the tray until they touched one another. They were at least 50 per cent bigger than the hand-kneaded, which sat stingily separate, looking more like large cookies than dough balls.

I could not only feel the difference – the machine-kneaded were far springier and more elastic – I could see it. The machine version was speckled with airholes that would easily spread cooking heat throughout the crust and expand to give that characteristically Neapolitan bubbled surface. Chris and I held and stretched out examples of each – like two wives in a washing powder commercial comparing shirts – but it was already obvious which way we'd be kneading our pizza dough. So many times in the *Perfection* series I'd ended up recommending a slower, less mechanised approach; it was quite refreshing to be able to advocate a technological advance that was not only quicker and easier but also better for the end product. Maybe I wouldn't need the Sweatometer™ after all.

IN THE CAN

It had sat on the shelf for weeks, tempting me with its vibrant primary colours and the promise of what was inside. I had resisted manfully, and now the moment had come when I could let the genie out of the bottle, or in this case out of the can: I was going to compare the famous San Marzano tomato with a number of other varieties to see if canning gave it a superior texture or flavour.

I lined up Solania's San Marzano alongside cans of peeled plum tomatoes from Sainsbury's, Tesco, Waitrose, M&S and Napolina. In Naples pizzerias most chefs take tomatoes straight from the tin and crush them by hand before popping the lot on the pizza, so I did the same and tasted the results.

Things got bloody almost as soon as I began. I misjudged the first squeeze and ended up with my chef's whites covered in red, as though I'd secured a walk-on part in a splatter movie. Proceeding more gingerly, I squashed each tomato into a bowl, then speared some on a fork and chewed, trying to discern its characteristic flavours.

A couple were far too liquid: they would never dry out sufficiently during a ninety-second cook, no matter how high the heat. The pizza base would be drowned. What I was looking for from the others was the right balance of flavour and acidity. If the flavour is bland, the acid dominates, giving an unpleasant taste in the mouth. If, on the other hand, there's a big fruity flavour, then the acid does a valuable job of cutting through the sweetness. The San Marzano definitely had the best balance: the canning had concentrated its taste (the heat involved in the canning process effectively cooks the tomatoes, giving them some of the flavour dimensions of oven-roasted tomatoes) to produce something sharp but sweet. It was the taste I remembered from Neapolitan pizzas.

Yet both M&S and Waitrose peeled plums could give it a run for its money – a big consideration given that San Marzano tomatoes are difficult to get hold of in Britain and can cost up to six times more than a supermarket brand. I was sure that I could get equally good results using a tin of M&S tomatoes. But could I get better results going down a different route altogether? When I'd visited the tomato fields beneath Vesuvius I'd discovered that the San Marzano was less flavourful than other tomatoes I'd tasted. I decided to try pressure-cooking some of those to see if they'd add something extra.

Mozzarella-tasting turned out to be a similar experience. In Naples airport I had eaten some of the best mozzarella I've ever had: a smooth, creamy, melt-in-the-mouth texture allied to a rich depth of flavour and just a delicate hint of acidity. I arranged for Enzo Caldarelli to send some over to my development kitchen: I wanted to blind-taste it against the best I could obtain in Britain – Blissful Buffalo, Mandara and Garofalo Mozzarella di Bufala Campana – to find the right cheese for my pizza.

Maybe I had just got lucky, or maybe mozzarella's one of those things that 'doesn't travel well': Enzo's next batch had none of the same magnificence. It was still very good, but so was Garofalo, which is a lot easier to get hold of. In some ways this was a relief, as I already felt a little guilty about the hoops I would be putting home cooks through as they scoured the country for Bresse chickens, artisanal pasta and Japanese brown rice malt syrup. I was glad to be able to recommend something that might be picked up in a shopping trolley rather than via a website.

SOME LIKE IT HOT

The EU pizza copyright proposal specifies an oven-surface tempera-ture of 485°C and a cooking time of between sixty and ninety seconds. As I've said, this speedy, high-temp approach has a profound effect on the end result: one of the reasons British pizzas tend to taste different from the Neapolitan version is that the pizza ovens here often peak at a far lower temperature and thus take five minutes to cook, which changes the character of the dish.

So my goal was a sixty-second pizza, and to achieve it I'd need to make an oven as hot as I possibly could. I bought a proper *pizzaiolo's* peel and a very smart, boxy, brushed-steel Gaggenau cooker, and I set to work.

I was all for disassembling the thermostat and bunging in a few anthracite coals to whack up the temperature, but when people suggested it would melt the seals and crack the glass it seemed sensible to devise an alternative.

How else could I buck the oven's top temp? I programmed 300°C into the oven and placed a pizza stone inside. Once the LCD told me I'd got to 300, I turned off the oven and turned on the grill. As expected, that extra burst of heat upped the temperature rapidly. I checked the fast-paced scramble of the temperature gun's read-out: 320 … 353 … 370. That's where the thermostat lost our game of 'Chicken', shutting off the grill to cool things down. But the pizza stone would retain the heat for a while, and I could turn on the grill again in a minute for a final blast.

It wasn't 485°C but it was a start. With a temperature gun and split-second timing, we had a small window of opportunity during which we could cook a pizza base at a reasonably high heat. Chris grabbed the peel, I clutched the temperature gun and we waited – like sportsmen ready for the off – until the heat reached 370°C again.

'GO!'

Dough disc was scooped on to peel I flipped open oven door in it went with a shove and jerk on to stone and *slam!*

The door was shut. We all stared through the glass – me, Chris, the director, the cameraman, the researcher – waiting to see what would happen, willing it to work.

The dough bubbled up just like a Naples pizza before puffing out like a poppadom – time to take it out. It had been in there for ninety seconds.

It looked great, nicely browned in places and retaining a lightness of structure. And it tasted great, too: the distinctive sweet, toasty bread flavour I remembered from Naples. I still had to get the topping right, but already the dough base seemed to me to be really authentic.

Intoxicated by success, Chris and I flipped one dough base after another into the oven, testing the cooked taste of hand-kneaded dough against machine-kneaded. As expected, machine-made had the edge: the more generous rising meant bigger bubbles that made for a less dense, more elastic texture. It had the crisp crust and tender interior of a genuine Naples pizza. Technique and ingredients were starting to come together. It was all very exciting.

Later, it momentarily became even more exciting when we discovered that the oven's cleaning cycle actually went up to 470°C. Problem solved! We'd got access to the temperature we wanted and there couldn't be any danger of the glass door cracking or the seals melting because the oven was designed to handle that kind of heat. We were on track at last for the sixty-second pizza ...

Except that the Gaggenau's door automatically locked during cleaning. Technology isn't always your best friend. The perfect recipe was still a few hurdles away.

---

* Umami The Fifth Taste

There's a fundamental difference between taste and flavour. Crudely speaking, we taste with our mouths but we discern flavours with our nose (via an olfactory bulb situated behind it). If this seems counter-intuitive, put onion purée and apple purée in bowls and don a blindfold. Pinch your nose while eating from one of the bowls and see if you can guess whether it's onion or apple. The chances are you'll find it impossible to distinguish one from the other until you stop pinching your nose. This is because flavour is registered by the olfactory bulb as flavour molecules pass up into it. When we pinch our nostrils, denying air to the olfactory bulb, our brains can't decipher the information received.

The olfactory bulb can distinguish between thousands of different flavours. But the mouth can only distinguish five tastes. (That's why wine tasters spend more time sniffing than swilling.)

At least, that's the current thinking. But this is an exciting branch of science in which new discoveries are being made all the time: scientists only recently established that we have more than 600 genes that can register flavour – double the previous estimate. There is still debate over whether the concept of five tastes is too simplistic: for the bitter taste alone, for example, there are more than twenty receptors, which respond to different things and in different combinations. And some scientists are pushing for fat to be identified as a taste.

Even the fifth taste was only discovered in the last one hundred years. Up until then, scientists had only formally recognised four tastes distin-guishable by the tongue: salty, sweet, sour and bitter. But Professor Kikunae Ikeda of the University of Tokyo became interested in the brothy, savoury taste generated by kombu, or giant kelp, which grows up to 30 feet long off the northern islands of Japan and has been flavouring their food for at least a thousand years. In 1908 he discovered that the savoury taste was caused by the presence in kombu of glutamic acid, and decided to name that taste 'umami' (which translates roughly as 'delicious'). Since then, scientists have discovered several other substances in food that provide the umami taste: inosinate (which is present in bonito and many meats), guanylate (more abundant in plants: shiitake mushrooms have high concentrations) and adenylate (which occurs mainly in fish and shellfish).

Ikeda went on to develop a new flavouring based on glutamic acid. In 1909 he marketed monosodium glutamate (MSG), which has since been readily accepted in Asian countries (where it appears in kitchens much as salt would, in fine pale flakes in a jar) but has provoked concern in the West. A phenomenon known as 'Chinese restaurant syndrome' (CRS), the effects of which include dehydration and headaches, is thought to be caused by MSG.

Admittedly, monosodium glutamate's acronym has done it no favours, making it sound especially synthetic and unnatural. But the truth is that the scientific tests that led to the identification of CRS were unrigorous, and more recent tests have found that earlier conclusions were largely without foundation. Food writer Jeffrey Steingarten made a succinct defence of MSG in the title of his essay 'Why Doesn't Everybody in China Have a Headache?' This might seem flippant, but many people who consider MSG harmful wouldn't think twice about putting ketchup on their chips or adding a stock cube to their sauce, both of which are rich in umami.

What's all this got to do with pizza?

Although umami was identified in Japan, it's not an Eastern phenomenon. It is present in all kinds of foods familiar to us: anchovies, bouillon, bouillabaisse, gumbo, soy sauce, ketchup, Marmite, and those pizza staples, Parmesan and tomatoes. (Try this next time you have a really ripe tomato: take a bite of the outer flesh on its own, and then of the stuff around the seeds. There'll be a big difference in taste, and it'll be the inner part that gives the big, savoury, meaty mouthfeel. That's umami. As you can probably tell, this a subject close to my heart. That's why my first research paper investigated precisely where in a tomato umami *compounds are most highly concentrated, and which factors influence the presence of such compounds.)*

What is more, in combination the umami chemicals have a magnified effect: if you add a food rich in glutamic acid to another that has, say, traces of inosinate, the umami taste is massively intensified. This plays a huge part in the recipes in this book. Put mushroom ketchup on a steak, simmer meat and tomatoes in a bolognese, add Parmesan to a Margherita, and you get a taste explosion!

Pizza Margherita Serves 5

By pressure-cooking and oven-drying tomatoes, I managed to get the big, meaty umami taste I'd been looking for, and using a smoked salt captured that provolone touch, but the key features of this pizza are still heat and dough.

Making dough involves a number of conflicting demands: the longer it's left the more its flavour develops, giving that wonderful yeasty, bready note. But, over time, the gluten loses its elasticity and becomes wet, flabby and difficult to work. The answer to this dilemma is a pre-ferment: a small amount of dough, prepared for its flavour, which is then added to a larger amount of dough that still retains its extensibility. The best of both worlds!

It's essential to get the heat above and below the pizza as hot – and as even – as possible. The secret is a heavy cast-iron frying pan, which can get much hotter than a ceramic pizza stone and holds that heat for longer. Whack the grill on full for a while, put a preheated pan under it and you've got yourself a serviceable pizza oven that should cook a Margherita in a couple of minutes. The speed's vital because the character of the ingredients changes with a longer cooking time. It might take a bit of experimentation to get it just right, but after that the pizzas will come fast and easy – as in an authentic home pizzeria, especially if you've got hold of a pizza peel for that final Italian touch.

Special equipment
Food mixer, pressure cooker, cast-iron frying pan (at least 26cm in diameter: large enough to accommodate a pizza on the base), short-handled pizza peel (optional)

Timing
Making pizza dough is as easy as making bread – a matter of a few minutes' mixing and a few hours' proving (rising). You need to start a day in advance, but only so the pre-ferment dough can prove overnight. Peeling, cutting and deseeding the tomatoes takes a while, but

after that there are no complicated cooking techniques: the tomatoes can be put in the oven or pressure cooker until done. (And you can do it all the day before to stagger the workload.) The pizza itself is incredibly quick. Once the pan is hot enough and the dough ball has been flattened out, it takes only a couple of minutes to put on the toppings and cook the pizza.

For the pre-ferment
150g pizza flour (such as Caputo, or a flour with a medium-to-high protein content – about 12% – such as Alimonti Organic '00' pasta flour) _ ¼ tsp malt syrup _ 85g cold water (for accuracy, it's important to weigh the liquid in grams rather than using a measuring jug) _ 3.5g (½ sachet) fast-action bread yeast _ ½ tsp table salt

For the dough
350g pizza flour _ ½ tsp malt syrup _ 195g cold water _ 7g (1 sachet) fast-action bread yeast _ 1 tsp table salt _ reserved pre-fermented dough

For the tomato toppings
45 (about 1kg) large cherry tomatoes, on the vine* _ extra virgin olive oil _ 2 large cloves of garlic _ 20 fresh basil leaves _ 20 fresh thyme sprigs _ 2 fresh bay leaves _ 1 tsp unrefined caster sugar _ table salt and freshly ground black pepper

For each finished pizza
1 ball of reserved pizza dough _ 50g tomato sauce _ 10 oven-dried tomato halves _ 125g buffalo mozzarella (such as Garofalo Mozzarella di Bufala Campana), drained _ extra virgin olive oil _ 4 fresh basil leaves _ smoked sea salt

PREPARING THE PRE-FERMENT
Flours vary, hydrating at different levels. If, at the end of mixing, the dough is still too crumbly, add a little extra water and mix a little

---

* As with all recipes in this book involving tomatoes, it's very important that they are ripe and of good quality. It's equally important they're not stored in the fridge: low temperatures actually kill off the flavour of tomatoes.

longer so that it forms into a cohesive ball. Conversely, if it still seems 'wet' at the end, add a little more flour.

1. Tip the flour into the bowl of a food mixer. Using the dough hook, begin to mix on the first (lowest) speed.
2. Stir the malt syrup into the water, then pour the liquid into the flour. Mix on the first speed for 3 minutes, then stop the mixing and allow it to rest in the bowl for between 10 minutes and 1 hour. (An hour is best, if the time is available. It improves the flavour of the dough and its stretchiness.)
3. Add the yeast and salt and mix on the second speed for 7 minutes. (If, halfway through this process, the dough does not look as though it is coming together, stop the mixer and scrape the flour from the sides of the bowl.)
4. Transfer the dough to a large, clean mixing bowl and cover tightly with clingfilm to prevent a skin forming on the surface. Place the bowl in the fridge and leave to ferment for 12 hours.

MAKING THE DOUGH

1. Tip the flour into the bowl of a food mixer. Using the dough hook, begin to mix on the first speed.
2. Mix the malt syrup into the water, then pour the liquid into the flour. Mix on the first speed for 4 minutes, then stop mixing and allow it to rest in the bowl for between 10 minutes and 1 hour. (As with the pre-ferment, an hour is best.)
3. Add the yeast and salt and mix on the second speed for 4 minutes.
4. Stop the mixer. Add the pre-ferment to the bowl and mix for 4 minutes on the second speed.
5. Remove the dough (it should pull away cleanly from the sides of the bowl: if it doesn't, try adding a little more water and mixing for a further 2–3 minutes). Place it on a clean work surface, shape the dough into a log and then cut into 5 pieces, each weighing about 150g.
6. To make the dough balls, first place your palm on a work surface, then arch it up into a kind of claw shape. Place a piece of dough within it. Move your hand round and round – your fingertips should be touching the work surface and your palm pressing gently on to the dough. This motion will form perfectly round balls – the more round your dough is, the better the shape of the

pizza base – and, more importantly, it won't squeeze the air out of the dough.

7. Place the balls on a plastic tray that has been brushed with oil (or a baking tray lined with oiled clingfilm), leaving at least 4cm between each ball. Cover well with a large piece of oiled clingfilm. Leave to prove for 2 hours in a warm place (or refrigerate for 12 hours). The dough balls will double in size and should look moist, light and airy.

MAKING THE DRIED TOMATOES AND TOMATO SAUCE

1. Preheat the oven to 110°C/225°F/Gas ¼. Bring a large pan of water to the boil. Fill a large bowl with ice-cold water.

2. Pull the tomatoes off the vine, reserving the vines. Remove the cores with a paring knife. Blanch the tomatoes by dropping them into the boiling water for 10 seconds and then carefully transferring them to the bowl of ice-cold water. Take them out of the water immediately and peel off the split skins. (If the tomatoes are not ripe enough, make a cross with a sharp knife in the underside of each, to encourage the skins to come away. They can be left in the hot water for an extra 10 seconds or so, but it's important that they don't overheat and begin to cook.)

3. Cut 25 of the tomatoes in half vertically. Scoop out the seeds and membrane.

4. Place the tomato halves in a bowl and drizzle with olive oil. Toss the tomatoes in the oil and then, using a slotted spoon, transfer them to a baking tray lined with foil, cut side up. Slice the garlic and place a slice on each tomato half. Tear the herbs and scatter over the tomatoes, along with a drizzle of olive oil. Season with salt and pepper and sprinkle over the sugar.

5. Cook the halves for approximately 2–3 hours (the ripeness of the tomatoes can make a big difference to the cooking time), turning them over about halfway through cooking. When they are ready, the tomatoes will have shrivelled slightly and turned a deep, vibrant red, but they should still be moist rather than 'sun-dried'. (If, during cooking, some appear to be drying more than others, remove them from the oven early.) Allow them to cool, pick off the garlic and herbs, and store the tomatoes in a container, covering them with extra virgin olive oil.

6. Cut the remainder of the blanched tomatoes into eighths and place in a sieve over a bowl. Sprinkle over 1 teaspoon of salt and leave until 5–6 tablespoons of tomato juice have collected in the bowl.

7. Place the tomatoes and their juice in a small pressure cooker. Put on the lid and cook over a high heat at full pressure for 12 minutes.

8. Remove from the heat and leave to cool. Once cool, remove the lid and place the tomatoes back on the heat. Cook over a high heat, stirring frequently, for 10–15 minutes, or until there is very little liquid left.

9. Leave the sauce to cool again, then tip into a container. Add the reserved vines (plus any extra that are to hand) and cover. Leave at room temperature if cooking the pizzas straight away; otherwise store in the fridge for up to 24 hours. (The vines seem to contain a lot of that wonderful fresh tomato smell. Adding them here allows that aroma to permeate the sauce. It's a technique that can be used in other dishes – try orange, lemon or mandarin leaves – bearing in mind that the leaves may be heat-sensitive, so are best added to slightly cooled ingredients.)

ASSEMBLING THE PIZZA

1. Preheat a cast-iron frying pan over a high heat for at least 20 minutes. Preheat the grill to the highest temperature possible. Generously flour the work surface and a baking sheet or pizza peel.

2. To shape the pizza base, put a ball of dough on the floured surface, then place your fingertips 1.5cm in from the edge and push down as you move the ball around in a clockwise direction. Continue pushing and turning until a rim (the *cornicione*) forms that will ensure the sauce collects in the centre of the pizza.

3. To finish, place the palms of your hands on the dough and gently stretch it in opposing directions. Rotate the pizza through 90° and repeat this action. Continue to rotate and stretch until the pizza is 20–25cm in diameter. (Make sure it's not bigger than the base of the frying pan!) If you're gentle, this process should preserve the circular shape of the pizza. Be careful not to squash the rim or leave a dome in the centre.

4. Carefully lift the pizza base on to a baking sheet or pizza peel. Spoon the tomato sauce on to the centre of the pizza and swirl it

outwards in a circular pattern to cover the dough thinly, making sure you don't spread it over the *cornicione*. Scatter the oven-dried tomatoes on top. Tear the mozzarella into chunks the size of a gobstopper and dot over the pizza. Finish with a generous drizzle of olive oil and a sprinkling of smoked sea salt.

5. Remove the frying pan from the hob, turn it upside down and place under the grill. (It needs to be very close to the grill but with enough space left for the pizza to rise slightly: you don't want the topping to end up stuck to the grill's element.) Let it heat up for several minutes before carefully sliding the pizza on to the base of the frying pan. (This must be done while the pan is under the grill so as not to lose valuable heat.) Cook for 90 seconds or until the dough has cooked and turned golden brown and the mozzarella has melted and started to bubble but not brown. Add the basil leaves and serve.

Risotto

'Risotto is such a simple and satisfactory dish,
so universally appreciated.'

Elizabeth David, *Italian Food*

History

Rice has its origins in Asia. The earliest known remains of cultivated rice come from the Yangtze valley and are about 8,500 years old. Further evidence of its early use has been found in pottery fragments from the sixth millennium BC, which show the imprint of rice grains on their surface. The spread westwards took time, perhaps because rice is a demanding crop that requires the organisation and stability of a settled community, but gradually it made its way from the Far East to India, the Philippines, Japan and the Middle East. It is the Muslims who are credited with increasing the area devoted to rice cultivation: knowledge of the staple was a by-product of conquests in Persia and India in the seventh and eighth centuries, and it accompanied their rapid expansion through the Western world so that, by AD 1000, rice was being grown in Spain and exported to Sicily. Henry III's household accounts show that rice had reached England by 1234, and around the same time there are references to it in the book-keeping of the Duke of Savoy. In Milan rice was already heavily taxed as 'spice brought through Greece from Asia'.

It's not clear exactly when rice reached the flat, humid, well-irrigated plains of Lombardy and Piedmont that turned out to be a perfect environment for its cultivation (the area now produces 90 per cent of Italy's rice) but historians quote a 1475 letter from Galeazzo Maria Sforza to the Duke d'Este of Ferrara concerning the expected output from a sack of rice seed as evidence that rice was being grown in the Po valley by the fifteenth century at the latest. (Sforza's advice must have been good because by 1543 'Sicilian-style rice' was being served at an Este family banquet.)

A much-circulated story has it that risotto Milanese was invented in 1574 by Valerio, an apprentice artist working on Milan's duomo. Fed up with being teased by his master for the amount of saffron he used in his stained-glass colouring – 'You use so much you'll end up using it even in risotto!' – Valerio actually added saffron to the rice to be served at his master's wedding, and the idea instantly caught on throughout the city.

This story needs to be taken with a pinch or two of salt. Although TV chefs occasionally cause a run on cranberries or goosefat, in general food trends don't have a single, dramatic starting point. The pairing of rice and saffron was surely already familiar to Italians since it was common practice in Arab cuisine, and had appeared in recipe manuscripts in France (*Le Vivendier de Taillevant*) and England (*Form of Cury*), and even in Maestro Martino's *Libro de arte coquinaria*, which pre-dates Valerio's wedding joke by 100 years and had a huge influence on Italian cuisine.*

In *The Oxford Companion to Food*, Alan Davidson says that the first risotto recipes appear in the mid-nineteenth century in the work of Giovanni Vialardi and Pellegrino Artusi, implying that risotto was originally a peasant dish that therefore went unrecorded: only after it evolved into something more sophisticated did it acquire a body of literature. Websites try to extend this, tracing a line from *Oniatologia* (*Science of Food*, published in the late 1700s) with its recipe for 'rice soup in the Milanese style', through Antonio Nebbia's *Il cuoco Maceratese* (1784), which talks of soaking and frying rice, and on to Felice Luraschi's *Nuovo cuoco Milanese economico* (1829), in which rice is cooked in a manner close to modern practice, though the addition of wine comes later. It first appears in Artusi's recipes, confirming just how incrementally the dish has adapted and evolved.

The Quest for the Best

RISOTTO CRACCO

From the outside, Carlo Cracco's restaurant doesn't look like one of the most inventive in Italy. It presents a sleekly anonymous façade of glass, pale stone and claret-coloured steel, as though it were the

---

* It contributed much to Platina's *De honesta voluptate et valetudine* (1472 or 1475), which has been described by Gillian Riley as 'the first best-selling cookery book in history'.

headquarters of some discreet international company. The nameplate, however, suggests otherwise. It spells out Cracco-Peck – Ristorante in Milano, but does so in reverse, as if to tell you to expect the unexpected. Given the surprises Carlo manages to pull off with his food, it's sound advice. And for me the reversal was doubly appropriate because my Italian journey in search of the foundations of a proper risotto Milanese was going to be conducted backwards, beginning with two thoroughly modern reinventions of risotto, before I visited the rice fields of Piedmont and then sampled a classic version of the dish.

Carlo poked his head out of the door and beckoned me downstairs. (The last time I had seen him his head had been shaved. Now his hair was long and carefully brushed, and he looked like a 1980s movie star – another reversal.) The restaurant has been brilliantly designed to ensure that, despite being below ground, it doesn't feel in any way cramped or confined. Most of the dining area is double-height, giving a breathtaking sense of vertical space. The mezzanine allows a series of unexpected viewpoints, in the manner of a modern art gallery, and, indeed, as Carlo escorted me downstairs, I was confronted at each level by a work of art. A vast trapezoid of upholsterer's webbing and coloured bobbins accompanied my first steps, and further down the mezzanine presented a framed square of metal, bashed and flattened and folded over itself as though rescued too late from the breaker's yard. Facing the foot of the staircase was a black stone plinth topped by a ripple of bronze. Against the ribbed cherrywood panelling and stone-coloured walls it all gave a feeling of grandeur and solidity, of something monumental.

Carlo had already laid out what he needed for the first of two risottos he was going to show me. In eight small white oval bowls, arranged like an artist's palette in a semicircle, were the ingredients, some of which were unexpected or unidentifiable, such as the pale, milky liquid in a plastic tub to one side. I had been hoping for something unexpected, and it looked as though he wasn't going to disappoint.

He took a small, heavy copper saucepan and placed it on a burner set to a fairly high heat. Slooshed in a swirl of olive oil and then a spoon-sized dollop of onion that had been diced to a paste.

'Molto fino.'

'Very finely chopped,' I translated. 'I'm learning Italian as well as risotto.'

'*Bene*. Once the onion has softened – which is quick because of the *molto fino* – we add Carnaroli rice.' He up-ended a bowl into the pan and stirred.

'Do you always use Carnaroli?' This was one of the key things that I wanted to canvass opinion on. There are several different varieties of risotto rice available: each of them must be cooked in a slightly different way, each gives different results, and each suits a different type of risotto. At the Fat Duck I had experimented with aged and par-cooked rice, talked to many chefs and explored all kinds of techniques. I had discovered that risotto provokes strong opinions that are often based more on lore and tradition than hard fact.

'Well, as you know, Heston, I come from Vicenza. There the risotto has to be very liquid, very … '

'Emulsified?'

'Yes. So we utilise only Vialone Nano. It's better *in bocca* … in the mouth. But here in Milan I always utilise Carnaroli because it's typical of this region. Mine is from Lomellina, about 40 kilometres from here. It's a very long rice, very strong.'

'Which makes it more creamy?'

'No, it's more that it gives a finer texture. OK, now I'm going to add liquid. The normal choice would, of course, be stock or milk, but as this is not a traditional recipe, I'm going to utilise water. I prefer it because it makes the risotto very flat.'

'So it's just a base for the other ingredients – it doesn't mask their flavours.'

'Exactly.'

Carlo added a lot of the water straight away. Over the next twelve minutes he would top it up from time to time, but there was no continuous stirring. As the rice cooked, we discussed the benefits of using rice that has been allowed to age for a year or so, a practice that I suspected might be another key to giving the dish an extra dimension. I was using aged rice at the Fat Duck and it gave a fantastic al dente texture. Could it also work in a Milanese?

'Italians cook risotto only with fresh rice, but that's because that's how it has always been done. For me that's never a good reason not to try something new. And, in fact, fresh rice is very delicate – it doesn't stay al dente very long. In this respect, aged rice would certainly be better – the risotto would stay at the right consistency for a much longer time. But, in my experience, this comes at a price. You lose some of that lovely aroma you get with fresh rice, and this is also very important in something as simple as a risotto.'

Hard experience and a sense of adventure gave Carlo's words an urgency, even in translation, that was infectious. 'How about this, then?' I challenged. 'Make a broth using new rice, then use that liquid to cook the old rice. The best of both worlds – the aroma of one, the texture of the other. Has it been done before?'

'No. No one has done this. But I think we could do it together,' he said, breaking into his high peal of laughter.

The rice was ready and Carlo pulled the pan off the heat. 'It must rest for one minute because the rice is stressed from cooking. And it must never go back on the heat. Never. Now we go to the *mantecatura*, how is it called … ?'

'The emulsifying. The addition of the ingredients that'll bring it to life.'

Carlo lifted the lid on the small plastic tub he had set aside and flourished a small glug into the pan. He handed over the tub for me to smell. Zing – each nostril was hit by a sharp scouring cleansing freshness. Horseradish juice.

'After this, Heston, I add finely grated Parmesan, of course, and then butter and mascarpone.' He scooped up a thumb-sized lump and began folding it into the mixture with a wooden spoon. Three quick stirs to the left; one bigger slower stir to the right. 'Mascarpone is a typical cheese of Milan. Not many people know that it was born here. For me, this is one of the most important things for the risotto. Mascarpone makes it very creamy but without too much fat.'

The ingredients were no longer separate but had come together as one. Putting the mixture back on the heat would have split out the fat and spoiled that careful combining. Carlo was ready to serve. He began by painting a thin layer of pale caramel-coloured paste on to the plate.

'Anchovies,' he explained, working the pastry brush in quick strokes. 'I cook them in olive oil for an hour, then push them through a fine sieve to get rid of all the filaments.'

The aroma was fantastic, and was soon joined by the tang of the fresh lemon that Carlo grated on top of the anchovy undercoat, using the photo-etched sharpness of a Microplane to ensure he got only the skin and not the bitter pith. 'It gives a lovely smell – and it's cheaper than truffles!' Another volley of laughter. He poured the risotto into the centre of the plate and shook it back and forth until the rice settled to the rim in a smooth, flat circle. Satisfied, he tapped the plate on the work surface a few times, then reached for the final white bowl and the finishing touch: a small disc of 99 per cent bitter chocolate.

Bullseyeing the centre of the risotto with something unusual seems to be something of a tradition in Italy, and before I left Lombardy I would encounter an even more extravagant centrepiece. It undoubtedly conferred a visual elegance on the dish, a counterpoint of colour that tempered the possible monotony of a whole plateful of white rice. Carlo's dark brown disc softened to take on a shine and the nubbed impression of the rice below. It was very picturesque, geometric, sculptural.

'I wanted to preserve part of the classic risotto,' he explained, 'but with a completely new taste.'

I turned my spoon upside down and scraped it in to catch the edge of the chocolate and the rice, lemon and anchovy below. Including chocolate in a risotto might seem strange to some people, but here it was far from sweet and had a piquancy that sneaked up on you. And the balance of flavours was fantastic. The richness of the rice and the chocolate was offset perfectly by the saltiness of the anchovies and the fragrance and acidity of the lemon.

'You've succeeded, Carlo. That really is a new taste, and it's delicious. But I believe you've got something else to show me – something that could never be called a classic risotto?'

If the raised eyebrows and grin on Carlo's face hadn't confirmed this to be true, then a quick glance at the new ingredients he'd put out would have given the game away:

olive oil
cream
sea urchins
basmati rice
instant coffee

My first spoonful of Carlo Cracco's undeniably unconventional sea urchin risotto.

'I love the fragrance of basmati rice and I wanted to capture it in a risotto but the texture was a problem for people.'

'Yes. This must be one of the most difficult countries to be creative in because it has a culinary tradition that is so strong.'

'And the people are strong too. When I started this restaurant I didn't do recipes like the one you're about to see. I stayed traditional for the first three months. Then I changed and people weren't happy about it. But I was happy, and slowly I altered the menu, adding a few more twists each month. I conserve tradition – sure! – but it's inside the dish. Here's what I mean … '

He put a plug in a socket. One of the most innovative features of the dish was the technology used to create it: a Bimby thermomixer that slowly mixes and heats at the same time. It's a great machine, but its potential is only just being recognised by chefs.

'In this … ' Carlo waved at what looked like a high-tech blender or juicer – a lidded steel jug slotted into a chunky square housing with a couple of calibrated knobs and an LCD. 'I have put basmati rice and cream. Very little rice. About 40 grams to 1 litre of cream.'

'Otherwise, I guess, there'll be too much starch released into the mix from the rice. And it'll end up far too thick.'

'Exactly. I set the heat to 90°C and let the rice mix slowly for forty minutes. It should be ready now. Here – smell.' He unscrewed the lid and inhaled the aroma before handing it on. The basmati was intensely perfumed, intoxicating.

'Now I take Nescafé— '

'Maybe this is even braver than using basmati, Carlo. An Italian, in Milan of all places, using freeze-dried coffee.'

He sprinkled coffee granules over the bottom of the bowl. 'I utilise this to counter the cream, which is very fatty.' On top went the rice-cream, a smooth, almost liquid purée, releasing a cloud of basmati fragrance. Plump sea urchins were delicately spooned on top of this, one by one – dotted brown counterpoints to the chalky whiteness of the rice – and sank slightly into the surface. The dish was finished with a swift zigzag of olive oil, a scribble of shimmering green to complement the other colours. 'Coffee and sea urchin is for me perfection. The sea urchin is sweet— '

'And it has that iodine note – it's a very complex flavour on the tongue.'

'Such a sharp taste, but even. And the coffee explodes but extends the flavour.'

I knew exactly what Carlo meant. Sea urchins are very aromatic but they need another flavour – like the bitterness of coffee – to boost them. The coffee brought this dish together, emphasising the flavour of the sea urchins while at the same time cutting the rich creaminess of the rice-cream. The balance of flavours was, again, amazing: the aroma of sea urchin succeeded by the aroma of rice, and finally that touch of bitterness with, all the while, the slight pepperiness of olive oil. Together, the five key ingredients were much more than the sum of their parts. It was beautiful.

'Bellissimo,' I told Carlo.

'Grazie,' he giggled.

* Starch in Rice

Starch is a carbohydrate: a molecule produced for the purpose of storing chemical energy. In rice, the parent plant lays down starch molecules in microscopic solid granules that fill the cells of the grain's central core (the endosperm). Whether brown or white, about 80 per cent of the rice grain is starch.

The simplest carbohydrates are sugars, such as sucrose (table sugar), lactose (the sugar in milk) and glucose (also known as dextrose), the most common sugar from which living cells get their chemical energy. Starch, a more complex carbohydrate, is formed from a long chain of glucose molecules. (Such sugar chains are called polysaccharides: other examples are cellulose, gum arabic and the pectin in jam.)

Starch granules contain two different kinds of starch molecule, each of which is constructed differently:

AMYLOSE – made from about 1,000 glucose sugars and constructed in a long chain with few branches

AMYLOPECTIN – made from 5,000–20,000 glucose sugars in hundreds of short branches

Amylose is therefore a simple molecule, the neat structure of which allows it to form in a strong, orderly pattern. So it behaves like a well-trained soldier, whereas amylopectin is more like a raw recruit – it doesn't cluster easily or tightly. These differences in structure have a marked effect on how rice behaves as it cooks.

The starch granules absorb water, swelling and softening as the water penetrates them and pushes the molecules apart. This happens quickly and easily to the loose-structured amylopectin, but the tightly packed amylose molecules require a higher temperature, more water and a longer cooking time to prise them apart.

Clearly, the ratio of amylose to amylopectin in the rice is going to have a significant effect on the end result. Long-grain rice, for example, has about 25 per cent amylose, while sticky rice is almost all amylopectin.

Risotto rice is high in amylopectin, but it varies from type to type, and this has to be taken into consideration when cooking.

Arborio has the highest concentration of amylopectin. A lot of its starch, therefore, breaks down easily, which makes it great to add to soups and stews in small quantities. Arborio is the most commonly used for making risotto.

Vialone Nano has more amylose than Arborio, making it more robust. It will take longer to cook, it will absorb more liquid and it will be more al dente. Italians often choose Vialone Nano for a dish that has a variety of ingredients, and keep Carnaroli for simpler, more delicate risottos. Carnaroli has a good balance of both starches, which in turn gives a good balance of creaminess and texture in the finished dish.

RISI E BUSY

The next morning we headed east towards the rice fields of Piedmont, where there were two producers I particularly wanted to visit: Michele Perinotti of Gli Aironi, and the Rondolino family of Acquerello. Piero and Rinaldo Rondolino are acknowledged experts in their field, consulted by local universities and the Slow Food movement. The Carnaroli they sell has been aged for a year, and they have done extensive research on rice aged for longer. I was hoping their technical specialisation would help guide my own research.

I know just how good the Rondolinos' rice is because I use it in a risotto at the Fat Duck. Michele Perinotti's product, on the other hand, had come as an exciting surprise. In preparation for this trip, I had tasted dozens of examples of risotto rice in order to establish a benchmark for comparison. Gli Aironi's Carnaroli was utterly distinctive, with an intense, nutty note that I really valued. I realised straight away that I would have to visit Michele and find out how he got that flavour.

Soon after we left Milan the reason for our trip became visible all around us. On either side of the A4 spread a gridwork of what looked like vast sheets of glass – the shallow pools in which rice was germinating. The pattern continued virtually without a break during the 80-kilometre drive to Vercelli, the mirrored sheen of irrigated fields alternating with the sump mud of fallow ones and the acid green of

Michele Perinotti's father beside a rice field and the spike-wheeled tractor used to farm it.

those in which the rice plants were already well grown. Eventually we pulled into the large gravelled courtyard of the Perinottis' farm.

In his red jeans, docksiders and multistriped shirt, Michele wouldn't have been out of place at Henley Regatta. His dad looked more the part, dressed in heavy denim and a pair of green waders that he had folded to the knee in thick cuffs, giving him a faintly piratical look. 'Come,' Michele encouraged me, shaking hands, 'there are some small fields at the back where the seed is to be sown.'

We walked past rusting machinery, then threaded our way slowly along one of the tussocky raised strips that bordered each of the fields. The smell of mint, released by plants crushed underfoot, suffused the air. Disturbed by our progress, herons took flight with lazy flaps, presenting strange, elongated silhouettes. Gli Aironi is Italian for 'the herons'. Michele's company was well named.

'The seed is sown in water,' he explained. 'At this stage it's very delicate and the water acts as a kind of protection. We call it *la coperta termica* – the thermal blanket. However, after a week, ten days maybe, when it's a bit stronger, we drain off the water, let the seed germinate. Later we bring the water back in to keep the shoots from blowing around and to stop weeds from growing.'

'Your rice has a lovely, distinctive taste – nutty, full-flavoured. Is there something going on in the fields that accounts for that?'

'It's important that the rice doesn't sit in stagnant water, and we've worked hard to make the irrigation as efficient as possible. As well as the canals here that service every property, my father and I have dug underground tubes to feed our fields. These can be closed or opened with sluice gates. The temperature of the rice is crucial at all times: a warm day or a cold night can really damage it. Our system means we have much greater control of this. But what you're interested in, Heston, is as much to do with taste as cultivation. And for that we have to go to the silos.'

We made our way back along the edge of the field, the looping calls of lapwings in our ears, and Michele outlined the storage process. 'The rice matures in the fields, but this continues after harvesting, in the silo. The rice becomes more acidic and firms up as it does so. This gives a good texture, but the density reduces the aroma; and as the starch content reduces, so does the taste. It's a question of balance. There's an optimum point where all these things work together. That's the real skill of the rice producer – judging when it's ready. For me it's somewhere between four and eight months after harvesting, and I check small batches regularly to see how the rice is coming along.'

By now we had once more passed the rusting farm machinery and crunched across the gravel to reach a large concrete and metal hangar with a long steel tube sticking out of one side, presumably to feed rice that had reached the optimum point into waiting lorries to be taken off to the mill. Passing a complicated set of pipes and hoppers, we climbed up a narrow, vertigo-inducing metal staircase to reach a set of gangplanks that criss-crossed the building just beneath the roof. Below us hillocks of unhusked rice thrust upwards from four two-storey concrete wells, spilling over the walkways in places. The air was thick with the same rich nutty aroma that I'd noticed in the polished rice I'd tasted back in Bray. Stretching, I could reach down far enough to pick up a handful of grains. They looked like tiny slim nuts, the skin papery to the touch, each with a dark plume poking out of it.

'That's the moustache,' said Michele. 'Only the Carnaroli has it. What you see here, Heston, is 600 tonnes of rice – half our yearly produce. It stays here, temperature-regulated, until it's ready, then goes off to be milled, which is the final key to quality. You have to mill delicately to keep as much as possible of what's under the outer skin. There's lots of protein and fat there, and that's what provides the flavour.'

THE MILLER'S TALE

As Michele said, milling is a crucial factor in the quality of rice. On the short drive to Acquerello's estate near Livorno Ferraris, I read through the notes I had made on the process of transforming it into shiny white kernels.

At harvesting, the kernel is surrounded by two layers – the outer (or husk) and the inner (the bran). This rough rice is called the 'paddy', and that's what's delivered to the mill, where it's passed through some form of coarse and fine filter (screen sieves or specific gravity tubes) to get rid of impurities larger than the rice (straw, stones, feathers) and anything smaller (weed seed, dirt, grit). Just the paddy remains.

The next stage, husking, is relatively easy because the husk isn't tightly attached to the kernel. Usually the rice is fed through two rubber rollers spinning at different speeds, and these strip off the outer layer, leaving rice that still retains the bran: brown rice.

The bran is more securely attached than the husk and requires more abrasive milling to produce kernels of a smooth, fine whiteness (often known, therefore, as 'pearling'). Great care must be taken to protect the kernels. This is the heart of the miller's art. Many large commercial concerns cut corners in the interests of economics, husking and removing the bran in one aggressive process that weakens the structure and limits the flavour. At the other end of the scale, there are producers who mill their rice seven times. More usual is a double process – milling first with an abrasive stone and then with a metal roller.

Over time rice production has become a singularly high-tech business. I had visited a mill not far from here, Tenuta Val del Serpe, where the Zanotti machinery was compact enough to fit in one small room, but nonetheless put the rice through a fantastically complicated vetting process that separated off, in succession, the green bits (for fuel), the over- and undersized rice (for rice crispies etc.), the bran (for animal feed), more bran (more animal feed), before sending the product past an electronic eye that detected differences in colour and graded the rice accordingly. A burst of pressurised air shunted the grains to the appropriate tube. The rice eventually ended up in a small hopper and the smell was absolutely out of this world: as complex as it would ever be, with an aroma of nuts, oats and honey, and a grassiness, even a touch of damp leaf, recalling the fields from which it had come.

Over the years I have encountered many people who think science has no place in the kitchen. I wondered whether they'd feel differently if they knew what went into the grains of rice on their plate.

ROCK 'N' CARNAROLI

My reading was interrupted as the car was plunged into darkness by the shadow of a huge archway – the entrance to the seventeenth-century splendour of Tenuta Colombara, home of Acquerello rice. The building had the dimensions of a Renaissance palace: on each of three sides a double row of twenty or so windows looked on to the cobbled courtyard and the swallows wheeling around the pantiles. The fourth side had a succession of airy barnlike structures big enough to house a fleet of carriages. It was all testament to a time before mechanisation when more than a thousand people would have lived and worked here. Now the only permanent inhabitant was an artist-in-residence. (Occasionally, peering in through a dusty barred window, I would catch sight of sinuous white sculptures suspended by threads on metal frames and begin to feel as though I had stumbled into a David Lynch movie.) The Rondolino family have apparently been patiently preserving and restoring the place to make a kind of 'living museum'.

Despite the backdrop, Rinaldo Rondolino didn't play lord of the manor. Slight, and clad in jeans and a grey T-shirt with *Stomp* printed across it, he looked more like one of the students from Pollenzo's University of Gastronomical Sciences who regularly visit Colombara for instruction.

A few seconds' conversation soon altered this impression. Rinaldo is an apostle for his product. Serious and seriously knowledgeable, he talks about rice with the precision of one determined not to be misunderstood. He led me through another arch to where the green of his rice fields stretched to the horizon, interrupted only by another vast and ancient building in the distance.

'Do you plant only Carnaroli?' I wanted to know.

'Yes. Many commercial concerns go for Arborio because it has a higher yield.' Rinaldo plucked a one-month-old plant from the field and stared at it intently, his dark eyebrows narrowed. 'In another four months this little green strand will produce about 150 rice grains. Arborio produces above 200.'

'But you still prefer Carnaroli.'

'It's the best for our interpretation of how a risotto should be. The type of starch in Carnaroli develops two very important characteristics during maturation: it absorbs the flavours of the other ingredients, while at the same time it doesn't overcook easily. So it's logical that we now go and see where the rice ages. Come, Heston.'

We made our way to a modern, red-painted hangar with another narrow, vertiginous metal staircase. As I climbed I could smell again the malty, nutty aroma that I'd encountered in the silos at Gli Aironi, and eventually I reached a similar set-up of crawl spaces above fifteen deep wells of ridged galvanised metal. The heat was dry, stifling. Above our heads was a constant clatter of what sounded like rats' feet on the hangar roof.

'What's that?' I bellowed above the noise.

'Water,' Rinaldo explained. 'It runs in pipes below the roof to keep the temperature down. It's important that it stays below 30°C.'

'Where did the idea of ageing rice come from?'

'It's not our idea. In fact, my father read somewhere about a Sanskrit manuscript that talked about the perfect maturation of paddy rice and decided to explore the possibilities. We have tried ageing rice right up to three years, just to see what happens. A year seems to be the most effective.'

'So what happens? How does it work?'

'The rice is picked and put in here still in its husk. The ageing allows various things to develop. Sugars present in the starch – glucose and fructose – increase, making it sweeter. At the same time, lipids in the rice are oxidised, releasing fatty acids. The rice becomes more acidic and so hardens up.'

'Which is why there's less danger of it overcooking. It takes longer to absorb the water,' I said. 'I understand that in stored rice grains the surface proteins also oxidise and bond to each other. A thin skin forms on the grain that limits both the water penetrating the grain and the starch leaking out. The result is less stickiness.' (It seemed I could talk like a PhD student too. I hadn't been awarded an honorary degree by Reading University for nothing!)

'You are right, Heston. Finally, as well as taking longer to absorb water, rice that has been aged for ten months absorbs more water during cooking and the kernel swells up more.'

'And does this continue over time? Does two-year-old rice exhibit particular characteristics?' I knew that ageing beef brought all kinds of interesting flavours and reactions into play, something I'd used to develop my steak recipe. I was hoping to pull off the same trick with rice.

'No. The difference between fresh rice and year-old is huge. Between one and two years, however, is negligible. Ninety per cent of the positive effects of rice ageing happen in the first year. The remaining 10 per cent take a further six years to develop.'

Back to the drawing board. We clattered back downstairs, the rats' footsteps still pattering in the background, and finished by discussing the milling, which is another crucial feature of Acquerello's quality.

'Usually, big rice companies grind twice, briefly – six seconds maybe – using stones. And that's it. But we follow this up with a system that grinds rice on rice. It's a process unique to Acquerello and it provides a much more gentle abrasion. You have to be very careful and delicate towards the end of milling or you'll get fractures and the rice won't cook evenly because water won't enter it in a uniform way.'

'I guess it's a little like polishing with successively finer grades of sandpaper to get a smooth finish.'

'Yes, exactly. This final grind takes ten minutes, during which the temperature reaches 35°C. The fine powder created by this milling is then absorbed in the fine cracks that open up under the heat created during this process. This means our rice needs very little in the way of *tostatura*. A minute maybe. Not more. This absorption is also what gives the kernels that ivory-white colour that is always a sign of good rice. If the rice is too white, then too much has been removed. I can show you, if you like.'

Like? Showing me involved a cool piece of kit: a chunky, black plastic cube that looked like a Polaroid camera until Rinaldo pressed a button and it flipped open to reveal a lightbox and magnifying glass. What was not to like? I had noticed it earlier sitting on a table alongside a set of super-sensitive scales, several sorting trays and sealed plastic packets of rice samples and had hoped that it would somehow get involved in the afternoon's explorations. I hunched over, screwed one eye shut and peered down at the blue glow of the lightbox while Rinaldo told me what to look for.

'On the left you have rice polished the conventional way, Heston, and on the right is rice that uses our process. Can you see the difference?'

This was a very modest question because the difference was in fact marked. Under the magnifier the grain on the left had dark lines and patches, evidence of fractures. Rinaldo's rice was pristine bar the faint stripe of shadow caused by the grain's oval shape. It threw into sharp relief just how important the very structure of the rice would be to a perfect risotto. My dish would stand or fall by the rice I chose.

RISOTTO CLASSICO

It might seem perverse to seek advice on the classic risotto from a chef who, when his restaurant first opened in Milan, served neither rice nor pasta, declaring, 'Pasta is for when you are hungry.' Nonetheless, I was driving past the generously proportioned houses, manicured lawns and gently sloping vineyards of Franciacorta on my way to visit one of the restaurants run by that very chef – Gualtiero Marchesi.

Marchesi is widely regarded as the father of modern Italian cooking. He was not only the first Italian to gain three Michelin stars; he was also the first non-Frenchman to do so. To achieve this in a country that clings so tenaciously to its culinary roots requires a talent not only for cooking but also for self-promotion. The pasta ban was, at least in part, a gambit – a piece of gamesmanship. Two years later, the final course of a meal at his restaurant was served under the brand-

new cloche he had just designed for Alessi. The lid was lifted to reveal
… a tiny portion of tagliolini with fonduta and truffles. Marchesi does
pasta! It began a tradition of 'surprise' pasta dishes, such as the 7/20/7
with its 7 grams of penne, 7 grams of asparagus and 20 grams of
black truffles. His trademark risotto, *riso e oro* (literally, rice and gold)
was equally flamboyant and extravagant. I could hardly wait to see it
being made.

The car swung through the imposing gates of L'Albereta hotel and
spa and headed up between rows of towering cedar trees to emerge
before what looked like the villa of an art-loving millionaire. Framed
by the last of the cedar trees was a two-storey building crowned by a
tall tower swathed in ivy. To the left a colonnaded gallery made its
way into the trees, past the rain-streaked, sullen-faced bronze *Bather*
by Giuseppe Bergomi. Behind me was *Polifonia* – a large marble female
nude lopped off at shoulder and knee and flanked by five thin marble
pillars. The splashing of a fountain vied with the constant twitter
of birdsong. At the entrance, bushy purple and green acers were
dominated by the flare of jasmine that grew up and over the doorway,
its flowers spreading a rich, heady scent as you approached.

The art theme continued in the restaurant itself. The walls had
canvases by Joan Miró and Gaston Chaissac, the self-styled 'Picasso in
clogs'. Huge windows looked on to a garden that housed a stylised
sculpture of a motorbike – sleek and slippery, half Dalí, half Boccioni.
Beyond was a breathtaking view of Lake Iseo, with the island of Monte
Isola at its centre and Monte Guglielmo rearing up behind. Each table
had as its centrepiece a work of art – Joe Tilson's wooden egg marked
'Eros'; a miniature version of Gianfranco Pardi's *Danza* – because
Marchesi saw that as part of the dining experience. Fanned out on
a piano in the corner were copies of the magazine *Stile Arte* with
examples of Gualtiero's recipes inspired by art: 'La forma del formaggio'
incarnated Dalí's surreal melting point.

And suddenly, there was the man himself, making light of our
need for an interpreter: 'I don't speak English. French, yes. German. A
little Italian also … ' The rimless glasses and swept-back grey hair
made him look like a musician, an impression that fitted with how he
sees the kitchen at work. 'I am the conductor. My chefs are my orchestra,'
he told me, and this perspective is reinforced by the way the *brigade*

de cuisine is on show to the customers. Between dining room and kitchen is a large wide window covered by a screen. As service begins, a button is pressed and the curtain goes up, revealing the chefs going about their business and a long shelf with copper pans ranged in order of height, at the dead centre of which is a model of the Michelin man perched on top of a Red Guide.

'Come, Heston. Let's go behind the curtain.'

Marchesi's ingredients were neatly lined up in two straight rows on a metal tray – rice, saffron, Parmesan, butter, acid butter, salt, white wine. Spoons stuck out of all but the wine, ready for action.

Chicken stock was already warming on the stove. Gualtiero placed a small copper pan on a burner, scooped in a big tablespoon of butter, cranked up the heat, let it warm, then added the rice and agitated it back and forth for a while.

'What rice do you use?'

'Carnaroli. Aged for a year.' He slapped in a ladleful of stock, provoking an angry hiss from the pan. Pinches of salt and saffron were added and the heat taken right down.

'I see you don't add any onions … '

'They're present in the flavour of the butter that I add later, but that's all. I try to take everything unnecessary out of the risotto, to keep the flavour of the rice and the saffron as pure as possible.'

'What's your view on stirring, Gualtiero? Does the rice need a constant massage to release the starch?'

'A lot of myth surrounds the stirring. The key is a slow boiling. With the right heat, the rice will amalgamate on its own.' As he talked, Marchesi tweaked constantly at the dial controlling that heat. 'Add the stock a little at a time. It has to be exactly right at the end – there's a very thin line between liquid … and soup! So put more in at the start. Be sparing later on. The Milanese style is *all'onda*: the risotto is ready when you can shake the pan and see the ripple – like a wave – across the top. Then you know it is done.' He shook the pan and a ripple rolled obligingly across the surface. 'OK, it's ready to *mantecare* – *com'un gelato*. You know why I say this, Heston? It's because *mantecare* means something similar to churning, like with ice cream. For me the *mantecare* is all about adding *burro acido* – butter flavoured with white wine, onions and vinegar.'

Gualtiero Marchesi ladles out his trademark risotto, riso e oro, which contains real gold leaf.

The butter was added to the pot and left unstirred. A white napkin was placed on top.

'So acid butter is what makes the difference? That's your secret ingredient?'

'I got the idea from beurre blanc. It's great because it gives a slight sweetness and it means you can use less Parmesan in the dish, which makes it lighter. Normally the acidity that is essential to risotto comes from the addition of Parmesan, but in my version the acidity comes from the wine and the vinegar.'

'Why is it left unstirred? And why the napkin?'

'That's just how we do it. Under the napkin for two minutes.' With mock ceremony he took a tea towel and buffed up a spoon before handing it to me.

'I'm like a kid getting a treat. A risotto Milanese from Marchesi.'

Gualtiero inclined his head graciously, then ladled out a small cone of risotto on to a white plate with a black and gold rim, and knocked it against the table until the risotto lay flat. Picking up a small square booklet, he detached a page, peeled back the edges and gently let a fine sheet of gold leaf float on to the centre of the risotto. 'To make it beautiful,' he said, and indeed it looked great against the gold rim. The risotto itself looked fantastic too – a deep orange-yellow flecked with red from the saffron strands. A real work of art.

There was a pause while the camera tried to capture Marchesi's dish on film. I could see Gualtiero out of the corner of my eye, politely patient but at the same time keen for me to tuck in. The pleasure in cooking for people, the excitement at watching them taste his food, was as strong as ever.

And that passion, it seems to me, is the key to great cooking – as important as the science, the technique, the intuition, the invention. That is part of perfection too.

WHAT'S IN A NAME?

Gualtiero Marchesi puts an artwork on each table in his restaurant, believing it to be an essential part of the experience. Did it alter his customers' appreciation of the menu? I'm sure it did. The taste of food depends on all kinds of things that aren't experienced on the tongue or in the nose, yet affect the brain's perception of what is being eaten, so, with the help of Professor Charles Spence, I set up a little experiment to explore the idea.

In his cramped lab, amid the ranks of amplifiers and spools of cable tentacling across the floor, I placed a rickety desk at which sat Alberto, the guinea pig for this test, waiting to taste and compare three dishes that I had prepared: a strawberry risotto which, as an Italian, he'd be familiar with; a tomato risotto; and a strawberry rice pudding. Kyle brought all three in and placed them before him. The rice pudding had an attractive scatter of diced strawberries dimpling its surface. Alongside it was the tomato risotto, with its delicate pinkish blush, and next to that was the gentle pink hue of the strawberry risotto. To me they looked very appealing, but what would Alberto make of them?

He spooned up a mouthful of tomato risotto, nodded and grinned. 'It's a bit acid, I have to say.'

Not so good. I invited him to try the other risotto, eager to see whether he preferred it.

'That's better. I don't feel so much the strawberries, but it's good.'

I expected Alberto to find the final dish a bit unusual. After all, rice pudding doesn't get served in Italy, and he confirmed that he had never eaten it before.

'Strange, but not bad,' he granted, perhaps not wanting to let me down.

He hadn't let me down because what I had kept from him was the fact that all three dishes were exactly the same. Alberto had been served three plates of strawberry risotto. Apart from strawberries dotted on the top of one, the only difference was the name given to each, and that had had a major influence on what his brain told him he was tasting.

I wasn't about to change the name of risotto Milanese to risotto Hestonese or anything like that. Risotto had simply presented the perfect opportunity to illustrate how important it is to consider every aspect of a dish's presentation because the perceived flavour depends on much more than just a set of tastebuds in the mouth and receptor neurons in the nose.

Risotto Serves 6

The most pared-down risotto dishes, such as Milanese, are in effect a celebration of rice. I wanted my recipe to capitalise on that, combining the properties of aged rice with the marvellous aroma of basmati and the nuttiness of Gli Aironi's product, and, indeed, any other aspects of rice that would suit the dish.

Basmati's aroma is surprisingly delicate and can easily get lost. The efforts to introduce it to the dish in a form that preserved its character all too often took the recipe too far from what people might accept as a risotto. In the end a basmati-infused chicken stock best allowed its flavour to come through uncompromised, and a conversation with my friend the food science writer Harold McGee led to a fantastic finishing touch – pandanus leaf crème fraîche. The aroma in basmati comes from a molecule called 2-acetyl-1-pyrroline (2AP). Harold had come across research that had discovered high levels of 2AP in the pandanus leaf, or screwpine, a herb used as a flavouring in Asian cooking. Adding it to the risotto perfectly reinforced that delicate aroma I was trying to capture.

I also wanted to include the nuttiness of Gli Aironi's Carnaroli rice in my recipe, and after many trials it found its way into an acidulated beurre noisette, added at the end of cooking to give the dish a marvellous freshness. (This also avoids one of the significant pitfalls of softening onion at the start: an overbrowning that affects the final balance of flavours.)

One of the fascinating things about experimenting with risotto was the opportunity it gave to test some of the inviolable lore surrounding its cooking. We did numerous comparisons of different approaches to adding stock – calculating the exact amount of liquid needed and putting it all in at the beginning; ladling in a little at a time and massaging it into the grains; pouring in most of the stock at the start and then topping up occasionally. Tastings showed that the last two techniques worked well – the key was monitoring the crucial final minute or so of cooking and making whatever adjustments were necessary.

The *tostatura* – the toasting of the rice in oil before adding the liquid – turned out to have an even more decisive effect on the finished dish, encouraging the rice to absorb the stock evenly. Untoasted grains tended to go plump and mushy.

Special equipment
8-litre pressure cooker, oven thermometer, drum sieve, food processor, hand-held blender

Timing
Preparation takes about 10 hours. Cooking takes about 35 minutes.

For the basmati-infused chicken bouillon
8 legs or thighs of organic, free-range chicken, chopped (to increase exposed surface area) _ 250g thinly sliced carrot (about 2 large carrots) _ 250g thinly sliced onion (about 1 large onion) _ 125g thinly sliced leek (about 1 leek), white and pale green parts only _ 2 cloves of garlic, crushed _ 5 whole peppercorns _ 100g basmati rice _ 1 bunch of parsley

For the puffed rice
100g basmati rice _ 500g water _ 1 packet saffron (about ½g) _ 500g grapeseed or groundnut oil _ fine salt

For the velouté stock base
50g butter _ 250g button mushrooms, cleaned and sliced _ 50g white wine _ 20g Madeira _ 1kg reserved chicken bouillon

For the finished velouté stock
1kg reserved stock base _ 250g reserved basmati water _ 450g whipping cream _ 80g white wine _ 20g thinly sliced shallot (about 1 shallot) _ 250g basmati rice

For the butter emulsion and toasted rice
200g diced onion (about 1 medium onion) _ 375g dry white wine 375g white wine vinegar _ 200g butter _ 50g Gli Aironi Carnaroli rice _ 300g butter, cubed and chilled

For the toasted rice tuiles

reserved toasted rice _ 190g whole milk _ 70g double cream _ egg whites (see step 5) _ caster sugar (see step 5) _ salt (see step 5) _ reserved puffed rice

For the saffron butter

100g butter, softened to room temperature _ 1 packet saffron (about ½g)

For the Horlicks and coffee salt cubes

10g freeze-dried coffee granules _ 250g fleur de sel (hand-gathered sea salt, available from steenbergs.co.uk) _ 25g Horlicks _ 115g water

For the dried mushroom powder

100g (about 8–10) button mushrooms, cleaned

For the pandanus crème fraîche

100g crème fraîche _ 10g pandanus leaves (available from Thai markets), washed and cut into 2cm strips

For the finished risotto

20g butter _ 300g Acquerello rice _ 100g dry white wine _ reserved chicken bouillon _ 80g reserved toasted rice butter _ 20g finely grated Parmesan cheese _ reserved velouté stock _ salt _ reserved cubes of frozen saffron butter _ reserved pandanus crème fraîche _ reserved mushroom powder _ reserved salt cubes (about 12) _ reserved toasted rice tuiles

MAKING THE BASMATI-INFUSED CHICKEN BOUILLON

1. Place the chicken in a large pan and cover with cold water (about 2kg). Bring to a simmer and immediately drain the water. Cool the chicken pieces under cold running water. This removes the blood and impurities from the bones and meat that would otherwise go into your final broth.
2. Place the chicken in an 8-litre pressure cooker and add enough water to cover (about 3kg). Put the lid on and place over a high heat. Bring to full pressure, then lower the heat and cook for 1 hour.

3. Allow the pressure cooker to cool, then remove lid and add all the remaining ingredients except the parsley and rice. Return to full pressure for 30 minutes.
4. Rinse the basmati rice under the cold tap until the water begins to run clear.
5. When the pressure cooker is still warm but not hot, add the parsley and allow to infuse for 30 minutes.
6. Strain the stock through a sieve into another pan. Add the rice and bring the stock up to a simmer. Simmer for 20 minutes, then strain through a sieve. Discard the rice.
7. Chill the stock in the fridge for later use in this recipe.

MAKING THE PUFFED RICE
1. Rinse the rice under the cold tap until the water runs clear.
2. Place the rice and water in a pan and bring to a simmer, stirring regularly. Simmer until the rice is thoroughly cooked but not mushy, approximately 8 minutes. Strain through a sieve, reserving the water (for use in the velouté recipe) and the rice.
3. Preheat the oven to 60°C/140°F.*
4. Using a rubber spatula, toss the rice with the saffron in a bowl until the mixture is evenly pale yellow.
5. Spread the rice in a thin, single layer on a parchment-lined baking sheet and dry in the oven for 45 minutes.
6. Remove from the oven and allow to cool to room temperature, breaking up any clumps that have dried together into individual grains.
7. Meanwhile, place the oil in a pan and heat to 190°C/375°F. Alongside it place a second pan, a mesh sieve, a tray lined with several layers of kitchen paper and a container of salt.
8. Begin frying the rice in small batches. It should puff as soon as it hits the oil. If it sinks to the bottom and does not puff, it simply means that too much moisture has been driven off in the drying process.
9. Strain the oil through the sieve into the second pan, then turn all the puffed rice on to the lined tray. Sprinkle with salt. Repeat the process until all the rice has been fried.

* If you don't have a convection oven, set your oven to the lowest it will go. You may need to prop the door open and use an oven thermometer to get the temperature down to 60°C/140°F.

10. Allow the puffed rice to cool completely, then cover and reserve for making the toasted rice tuiles.

MAKING THE VELOUTÉ STOCK BASE
1. Melt the butter in a pan wide enough to hold the mushrooms in a single layer. When the butter is foaming add the mushrooms and cook over a medium heat until they are evenly caramelised (about 15–20 minutes).
2. Add the wine and Madeira and reduce the liquid to a syrup.
3. Add the bouillon and heat until simmering. Simmer for 1 hour.
4. Pass the stock through a sieve and discard the mushrooms. Chill over ice and keep refrigerated or use immediately.

FINISHING THE VELOUTÉ STOCK
1. Place the stock, basmati water, cream, wine and shallot in a pan. Bring to a simmer over a medium heat and cook for 20 minutes.
2. During the simmering, rinse the rice under running water until all the starch has washed away and the water runs clear.
3. When the stock mixture has simmered for 20 minutes, add the rice and simmer for another 10 minutes.
4. Strain and chill over ice. Keep refrigerated until ready to use.

MAKING THE BUTTER EMULSION AND TOASTED RICE
1. Place the onion, wine and vinegar in a pan and cook over a high heat until the liquid has reduced.
2. Meanwhile, melt the butter in a sauté pan and add the rice. Cook, stirring frequently, over a medium heat until the butter becomes dark brown and nutty and the rice is toasted golden brown.
3. When the wine and vinegar have reduced to a thick syrup, begin to whisk in the chilled butter a few cubes at a time to keep the mixture emulsified. (This process is the same as for a beurre blanc type of sauce. You must maintain enough heat to melt the butter thoroughly, but not have it high enough to split the emulsion. You must also whisk constantly when making each addition of butter.)
4. Strain out the onion and discard it. Return the emulsified butter to the same pan.

5. Whisk in the brown butter and toasted rice until evenly incorporated. Allow this mixture to infuse off the heat for 10 minutes.
6. Pass the butter emulsion through a sieve, reserving the rice for the tuiles. Chill the emulsion over ice, then store refrigerated until needed.

MAKING THE TOASTED RICE TUILES

1. Rinse the toasted rice under tepid water until all the butter has gone.
2. Place the cleaned rice, the milk and the cream in a saucepan, bring to a simmer and cook over a low heat until the rice is tender (about 12–14 minutes). Strain, reserving both the cooking liquid and the rice.
3. Purée the rice in a blender with about one-third of the cooking liquid until you have a smooth paste.
4. Pass this rice batter through a sieve (preferably a drum sieve) to separate the larger pieces.
5. Weigh the rice batter and fold in 10 per cent of this weight in egg whites, 1.5 per cent of it in caster sugar and 1 per cent of it in salt. Fold all the ingredients together until evenly mixed. The batter should be easily spreadable.
6. Preheat the oven to 140°C/275°F/Gas 1. While the oven is heating, cut out a plastic stencil no thicker than 3mm in the shape of a tuile (a rounded rectangle about 11cm long and 3cm wide).
7. On a baking sheet lined with a silicone mat or baking parchment, spread your batter inside the stencil until the surface is covered in tuile shapes. Sprinkle the puffed rice over each one. (The batter will yield more than the 12 tuiles needed for this recipe, but some may break, so it is best to make extra.)
8. Bake in the oven until golden brown. Allow the tuiles to cool for a few minutes, then transfer with an offset spatula to a sheet of baking parchment and reserve.

MAKING THE SAFFRON BUTTER

1. Place the softened butter in a mixing bowl.
2. Put the saffron in a small bowl or ramekin with 1 tsp of hot water.
3. Pour the saffron infusion into the butter and mix well.

4. Place a piece of clingfilm over a small chopping board about 30cm long. Spread the butter over the film with an offset spatula to a thickness of 5mm. Cover with clingfilm and refrigerate until completely set.
5. Once the butter has hardened, unwrap and cut into 5mm cubes. Place them in the freezer until you're ready to serve.

MAKING THE HORLICKS AND COFFEE SALT CUBES
1. Preheat the oven to 100°C/212°F.
2. Using a food processor or mortar and pestle, grind the coffee into a fine powder.
3. Add the salt and Horlicks and grind together again.
4. Heat the water in a pan over a low heat and add a quarter of the salt mixture, stirring to dissolve.
5. Remove the pan from the hob and stir in the remaining salt mixture. Pour into a 10 x 12cm loaf tin and place in the oven until the liquid has evaporated and the salt mixture is crisp (about 1 hour).
6. Break the salt into small cubes (about 5mm square) and reserve.

MAKING THE DRIED MUSHROOM POWDER
1. Preheat the oven to its lowest setting (around 60°/140°F if possible).
2. Boil a pan of water. Place the mushrooms in a bowl and cover them with the boiling water. Strain immediately and discard the water.
3. Plunge the mushrooms into a bowl of iced water, then drain again.
4. Thinly slice the mushrooms with a mandolin or sharp knife.
5. Arrange the mushroom slices in a single layer on a parchment-lined baking sheet.
6. Place in the oven and allow the mushrooms to dry thoroughly until they are crisp (about 2 hours).
7. Grind the dried mushrooms to a powder in a food processor, then pass through a sieve to yield a fine powder. Discard any large pieces.
8. Store the powder in an airtight container until needed.

MAKING THE PANDANUS CRÈME FRAÎCHE

1. Place the crème fraîche and pandanus in a small pan and heat, stirring constantly for 2–3 minutes.
2. Using a hand-held blender, whisk the mixture to release more of the flavour and to give a pale green colouring.
3. Press the mixture through a sieve, discarding any bits of pandanus left behind.
4. Cover and store the crème fraîche in the fridge until needed.

FINISHING THE RISOTTO

1. Place the butter in a saucepan and melt over a medium-high heat.
2. Add the rice and toast over a medium-high heat, stirring constantly with a rubber spatula or wooden spoon (3–4 minutes). Although it is essential that the rice is toasted thoroughly, take care not to overbrown or scorch it at this stage.
3. Add the wine to deglaze the rice, then reduce the liquid until it has almost completely evaporated.
4. Add a ladleful (250g) of the hot bouillon to the rice and simmer, stirring regularly but not constantly.
5. When the liquid has reduced by half, add another 250g ladleful of the bouillon and stir in, preventing any grains from sticking to the bottom. Continue adding the bouillon a ladleful at a time when the previous batch has just about disappeared.
6. At this point you must start adding smaller quantities of bouillon and stirring more regularly. As the liquid is absorbed, taste the rice and add more bouillon as necessary. You're aiming for an al dente texture. The grains of rice should have a resistance in the centre but no chalkiness. This process takes approximately 20 minutes.
7. For the final stages keep the consistency quite loose as you work to finish the risotto. The grains should be cooked through but not soft or mushy. Keep in mind that the risotto will continue to cook after being taken off the heat.
8. Add 60g of the toasted rice butter and all the cheese, stirring quickly.
9. Cover the pan with clingfilm and allow to rest off the heat for 5 minutes.
10. Meanwhile, heat the reserved velouté stock to a simmer.

11. Remove the clingfilm from the risotto, then stir and add salt as necessary.
12. Divide the risotto between 6 warmed plates. Slap the bottom of the plates with one hand while holding firmly with the other to make the risotto spread out evenly.
13. Dot the risotto with pieces of the frozen saffron butter.
14. Using a teaspoon kept in a container of warm water, scoop up some crème fraîche and place in the centre of the risotto. Dip the teaspoon back into the warm water between each scoop.
15. Using a hand-held blender, add the remaining toasted rice butter to the velouté, frothing the mixture as you incorporate it.
16. Pour the velouté out into warm cappuccino cups and spoon the foam over the top. Sprinkle the top of the foam with a dusting of the mushroom powder.
17. Place the salt cubes on the side for each person to add to their taste (the velouté has not been seasoned to this point).
18. Place 2 of the tuiles at the side of each cup.
19. Serve the velouté and risotto together at the table.

Black Forest Gateau

'A gin and tonic says a lot about you as a person.
It is more than just a drink, it is an attitude of mind.
It goes with prawn cocktail, a grilled Dover sole,
Melba toast and Black Forest Gateau.'

Nico Ladenis, *My Gastronomy*

History

Although the *Schwarzwälderkirschtorte* was created less than a hundred years ago, its history is as impenetrable as parts of the Black Forest. Even the name is open to interpretation: pragmatists say that it's a tribute to the kirsch (cherry distillate) that plays such an important role in the cake's distinctive flavour and is made in some 14,000 distilleries in the region. The more romantically minded suggest that the dark shavings of chocolate on the top remind people of the thickset trees of the forest itself. Those with a historical bent argue that the name is in recognition of its precursor, the *Schwarzwaldtorte*, though this cake is largely Swiss in origin.

The combination of cherries, cream and kirsch was already familiar in the southern part of the Black Forest, though as a dessert rather than a cake. The cherries would be boiled down and served with cream, sometimes laced with spirits. The addition of chocolate is supposed to have occurred not in the Black Forest but in Bad Godesburg, near Bonn – the work of the pastry chef Josef Keller in his famous Café Agner in 1915. But, like the *Schwarzwaldtorte*, this recipe is more close relative than mother-lode. Keller's confection had only one layer and used *Murbeteig*, a kind of sweet, crumbly pastry, for its base.

In the Black Forest region these stories conflict and coalesce, depending on whom you're talking to. There is also the story – vague enough in its details to feel like yet another myth – of an obscure Dutchman who settled in the forest and developed the cake. The pre-eminence of the Dutch in the cacao trade makes this a possibility, and there is a Dutch cherry cake that has similarities to the *Schwarzwälderkirschtorte*.

Whatever its origins, the first recipe for the cake appeared in 1934 in J.M. Erich Weber's *250 Konditorei – Spezialitäten und wie sie entstehen* ('250 Pastry Shops – their specialities and how they came to be'). From this start, its rise was meteoric. In 1949 Black Forest gateau was only the thirteenth most popular cake in Germany. Over the next fifty years it beat off the competition to become the best-selling cake in the country, and one of its most famous exports throughout the world.

The Quest for the Best

CHOCS AWAY

To research spaghetti bolognese I had, naturally enough, gone to Bologna. So for Black Forest gateau I went to … Pisa.

It was vital that my Black Forest gateau used the best chocolate possible. In my development kitchen we had tried out several varieties – Valrhona, Domori, Scharffen Berger, Green & Black's – and one had fitted exactly with my vision of how a Black Forest gateau ought to be: Chuao by Amedei. It was rich and dark, with a tobacco aroma and a plum or cherry stone note that would complement the dish's other ingredients. Indeed, it was so good I was in danger of getting carried away: I almost said on camera that it captured the romance of the Black Forest – and I'd still not been there!

As it turned out, Amedei's chocolate had that effect on most people. At the 2005 World Chocolate Awards in London, it dominated the medals roster, gaining three golds, two silvers and a bronze. I had already made my choice, and was in fact at their factory near Pisa when I heard this news, but it was still gratifying to have my taste-buds vindicated in this instance.

And I was extremely pleased for the founders of Amedei – Alessio and Cecilia Tessieri – because they truly deserved it. They set up the company a mere fifteen years ago with the intention of producing the best chocolate in the world. To do so they worked on a different and, to my mind, fairer approach to the manufacture of their product.

Instead of employing a broker to buy the cocoa and sell it to them (which would keep down Amedei's costs and avoid burdensome commitments to particular plantations), Alessio and Cecilia wanted to set up a relationship with their cocoa farmers and invest in their plantations: a partnership. For the Tessieris this increases quality control and gives them exclusive access to some of the best beans in the world (for which they pay above the market price). For their farmers it provides a much-needed economic stability. The chocolate market is exceptionally volatile: cocoa trees are highly susceptible to disease and weather damage, and market speculation further exacerbates price fluctuations. If cocoa farmers are to have an existence beyond precarious subsistence, it is absolutely crucial that they have some form of ongoing support from their buyers. Valrhona was the first to eschew wholesalers and foster relationships with the producing countries. So far, however, Amedei is the only company to own its own plantations.*

In the early stages of Amedei's operations, wholesalers had refused to take Alessio's negotiations seriously, and then dismissed them as presumptuous. Valrhona was resistant too. When Alessio tried to buy some of their chocolate for processing, he was kept waiting at the Lyon offices and eventually turned down because it was considered that the Italian market couldn't appreciate high-quality dark chocolate. Such humiliations only strengthened the Tessieris' resolve to take matters into their own hands and negotiate directly with the Chuao Impresa Campesina, the local farmers' cooperative organisation. It wasn't an easy process: the Venezuelan government was understandably protective of the Chuao plantation, which is considered a national treasure (there are moves by Unesco to make its hacienda a Heritage of Humanity because of its cultural value), but on 3 November 2000 a contract was signed with the Campesina.

Venezuelan cocoa farms seemed a long way away, however, as I drove from Pisa to the small village of La Rotta, amid rolling hills across which cypress trees marched, like straight-backed soldiers: a

---

* The Tessieris' 'integralist' philosophy highlights an issue that runs through this book. The best products cost a lot of money. All of Amedei's chocolate is expensive (the Porcelana variety is, in fact, the most expensive in the world). Chefs – including me – will often exhort you to buy the best you can afford, as though our only aim is to empty your pockets. Certainly there's an aesthetic consideration at work here – generally, with a reliable artisan, you get what you pay for – but there's also a moral dimension. A cheap chicken has been treated badly: it's an almost inevitable by-product of cost-cutting. It may be that you're relatively unconcerned by the fate of dumb animals, but it's worth considering where the savings are made on cheap chocolate (or, for that matter, on affordable vegetables and fruit that have been flown halfway round the world). While the multinationals' hold over processing and the supermarkets' control of retail allows them to artificially inflate prices, the cocoa farmer gets only a tiny percentage of this – often as little as 0.5 per cent. (The situation has been described as 'a contest of unequals, with the end buyer and seller barely even aware of each other's existence'.) In a market as unstable as chocolate's, this means a hugely insecure working environment and widespread poverty for the producers. It means farmers' kids working in the plantations rather than going to school, limiting prospects for the next generation. It's better than the fate of battery chickens, but it's still far from equitable or humane.

classic Tuscan scene. The Amedei factory fitted perfectly into this landscape: on its front was a painted mural; against a terracotta-pink background was a riot of deep green foliage and clusters of bright yellow fruits. It took a moment to realise these were not lemons but cocoa pods, a gentle reminder perhaps that, although South America is far away, it's an important part of the Tessieris' venture.

I was met by Cecilia Tessieri (her brother Alessio was in London, receiving their clutch of medals), who managed to look glamorous even in a white lab coat and funny regulation hat. Like many of the experts I'd met on these trips, she was extremely shy, but came alive when the subject turned to her passion for chocolate. Her hands fluttered as she talked, and I'd be gently mocked whenever my questions seemed too obvious to her.

'Three steps are essential to good chocolate: the selection and fermentation of the beans, the roasting and the recipe,' she told me. 'Only *I* do the roasting,' she added, with that mixture of pride and determination I've often seen in chefs and artisans who want to get to the top.

The fermentation takes place at the plantations. Although it's an essential step in the development of chocolate flavour and a highly unpredictable one, it's often poorly overseen, which is why Cecilia and Alessio were keen to become involved in the plantations they bought from. The cocoa pods are broken open after harvesting, and the beans and pulp piled together in wooden tubs covered with banana leaves for several days while microbes work on the pulp. In the beginning, yeasts take precedence, converting sugars to alcohol and altering some of the pulp acids. They are succeeded by lactic-acid bacteria and then acetic-acid bacteria that consume the yeasts' alcohol and convert it to acetic acid.

The acetic acid is important because it eats away at the beans, boring into cells and causing the contents to mix together and react, forming molecules that are much less astringent. This process is complemented by the beans' own digestive enzymes, which break down proteins and sucrose sugar into amino acids and simple sugars – substances that are far more reactive and will play a major part in the development of aromas during the roasting process. The perforation of the beans also allows a kind of flavour exchange between pulp and bean: flavour molecules from the fermenting pulp travel to the bean, adding sugars, acids, and fruit, flower and wine notes. Thus fermentation turns the sharp, bland beans into something already tastier, and creates some of the chemicals essential to the browning reactions that occur during roasting.

On the plantations, the fermentation process can be scented on the air, as smells of toast, tobacco and spices waft through the village. Once ready, the beans are dried and shipped to Amedei's factory. 'The dried bean has taste, but it's still unbalanced and underdeveloped. It has a distinctly vinegary flavour from the acetic acid. Roasting helps to change that,' explained Cecilia. 'It fixes the flavours that are already there, and develops new ones through the browning of the beans, just as browning sugar gives it that caramelised effect. The process is a delicate one: the right balance of time and temperature is essential to great chocolate. A bad roast will give you bad chocolate, no matter what you do to it afterwards.'

As we talked, Cecilia led me down a white corridor towards the roasting department. A mild chocolate odour, a smell of red berries and leather, hung in the air; and a rhythmic, gloopy ker*plunk* rang out from machines somewhere in the factory. The sound seemed to follow us down each passageway, unearthly and insistent, until eventually I found myself unwittingly trying to keep in step with the tempo. We'd escape each time Cecilia opened the double doors to a different department in the factory. But it would be waiting for us when we re-entered the corridors, and each time it was a little louder.

Cecilia opened a set of double doors now. In front of me was a large spherical hopper. Peering over the rim, I could see thousands of beans crowded together, looking above all like a mulch of wood chips. A turning arm ploughed a furrow through them, keeping the beans moving so that they roasted evenly.

'I taste throughout the roasting, and it is only when I say the beans are right that they are released into the collection bin.'

'What temperature are they roasted at?' I asked tentatively. Most of the places I visited were among the best, if not *the* best, in their field, so had rivals. Often they kept their edge by keeping certain things secret. It was hard to know when I was straying into such territory.

Cecilia's secrets obviously lay elsewhere. 'The temperature varies, depending on the quality of the bean and the region it comes from. It's about 120°C. Try tasting one … It's good, yes?' she said, cocking her head and looking at me, tentative in her turn.

She needn't have worried. I'd chewed roasted cocoa beans before but none of this quality. It was still very unlike chocolate – very acidic and bitter – but it had lots of flavour. Cecilia's vigilance during roasting really paid off. Already you could taste the bean's potential, ready to be brought out further by the next stage in the process.

'We refrigerate the beans, after which they are put through a grinder to crack open and remove the shells, leaving the nib. We also take out the germ – the bean's embryo – which few other manufacturers bother to do because it's difficult and expensive. The law allows for up to 50 per cent of the chocolate to consist of the skins. But we get rid of the lot.'

In the roasted bean, the cocoa butter is locked inside a structure of carbohydrates and protein. Grinding begins the process of breaking down these rigid structures so the cocoa butter can escape. Removing the germ hugely improves the quality of chocolate, but it's an unbelievably labour-intensive process. The fact that Cecilia and Alessio undertook to do it was a sign of their commitment and dedication to the task of producing the perfect chocolate.

Cecilia drew up in front of the grinding machine where flat metal funnels channelled brown powder into large plastic tubs. She stooped and cupped her hands under one brown stream, as though at a fountain. There was a kind of reverence to her actions. She raised both hands and lowered her head to take in the bouquet before holding them out to me.

The smell was incredible. 'It's the aroma of plum … ' she suggested, 'of marmalade … '

'Yeah, plums,' I agreed, 'but ripe ones, even slightly fermented. And there's something of the plum stone too.' I recognised the aroma: these had to be nibs of Chuao, the chocolate that had captured my imagination in our taste test and brought me to Italy in the first place.

'OK,' said Cecilia, interrupting my reverie, 'now we go to another department where the nibs are turned into cocoa liquor.'

Another white corridor. Ker*plunk*, ker*plunk*, ker*plunk* – the machine noise followed us down it. Another set of double doors.

Inside was a knobbly, bolted-metal column with a cream-coloured conical hopper attached to it. Using a saucepan as a scoop, Cecilia poured nibs in at the top. They ground rapidly, reducing to a fine powder and releasing their stores of cocoa butter. From the bottom of the machine a slow and sludgy flow advanced, like lava. 'That's 100 per cent cocoa liquor,' she told me.

I dipped in a finger. 'That's 100 per cent bitterness.'

'Yes. It's not chocolate,' Cecilia said.

No, it wasn't chocolate. Not yet. But I guess it was close to what the Maya and Aztecs would have drunk. They ground the cocoa beans and added water and flavourings – maize, chilli, pepper – presumably to cut the bitterness. That's the drink Cortés would have come across when he invaded the Yucatán in the early sixteenth century. So far, my tour of the factory had shown me a mechanised version of ancient Central American practices. The rest would show what Europeans did to turn chocolate from bitter drink to addictive bar.

'Next we add sugar and vanilla and mix it well,' explained Cecilia. 'But it's still grainy – you can feel the particles of nib and sugar on your tongue – so it has to be blended and refined, which also helps to release the chocolate aromas. We pass the mixture through big rollers until the particles are microscopic in size. Most producers grind to about 24 microns, but we go down to 12. To give you an idea what this means: water is 0 microns, so reducing to 12 gives the chocolate a smoother, more liquid feel in the mouth.'

At the blender a man was scooping the liquor–sugar–vanilla mix out of a plastic vat and pasting it across a metal grid with a hand trowel until it dropped through to the machine's innards. Walking to the other end of the blender, I could see the paste emerging in thick soft twisted braids. It was paler in colour and far less sludgy. Already it looked a lot more like chocolate. (In fact, it looked like Cadbury's Flake.)

It also tasted more like chocolate. 'It's now smooth.'

'Yes,' said Cecilia. 'But it still has some of the acids that developed during fermentation. So the work is not finished yet. It must go to the conching room.'

Conching would heighten and mellow the chocolate's flavour. The machine was invented in 1879 by Rodolphe Lindt, and named after its shell-like shape. Conches roll and smear the mixture while submitting it to a stream of warm air. The friction-heat and air-blast carry away up to 80 per cent of the volatile aromatic compounds developed during processing (including many of the acids and aldehydes that had previously made the chocolate bitter and astringent: acidity declines significantly during conching). At the same time, the friction grinds and separates the solid particles, allowing a proper blending with the cocoa butter; and the heat increases the roasted, caramel and malt aromas we associate with top-quality chocolate.

The conching room at Amedei was the one that most reminded me of Willy Wonka's chocolate factory. Like the pasta-maker Luigi Donnari, Cecilia and Alessio had searched the disused factories of Europe for old machines that would process chocolate in the way they wanted, machines that reacted with the product in a particular fashion and handled things at a slower speed. Their conching machines took seventy-two hours to perform their task (modern large-scale concerns do the same job in eight to thirty-six hours) and had a Dan Dare quality to them. Instead of gleaming stainless steel and sleek, angular simplicity, these machines were oversized and heavily riveted, their cream paintwork scuffed and striated from use. The surreal, sci-fi element was reinforced by the fact that the workers padded around in blue plastic overshoes and white lab coats. Their actions were accompanied by that steady, inexorable ker*plunk*. This was its source. It was the sound of conches slopping chocolate.

In a blocky, rectangular tank, what at first looked like a huge vacuum-cleaner attachment clawed back and forth. As I got closer, a better analogy, from a different area of homecare, came to mind: DIY. By now the chocolate had the runny, glossy appearance of paint, and I could see that the clawing arm was in fact a roller, which rubbed and spread the chocolate exactly as you would emulsion in a tray.

Cecilia had a different frame of reference: pampering rather than painting. 'The longitudinal movement gives the chocolate a kind of long massage,' she said.

'The smell is absolutely out of this world. It's like pipe tobacco. Can I taste it?'

Although I'd been to chocolate factories before, it was only here at Amedei that I got the opportunity to try chocolate at each stage in the process, from bean to roast to nib to liquor to blended and refined. It was a real education, and I wanted to see it through to completion. Cecilia dipped a long wooden spoon into the tank and passed it to me, twisting as she did so to prevent it dripping. The only way to avoid a mess was to stand holding the spoon high above my mouth – as though posing for a Soviet propaganda poster – and let the chocolate run off it.

Cecilia glanced quizzically at me. It wasn't clear whether this was because I looked ridiculous or because she was concerned at what I thought of her chocolate. When I chewed and then shook my head, though, she misunderstood and began to look worried.

'No, no,' I assured her, 'I could only shake my head at how good it now is. I love the tobacco note on it. It's deep, rich, complex. Does it stay like this when it's cooled down and turned into a bar? Does it retain this complex mix of flavours?'

'Yes, of course. If you liquefied one of our chocolate bars, it would be just like this.'

The final part of the process is about controlling that kind of lique-faction. The chocolate has to undergo the tricky process of 'tempering' or 'pre-crystallisation': cooling and rewarming to particular tempera-tures until the cocoa-butter crystals form in a type that stays solid at room temperature – that really does melt in your mouth, not your hand.*

* Untempered chocolate will melt at 18°C, a low room temperature. Pick it up in your hand and within a few seconds you'll have sticky, chocolatey fingers. What's melting are crystals of cocoa butter.

Fortunately for chefs and chocoholics, cocoa butter can form into six types of crystal, all of which have a different melting temperature, and a different hardness. One of these types – known as Beta 2 or Form V – has the right combination for chocolate: strong yet breakable, with a high melting point (32–34°C). Tempering makes the cocoa butter form into stable Form V crystals rather than other unstable types. It's a process in three stages. First, the chocolate is heated to 50°C (if it's dark chocolate; milk and white chocolate have slightly different temperature ranges) to melt all the cocoa-butter crystals.

Second, it's cooled to 27°C, a temperature low enough to allow Form V crystals to form quickly, but high enough to prevent most of the other crystal types from forming (because their melting point is 16–26°C). At this stage the chocolate is stirred to break up and increase the number of crystals, which ensures that the final product is smooth and glossy rather than gritty. But you still need careful control over crystal formation: too many of even the right crystals will result in too solid a matrix, so the third stage is a reheating, to 31°C, which slows down the formation of Form V crystals while at the same time getting rid of any unstable crystals that have developed during cooling, leaving the stable crystals to grow into a network of the right density and hardness.

After which it's ready for wrapping, boxing, shipping and selling. Cecilia took me to taste the finished products and see which best suited Black Forest gateau.

In the last room on our tour, the finishing touches were being added to various chocolates. A woman placed chocolate balls called *deliziosi* on a conveyor belt that ferried them through a curtain of dripping chocolate, after which another woman hand-piped a zigzag of fine chocolate lines on top, like a miniature Jackson Pollock. It was highly manual labour that resulted in each chocolate being different. Here was food that came from the heart, that had been made with love and care, like the rough-edged pasta in Massimo Bottura's *ragù*. This ethos was evident throughout the factory: everyone I met took pride in their work – they were enthusiastic to show me the machines and how the chocolate tasted.

Cecilia placed on the work surface four slabs of chocolate wrapped in waxy black paper: two versions of Toscano Black, one containing 63 per cent cocoa, the other 70; the renowned Chuao (another 70 percenter); and Number 9, a blend from nine plantations with 75 per cent cocoa, the highest Amedei has ever marketed. She unwrapped them and effortlessly cut off brittle chunks with a knife. 'You want to taste?'

I did, and it was an extraordinary quartet: the Number 9 smelt of molasses and had earthy, coffee flavours; the Toscano Black 70 was equally uncompromising, with an almost woody scent and cherry and almond notes in it. I recognised Chuao's red-fruit aromas and creamy smoothness, and appreciated its long finish: the flavours really stayed and developed in the mouth. The Toscano Black 63 was a milder experience but no less pleasurable for that. It was almost fragrant, with notes of lemon and dried fruit, a touch of toffee. I felt as though I were at a wine tasting (and I was beginning to sound like that too): all four had a flavour complexity that really stimulated the tastebuds. I could see virtues in each one that would add something special to a Black Forest gateau. Was that what made it difficult to choose between them? Or was it the fact that it's not often you go into a sweetshop to be told 'Have as much as you like.'

I took the lot.

GATEAU LIFE

So I had four types of chocolate to test. Now it was time to discover how a *Torte* oughta taste. Time to visit the Black Forest.

Like many spa towns, Baden-Baden is a magnet for retirees. It is reputed to have the country's highest concentration of millionaires. Drive through the outskirts and the steeply winding streets are lined with vast mansions, each with its complement of marble statues and security cameras. The town centre is full of fur shops and classy art galleries, and elderly couples walk at the slow pace of people with time – and money – on their hands. Forget the ladies who lunch; here are the ladies (and gentlemen) who *indulge.*

What better place to have a *Konditorei*, that excellent German combination of cake shop and café? The Café König opened in Baden-Baden some 250 years ago and is still going strong. As I stood beneath its grey and pink striped awning, gazing in through the window, I felt like a small boy with his pocket money hotly clasped in his hand, trying in vain to decide what to choose. Laid out in inviting rows were pastries, petits fours and cellophane-wrapped chocolate geese and hedgehogs with orange bows. I could have *Kirschtorte, Zuger Kirschtorte, Pralinentorte, Baumkuchentorte, Sacher Torte, Malakoff Torte* or *Sonnentorte.* If any place was going to come up with a worthwhile *Schwarzwälderkirschtorte*, surely this was it.

Although it was a mild autumn with a weak sun filtering down, it was still too cold to sit outdoors for long. I walked past the small court-yard with its white marble-topped tables and curlicued chairs and took a seat inside. The café had a genteel, mock-Regency feel to it. Cream and white colours predominated, with decorative plates and paintings of flowers in oils or pastels on the walls. A couple of aspidistra stood in pots, and there was the faintest undercurrent of piped classical music. Well-groomed people sat at small round tables on cane-backed chairs. Opposite me were two silver-haired gentlemen in tweed jackets with silk handkerchiefs deftly tucked into their top pockets. One even wore a cravat. In the corner a single woman with an immaculate chignon earnestly studied the newspaper through a magnifying glass. I gave my order and pushed a silver sugar pot the size of a sporting trophy to one side, in anticipation of the delicacy about to come my way.

Although I disagreed with Nico Ladenis's sniffy dismissal of the cake as a middle-class pretension, I was still slightly worried about what I was going to eat. What if it was as disappointing as the British version of the 1970s, with leaden cream, dry sponge and cheap cooking chocolate? What if the idea of a good Black Forest gateau turned out to be an illusion, a vain fancy that had never really existed, turning my journey into a fool's errand? As it turned out, I needn't have worried. What arrived at my table bore little resemblance to the ersatz versions of my youth.

The König's gateau was a tall sharp wedge crowned with chocolate flakes and a rounded hillock of cream topped with a cherry half. Beneath this at least six layers of light and dark alternated. It wasn't a cake so much as an architectural creation, inviting me to explore its construction, to taste each part separately. The cream was rich, the mousse powerful but delicate; the kirsch had the sweet sharpness of a well-balanced spirit rather than the mule kick of a cheap one. The frozen cherries had an abundance of malic acid (an acid found in many fruits, especially apples: think of biting into a Granny Smith) which provided a perfect counterbalance to the fat of the cream. The chocolate had a cherry note that went well with the other flavours. All of it rested on a classic biscuit base.

I was surprised and pleased by what I'd found. Although the true *Schwarzwälderkirschtorte* was very different from the Great British gateau, I could see how one had gradually been transformed (and traduced) into the other. I was looking forward to fooling around with the *Torte*'s complex architecture, and I could see ways in which I might still be able to summon up – in a pleasant form – some of the nostalgia surrounding the humble, misconstrued gateau. Combining the two would make a cake that was really special.

GETTING ROMANTIK

The fine arts are five in number, namely: painting,
sculpture, poetry, music and architecture, the principal
branch of the latter being pastry.
Antonin Carême

I had said to camera that I wanted to soak up the atmosphere of the
Black Forest and somehow put it into my recipe. My overnight stay in
Oberkirch gave me a taste of what the forest had to offer. Most of the
town looks like anywhere in *Mitteleuropa* – sturdy concrete buildings
with steeply pitched roofs – but turn off the main road down one of
the shadowy arched passageways and suddenly you are confronted
by a soaring church or maze of cobbled streets. The modern buildings
occasionally give way to a house from another era, with shutters and
timbered lattice-work. I was glad to discover that my hotel, the
Romantik Hotel zur Oberen Linde, was one of these.

Like the English 'heritage' you find in B&Bs and tea shoppes,
German heritage is both charming … and slightly twee. The hotel
room's thick stone walls, low ceilings, extravagantly carved wood-
work and swagged four-poster were snug and welcoming; it was the
kind of place you'd gratefully retreat to as the cold took hold outside.
The bar, on the other hand, plundered a rustic theme: table decorations
of browning leaves, wrinkled berries and walnuts; wagon wheels
propped against the walls and milk churns on the floor. The waitresses
sported a Heidi look: red print dresses with bodice tops, lace collars and
leg-of-mutton sleeves. There was a kitsch element to it that I realised
I'd have to try to evoke in my gateau, especially since a vein of kitsch
ran equally through the British BFG of the 1970s.

However, I was principally here to visit Volker Gmeiner, owner of
the Café König and also the Confiserie Gmeiner in Oberkirch, who was
going to show me the building blocks of the delicious Black Forest
gateau he serves in his cafés. As with many of the artisans in this
book, he turned out to be part of a long-standing family tradition: his
grandfather was a baker, his father a baker and confectioner. His
experience showed in the kitchen, where the cooking proceeded with
the smoothness of a well-oiled machine.

I thought it best to confess up front to what we had done to his country's most popular dessert. 'In Britain, Black Forest gateau tends to come out of a box. It's got dodgy sponge, overwhipped cream, cheap alcohol, and glacé cherries that have an unnaturally bright red colour, as though they've been subjected to a dose of radiation. You don't even want to put them in your mouth.'

'I get the impression they did everything wrong that they could,' Volker replied. His pink cheeks gave him a boyish look, and he seemed more amused than shocked. 'I'll show you the traditional good way to do it. I was taught that the dish has to have a bit of all tastes – sweetness and bitterness from the chocolate; salt from the sponge and the base; acid from the cherries. And a bit of many different textures, too. A crispy base balanced by smooth chocolate, and cherries for bite. For me, it's important that you can taste each ingredient separately, that you can get a sense of the components of the Black Forest gateau.'

As he talked, Volker made a *pâte à bombe*, to stabilise the mousse. He put sugar and water in a pan on a gas ring and let it heat up to 120°C. In the meantime, he beat whole eggs until thick, and then slowly and delicately added the sugar syrup, leaving the machine running until the mixture cooled.

'OK, we're ready to make the mousse.' Volker removed the *pâte à bombe* and set it aside while he melted chocolate in the microwave – a mixture of Valrhona's Araguani and their Manjari, which we use at the Fat Duck; it has citrus and cherry notes that would go well in the gateau. Once it was warm but soft, the chocolate was poured into the *pâte à bombe*. Volker mixed it with a spoon, spreading delicate stripes of pale brown around the surface in a rings-of-Saturn effect. 'Now I add cream, but as you know, the important thing for the perfect mousse is not to beat the cream too much as it's added or you'll lose the volume as the air is knocked out.'

'Yes. And it'll get too grainy and noticeably fattier as beating forces the fat out of the emulsion. You don't need to beat it a lot because the chocolate'll hold in air as it cools down.'

Volker got stuck in, plunging his hand into the mixture and turning it over. When it was ready he let me taste what was in the bowl, as though we were in a mother-and-child baking session. It had exactly the right sweetness – light but preserving the flavour and strength of the ingredients – and already there was a welcome cherry note from the dark chocolate.

The mixture was put into a piping bag and smoothed over a layer of dark sponge. On top of this, Volker piped three concentric circles, as though drawing an archery target. 'OK, now for the cherries,' he said. 'I use sour cherries from the Black Forest,' Volker told me. 'They have a short season – the end of July to the start of August – during which they're generally frozen for use all year round. You can't use sweet cherries: they would make the *Torte* too sweet, cloyingly so. We defrost the cherries a day in advance, then cook them with cinnamon and salt.'

The cherries were piped between each ring. The ridges of mousse prevented the cherries from falling out as you cut into the cake; that's why you had to resist the temptation to put one cherry dead centre as the bull's-eye. (It brought home to me, once again, the architectural aspect of the true Black Forest gateau, and it triggered a memory. I had an honorary uncle called John, and my one good memory of the cake is going to his house in Brixton for Sunday lunch and eating a home-made version there. He was a retired architect, and maybe the BFG's elaborate superstructure was what fired up his culinary instincts. It was certainly his proudest culinary showpiece.)

Another 'floor' was then added to the construction, this time a disc of white sponge, which was squashed down so that the chocolate mousse squidged out and up the sides. (This is a neat trick that chefs use all the time: make the sponge discs slightly smaller than the cake tin so that, as each layer is pressed down, mousse is forced out and up. It's far easier than taking the cake out of the tin later and trying to apply chocolate to the sides.) With a squeezy bottle, Volker then drizzled the sponge with a mixture of half kirsch, half sugar syrup.

'You can't just use kirsch on its own. It's too strong and it flies away – "evaporates", I think you say. The quality of the spirit is very important: it mustn't be too sweet. I like to use one with 50 per cent alcohol – strong enough to stand up to the chocolate.'

Kirsch was also integral to the next stage. Volker added it to a pan containing hot water, sugar and gelatin and warmed it up. 'The gelatin holds the liquid in a kind of net,' he said. 'Another example of your architecture, Heston.'

I got the impression he might be teasing me just a little.

The intoxicating scent of kirsch suffused the room. Volker added a blob of cream to the pan and then poured the whole lot slowly back into a bowl containing more cream. 'The juggling of cream and kirsch here makes it an easier consistency to mix, and ensures not too much volume is lost,' he explained. 'As before, you've got to make sure the cream isn't overbeaten. You'll end up with too many air bubbles with thin walls that break and so reduce the volume.'

He scooped out the by-now sluggish white mass, plonked it on top of the sponge like a lick of shaving foam, and spread it out.

Another floor of dark sponge; another cream-splurge out the sides; another drizzle of the squeezy bottle in a spiralling motion towards the centre. The edifice was almost built. A final slop of kirsch cream and smoothing with a palette knife and it was done. A hat of grease-proof paper was placed on top and it was put in the fridge to cool for a couple of hours until the mousse set.

Once cooled, the gateau must be put on its foundation. Volker took a biscuit base and spread jam over it. 'It fixes the bottom of the cake to the base.'

'A kind of fruit glue,' I suggested.

'Architecture again,' he observed, as he placed the cake in position and smoothed more cream on top. 'You know, Black Forest gateau is hugely popular here. I couldn't open my shops for the day without it. Any other cake, yes, but not the Black Forest gateau. The elderly population in Baden-Baden keeps up the tradition of high tea. It's a good place for a *Konditorei*.'

'So the gateau is steeped in kirsch *and* tradition,' I offered, pleased with my wordplay.

In response, Volker fired up a blowtorch.

For a moment I wondered if I'd overstepped the mark, but he was just heating the cake tin a little to help the gateau slide out easily. On top of the cake he now placed a cutter that looked like a spoked wheel – 'I have to get it lined up with the centre; otherwise there will be pieces for rich people, and pieces for poor people' – and pressed down. Spot on. Equal shares for everybody this time.

A piped blob of whipped cream went on each portion, along with chocolate shavings and 'a little bit of snow' in the form of sifted sugar.

The final touch was a few chocolate Christmas trees and some candied sour cherries.

'There you are,' Volker announced, 'the traditional Black Forest gateau.' He didn't tinker with the sides but left them as they were. 'I don't care if there are a few holes and suchlike. I like the irregularities. The customer should be able to see that it's handmade.'

'So imperfection can be perfection?'

'Exactly.'

THE TUSCANY OF GERMANY

It was ironic really. It had felt odd beginning an exploration of Black Forest gateau by travelling to Pisa. And now here I was, in the Black Forest, being told that it was the Tuscany of Germany.

Hans-Peter Fies had a point, though. Olive trees grow in the region and, in season, you can get apricots, as well as pears, apples, wild plums and cherries. It's a fertile, farmers' landscape: Ringelbach still has a lot of rackety barns with firewood stored under the eaves. The bleat of sheep carry on the wind, and you can see people doubled over in cultivation on the steep hillsides that hem in the village.

By the main road, a waystone declares: *Wein – obst & honig – schnapps*. The area is famous for fruit and alcohol, and that's why I had come here. Volker Gmeiner had made it clear how easy it was for bad kirsch to swamp the virtues of the Black Forest gateau, so I'd travelled to Ringelbach to visit the Franz Fies distillery and discover more about the process of turning fruit into a full-blooded spirit.

The distillery's presence is felt – or rather, smelt – before it's seen: the sweet sharp smell of high-proof alcohol catches in the nostrils as you walk through the village. I entered the reception room and noticed that, like Amedei, Franz Fies has its clutch of gold, silver and bronze. The walls were full of framed certificates attesting to the company's excellence. Hans-Peter's father set up the distillery after the war as a small farm concern, and it had clearly come a long way since then.

The basic principles and science of distilling are relatively straight-forward. First, fermentation. Yeast fungi convert sugars to energy, producing alcohol as a by-product of that process. Add yeasts to a fruit (or grain or other carbohydrate source), therefore, and they will prey on its sugars, producing a mildly alcoholic liquid as they do so (between 5 and 12 per cent alcohol by volume, or ABV).

Second, evaporation. To create a spirit, the percentage of alcohol needs to be increased. Since alcohol is more volatile than water, and more easily brought to the boil and evaporated, if you heat up the fermented liquid, the alcohol turns to vapour first, so can be collected as it condenses.

The processes involved in producing a well-balanced spirit rather than toxic poteen or moonshine are, however, a lot more complicated than that, as I could see when I entered Hans-Peter's distillery. The dizzying aroma of liquor was even stronger in here, and the place looked like Frankenstein's laboratory: 20-foot-high stainless steel drums towered over me, and a tangled network of pipes fed in and out of what looked like a giant deep-sea diver's helmet of burnished copper, with riveted portholes and pressure gauges.

'It's like something from *20,000 Leagues under the Sea*,' I exclaimed.

The diver's helmet turned out to be the still. 'First the fresh cherries are picked,' Hans-Peter said. 'This is in fact the most important part of the whole process. More important than all this machinery. The quality of the fruit is absolutely essential. The cherries must be very fine, no flaws. Bad fruit makes bad kirsch. It's as simple as that. After picking, the cherries are crushed and fermented in our upper factory. Then the mash comes down to the lower factory and is left for ten to twelve weeks. And then it comes into this copper still, where we heat it to about 78°C, at which point what we call the "ghost" flies away. It goes up that pipeline and into a closed room.'

'Yes. The alcohol vaporises.'

'*Ja, ja. Genau.*'

'The smell is really wonderful.'

'Yes? OK.' Hans-Peter sounded almost surprised. It was as though he'd got so used to it that he didn't really notice any more. He took me over to the still's porthole. Peering through, I could see a briskly roiling liquid illuminated by a pinkish glow. 'The smell is from the cherries. And so is that colour. Later, as you'll see, it will be clear.'

'Is the temperature a crucial part of the process?' I wanted to know.

'I must heat very slowly, not too strong,' he explained. 'Between 75 and 80°C the pure alcohol comes off, along with some flavour and aroma compounds.'

'So by controlling the temperature you avoid collecting the water vapour?'

'Yes. But eventually the temperature does reach about 100°C, and then there is more water vapour, of course.'

'And this is the end of the first distillation?'

'Yes. Once all the alcohol is gone I can stop, and the rest of the mash is removed.'

The 'ghost' meanwhile has floated along pipes to the cooler. As its temperature reduces, it condenses and reverts to a liquid. It is now much purer and so no longer dark-coloured but clear.

'At the end of this cooking the alcohol is about 35–40 per cent ABV,' Hans-Peter told me. 'To increase the alcohol content and the flavour, we repeat the process: a second distillation that gives us about 70 per cent ABV.'

'And yet you then add spring water to dilute the spirit back to 40 per cent, so what's the point of this second distillation?'

'The quality of this distillate is very much better. The impurities and harshness of the first distillation are removed. It is purer and the taste is finer. You know, fermentation produces many volatile substances, not all of which you would want in the final product. Some – like methanol – are actually bad for our bodies! We class these substances into groups, according to how volatile they are, and during distillation we can use the variations in volatility to separate them from each other, leaving just the fraction that is richest in alcohol.'

It was hard to hear him over the insistent, almost melodic rattle of glass bottles, which shunted along a conveyor belt in the centre of the factory to be filled, sealed and boxed.

'The most volatile – and therefore the quickest to evaporate – include methanol and acetone. Because they're the first, you call them, I think, the "heads". These are removed as they cool and condense. Then comes alcohol, which is collected separately. Lastly there are the "tails", the things that are less volatile than alcohol. These are more difficult to deal with because you don't want to remove them completely: many of the substances give spirits character. For example, the tails include fusel oils. In small amounts these supply a desirable, slightly oily body to the product. Too much, however, can render it rough and unpalatable – *Fusel* is actually German for "rotgut". You'd know about it the next morning!'

'So after the first distillation the liquid is volatile and aggressive and not particularly complex. The second distillation brings out the intensity of the alcohol as well as an intensity of taste and flavour?'

'Yes, exact, exact.'

'Could I try the second distillation?' I asked.

'Of course. I would be happy for you to do so.' He took a spirit glass – a long-stemmed flute with a bulbous bowl – and dipped it in a metal barrel, then handed it over to me. 'It's a very intensive taste. Very pure. Very strong. Be careful. Have only a little bit.'

He wasn't kidding. Even a brief sniff of the contents made me want to lie down. My eyes started to water. It tasted very strong indeed. 'What percentage ABV is that?'

'About 75 per cent.'

'A few years ago I went to Armagnac to see a distiller. He told me that a good way to test the product is to pour some on your hands, rub them together, then cup them over your nose. Shall we try it?'

With his neat silvery hair and full moustache, Hans-Peter looked a bit like a movie actor from the 1920s, an impression reinforced by his tweed jacket and checked shirt. He had a sense of humour but he was also quite correct, so I wasn't entirely sure how this suggestion would be taken. It turned out he was entirely game, so we tipped our glasses on to our palms and then rubbed, as though about to apply aftershave. I put my hands up to my nostrils. As the alcohol vaporised I got a real hit of complex, intense cherry smell – including the cherry stone note that I liked so much and had found in Amedei's chocolate. It was something I definitely wanted to capture in my Black Forest gateau, so I was very pleased to discover that kirsch could summon it up too.

It was another example of how instructive this trip to the source had been: everybody I had met had passed on insights that magnified the gateau's potential. Even just wandering around Ringelbach and catching the faint wafts of alcohol in the air had prompted ideas: if I put kirsch in a spray bottle and squirted it around before serving the gateau, would that provide an atmosphere of the Black Forest and heighten the eating experience, making it a little more authentic? I didn't know, but it would be fun trying it out back in the lab.

LAYER CAKE

'You've been a busy boy, Jocky.'

It sounded like a line from a British gangster flick – the sort of thing the boss says before punishing an underling who's been a bit too handy with an Uzi – but it was true: my pastry chef had been busy.

The work surface of the Fat Duck development kitchen was covered with slabs and strips ranging in colour from pale cream to darkest brown. They looked like planks and blocks from a child's building set – a reminder of the architectural aspect of the BFG. Jocky had consulted every cake and mousse recipe he could find, and baked them at a variety of temperatures and percentages in order to give us the widest possible choice from which to construct our gateau. There were jacondes and financiers, dacquoises and génoises, along with tubs of fresh cherries, compotes and purées, and even cherry and apricot pits. Nestling among them were ganaches and parfaits made with the chocolate we'd brought back from Amedei. Each item sat on greaseproof paper, labelled like an exhibit.

From this fantastic spread we had to choose the layers of our gateau, and their order and thickness, bearing in mind the chocolate and cherries that would cement it all together. I didn't even want to think about the maths of the maximum number of possible combinations.

'I've got the Black Forest gateau that Volker made for me as a starting point,' I said to Jocky. 'Let's begin with his basic structure of seven layers and then play around with the rest. Three things really struck me while I was in Germany: Volker said that the gateau should contain four tastes – sweet, sour, salt and bitter – and emphasise the contrasts of dark and light. I'd like to capture both of those, if I can. And above all I want to somehow incorporate exactly the kirsch-memory I have from being there. If this is going to work, we've got to get the kirsch right. We'll start with the base and build upwards, trying to get the right balance of taste and texture.'

And so began an afternoon of spooning out mousses and compotes and putting them between sponges and biscuits. It took me back to a time when, as a kid, I'd try to construct an enormous sandwich containing only my favourite things: jam, jelly, Nutella, peanut butter, hundreds and thousands. Some of the results here were equally anarchic and inedible, but gradually we started to whittle down the choices.

Jocky had prepared a dried madeleine that had a really interesting texture, rather like a langue-de-chat biscuit. It was both light and crunchy, so could make a great base. And the chocolate sablés he'd cooked were promising too: they gave us the opportunity to incorporate milk chocolate as well as the dark, and had a thinness that meant we could increase the number of layers in the cake. I wanted in any case to cut down the height of the gateau, for it seemed to me that if it was too big to fit in the mouth then some of the flavour combinations would be lost.

So we had a tentative shortlist for the base. The sponge layers proved trickier. Many just didn't seem to fit in with my mental picture and taste-map of the Black Forest gateau: they didn't match up to my memories of the German version, though we'd have to see how they responded to soaking in kirsch. A soft almond cake had the right kind of chewiness, and cherries and almonds certainly complemented one another, though I wondered if the almond took it too far in the wrong direction, too far from what people thought of as a Black Forest gateau. I wanted to include as many contrasting textures as possible – stimulation for both head and palate – so anything a bit different had to be considered.

We built combinations into toppling towers. We tried out cherry and apricot preserves and found the apricot gave a better balance of acidity. On top of this went a chocolate sponge without flour that had a really pleasing delicacy to it. Jocky and I were unsure about which was the most suitable chocolate – Porcelana probably gave the best chocolate experience but Chuao accentuated the cherry character – so decided to try to incorporate both. We found an unaggressive kirsch that instantly took me back to the Black Forest itself.

Things were coming together, but the maths of testing combinations wasn't the only factor we had to contend with. Normally, at the Fat Duck, experimentation is just like this – a mixture of instinct, blind alleys and continual testing – but there's no time limit involved.

Recipes can take years to perfect, and often go through several metamorphoses to get there. Here we had a deadline: the eight dishes had to be finalised for filming in a week, and the Black Forest gateau was proving to be the most difficult of the lot. I still had sponges to soak, vanilla stalks to dry out, and an idea about chocolate snow that I wanted to follow through … Were we going to be ready in time?

Black Forest Gateau **Makes 3 cakes**

My Black Forest gateau is composed of six delicious layers: biscuit base topped with aerated chocolate, chocolate sponge, kirsch cream, ganache and chocolate mousse. More than any other dish, perhaps, this one can be let down by its ingredients. The salt plays a pivotal role, enhancing the flavours and tempering the cake's sweetness. And it's absolutely vital that you use the best chocolate, sour cherries and kirsch that you can get. The kirsch is especially important: I recommend Franz Fies' (their address and website are included in the Directory), but if you can't obtain this, it's worth taste-testing a few – surely no hardship – to find one that works. It needs to be smooth, aromatic and full-flavoured.

One of the beauties of this recipe is its adaptability. The layers don't have to be assembled into a cake: many can be served up as desserts in their own right. Kids and grown-ups alike will love the chocolate mousse and aerated chocolate. Serving kirsch cream with a bowl of cherries would be an interesting echo of the cake's origins. This really is six recipes in one – and the possibilities are almost endless.

And the final touches, as always, make a difference. Spray a little kirsch round the dining room and serve the gateau on a wood-effect base and you have a context that, to my mind, makes it taste all the better.

Special equipment
21.5 x 31.5cm brownie tin(s),* food mixer (optional), oven thermometer, 2.6 litre hard plastic container with lid (into which you have bored a small hole using a corkscrew), microwave (optional), whipping-cream canister and charges, vacuum-seal storage bag with one-way valve, vacuum cleaner, digital probe, wood-effect painting tool, non-stick

---

* A centimetre either side of these dimensions doesn't matter as the base will be trimmed after baking.

silicone baking sheet (e.g. Silpat), 9 x 19cm loaf tin(s) with a depth of 5cm, piping bag, melon baller, large cardboard box, paint gun (optional), atomiser (optional)

Timing
Lots of layers mean lots of different cooking techniques. To assemble a whole cake in one day would undeniably be a fair amount of work. Better to think of this as architecture – a flatpack gateau – and spread out the building tasks. Prepare the chocolate sponge and kirsch cream up to a month in advance and keep them in the freezer; make the biscuit base up to a week in advance, keeping it in an airtight container. The aerated chocolate can be prepared anytime: it will keep well in the fridge if sealed properly. That leaves only two layers to prepare on the day – the chocolate ganache and the chocolate mousse – neither of which is particularly laborious.

Ingredients list
This is broken down into quantities for each component part below, but here's the entire shopping list for three cakes:
6 plump vanilla pods _ 50g sea salt _ 120g unsalted butter _ 18 large eggs _ 60g honey _ 120g plain flour _ 60g icing sugar _ 10g baking powder _ 380ml whole milk _ 500g top-quality milk chocolate (such as Valrhona's Tanariva) _ 565g top-quality dark chocolate (such as Amadei's Toscano Black 66%) _ 95g top-quality dark chocolate (such as Amadei's Porcelana) _ 150g top-quality dark chocolate (such as Amadei's Chuao) _ 215g groundnut oil _ 210g unrefined caster sugar _ 115g good-quality cocoa powder _ 2 sheets of leaf gelatin _ 50ml top-quality kirsch (e.g. Franz Fies) _ 515ml whipping cream _ 1 tsp glucose syrup _ 1 jar of apricot baking glaze _ 1 jar of top-quality sour cherries in syrup (e.g. Amarena Fabbri)

For the madeleine biscuit base
If making the wood-effect base at the same time, then double these quantities and set aside half the mixture to use in that.
50g unsalted butter _ 1 large egg (60g) _ 30g honey _ 60g plain flour _ 30g icing sugar, sifted _ 5g (½ tsp) baking powder _ pinch of table salt _ 15ml (1 tbsp) whole milk

For the aerated chocolate layer
500g top-quality milk chocolate (such as Valrhona's Tanariva) _
65g groundnut oil

For the flourless chocolate sponge
65g top-quality dark chocolate (such as Amedei's Toscano Black
66%) _ 7 egg yolks (140g) _ 130g unrefined caster sugar _
15g good-quality cocoa powder (such as Green & Black's Organic),
sifted _ 5 egg whites (150g)

For the kirsch cream
2 sheets of leaf gelatin _ 5 egg yolks (100g) _ 90g unrefined
caster sugar _ 250ml whole milk _ 220ml whipping cream _
20ml top-quality kirsch (e.g. Franz Fies)

For the wood-effect base
100g good-quality cocoa powder (such as Green & Black's Organic) _
200ml water _ reserved madeleine biscuit base mix

For the dried vanilla pod stalks
6 plump vanilla pods

For the chocolate ganache
95ml whipping cream _ 1 tsp glucose syrup _ pinch of table salt _
95g top-quality dark chocolate (such as Amedei's Porcelana) _
20g unsalted butter, diced

For the chocolate mousse
4 egg yolks (80g) _ 200g unrefined caster sugar _ 100ml whole
milk _ 150g top-quality dark chocolate (such as Amedei's Chuao) _
generous pinch of table salt _ 200ml whipping cream

For the finished gateau
The quantities below are enough for three cakes. You can either freeze
the cakes you don't want to use at once, or make up one cake and save
the rest of the prepared ingredients. For one cake, simply halve the
chocolate ganache and chocolate cream recipes.

reserved madeleine biscuit base rectangles _ reserved flourless chocolate sponge rectangles _ reserved aerated chocolate _ 1 jar of apricot baking glaze _ reserved chocolate ganache _ reserved kirsch cream _ 1 jar of top-quality wild cherries in heavy syrup (Amarena Fabbri cherries are ideal but difficult to obtain. Griottines are more readily available, though they'll take the gateau's taste in a slightly different direction.) _ 30ml top-quality kirsch (e.g. Franz Fies) _ reserved chocolate mousse _ 500g top-quality dark chocolate (such as Amedei's Toscano Black 66%) _ 150g groundnut oil _ reserved wood-effect base _ reserved dried vanilla pods, to decorate

MAKING THE MADELEINE BISCUIT BASE

1. Heat the oven to 200°C/400°F/Gas 6. Line a 21.5 x 31.5cm brownie tin with greaseproof paper or a little butter.
2. Melt the butter over a low heat, then leave to cool a little.
3. Beat the egg and honey together for 5 minutes, or until white and thick. (A food mixer with a paddle attachment is ideal for this job.)
4. Gradually add all the dry ingredients, then the cooled butter and finally the milk. Mix until they're all just combined. Do not overbeat.
5. Pour the mixture into the brownie tin. (But if you've doubled the quantities to make enough for the wood-effect base, set aside half the mixture for this.) Bake for 10 minutes, or until a pale golden brown.
6. Turn the oven down to 100°C/212°F. (Use an oven thermometer to check this.) Cut the biscuit base into three 8 x 18cm rectangles. (It's not essential that they're exact at this point, as they will need to be trimmed again when assembling the gateau.) Lift these out of the tin and place on a baking sheet.
7. Bake in the preheated oven for 20 minutes, or until deep golden brown and crisp. Leave to cool, then store in an airtight container until required.

MAKING THE AERATED CHOCOLATE

Here it is an especially good idea to get all the ingredients and equipment ready beforehand so that the chocolate goes through the process quickly, stays liquid and gets well aerated.

1. Line the 2.6 litre plastic container with greaseproof paper.
2. Break the chocolate into chunks and place in a medium-sized glass bowl. Place the bowl over a saucepan of simmering water and let the chocolate melt. (The bowl needs to be large enough to sit on top of the saucepan without its base touching the water: the aim is to soften up the chocolate on the gentlest of heats so that it doesn't go grainy.) Alternatively, melt the chocolate at high power in a microwave for 1½–2 minutes. (Again, be careful not to overheat it.)
3. Place a whipping-cream canister in a bowl or pan of boiling water. (Warming the canister ensures that the chocolate stays molten when poured into it.)
4. Stir the oil into the bowl containing the melted chocolate, then pour it all into the whipping-cream canister. Attach the canister cap and charge with three charges.
5. Shake the canister, then squirt the chocolate on to the base of the lined plastic container. Cover the container with its lid, then place in the vacuum storage bag. Position the storage bag's valve over the hole in the container's lid. Switch on the vacuum cleaner and place the hose on the valve to suck the air out of the bag. The chocolate should rise and be riddled with small bubbles. As soon as it does so, remove the vacuum and close the valve as quickly as possible. To set the chocolate, place the box – still in the vacuum bag – in the fridge until required.

MAKING THE FLOURLESS CHOCOLATE SPONGE

1. Preheat the oven to 180°C/350°F/Gas 4. Line a 21.5 x 31.5cm brownie tin with greaseproof paper or a little butter.
2. Break the chocolate into chunks and place in a glass bowl. Place the bowl over a saucepan of simmering water and let the chocolate melt (or heat the chocolate at high power in a microwave for 1½–2 minutes). Leave to cool.
3. Beat the egg yolks with 65g of the caster sugar for 5 minutes, or until white and thick. (A food mixer with a whisk attachment can be used for this.) Stir in the cocoa powder and melted, cooled chocolate.
4. Whisk the egg whites with the remaining sugar until soft peaks form. (The mixer can do this job too. If you have only one mixer bowl, a similar-sized stainless-steel or glass mixing bowl will work.

Make sure it is spotlessly clean: a dirty bowl is one of the commonest reasons for egg whites not stiffening.)

5. Gradually fold the egg whites into the beaten egg yolks, then pour this mixture into the brownie tin and bake for 20–25 minutes. The surface of the cake will look a little dry when removed from the oven, and it may sink slightly. Leave it to cool before cutting into three 8 x 18cm rectangles.

MAKING THE KIRSCH CREAM

1. Line a 21.5 x 31.5cm brownie tin with clingfilm.
2. Place the sheets of gelatin in a small bowl and pour over 100ml cold water. Leave for 15 minutes, or until soft.
3. Beat the egg yolks with the sugar for 5 minutes, or until white and thick. (The food mixer can do this job.)
4. Gently warm the milk in a small pan. Remove from the heat and stir in the beaten egg yolks. Return to a medium heat and cook for a further 2–3 minutes, stirring frequently. Use a digital probe to monitor when the temperature of the mixture reaches 80°C/175°F, at which point it should be taken off the heat. (It will have become thicker, with tiny bubbles appearing on the surface.)
5. Drain the gelatin and stir it into the warm mixture. (Make sure the mixture is not too hot or the gelatin will break. Make sure too that all the gelatin dissolves.) Leave until lukewarm.
6. Meanwhile, lightly whip the cream, then add the kirsch. Fold this into the cooled gelatin mixture, then pour the mixture into the brownie tin and place it in the freezer to set for at least 1 hour.

MAKING THE WOOD-EFFECT BASE

1. Preheat the oven to 200°C/400°F/Gas 6.
2. First make the madeleine mix (if you haven't already reserved some earlier – see page 391) using the ingredients listed on page 389. Melt the butter over a low heat, then leave to cool a little. Beat the egg and honey together for 5 minutes, or until the mixture is white and thick. (A food mixer with a paddle attachment is ideal for this job.) Gradually add all the dry ingredients, then the cooled butter and finally the milk. Mix until they're all just combined (do not over-beat). Set this madeleine mix aside.

3. Mix the cocoa powder and water and pour on to the far end of a non-stick silicone baking sheet set on top of a rigid baking sheet.
4. Drag the wood-effect painting tool over the batter and towards you, pivoting it back and forth as you go. (It's a process similar to pouring paint into a tray and dragging a roller through it to spread it out.) Place in the fridge and leave to chill for 1 hour.
5. Take the butter out of the fridge and, using a spatula, spread the madeleine mix over it. Place in the oven for 10 minutes, or until a light golden brown.
6. Remove from the rigid baking sheet and allow to cool. Once cooled, invert the wood-effect base on to the plate that will be displaying the gateau, and peel away the silicone baking sheet.

MAKING THE DRIED VANILLA POD STALKS
1. Cut the vanilla pods lengthways into four.
2. Tie a knot at the end of each strip, then twist it to give a gnarled effect.
3. Place on a plate and leave to dry overnight at room temperature.

MAKING THE CHOCOLATE GANACHE AND CHOCOLATE MOUSSE AND ASSEMBLING THE BLACK FOREST GATEAU
1. Line a 5cm deep, 9 x 19cm loaf tin with clingfilm.
2. For the chocolate ganache: gently heat the cream, glucose syrup and salt. Break the chocolate into a bowl, then stir in the warm cream. When the chocolate has melted entirely, add the butter and stir until that too has melted. Spoon the mixture into a piping bag and place it in the fridge for at least an hour to stiffen up.
3. Meanwhile, if need be, trim the madeleine base so that it fits the bottom of the loaf tin, leaving a ½cm gap between it and the sides of the tin. Trim the flourless chocolate sponge to the same dimensions as the madeleine base. Cut the aerated chocolate to these dimensions, and trim it so that it is no more than 1cm thick.
4. Before putting the madeleine base in the tin, spread it with a generous layer of apricot baking glaze. Put the aerated chocolate on top and place these in the bottom of the tin. (If you're making the cake without the aerated chocolate layer, replace it with a piece of flourless chocolate sponge.)

5. Remove the piping bag containing the ganache from the fridge. Along the top of the aerated chocolate, about 2–3mm from the edge, pipe a thick line of ganache. Repeat on the other side. (Looked at from above, the rectangle of aerated chocolate should now have two stripes of ganache, each of which runs parallel to the longer edges.)

6. Drain the cherries and reserve the syrup. Fill the gap between the two lines of ganache with a double row of cherries. (The idea is that every person is served a slice containing a pair of cherries, so calculate the number you'll need accordingly and be sure to space them well. Keep in mind roughly where you've placed them, which will make step 14 easier.)

7. Mix 60ml of the reserved cherry syrup with the kirsch.* Dip the chocolate sponge in this soaking syrup, then position it on top of the ganache and cherries.

8. Remove the kirsch cream from the freezer and trim it to the same dimensions as the other layers. Manoeuvre it on top of the chocolate sponge using a palette knife or fish slice. Put the gateau in the freezer while you prepare the chocolate mousse.

9. To make the chocolate mousse, beat the egg yolks with the sugar for 5 minutes, or until white and thick. (A food mixer with a paddle attachment can be used for this.)

10. Gently warm the milk in a small pan. Remove it from the heat and stir in the beaten egg yolks. Return to a medium heat and cook for a further 2–3 minutes, stirring frequently. Use a digital probe to monitor when the temperature of the mixture reaches 80°C/175°F, and remove from the heat.

11. Finely chop the chocolate and place it in a medium-sized bowl. Pour the warm milk and eggs over the chocolate and stir until the chocolate has melted. Add the salt and leave to cool.

12. Whip the cream until soft peaks form. Fold the cream into the cooled chocolate mixture.

13. Remove the gateau from the freezer. Make sure the clingfilm is taut against the sides of the tin. Pour the chocolate mousse down

* Taste the cherry syrup before mixing it with the kirsch. If it is rather flavourless, tip it into a small pan, add a tablespoon of unrefined caster sugar and bring to the boil. When it has reduced by half, take it off the heat and leave to cool slightly before stirring in the kirsch.

The delicate final touches can make all the difference – in Black Forest gateau cherry syrup is pipetted into the cake and two rows of sour cherries are carefully positioned with tweezers.

the sides of the tin until it reaches a level 1cm above the kirsch cream layer. Return the gateau to the freezer and leave it for at least an hour to firm up the layer of mousse.

14. Using a melon baller, scoop out a double row of indentations along the gateau. (Ideally, they should be above the cherries that were added in step 6.) Return the gateau to the freezer for a least an hour: it needs to be properly frozen in order to get the right effect with the chocolate coating.

15. For the coating, break the chocolate into chunks and place in a small glass bowl. Melt the chocolate by placing the bowl over a pan of simmering water, or by heating it at high power in a microwave for 1½–2 minutes. Leave to cool slightly before stirring in the groundnut oil. (If you don't plan to coat the cake with the paint gun, take 100g of this chocolate, cut it into shavings and scatter over the cake just before serving.)

16. Fill the base of the paint gun with the melted chocolate mixture and attach the nozzle. To avoid redecorating the kitchen in chocolate brown, set the large cardboard box on its side (which effectively

provides a protective roof and walls to work in). Remove the gateau from the freezer. Carefully lift it out of the loaf tin and on to a plate. Remove the clingfilm and place the gateau in the cardboard box. Spray the gateau with the chocolate, turning carefully as you go. Return it to the freezer until 20 minutes before serving.

17. To serve, place the gateau on the wood-effect base. Use a skewer to bore a small hole 2–3 inches into the centre of the bottom of each indentation, down towards the cherry below. Agitate the skewer a little to increase the hole's diameter. Pipette in the cherry syrup until it reaches the top of the bore-hole (but doesn't spill out into the indentation itself). Place a sour cherry, stalk end up, in each indentation, and sit a dried vanilla pod in each cherry, to make a decorative stalk. For the full effect, fill an atomiser with kirsch and squirt it round the room just before serving the gateau – it will magically bring a little of the Black Forest to the dinner table.

Treacle Tart

& Ice Cream

'... he felt it was a better use of his time to eat his way steadily through his steak and kidney pie, then a large plateful of his favourite treacle tart.'

J.K. Rowling, *Harry Potter and the Order of the Phoenix*

History

TREACLE

'They lived on treacle,' said the Dormouse,
after thinking a minute or two.
Lewis Carroll, *Alice's Adventures in Wonderland*

Although treacle was slow to catch on as a sweetener, its name originates from ancient times. It comes from the Greek *theriake*, meaning 'an antidote to the bite of wild beasts', and was employed as a cure for all kinds of poisons, right up to the Middle Ages.

Perhaps the slow spread of the product is a result of its medicinal history. At first, apothecaries made treacle from their own secret recipes. But as demand from chemists and distillers grew, it became a valuable article of trade. For a time, Venice had a virtual monopoly on production, but by the fifteenth century, Genoa and Flanders were supplying most of England's treacle. Eventually, sugar refineries were set up in London, and the home-manufactured product supplanted the imports. London treacle was born.

Refining raw sugar cane involves crushing and then boiling the cane until it has thickened sufficiently to allow the growth of the sugar crystals that will eventually become sugar. Treacle was made at this stage with what was drained off from the sugar cane during successive boilings. It was almost black in colour and had a faint burnt-caramel flavour, like molasses. (This is now called 'black treacle'. 'Light treacle', better known as golden syrup, is made from the syrup obtained during the first boiling of sugar cane, a refining method that was only introduced around 1880.)

Mass production led to supply outstripping demand from distillers and apothecaries, and by the seventeenth century the excess was marketed in its natural state as a sweetener. For the poor, especially in the north, a spoonful of treacle helped their meagre diet go down: it was added to parkin and oatmeal biscuits, and puddled on top of porridge.

As the number of British colonies grew (and access to cheap labour along with them), the gathering and processing of sugar cane became more economical. Once refined sugar was affordable, it soon replaced treacle as the masses' sweetener of choice. This and the development of golden syrup heralded treacle's transition from sweetener to dessert ingredient, adding colour, moisture and taste to a variety of dishes.

It is not known when and where treacle tart was thought up – when treacle went from walk-on part to star performer in a dessert – but one of treacle's early roles provides a possible clue. By the reign of Charles II, treacle rather than liquorice was being used to make gingerbread. The royal recipe called for large amounts of candied peel and coriander seed, but the domestic version couldn't possibly afford that level of spicing, so relied far more heavily on treacle for flavour. Somewhere a chef with an inventive imagination may well have tasted festive gingerbread and decided that putting it in a pastry case would add something special.

ICE CREAM

I doubt the world holds for anyone a more soul-stirring surprise than the first adventure with ice cream.
Heywood Broun

The story of ice cream satisfyingly encapsulates two themes of this book: the way in which much of food history soon becomes a frothy confection of myth, exaggeration and romanticism; and the importance of science in the kitchen.

Authoritative books will tell you that Arabs in Sicily began by icing their sweetened aromatic drinks known as *sharbats* with snow from Mount Etna, and ended up inventing granitas and water ices. They will say that Marco Polo saw ice cream being made in China and brought the idea back to Italy, and that Catherine de' Medici hired an Italian chef, Buontalenti, who introduced the French court to ice cream in 1533. Legend also has it that two more Italians, de Mirra and Marco, brought ices to the court of Charles I, who later gave his official ice-cream maker a lifetime pension with the proviso that he reveal the recipe to no one.

Historical evidence contradicts all these stories. It's now commonly believed that Marco Polo never actually reached China in his travels, and there's no record of Charles I's supposed ice-cream supremo. If he did actually exist, then it's a very well-kept secret indeed. Most of these tall tales appear only in the nineteenth century, and seem to be generated by marketing men and ice-cream makers and vendors, as though they felt the need not only to churn their product, but to give it some spin as well.

The final disproof is not historic but scientific: before the middle of the seventeenth century, almost no one in Europe could make ice cream because they didn't know the chemical process that makes it happen.

The most basic technique for manufacturing ice cream depends on the 'endothermic effect': if you add some form of salt to ice, it significantly lowers the freezing point of the mixture. Add another liquid to the mix, and this too will freeze and solidify via conduction.

It is true that Arabs and Italians played a significant part in the dissemination of this crucial culinary know-how. In the thirteenth century, the Arab historian of medicine Ibn Abu Usaybi'a talks of making artificial ice from cold water and saltpetre, and indeed historians largely agree that the Arabs acquired their knowledge from China and passed it on during their occupation of Spain. The first reference to this process in Europe is in the Italian physician Zimara's *Problemata* in 1530, but it remained the province of doctors and scholars for another century or so. Water ices began to appear in Italy, France and Spain in the 1660s, and the earliest French recipe was published in 1674. The earliest English version came some forty years later, in *Mrs Mary Eales Receipts*, a cookbook by Queen Anne's confectioner.

As the frequent mention above of courts, kings and queens suggests, ice cream was at first a pleasure only for the wealthy. Making ice on a commercial basis was enormously costly, so enthusiasts tended to harvest and store natural ice in specially constructed ice houses. By 1800 these were a feature of many European stately homes, but ice cream was still largely denied to those without the money and space to indulge themselves. Once again it was science that introduced ice cream to a new audience: in 1843 machines were invented in both England and America that froze and churned the mixture – the first step towards mass production. And the market for this increased output was in part the result of the upheavals and unification of Italy in the mid-nineteenth century: many Italian emigrants ended up in England and brought their ice-cream expertise with them. The British masses soon acquired a taste for their wares, made possible by the importation of farmed ice, initially from the United States and later from Norway.

More scientific revolution followed. By the beginning of the twentieth century mechanical refrigeration had largely superseded the ice-and-salt approach, meaning manufacturers were no longer at the mercy of warm winters or fluctuations in salt production.* This, allied to the development of refrigerated railway trucks, massively expanded the opportunities for manufacture and delivery. Once domestic freezers were invented, liberating the consumer from the need to eat it immediately, ice cream's popularity became unstoppable.

The Quest for the Best

MILKING IT

The fat in milk and cream is part of the magic that makes ice cream. It keeps the ice crystals from becoming too large, and it accounts for the richness and smoothness of the end product. To make really delicious ice cream, it was vital that I got hold of the best milk I could, so I went to the village of White Waltham in Berkshire.

Over the last decade, Waltham Place Farm has worked hard to become biodynamic – an agricultural approach that is far removed from the intensive farming that has shrivelled the environment and the food it produces. Biodynamics developed from a series of lectures given by the philosopher Rudolf Steiner in Koberwitz (now Kobierzyce

---

* In many parts of the world, however, salt and ice are still used. Making ices using salt, ice and a hand machine is a very satisfying way of doing it, and a rewarding piece of practical science.

in Poland) in 1924. At its heart is the belief that there should be an integrated relationship between farmers and the plants, animals and soil they work with. The aim is to have a self-sufficient farm, maintaining a mix of habitats. The fields should be managed in a way that supports animal life, and the soil nourished with therapeutic preparations. Biodynamic farmers are aware that their farms are part of the wider natural environment and act accordingly. Even the planetary rhythms and their influence on the growth of animals and plants are considered. Quality not quantity is a fundamental part of the biodynamic vision, and I had enjoyed the benefits of this at the Fat Duck: Waltham Place supplies us with fruit and vegetables, and I was hoping that it would start planting for us in the near future.

The farm has another thing to recommend it: it's only a ten-minute drive from my home, which is fortunate because milking means an early start.

Although it was barely light when I arrived, Chris Stevenson was already waiting impatiently for me. Chris is about as far from the traditional image of the milkmaid as you are likely to get. With his long moustache and sideburns, he looked more like Lemmy from Motörhead. His eyes glittered with nervousness or amusement, I wasn't sure which. 'Right, let's go and see the cows,' he said, and plodded off.

The mist of early morning was clearing to reveal a classic English scene. We walked past solid outbuildings of weathered red brick and purple clapboard. A cluster of turkeys stalked us, expecting food. Although it was late autumn, the vegetable gardens spread out lush and colourful: squashes and beets were neatly flanked by dahlias and marigolds, grown to attract insects and ward off bugs with their heady scent and bright blooms. Rare breeds of sheep – Jacob and Castlemilk Moorit – foraged happily in fenced enclosures. The Jersey cows looked magnificent. They were a glossy caramel or clotted-cream colour and still had their horns, which somehow made them look nobler. (Intensive dairy farms saw off the horns. Although it's claimed this is for safety, there's also – as always – an economic consideration: without horns you can cram more cows into a shed. To me it seems a sorry desecration of the animal's dignity.)

I had chosen Jersey cows because their milk has 25 per cent more butterfat than milk from most other breeds, allowing me to have the 'clean' taste that milk gives to ice cream as well as a real creaminess. As we walked along the muddy track towards the milking shed, however, Chris told me to expect other differences in the milk from their biodynamic cows. 'Intensive farms have an increased risk of contamination, so they pasteurise the milk – heating it to kill off any bugs. The problem is heat kills off lots of good things along with the bad. The milk lacks vitality and flavour. Here at Waltham Place we're small enough to keep proper control over hygiene, so we don't have to pasteurise.'

As any mother who has breastfed will know, what you eat affects the taste of milk. Most commercial dairy operations give their cows only one type of grass. 'This is at odds with nature, so it's not good for the cows or their milk,' said Chris. 'If you think back to a time before intensive cultivation, fields for grazing had a huge variety. There'd be herbs, rye, wild flowers and other stuff in there, and the cow would instinctively select what it needed for a healthy balanced diet. Here the Jerseys graze on grass leys that are as near as possible to what they would feed on naturally. And you can taste that in the milk. No question.'

As we arrived at the milking shed and Peggy, Becky and Cathy trotted inside, Chris explained that we'd be milking by hand. He claimed the machine had broken down, though I wondered whether he was tricking me into a very literal 'hands-on' experience. He still had that amused glint in his eye. Anyway, it seemed appropriate, in such a timeless setting, to be doing things the old-fashioned way. I rolled up my sleeves, while Chris showed me how to do it.

First, he 'stripped out' the cows: squeezing their teats to get rid of the milk that had collected in them overnight and then washing and drying them. Then, squatting on a large red plastic jerrycan and resting his head affectionately against Peggy's flank, he began pulling, gently but firmly, on two of her teats. He settled into a piston-like rhythm, and the shed was gradually suffused with a rich, milky aroma. All too soon he had filled half a bucket and it was my turn. I knew already this would be one of those things that looks simple until you try it.

Most difficult was knowing how much force and pressure you could exert without hurting the cow. Peggy sensed she was in unfamiliar hands and Chris had to call out 'Good girl' a few times to steady and reassure her. Under his guidance I became more skilful and the trickle of milk became if not a stream, then at least a runnel.

'How much do you want?' I asked. Already my fingers were beginning to ache.

'Well, there's enough there for a cup of tea. But we won't be getting any milk on our cornflakes at this rate,' Chris replied.

I let him take over. Even at his speed, hand-milking took about twenty minutes per cow (a machine can do the same job in two), and by the end, even his fingers were aching. But we had 11 litres of fresh milk to play around with. The next stage was to turn it into cream.

Chris had already put a bucketful of fresh milk into a sink of hot water. 'While milk and cream are inside the cow,' he explained, 'they're at a warm enough temperature that the two mix properly. As soon as milk leaves the cow and cools down in the bucket, the cream begins to separate out. You can't just stir it back in because it'll become too lumpy. Instead you have to warm it again until the cream and milk recombine.' As he talked he assembled the parts of the creamer, attaching a series of silver metal attachments to a small motor, on top of which he placed a metal basin. The contraption looked no bigger or more complicated than a food processor, and by the time he'd finished, the milk was ready to be poured in the top.

Different attachments determine whether you get double cream and skimmed milk, or single cream and semi-skimmed. Eventually I wanted to try out each of them as the basis for my ice cream, but we began with double and skimmed. The rotor whirred into life and, minutes later, a thick yellow paste was oozing out of one nozzle while a white stream flowed out of the other.

The double cream was delicious, but the skimmed milk was a revelation. Normally skimmed milk is thin, watery and characterless – useful if you're looking for milk that has no danger of overpowering other tastes but hardly a satisfying drinking experience. This, on the other hand, was smooth, rich and full-flavoured, almost chewy, and with subtleties of taste. Using Jersey milk or cream in an ice cream was going to be really interesting: I could hardly wait to get back to the Fat Duck and start trying it out.

As it happens, I didn't have to wait, thanks to liquid nitrogen. One of liquid nitrogen's properties is that it boils at −196°C/−320°F. (We use it at the Fat Duck to make nitro-poached green tea and lime mousse, a fantastic palate-cleanser at the start of a meal.) For ice cream you simply add liquid nitrogen to the mix and it boils, bubbles and chills almost immediately.*

Along with some of the usual chef's paraphernalia – hand whisk, mixing bowl – I'd also brought a canister of the stuff. As soon as Chris had separated the milk and cream, I put some of the latter in a bowl, added sugar and whisked while pouring in the liquid nitrogen. Gusts of white condensed vapour ballooned out over the table like low-lying mist in a spooky graveyard, then disappeared almost as swiftly to leave a bowlful of smooth, creamy ice cream. From cow to cornet in four minutes! Even Chris seemed impressed. 'Mmm, that's rich, that is,' he said as his face broke into a satisfied smile.

As I drove away from the farm I reflected on what I'd seen and learned – not just in terms of what would be useful for the perfect ice cream, but also in terms of wider considerations on the future of farming. Waltham Place does show us a kind of perfection. Certainly, if the taste was anything to go by, the farm yields far better milk than its high-production rivals. But it goes deeper than that. The quality of the produce goes hand in hand with the quality of life of the animals – they appear to be happy.

If you think this is simply dewy-eyed romanticism on my part (and there's no doubt that Waltham Place Farm can have that kind of effect), then consider this: on intensive dairy farms most cows are spent by the age of seven or eight, after which it's the cull market for them, to be turned into steak and kidney pies. Holsteins, which form about 80 per cent of British stock, often manage a mere two and a half years. Yet Peggy, the cow I'd milked that morning, was fourteen and still going strong. Waltham Place demonstrated that there are other – and better – ways to farm. Better for Peggy, certainly, but also better for us – for our morals, our health and the taste of the food we put on the table.

* With a substance this cold, care needs to be taken while handling it to avoid a nasty freezer burn. Make sure you understand what is involved and take the necessary precautions if you're intending to try this at home.

Making ice cream with liquid nitrogen, as a sceptical dairy farmer looks on.

'OUT OF THE STRONG CAME FORTH SWEETNESS'

My ice cream was taking shape, but I also had a tart to start. A trip to Tate & Lyle was in order.

It was only when I visited the company's factory in London's Docklands that I realised that, although the green and gold tin had an iconic status for me and was a vivid part of my youthful memories of Mum's kitchen shelves, I had never really looked at it properly.

At the entrance to the factory, however, there's a large stone bas-relief that makes you see the label anew. There's the motto, etched in large letters, and there's the lion. Only I now saw, for the first time, that he's a dead lion, and what look like flies are buzzing around his head.

The staff at Tate & Lyle are extremely loyal, enthusiastic and knowledgeable about their product and its hundred-year history (the syrup is often referred to there as 'Goldie', as though it were a character in its own right). They know by heart all the seminal facts and dates, and have a touching appreciation for the memorabilia – they showed me marvellous old cookbooks that ingeniously weaved treacle into every recipe, and a (full) tin from the First World War that had a metal base and lid but cardboard sides, so as to save resources. They of course knew that the flies are in fact bees, and that the motto and scene come from the Bible. They told me that, in Judges 14, Samson kills a lion on his way to the Philistines, and on the way back notices that bees have made a honeycomb in the carcass. This inspires him to set the Philistines a riddle: 'Out of the eater came forth meat, and out of the strong came forth sweetness.' It was hard to see how this related to treacle, except for the fact that it has an undeniable sweetness, but apparently Abram Lyle was a very religious man and the image was his idea. Despite – or perhaps because of – its idiosyncrasies, the trade-mark has remained virtually unchanged ever since, a true branding classic. Indeed, the lion is almost too powerful: many people believe it's called Lion's Golden Syrup.

Mr Tate and Mr Lyle never met. They began as rival sugar refiners in the 1860s, and the companies merged only in 1921. Lyle spotted the potential of golden syrup early on, feeding it first to his employees and, as demand grew, supplying it to shopkeepers in barrels. The company is still practically the only manufacturer of treacle in the country.

The manager, Ian Clark, took me on a tour of the factory. It was, as you might expect, a strange mix of old and new. We first visited the can-making room, which had none of the prefab functionality of modern industry: here there were high ceilings, solid brickwork and bolted iron girders, a feeling of space. As at Amedei, the machines had a satisfyingly retro look to them – bulky, weighty and painted a dour green or black. The room was dominated by three 10-foot-high Ferris wheels that gave each can a ride while testing to see if it was airtight. The rejects fell to the bottom.

The can-making room might have seemed like a museum piece (it reminded me of the East Hall of Kensington's Science Museum: the oversized Georgian and Victorian engines with their elaborate networks of pistons and pulleys), but the filtering and inversion room looked positively space-age. Steel silos soared upwards and a web of silver pipes spread and intertwined in all directions. Once again I was reminded of *Charlie and the Chocolate Factory*.

'All these tubes and vessels and dials. This is the Wonka room, isn't it?' I said.

'You could say that,' Ian giggled enigmatically, rather like Willy Wonka himself (an impression reinforced by the fact that regulations meant he was wearing a cobalt-blue hairnet under a moss-green baseball cap).

'There's a wonderful smell of molasses and toasted cereal. What's happening here?'

'This is the nerve centre of the Goldie process,' he told me. 'It's where the inversion takes place, the most important part of the procedure. I'll explain it to you later, in the lab: I've got some coloured balls that make it simpler.' (I told you the staff were keen.)

The heat was near tropical: through a small bolted port-hole in one of the pipes I could see a fierce red glow. 'That's the evaporator,' Ian said. 'We trickle the syrup through a carbon bed to make it a more attractive colour, then the evaporators feed it up to the next floor.'

Squeezed in below the roof are three huge steel drums lying on their side: the storage tanks containing some twenty-three tons of treacle. From here, gravity propels the treacle downwards to the syrup filling room, where the tins are rattled along racks and conveyor belts to be filled and sealed. The place is slightly sticky underfoot and the characteristic rich, sweet smell wafts through the room. Ian and I walked upstairs to the lab so he could show me the science behind that thick, sticky sweetness.

With its veneered cupboards and work surfaces, the Tate & Lyle laboratory would look like a large domestic kitchen, except that every available surface is filled with bottles of liquid marked with dates and percentages and intriguing combinations such as 'brandy & nutmeg' or 'rum & cinnamon'. The room is at the top of the factory, and through the windows I could see across large swathes of Docklands. One hundred years ago, the area must have been an industrial powerhouse, with the fug of different factories clouding the air with aromas. It has since become something of a wasteland – dominated by pylons and moribund pubs – but there are signs of renewal. A futuristic-looking DLR station has appeared, and optimistic estate agents advertise riverside apartments. Tate & Lyle seems to carry on regardless, secure in the integrity of its product and selling a whopping thirteen million tins a year.

Ian explained to me the process of inversion that is so central to the creation of golden syrup. 'Sugars come in many forms: sucrose, glucose, fructose, maltose and lactose, among others. The starting point for golden syrup is sucrose, which is the most common and one of the sweetest. That's what you've got in your sugar pot. It has the distinction of keeping its pleasant taste even in high concentrations. But for golden syrup we need to change the sugar's crystalline structure into something with a runny smoothness, and we do this by splitting it into other sugars. Here, take these.'

He handed me two balls, one red, one yellow.

'Sucrose is made up of two simpler sugars: glucose and fructose. Imagine the red ball is a fructose molecule, the yellow a glucose molecule. Hold one ball in each hand and bring the two together and you've got sucrose.' I stood there obligingly, like a magician setting up his next trick. 'Now, if you heat sucrose in the presence of acid, the sucrose splits into its constituent parts.' Ian pushed my hands apart; the trick was under way. 'This messes up the orderly crystalline structure, resulting in a thick liquid. And the disorder prevents the sucrose from re-forming – rogue molecules of glucose or fructose keep getting in the way.' He handed me a third ball and brought my hands back together. Hey presto! The presence of another ball meant the neat bonding of one glucose molecule with one fructose molecule was no longer possible. (Much as playing gooseberry tends to kill off romance: two's company, three's a crowd.)

This was the theory. Now Ian showed it in action. He mixed together 350 grams of demerara sugar, 150 millilitres of water and 750 milligrams of citric acid powder until he had a grainy brown soup. Then he heated up the concoction to about 80°C/175°F and let it simmer for fifteen minutes. Gradually the sweetness lessened and the mixture thickened.

'So, once the sugar's inverted, you've got a syrup with an acidic note to it. What's the next stage, Ian?'

'Add sodium bicarbonate to bring the pH back up to neutral and stop the inversion process.'

I tasted the results. It was syrup all right, but not quite what I was after. 'Lyle's Golden Syrup has got a particular flavour, a characteristic that's not what you get when you do this. So something else must be going on as well as inversion. How do you get that flavour?'

'Golden Syrup is a lot more concentrated than this. At our refinery, brown sugar is boiled under a vacuum, driving off a lot of the water and intensifying the flavour. But then, as it cools down and the white sugar begins to recrystallise, we remove that too, which concentrates the flavour further. The product of this process is known as a "Jet" and we can repeat the process as many times as we need to get the flavour, colour and consistency we want. To give you some idea: Golden Syrup is a mixture of Jets 2 and 3; Jet 5 is black treacle.'

'Have you got some here? I'd love to taste it.'

Ian fetched samples of Jets 2 and 3. There was a marked colour difference between the two: the dark caramel of the second Jet had transformed to a much darker reddy-brown in the third. The change in colour was mirrored by a noticeable difference in taste.

'Jet 3 has much more of the treacle flavour that you'll recognise,' suggested Ian.

'Yes, it's got a slight liquorice aspect, some butterscotch and a real nutty note that reminds me above all of monkey nuts, especially the shell.'

For me this was a pivotal moment: I'd not really registered the nutty flavour in treacle before, and I suddenly saw how I could use a technique from classic French cuisine to accentuate this in my treacle tart, adding to its complexity and depth of taste. It was one of those lovely epiphanies that you hope for during each research visit or experiment, and rarely get. With this recipe, I was at last beginning to see the way forward. Paradoxically, however, my next trip was pointed in the opposite direction – back into the past.

COURT ON CAMERA

There are always mysteries in old cookbooks, because even the most unpoetical depend on the existence of a living tradition for the cook to know when the result is correct.
Charles Perry, from *In Taste: Proceedings of the Oxford Symposium on Food & Cookery*

With its spacious courtyards, pleasing proportions and soaring octagonal red-brick towers, Hampton Court is one of the glories of Tudor architecture. It's thrilling to look at – but not half as thrilling for me as what's inside: the Hampton Court kitchens.

There are no Pyrex beakers or stainless-steel work surfaces, no distillator or centrifuge, but in many ways these are the ultimate research kitchens. (There's even a black witch's cauldron in one of the vast stone fireplaces, suggesting that a kind of alchemy really does take place here.) They can be rigged up as they would have been in the Tudor, Elizabethan or Jacobean periods. The aim is to 'learn from doing' – using recipes and utensils from the past, in the original setting, to see what light it sheds on a specific area of social history. You've heard of method acting? This is method cooking: historians investigate exactly what kitchen equipment was used and have copies made; they travel to the Canary Islands to obtain the right cochineal beetle for sixteenth-century food colouring; and they've been known to don waistcoats and breeches dyed with onion skins because that's what would have been worn at the time. For the last few years I've been working with them to develop historical British food for the Hind's Head.

My guides for the day, Marc Meltonville and Richard Fitch, were wearing black T-shirts rather than hand-woven hemp, but their immersion in culinary history was nonetheless impressive. If anyone could fill me in on the historical background of treacle tart, these guys could. They were a formidable double act, plucking dates out of the air for any ingredient you cared to mention and finishing off each other's sentences.

'We serve a treacle tart at the Hind's Head,' I began, 'and we've done a lot of work developing it. I originally wanted to recreate one of the earliest recipes, which had dark treacle, apple, dried fruit and ginger, but it turned out to be too far removed from what people now think of as treacle tart. So this time I wanted to see how far we can raid history but still keep within the boundaries of people's expectations.'

'The earliest thing we've found that looks like treacle tart is called "Tart of Bread",' Marc told me. 'It doesn't use treacle, but it's in the right style, so that's what we're making here.' He picked up an incredibly sculptural, solid, rounded cone of sugar and hammered at it with a wooden mallet. It sheared into large chunks that then had to be worked over using a pestle and mortar.

'That sugar's unusual. Where did you get it?' I wanted to know.

'It's from Iran,' said Richard. 'They boil down the cane juice, then pour it into cone-shaped moulds, where it's left to cool and crystallise. Before Henry Tate patented a sugar-cube cutter, sugar was always sold in the form of these "loaves" – that's how Sugar Loaf Mountain in Brazil got its name: it's the same cone shape.'

'You can really smell the molasses.'

'Yes. It's single-refined, so although some of the molasses would drain away while the cone was inverted, there'd still be a lot in there.'

Marc ground the sugar until it was a fine powder – a hard bout of manual work – then made equally fine breadcrumbs and mixed them together in a glazed earthenware bowl. Next, rose water was added.

'The recipe just says "some",' said Richard, 'so there's a lot of guesswork involved. That's part of the reason for experimenting here at Hampton Court.'

'When is this recipe from? What year?'

'It's from *The Good Housewife's Handmaid for the Kitchen*, published in 1594,' he said without hesitation.

Marc poured molten butter on to the sugar, breadcrumbs and rose water, and stirred until it was all thoroughly incorporated. By now it looked like a stodgy breadcrumb mix. Richard brought over a heavy pan in which he'd placed pastry. He scraped in the mix, pressed it down with his fingers, then trimmed the edges off the pastry.

'Would anything be added on top?' I wondered.

'You might sprinkle over sugar.' He placed the pan on a copper tray, and laid this on top of a tray containing hot coals. Above the two trays went a third, containing more hot coals. 'This oven's even more of an experiment than the rest,' he said. 'It should be 180–200°C. I reckon the tart'll take twenty minutes or so.'

'So, while that's cooking, tell me about the next link in the treacle chain after Tart of Bread.'

'Well, there is no direct link. We've looked through the extensive collection of books here and there's no treacle tart recipe until the 1920s.'

'The 1920s?! OK, what about the earliest use of the word "treacle" in a dish?'

'Well, as you know, Heston, the product golden syrup, sold and marketed as such, only appears in the 1880s,' explained Richard. 'But people have been getting that extraction throughout history whenever they've refined sugar. Traditionally, in England "treacle" meant any of the syrups you got from refining. So when it says "treacle" in a recipe, we haven't really got a clue what goes in it—'

'—in our collection,' Marc continued, 'the earliest use is in an eighteenth-century book called *A Collection of Above 300 Receipts* by Mary Kettilby. It's a recipe for thick gingerbread, and it continues in much the same form into the late nineteenth century, containing ginger, flour, treacle and eggs.'

By now, Tart of Bread was done. Richard lifted off the coals. 'The top's browned off nicely. Let's give it a try.'

'At least it looks like treacle tart,' observed Marc.

'Yes, it's the right texture,' I said. 'Like a slightly moist madeleine, with a cakey note. And the taste of rose water really comes through. It's very nice indeed. I don't think it's that far removed from the modern palate at all.'

'I agree,' Richard affirmed. 'It's definitely in the right area. It might not be the grandfather of treacle tart, but it's certainly a distant relative.'

'Could do with some custard, though,' Marc said ruefully.

Already, using historically accurate ingredients was reaping rewards: the low water content of the single-refined sugar meant the tart had a really good crispy crust on top – something you'd never have got using normal sugar. It was a small but valuable insight into past practices and kitchen lore.

Richard and Marc were not finished, though. They had other experiments for me to try.

'Before golden syrup was invented, references to treacle often had black treacle in mind, so we've tried a recipe using that. It calls for breadcrumbs again, plus treacle, currants and ginger—'

'—the amounts are all guesswork. Old recipes tend to give vague measurements such as "a small bigness". It's very much trial and error.' Richard mixed together the breadcrumbs, ginger and currants, then poured black treacle – glossy and viscous, like engine oil – into the bowl. It bonded thickly to the other ingredients. 'Now we add melted butter to loosen it up.'

'It's actually not so far from the Tart of Bread recipe, is it?'

'No,' Marc agreed.

'What about salt? I feel it has to have that to cut the sweetness and give a richer, more rounded flavour.'

'None of the old recipes mentions it—'

'—but none of the old recipes mentions what to them is blindingly obvious,' finished Richard. 'They'll just say "season" and leave it at that. And when they say "spice it", they mean the entire range of your spice box. It could mean sugar, as that's among the spices, or some-thing else—'

'—these books were written long before the era of coffee-table cookbooks that are used for inspiration. They're more of a reminder. That's why there are no precise measurements.'

Richard had been mixing the ingredients for some time. The result looked a lot like mincemeat. He put the concoction in a metal pan. 'No pastry case: at this time "tart" meant it was left open.' Sugar was sprinkled over and it went in the copper tray and into the oven.

'What's the date of this recipe?' I asked.

'The first half of the nineteenth century – early Queen Victoria,' Marc replied.

The smell told us when the tart was done. 'It's still soft,' said Richard. 'That's good. But it's not as crisp as the other was. That's the black treacle at work. I'm sad to say there's virtually no taste.'

'Yes,' I had to admit. 'It's bready, a bit toast-like. It's strange, but the Tart of Bread is in some ways closer to the modern treacle tart than this is, even though it's some 250 years older. It's as though we've come full circle.'

'But even in this recipe you can see the continuity,' Marc pointed out. 'Apart from the black treacle, this has a lot of things you might find in a modern treacle tart.'

Marc and Richard had also prepared Mary Kettilby's thick gingerbread recipe. It took some cutting with a sharp knife and proved to be not so much hard as dense, somewhere between a biscuit and a cake, and very different from what the modern palate would expect. 'Think parkin not Victoria sponge,' advised Marc. 'They're not into that kind of cake yet.'

It was a reminder of how important context is: this kind of gingerbread might seem strange and uninviting to us now, but it was a staple of the eighteenth and nineteenth centuries, when it would have been eaten sliced, with a cup of tea or a glass of sherry. Cooking is intertwined with custom and habit, the style of the times, and the Hampton Court kitchens are a great way of reminding yourself of this, and of seeing the change and continuity that surround cooking.

As always with a visit to Hampton Court, I had been given far more than I could possibly make sense of in one go. But already I'd got an idea of the backbone of the recipe, of the ingredients that had gradually coalesced into what we think of as treacle tart today. Playing around with those ingredients would be intriguing, especially if I could somehow give a nod to the dish's origins.

GETTING A READING AT READING UNIVERSITY

In Patrick Süskind's novel *Perfume*, Jean-Baptiste Grenouille has a nose so sensitive that it can distinguish different types of wood or smoke or stone by smell alone.

He had gathered tens of thousands, hundreds of thousands of specific smells and kept them so clearly, so randomly, at his disposal, that he could not only recall them when he smelled them again, but could also actually smell them simply upon recollection.

My sense of smell is pretty good, but many is the time I've wished I had Grenouille in my employ – and now that wish was all the keener because I wanted to differentiate between the many subtle aromas that make up golden syrup so that I could experiment with the composition of my tart. I could have done with Jean-Baptiste's nose. Fortunately, I knew a man with the next best things – Professor Don Mottram, who has access to a gas chromatograph and mass spectrometer. As the chilli chapter showed, the gas chromatograph gives you the opportunity to stick your nose in a tube and try to detect each successive aroma in a substance. The mass spectrometer, on the other hand, provides a computer read-out that shows, by means of graphed peaks, what compounds are present, and in what quantities. For me it has been a great way of searching out surprising but effective food combinations – white chocolate and caviar, for example, and foie gras, almonds and sour cherries. By isolating particular flavour compounds in one food, and then cross-referencing these against a database, I can discover which foods have a compound in common. Of course, this doesn't mean they're bound to suit each other, but the hidden connections revealed by the computer provide a great spur to creativity and culinary investigation.

It's serious science, but there is an undeniable Willy Wonka aspect to the technology, so it seemed appropriate that I'd be testing golden syrup with it. I'd brought with me a normal green tin's worth, along with a glass jar of seventy-year-old Tate & Lyle's Golden Syrup that Ian Clark had lent me so that I could explore the effects on flavour of ageing. Don set up the machines and I, effectively, set my nose to the grindstone ...

The high-tech scratch 'n' sniff approach eventually resulted in an intriguing list of foods that might go well with treacle: popcorn, butterscotch, cooked banana, candyfloss, dried fruit, coffee. Back at the development kitchen we stocked up on ingredients until the place looked like a farmers' market – fresh figs tumbled across the work surface in a riot of deep purple streaked with vibrant green, interspersed with clusters of black, green and yellow bananas and tubs of purée and compote – and then we tried out ideas, looking for a combination of texture and flavour that would bring something extra to a treacle tart.

Mary-Ellen made strips of fig and banana purée and baked them in the oven, while I smoked a banana in ginger essential oil and even froze a banana with liquid nitrogen so that I could grate it into fine flakes. We prepared each potential ingredient in every way we could think of, then added them to a batch of tarts and cooked and tasted. All of them were good – and the addition of coffee seemed to me outstanding – but all of them took the dish in a direction that was just too far from what we think of as treacle tart.

It wasn't exactly back to the drawing board, though. At Reading the seventy-year-old syrup had produced a really interesting result. The peaks of the computer read-out zigzagged across the page like a mountain range. The older treacle contained the same flavour compounds as the normal stuff, but each was intensified. Age had had a beneficial effect. I decided there and then to have a go at replicating that effect because it would definitely add something to the recipe.

So I put a tin of golden syrup in a water bath on a low heat for a couple of weeks, crossed my fingers, fought the temptation to tinker with it, and then tasted the results. The treacle definitely had more depth and individuality – perhaps not as much as three-quarters of a century might achieve, but certainly enough to enhance my tart. I'd found the ingredient that would make it special.

Treacle Tart & Ice Cream Serves 8–10

Here, the key is to keep the pastry as cold and relaxed as possible at all times. If it's too warm, the fat begins to melt. If it's overworked, the gluten develops too much and the pastry loses its lightness. So don't overdo the mixing and rolling: work quickly and briefly. Cool all the equipment – greaseproof paper, rolling pin, marble pastry board if you have one – in the fridge before you start. And return the pastry to the fridge whenever you feel it's getting too warm. The fridge's coldness will harden up the butter and the resting time will relax the gluten, after which it will be easy to work with once more.

Coldness is, of course, also the key to the ice cream. I'd had problems with domestic ice-cream makers because they didn't get the mixture cold enough. The stuff I used at Waltham Place Farm – liquid nitrogen – was one solution, but it's difficult to obtain and difficult to work with. I seemed to be stuck between a rock and a hard place – either too cold or not cold enough – and then I remembered dry ice. At -80°C/-112°F it would freeze the mixture properly without causing havoc in the kitchen. And, as the main source of eerie mist effects on stage and screen, it would be easier to obtain than a canister of liquid nitrogen.

The Fat Duck's nitro-poached green tea and lime mousse is served up surrounded by a swirl of vapour. With a bit of practice, this ice cream could be made at the table, providing a fantastic piece of theatre as the billowing mists of dry ice clear to reveal a cook, in goggles, bearing a bowl of ice cream that's out of this world.

Special equipment
Digital probe, oven thermometer, loose-bottomed tart tin (28cm diameter and 3cm deep), baking beans or several handfuls of small change, protective goggles, safety gloves, dry ice, food mixer

Timing
Making the pastry requires care and patience: it will take a few hours, though for much of this time the pastry is simply chilling in the fridge.

Once this is done, the tart should be relatively uncomplicated – the filling involves only a little heating and mixing. And, once you've got the hang of dry ice, the ice cream takes no time at all.

For the vanilla salt
2 plump vanilla pods _ 50g sea salt

For the pastry
400g plain flour _ 1 heaped tsp table salt _ 400g unsalted butter, chilled and diced _ 100g icing sugar _ zest of 1 lemon, finely grated _ seeds from 1 vanilla pod _ 2 large egg yolks (about 40g) _ 2 large eggs (about 120g)

For the treacle tart filling
half an 800g loaf of brown bread _ 200g unsalted butter _ 3 large eggs (about 180g) _ 75ml double cream _ 2 tsp table salt _ 2 x 454g tins of golden syrup* _ zest of 3 lemons _ juice of 2 lemons (or enough to make 60ml)

For the Jersey milk ice cream
500ml Jersey whole milk _ 300ml double cream _ 80g unrefined caster sugar _ 100g glucose syrup _ 1kg dry ice

MAKING THE VANILLA SALT
1. Split the vanilla pods with a knife and scrape out the seeds.
2. Work the seeds into the salt with your fingers and leave to infuse until needed.

PREPARING THE PASTRY
1. Tip the flour and salt into a large bowl. Using your fingertips, rub in the butter until the mixture resembles breadcrumbs.
2. Quickly stir in the icing sugar, lemon zest and vanilla seeds. Add the egg yolks and the whole eggs and mix until combined. Tip on to

---

* Ideally, this should be aged. Preheat the oven to 70–80°C/160–175°F (the latter temperature is the absolute maximum). Make sure the tin is well sealed, then place in the oven for at least 24 hours. (It can be left for up to 100 hours, during which it will continue to improve in depth and complexity. And it will keep for a long time, so it's worth doing several tins at once.)

a sheet of clingfilm, wrap it up and leave to rest in the fridge for at least 3 hours.

3. Meanwhile, preheat the oven to 150°C/300°F/Gas 2. Lightly butter and flour the tart tin and place it on a baking sheet.

4. Dust a piece of greaseproof paper with flour. Take the pastry out of the fridge and remove the clingfilm. Place the pastry on the grease-proof paper. Cut off one-third of the dough and reserve in case needed to patch holes in the pastry base. (If unused, it can be frozen or baked off as biscuits.) Shake over more flour, then top with a second piece of greaseproof paper. Begin to roll the pastry flat, moving the pin from the centre outwards. Keep turning the pastry through 90° every few rolls. Aim for a thickness of 3–5mm and a diameter of 45–50cm. Once the pastry is rolled out to the correct thickness, peel back the top layer of greaseproof paper, trim off any excess, then wind the pastry on to the rolling pin, removing the other layer of paper as you go. Unwind the pastry over the flan tin and gently push it into the base and edges. Chill it for 30 minutes.

5. Once the pastry has firmed up, remove it from the fridge. Prick the base with a fork to stop it puffing up. Take a new piece of grease-proof paper, scrunch it up and smooth it out several times (this makes it easier to put in position), then place it over the pastry base. Put baking beans or – even better – coins on top. Return the lined pastry case to the fridge for at least 30 minutes.

6. Remove the case from the fridge and put in the oven to bake for 25–30 minutes, until the pastry is a light golden brown. You may need to return the case to the oven for 10–15 minutes if, after removing the beans or coins, the base is slightly tacky.

PREPARING THE FILLING AND COOKING THE TART

1. Preheat the oven to 150°C/300°F/Gas 2. Remove the crusts from the brown bread and discard. Tear the bread into pieces and blitz in the food processor to make breadcrumbs. Weigh out 170g and set aside.

2. Make a beurre noisette by putting the butter in a pan over a medium heat. When the butter stops sizzling (a sign that the water has all evaporated, after which it will soon burn) and develops a nutty aroma, remove it from the heat immediately. Strain it into a jug and leave to cool until needed. Discard the blackened solids in the sieve.

3. Put the eggs, cream and salt in a bowl and whisk until combined. Pour the golden syrup into a pan and heat gently until liquid.

4. Pour 115g of beurre noisette into the warmed golden syrup, and stir. (Try to avoid tipping in any sediment that may have collected at the bottom of the jug.)

5. Pour the buttery syrup into the egg and cream mixture. Stir in the breadcrumbs and the lemon zest and juice.

6. Transfer the mixture to a large jug. Pour two-thirds of it into the pastry case. Slide the tart into the oven and pour in the remainder of the filling. Bake for 50–60 minutes, or until the tart is a deep brown colour. Remove from the oven and leave to cool before taking out of the tin.

7. Slice and serve with a few grains of vanilla salt and a dollop of Jersey milk ice cream.

MAKING THE ICE CREAM

1. Put the milk, cream, sugar and glucose syrup in a pan and heat gently until the sugar has dissolved and the glucose is liquid. Set aside.

2. Put on safety gloves and protective goggles and open the packet of dry ice. Wrap it in a tea towel and then a hand towel and smash it into a powder with a rolling pin. (Make sure that there are no large lumps as these will remain as lumps in the ice cream.) Unfold the towels and shake the powdered dry ice into a glass bowl.

3. Pour the milk and glucose mix into the bowl of a food mixer. (From now on you need to work reasonably rapidly to avoid freezing up the equipment.) Shake a little of the dry ice into the mixing bowl and, using the mixer's paddle, mix on the first (lowest) speed until the dry ice dissolves and its vapour clears. Continue to add dry ice a little at a time until the ice cream has absorbed all of it. (It may be easier to do this in two batches. It's important to add the dry ice in small quantities to prevent the ice cream going grainy.) Once the dry ice is absorbed, beat the ice cream on the second speed until smooth.

4. Quickly scrape the ice cream out of the mixer* and into a container. Store in the freezer until required. It is best eaten within 24 hours.

---

* If undissolved chunks of dry ice remain at the bottom of the mixer bowl, leave them to dissolve entirely, then run the bowl under hot water.

Super cold and super smooth – the end result of ice cream made with dry ice.

Baked Alaska

'People love baked Alaska because people are –
when it comes to culinary appreciation –
very often masochistic.'

Nicholas Kurti in 'The Proof of the Pudding', *QED*, 1982

History

It is largely agreed that baked Alaska (or Alaska, Florida, as it was originally known) was created by Charles Ranhofer, the legendary chef of Delmonico's restaurant in New York, to commemorate the American purchase of Alaska from the Russians on 30 March 1867.

But cuisine is in constant evolution. Even the most original dishes don't spring fully formed from a chef's imagination. It is difficult now to track down Ranhofer's antecedents and inspirations, but a Chinese delegation to Paris, the third president of the United States and the scientist who founded the Royal Institution appear to have contributed to the creation of baked Alaska.

Although there is debate over both the date (1866, 1867 and 1886 have all been suggested) and the particular roles of the protagonists (the dessert was prepared either by a French chef cooking for the Chinese, or a Chinese chef demonstrating to the French), one often-quoted landmark in the history of baked Alaska is a dinner at the Grand Hotel attended by a Chinese delegation. The famous food journalist Baron Léon Brisse apparently mentions 'baked ices' being served, though it has been suggested that these were encased in pastry rather than meringue.

The sense of occasion that attaches to this story highlights the dish's role as a party piece at formal gatherings. The hot–cold conjuring trick presented in pastry was already on the menu at the White House some fifty years earlier. A state banquet in the early 1800s featured 'ice cream very good, crust wholly dried, crumbled into thin flakes; a dish somewhat like a pudding'. President Thomas Jefferson served something similar on his Monticello estate. The visitors' book makes mention of ice creams 'produced in the form of balls of the frozen material inclosed in covers of warm pastry, exhibiting a curious contrast, as if the ice had just been taken from the oven'.

Jefferson's energetic engagement with the science of his day has been well documented, and Monticello is full of examples of his inventions: revolving chairs and bookstands, a folding ladder, a new type of dumbwaiter, 'automatic' doors. Inevitably, this scientific curiosity would have brought the President into contact with the ideas of Benjamin Thompson (Count Rumford), a brilliant physicist, whose energy and wide range of interests matched Jefferson's own. He made huge advances in our understanding of the properties of heat, and invented, among other things, a coffee percolator, the kitchen range and a more efficient style of fireplace. In the 1790s Jefferson altered the dimensions of the fireplaces at Monticello in accordance with the principles of efficiency established by Rumford. It is therefore possible that Jefferson's baked ice cream was a version of Rumford's 'Omelette Surprise', a dish said to resemble baked Alaska and created by the Count around 1804, while he was investigating the heat resistance of beaten egg whites.

The Quest for the Best

'You know who I used to be? Max Bialystock! The King of Broadway! Six shows running at once. Lunch at Delmonico's. Two-hundred-dollar suits … '
Max Bialystock in *The Producers*

THE FIRST RESTAURANT IN AMERICA

The restaurant has changed hands more than once, and even closed down a couple of times (first of all in 1923, when Prohibition forced those who liked a drink with dinner back into their own homes). Nonetheless, I wanted to begin my exploration of baked Alaska in the place that made it famous – Delmonico's.

Delmonico's is a huge landmark in American cuisine. Originally opened as a pastry shop in 1827, it was offering an à la carte menu by 1830, making it the first restaurant in America. (Previously, eating out had meant going to inns that offered a set meal at a set price.) It was the first of many firsts. The restaurant is reputed to have invented chicken à la king, lobster Newburg, eggs Benedict, Delmonico potatoes and Delmonico steak. With such a pedigree (and menu) it's not surprising that it had an impressive list of patrons – not only Max Bialystock, but also Mark Twain, Willa Cather, Oscar Wilde, Charles Dickens, Queen Victoria, Edward VII, Abraham Lincoln (who apparently loved those potatoes) and, of course, the mastermind of the Alaska purchase, William H. Seward.

Most of the places in New York that I had visited – Robert's Steakhouse, Bouchon Bakery, Shake Shack, Burger Joint – were situated in the latticework grid of midtown, all straight lines and long vistas, so it was almost disorientating to find myself in downtown's warren of narrow streets. At the busy five-point intersection of Beaver, William and South William, the pavement vibrated to the throb of cement mixers, while men in checked shirts and hard hats desperately waved flags to herd the backed-up traffic. The place was literally a building site. An advertising banner on a crane read: 'André Balazs says swing into William Beaver House – Supercharged Condos.'

Delmonico's stood opposite this, in the narrow triangle formed between Beaver and South William – a piece of Old World elegance amid the New World chaos. A row of red awnings ran down each side of the building, displaying the restaurant's laurel-wreathed D. Doors of polished dark wood, brass and etched glass were flanked by two white marble Corinthian columns, in front of which were four more stone columns curving around in a small colonnade, topped by an elaborate pillared balcony. Two antique black streetlamps stood like sentinels on either side of the doors.

Inside, the opulence continued. The entranceway was paved with flecked reddish-brown marble and lined with heavy wood panelling. It looked more like a country house than a restaurant. Beyond the greeter's lectern, an ornate staircase descended past a parade of 6-litre bottles of cabernet sauvignon – La Jota 1999, Far Niente 2000, Grgich Hills 1993, Dominus 2002. This, however, was not immediately what caught the eye. Above the fireplace, between frondy potted palms and two flared glass bowls containing a tumble of lemons, was a suitably flamboyant portrait of, I was told, the man who set the seal on Delmonico's celebrity, Charles Ranhofer. His chef's whites had a bohemian air: the jacket was cut like a suit, with lapels, and the toque flopped at a rakish angle, like a beret. In his hands Ranhofer held a plate containing something more like a Dutch still-life than a meal – a spill of artfully arranged grapes and citrus fruit, a dangle of peel spiralling over the plate's edge, above which lay a lobster with a crucifix-shaped knife handle protruding from its back. Whodunnit? I nominated the stern-faced chef who stared out of the picture, his formidable, jet-black mutton-chop sideburns hanging over the jacket's lapels.

I went and took my place at a table close by the glass case housing a leather-bound first edition of Ranhofer's mammoth, encyclopedic 1894 cookbook, *The Epicurean*.

Delmonico's head chef, Clinton McCann, explained to me that he was using the book to recreate the original recipe for baked Alaska. 'At a restaurant like Del's we've got to stay within the classical tradition. So to give myself a challenge, I like to go down the historical route.' He hovered near the table, waiting for the dessert to be served, his right hand clasping his left elbow, like a schoolboy awaiting the outcome of a test.

In fact, I was nervous too. I hadn't had baked Alaska since I was a kid, and I didn't know what to expect. I remembered it as a kitschy, show-off dish of the 1970s, and worried that it might now seem out-dated and unappealing.

A waiter in a gold-patterned waistcoat placed before me a white plate with the ubiquitous D stamped on its rim. At its centre sat a sculpted dome of meringue that wouldn't have looked out of place on someone's head at Ascot. It had all the kitsch magnificence I could have hoped for. The piped blobs of meringue were arranged in gradually narrowing tiers and resembled acanthus leaves on a Greek column, an impression reinforced by the sharp relief conferred upon them by the delicate browning that the oven had given the fluted edges. It seemed almost a shame to break into the meringue. I prised apart one side to look at the layers. There was an architectural aspect to it that reminded me of Black Forest gateau: it was carefully constructed to emphasise a series of contrasts. There was, of course, the balance of hot and cold, but there was also the chewiness of the meringue giving way to the softness of a sponge base, and a lovely balance of ice cream sweetness and apricot compote acidity.

'That's delicious, Clinton. Though I can't really remember back that far, I'm pretty sure that the ones I had as a kid weren't anything like this.'

Baked Alaska served in the restaurant where it was invented – Delmonico's.

He nodded earnestly. 'That's nice to hear, but I still feel it needs a little work before it goes on the menu. Less meringue. Maybe add almonds for texture. Come on, I'll show you how it's done.'

In the kitchen he took a thick disc of sponge and trimmed out the centre with a knife to leave a central well into which he spooned the chunky compote. On top of this went a half-ball of banana ice cream. Speed was now crucial if the ice cream wasn't to melt. Grabbing the piping bag, Clinton began squirting blobs of meringue in circles, one on top of the other, each circle a slightly smaller circumference than the last, until the dome was complete. He lifted it on to a small, oval metal dish, which he slid into the oven. 'Top shelf for seven minutes.'

It was amazingly simple – a good example, perhaps, of how the sound use of scientific principles can bring a bit of magic to cuisine. I wanted to preserve that simplicity while at the same time maximising the contrasts of taste and texture in the dish. Clearly, it was going to take a lot of scientific and culinary knowhow to pull that off.

---

* **Frozen Florida**

Cooking up a thermal contrast has continued to tempt scientists into the kitchen. In 1969 Nicholas Kurti gave a talk at the Royal Institution entitled 'The Physicist in the Kitchen' that is now seen as the starting point of the modern-day interest in the molecular properties of food. During the talk, Kurti demonstrated the relatively unfamiliar technology of the microwave oven by taking a hollowed-out block of ice, filling it with water and placing it in the oven. Thirty seconds later, the water boiled while the ice remained intact.

This is possible because microwaves are waves of electromagnetic radiation (as are radio waves and light waves; each type has a character-istic wavelength that gives it its particular properties). Some of the molecules in food (especially the water molecules) behave like electric magnets and line up with the direction of an electric field, much like a compass seeking north. The microwave oven produces an electric field that reverses direction billions of times a second, forcing the water molecules to realign their orientation at the same rate. The flipping and colliding molecules agitate their neighbours, and that energy produces heat: a fast-moving molecule is a hot molecule.

However, microwaves don't melt frozen water very efficiently: the water molecules are trapped in a rigid latticework, so they can't flip back and forth to produce the energy that makes them hot.

Kurti used these principles to create a reversal of baked Alaska – a cold meringue ball with a hot centre. A mix of apricot compote and apricot brandy (which would remain liquid at low temperatures) was poured into a meringue that was then placed in the freezer. When it was removed and put in the oven, the microwaves agitated the water molecules in the liqueur but not the immobile water molecules in the frozen meringue.

The result was named frozen Florida.

LOFTY THOUGHTS

We take all kinds of strange, one-off deliveries at the Fat Duck lab – sea shells, Venezuelan sand, 5,000 foam earplugs – but the courier had just handed over one of the more unusual: it looked like a giant, plastic-wrapped Swiss roll, but turned out to be Space Blanket DIY Loft Insulation. 'Quick, clean and easy – virtually itch-free' boasted the slogan. I opened the packaging, pulled off a piece of what looked like kapok and cut out a thick disc of it, which I placed next to seven others on the lab's work surface.

Baked Alaska is all about insulation – about protecting the ice cream from the oven's heat sufficiently that it remains an icy contrast to the warmed, browned meringue exterior. I wanted to find the spongy base that would best ensure that effect.* Six of the discs, then, were different types of cake-like base: chiffon, sponge, genoise,

---

* Sponge and meringue are both examples of foams: suspensions of gas bubbles in a liquid (the term still applies after the liquid has solidified). Other examples are marshmallows, soufflés, mousses, bread and the froth on a cappuccino. All of these are efficient insulators because the air bubbles they contain are poor conductors of heat due to the distance between the molecules (heat makes molecules vibrate more rapidly and they pass on some of this energy to other molecules as they collide; the further apart these molecules are, the lower the frequency of collision and thus the slower the rate of heat transfer). That's why a cappuccino cools more slowly than an ordinary coffee: the frothy head seals in the heat. It's also why the polystyrene cup the coffee comes in isn't too hot to handle: that too is a foam.

enriched sponge, supermoist and pound cake. In a short while I would be putting ice cream on top of these and seeing how soon it melted, but first I wanted to try the experiment with some proper loft insulation, as a kind of control. I had two hotplates on which gently simmered two foil-lidded beakers of water. On top of one I placed a disc of space blanket (which looked like a fluffy vol-au-vent) and on the other a disc of extruded polystyrene (which looked disturbingly like the other sponges). On top of each of these I perched a disc of ice cream and then told Kyle to start the stopwatch.

We stood there – Chris, Kyle and I – each of us hunched over like Rodin's *Thinker*, watching a faint glisten develop on the ice cream (or was that just a play of the light?).

'That's starting to go. It's softening at the edge,' Chris eventually declared.

It was about time. Kyle had just called out 3.55. I got a digital probe with the most needle-like attachment I could find, and spiked it into each of the insulation materials in turn. Both hovered around the 40°C mark.

'Six minutes forty-five.'

Ice cream was running off the edges of the space blanket and pooling on the foil. It had collapsed throughout. The extruded polystyrene seemed to be doing a better job. I probed the ice cream. It had a temperature of minus 6.5°C.

We re-prepped the experiment and decided to compare light with heavy – chiffon versus pound cake. This time I checked the ice cream temperature before we started – minus 16.5°C – and decided to check again after 6.45 minutes. We settled into RodinMode, discussed the wishlist for baked Alaska, and watched the occasional bubble break loose and rise to the surface of the beaker.

'Whatever base we choose'll need a lot of air,' said Chris.

'Yes,' I agreed. 'Air will absorb heat quickly.'

'But it's not a good conductor of heat.'

'Well, do we want the base to be warm and crisp or soft and melting? Do we want it to be frozen?'

'Yeah,' Kyle said. 'We probably need to check how our ingredients respond to freezing.'

'And remember,' I cautioned, 'we're looking for an insulator but we mustn't lose sight of the flavour. We've got to choose on that basis. It has got to eat well. If we disregard insulation, I'd probably go for something like a madeleine with its lovely, chewy crust— '

'Five fifty,' broke in Kyle. 'The excitement's killing me.'

'Maybe we'll cut in shots of tumbleweed,' said the director.

The cakes looked as though they were doing better than the loft insulation. The ice cream had acquired a sticky surface – a film of melt – but remained intact on top of both discs.

'Six forty-five.'

The probe went into the ice cream: minus 8.4°C for the chiffon and minus 8°C for the pound cake. A full couple of degrees better than loft insulation. Maybe we should be marketing our sponge cake to the building trade. Especially since the supermoist and genoise performed similarly well at minus 8.5°C and minus 7.8°C respectively. They were all efficient insulators, so that didn't need to be the determining factor in our choice. It could be down to flavour and texture alone.

HALF-BAKED ALASKA

I have a lot to thank Nicholas Kurti for. His talk on 'The Physicist in the Kitchen' gave a much-needed legitimacy to the idea of scientific culinary exploration (although in the early days of the Fat Duck, I had great difficulty persuading people that science has a crucial role in cuisine, and even now there are many who find the proposition unacceptable). It was by looking up the lists of those who had attended his workshops on 'Molecular and Physical Gastronomy' (I had originally tried to contact Nicholas himself, only to find he had died a few months earlier) that I eventually established a loose network of scientists in the Kurti mould with whom I could investigate food's potential.

It seemed appropriate to try to combine baked Alaska with his reversal of it, the frozen Florida. (It could be called 'Alaska, Florida', which would make it doubly appropriate by paying homage to Charles Ranhofer's original creation.) The reasons for doing this were as much gastronomic as historic: baked Alaska is all about contrasts, and this could provide a far greater range.

The central structure would remain the same: a sponge base and warm, chewy meringue with still-cold banana ice cream inside it. But within that there would be hidden bursts of heat and flavour and texture – something crispy, something oozing, something fruity.

The trick was to find ingredients that would respond well to microwaves. Essentially, they had to contain polar molecules: those in which the uneven distribution of electrons meant that the molecules had a slight positive charge at one end and a slight negative charge at the other. The changes would act as the 'handles' with which the microwaves performed their billions-of-times-a-second flip action. Water is a good example of a polar molecule. Were there others I could employ that would bring something to the dessert? I consulted scientists at the Campden & Chorleywood Food Research Association, who suggested I try alcohol, sugar and salt.

It's always very exciting when a dish starts to find its particular direction. I drew a crude visual plan of an ice-cream core in which were embedded tubes that held surprise ingredients – sugary raspberry sorbet and alcohol-laced fruit compote; salted butter caramel. Some of the tubes could be made from brick pastry (similar to filo, but finer and more crêpe-like), which would act as insulation, preventing the microwave-warmed caramel and compote from melting the ice cream. The sorbet could be enclosed in white chocolate, bringing yet another flavour dimension and a nice crunchy brittleness. Chris and I began work on bringing the drawing to life.

'These are a royal pain to do,' Chris declared later, brandishing a set of tubes.

It was just one of several problems that I had to solve if this was going to be accessible to the home cook. The current ice-cream recipe was also still a work in progress (we had just ditched a roast-banana-and-muscovado version – far too strong a liquorice note – in favour of something with a more green banana character), but it would do for testing. I sank the tubes in the ice cream and placed it all in a mould that I had fashioned from a sawn-off length of plastic guttering that had the kind of curve I wanted. Once the ice cream was frozen, Chris set it on a sponge base, pasted it thickly with meringue, then combed ridges on it with an artist's graining comb. I fired up the blowtorch and wafted it across the surface, the ridges rapidly browning and giving the dish its bas-relief. It looked great. Chris carried it over to the microwave, laid it gently inside and set the timer for thirty seconds.

It wasn't long enough: the insides hadn't melted. It went back in for another thirty.

This time it looked like one of Dali's floppy watches. A surreal joke – mainly on me. The top had slumped and slewed to one side because the ice cream, rather than the ingredients in the tubes, had melted. It was hugely disappointing, not least because I could tell, even in this collapsed form, that the components of the dish worked together. I was stuck not with a taste problem, but with a technical one. I hated admitting defeat, and I wasn't throwing in the (tea) towel just yet, but if I couldn't find a way to overcome it, I'd have to scale back my ideas for the dessert.

Baked Alaska Serves 6

Although I chose to move away from the Florida-in-Alaska concept, many of the ingredients and structural elements, such as the raspberry sorbet and chocolate tube, remained through various evolutions of this recipe. I introduced bitter orange marmalade to offset the confirmed sweetness of the other ingredients. Instead of the ice cream, I eventually settled on roasted banana parfait (ordinary bananas, even when fully ripe, had a starchiness that made it too grainy). Roasting got rid of that starchiness and introduced a lovely caramelised flavour. And I got the vivid emphasis on contrast I was looking for by a dramatic combination of fire and ice – a cascade of flambéd alcohol succeeded by billowing gusts of dry ice.

Special equipment
Food mixer, 1 acetate sheet, about 3kg dry ice, food processor, piping bag, sturdy plastic or cardboard, digital probe, blowtorch

Timing
Preparation takes about 4 hours, plus 6 hours for the parfait to harden. Cooking takes 1 hour.

For the cake (makes 2)
Only one cake is needed for the recipe; the second can be frozen for later use.

My cake calls for chlorinated flour (American cake flour) because the chlorination process changes the starch within the flour and makes it possible to incorporate more sugar than flour into the recipe, giving what is known as a 'high ratio' cake. Without chlorinated flour, a cake recipe that incorporates more sugar than flour will collapse during baking. Unfortunately, chlorinated flour is difficult to come by because it is no longer made within Europe. I've suggested a US alternative, but if you can't get it, use ordinary plain flour and reduce the sugar in the recipe to about 80 per cent of the weight of the flour. Note that the sugar isn't just for sweetness: it helps to lighten the cake and create a more delicate crumb.

A NOTE ABOUT EGG WHITES: As eggs age, the pH of the white increases, making it more alkaline. The more alkaline the egg white, the more readily the proteins in the white foam, and the lighter the meringue becomes. So, if possible, use eggs that are about two weeks old. If this isn't possible, it's best to add a pinch of tartaric acid to the whites. Surprisingly, slightly acidic egg whites also foam better than fresh egg whites. Although it might seem that more is better, don't add tartaric acid to an old egg white: they will cancel each other out and you'll be no better off than you were with a fresh egg. And if you have a copper bowl, by all means use it because it does help to create a lighter meringue, but don't bother adding tartaric acid because it binds to the copper and prevents the metal from stabilising the meringue.

60g unsalted butter _ 30g Trex (available at supermarkets, Trex is a vegetable fat used for pastry and bread) _ 45g vegetable oil _ 3 eggs, separated _ 170g chlorinated flour, such as Softasilk (available through the Overseas Buyers Club at obcusa.co.uk) _ 200g caster sugar _ 2g salt _ 5g (½ tsp) baking powder _ 100g whole milk

For the chocolate tube
100g white chocolate

For the raspberry sorbet
750g frozen organic raspberries _ 85g fructose (such as Tate & Lyle, available at supermarkets) _ 10g vodka _ crushed dry ice _ reserved chocolate tube

For the raspberry coulis
180g reserved raspberry purée _ 30g fructose

For the banana and praline parfait
115g skinless hazelnuts _ 375g caster sugar _ 500g very ripe bananas with brown skin _ 20g butter _ 30g unrefined caster sugar _ 50g rum _ 375g double cream _ 6 egg whites

To prepare the centre of the cake
reserved banana parfait _ reserved chocolate tube

For the Swiss meringue
This should be prepared just before serving the cake.
180g egg whites (about 6 eggs) _ 280g caster sugar

To finish the cake
200g reserved raspberry coulis _ 1 reserved cake _ 50g butter _
1 jar of Seville orange marmalade _ reserved frozen core _ reserved
Swiss meringue _ 300g rum

MAKING THE CAKE
1. In a pan on medium heat, brown the butter until a very nutty aroma develops, then strain it to remove the solids. Allow to cool.
2. Place the Trex in a pan with the oil and cooled browned butter and warm until just melted.
3. Put the egg yolks in the bowl of a food mixer and slowly whisk in the warm fats until a mayonnaise-like emulsion forms. Refrigerate this until very cold.
4. In the meantime, sift together the flour, 100g of the sugar, the salt and the baking powder.
5. Swap the whisk for the paddle attachment and add the sifted ingredients to the cold egg yolk mixture. Beat on a slow speed for 15 seconds, or until the dry ingredients are incorporated.
6. Add the milk and mix on a slow speed for another 30 seconds, until the milk has combined with the batter, then beat on a high speed for 4 minutes.
7. Transfer the batter to another bowl and set aside. Wash the mixer bowl with soap and hot water to remove any traces of fat.
8. Put the egg whites in the mixer bowl. Whisk on a high speed for 1 minute before adding 100g of sugar. Reduce the speed to low/medium for 5–10 minutes. The mixture should be creamy with soft peaks.
9. Preheat the oven to 170°C/325°F/Gas 3.
10. Using a large spatula, gently fold one-third of the meringue into the reserved batter. After this has been incorporated, add the remainder of the meringue and gently fold it into the loosened

batter. There should be no streaks of white meringue left, but be careful not to overdo this or the cake won't be soft and light.

11. Pour 400g of this batter into each of two buttered and floured 20 x 5cm loaf tins. Don't worry about levelling the surface – this will happen naturally during baking. Place in the preheated oven and bake for 20–25 minutes.

12. Remove the cakes from the oven and bang them down on the work surface before turning them on to a wire rack to cool.

13. If being used right away, keep the cakes at room temperature. If not, cool completely, then wrap in several layers of clingfilm and freeze until needed.

MAKING THE CHOCOLATE TUBE

1. Cut an acetate sheet into a strip 15cm wide and roll it into a tube with a diameter of 2cm. Use tape to keep the tube from unrolling.

2. Place the chocolate in a pan over a bain-marie and heat gently until it's just melted and can be poured.

3. Wrap one end of the tube with clingfilm, then pour the chocolate into the other end until it's filled (a funnel will make this easier). Twist the tube to make sure the chocolate covers all of it. Hold the filled tube for about 2 minutes, then invert it to drain out the excess chocolate. Place the coated tube in the freezer to harden the chocolate.

MAKING THE RASPBERRY SORBET

1. Thaw the raspberries, then purée them in a food processor or blender. Pass the purée through a coarse sieve to remove the seeds.

2. Weigh out 625g of the purée and add to a bowl containing the fructose and vodka. Stir until the fructose has dissolved. At this point the sorbet base can be refrigerated until needed. Reserve the extra purée for the raspberry coulis.

3. To prepare the frozen sorbet, pour the raspberry base into the bowl of a food mixer and, using the paddle attachment, begin mixing it at a slow speed. Crush the dry ice by wrapping in a tea towel and beating with a rolling pin. (Watch your fingers.) Slowly add spoonfuls of crushed dry ice. Continue mixing and adding dry ice a little at a time until the sorbet has frozen.

The delicate business of preparing tubes of chocolate-coated raspberry sorbet.

4. Scrape the sorbet into a piping bag and place in the freezer for about 20 minutes to harden slightly.
5. Use the piping bag to inject the sorbet into the chocolate tube. Return it to the freezer to harden. Any extra sorbet can be kept in the freezer in a sealed container.

MAKING THE RASPBERRY COULIS
1. Put the raspberry purée in a bowl, add the fructose and stir to dissolve. Set aside until serving the finished dish.

MAKING THE BANANA AND PRALINE PARFAIT
1. Preheat the oven to 150°C/300°F/Gas 2. Place the hazelnuts in a roasting tray large enough to hold them in a single layer. Roast the hazelnuts until lightly golden brown and very fragrant.
2. Tip the roasted hazelnuts into a frying pan on a medium heat and add 115g of the sugar to the hot pan. Keep tossing the hazelnuts until the sugar becomes caramelised and coats them. Tip the caramelised nuts out on to greaseproof paper and let cool. Once they've cooled, smash or grind them into coarse pieces.
3. Peel the bananas and cut them into slices 1cm thick.
4. Melt the butter in a pan, and when the foam has died down and the butter smells nutty, add the unrefined sugar. Stir with a spatula until a caramel forms.
5. Add the sliced bananas and sauté in the caramel.
6. When the bananas are coated and golden, add the rum. As vapours start to rise from the pan, use a match to light the alcohol, and continue to cook until the flame dies out and the caramel becomes thick enough to coat the bananas again.
7. Pass the caramelised banana mixture through a sieve and set aside.
8. Lightly whip the cream until it becomes thick, like yoghurt. Refrigerate until needed.
9. Using a stand mixer, whisk the egg whites on high speed until frothy, then add about one-quarter of the remaining caster sugar. Reduce the mixer to medium speed and continue whisking while slowly adding the remainder of the sugar. Whisk the egg whites for another 5–10 minutes until soft peaks form.

10. Add the hazelnut praline to the reserved banana purée, then fold in one-third of the meringue in order to loosen the mixture. Fold in the remainder of the meringue, but be careful to not overdo the mixing.
11. Finally, gently fold the whipped cream into the mixture.

PREPARING THE CENTRE OF THE CAKE

1. Begin by preparing a mould for the parfait. Cut two pieces of sturdy plastic or cardboard measuring 3 x 15cm. Cut two more pieces measuring 3 x 6cm. Use tape to join these pieces and form a rectangular mould.
2. Set the mould on a tray covered with a sheet of baking parchment. Fill the mould one-third full with cold banana parfait.
3. Take the chocolate-coated raspberry sorbet tube from the freezer. Remove the acetate from the tube and press it into the parfait in the mould.
4. Use a palette knife to fill in the rest of the mould with banana parfait, then scrape the surface smooth. Return this to the freezer for at least 6 hours to harden.

MAKING THE SWISS MERINGUE

1. Place the egg whites in a mixing bowl and set it over a pan filled with simmering water.
2. Whisk the whites over the water until they reach 55°C/130°F. Use a digital probe to check the temperature.
3. Remove the bowl from the pan and slowly whisk in the sugar until soft peaks form. It's helpful to do this with a food mixer.

FINISHING THE CAKE

1. Gently heat the raspberry coulis, then pour it into a jug and keep warm for serving.
2. Cut the cake into a rectangle measuring 15 x 6cm and 3cm thick.
3. Brown the butter in a sauté pan, then fry the cake on both sides. When the surfaces are brown, transfer the cake to a baking sheet and allow to cool for at least 10 minutes.
4. Spread a very generous layer of marmalade evenly over the top surface of the cooled cake.

5. Remove the frozen core from the freezer and unmould it. Place on top of the marmalade-coated cake and transfer to a small rectangular serving platter.
6. Preheat the oven to 180°C/350°F/Gas 4.
7. Using a palette knife, generously spread meringue over the entire surface of the cake and parfait, giving it a rippled effect. If you wish, you can use a piping bag to create peaks on the top surface.
8. Gently brown the surface of the meringue with a blowtorch, taking care not to have the flame too close.
9. Put the entire cake on its serving platter into the oven for about 2 minutes to warm the meringue.
10. Cover a large platter with dry ice and place the warmed platter of baked Alaska on top.
11. Just before serving, fill a jug with hot water and bring the rum to a simmer in a small pan. Pour the hot water on to the dry ice to create billows of vapour around the baked Alaska. When the rum is at a simmer, ignite the alcohol and carefully pour it around the edge of the smaller platter holding the baked Alaska.
12. When the flames die out, slice the cake into 6 pieces and serve with the warm raspberry coulis.

Trifle

'Trifles make perfection, and perfection is no trifle.'

Michelangelo

Historical Quest for the Best

A thin liquid flecked with froth slopped around the glazed earthenware bowl. It was supposed to be a syllabub, but it looked more like baby sick. Ivan agreed. 'In Yorkshire, that's called posset. Acid in the cider has curdled the milk. Very unappetising, especially with cow hairs and specks of bovine dandruff in it. An acceptable refreshment for a rude ploughboy, perhaps, though only after it had been put through a filter called a "sile". Which may be where the name "syllabub" comes from – a contraction of sile and "bubbles". Anyway, this proves I was right. It's virtually impossible to make a decent syllabub by milking the cow straight into a bowl of cider, even though several old cookbooks suggest it.'

We were in the milking shed of Low Sizergh, a beautiful organic farm in the Lake District. It might seem odd to labour at an experiment that you know will go wrong but, for a food historian like Ivan Day, the hands-on approach is often the only way to gain a true understanding of the cooking of the past. Removing an ancient recipe from the realm of abstraction and physically exploring how it was done offers important insights into both cuisine and the society that shaped that cuisine. Along with the historians at Hampton Court, Ivan had proved invaluable to me in the development of several dishes on the menu of the Fat Duck and the Hind's Head. Now I had come to Cumbria to explore the historical background of trifle with him in the hope that it would give me clues to the route I should take with the dish. Syllabub was at one time a key part of the trifle, and Ivan had brought me to Low Sizergh to show me what the original syllabub might have looked like.

'Of course, you could avoid curdling by adding cream to wine in advance,' he offered. 'There's a manuscript from about 1677 that tells you to do this and then "jumble it a pritie while" before milking directly on to it ... '

'Hmm. I think people might object to a recipe that begins: "1 cow, ready to milk".'

'In that case, let's drive over to my house. I've set up a shrine to trifle for you.'

Wondering what exactly was in store for me, I followed Ivan's car through winding hills and clusters of stone cottages, then inched up the narrow track that led to his seventeenth-century farmhouse. Rain fell in sudden bursts, giving the landscape the look of a washed-out watercolour. As the clouds massed and darkened, threatening another downpour, I parked and hurried towards the front door.

The rain made the fire blazing in the old-fashioned grate particularly welcome, though I knew it had been lit not for comfort, but for the cooking that was about to take place. The shrine turned out to be a long, sturdy oak table covered in a white cloth, on top of which was a fantastic display of all manner of material. The centrepiece was a highly decorated plate upon which lay what looked like a giant disc of shortbread stamped with the image of a whippet-thin stag bearing magnificent antlers. To its left was an elaborately engraved glass holding a syrupy yellow liquid, along with a plateful of macaroons, as though ready for the arrival of a maiden aunt. There were two bound books (slightly foxed) and a manuscript, which was open at the entry 'To make a triffell', written in spiky script. This was Robert May's *The Accomplisht Cook*. I'd got a facsimile copy of this, which I had consulted during the development of dishes such as quaking pudding. It was one of my favourite historical cookbooks, and it was slightly awing to have the original in front of me. Behind this were more plates and bowls containing all kinds of things that were unidentifiable but looked very tasty. At one end of the table was a syllabub pot, identifiable by the two handles and up-reared spout that gave it an elephantine look. I couldn't resist lifting the lid and peeking inside: it held a thickish custard, the surface puckered by traces of tiny air bubbles.

'So what do we have here?' I called after Ivan, who had shuffled off into the kitchen.

'The history of trifle in a series of books and dishes,' came back a disembodied voice. 'It makes much more sense if you can actually see and taste what I'm talking about. Originally, trifle looked something like this.' He reappeared holding a plate with a pool of cream-coloured liquid. A saucer for a Restoration cat, perhaps.

'May's recipe from 1660,' Ivan announced, 'served on a silver plate as he suggests. It's basically a junket – cream set with rennet and flavoured with rosewater and ginger. It's very, very simple.'

'Mmm, I like the floral note from the rosewater. It's really nice, but it's astonishingly different from what we now think of as trifle. How did it manage such a transformation?'

'The next stage was to add little pieces of bread.' He gestured at a lumpier cream on a blue and white china plate with an upturned rim. Each evolution of trifle appeared to require different tableware as its composition shifted. 'They used leftover bread for lots of dishes. Bread and butter pudding's a good example.'

I dug a spoon into the mixture. 'It makes it more texturally interesting, more substantial.'

'This would have been served at the end of a meal. As would much of this stuff.' He waved a hand vaguely over the table. 'In the medieval period it was believed that sweet foodstuffs at the end of a meal aided digestion. By the late 1600s this had developed into a spectacular "aftercourse" that included creams and junkets and syllabubs. Biscuits would be served as a counterpoint to all the richness.'

'Like these?' I asked, pointing at the plate piled with macaroons.

'Yes. Those are ratafia and Naples biscuits. They would be dunked in sweet wine, then eaten, just as Italians still do with vin santo and amaretti. Try them.' He proffered a glass.

'Yes, that's lovely. The biscuits have a hint of orangeflower that complements the wine.'

'And there's more. There would be marchpane – marzipan – made from grinding almonds to a paste and adding powdered sugar to form a soft, pliable material that could be moulded into spectacular centre-pieces like that stag over there. And comfits – seeds or nuts or spices enclosed in sugar. And redcurrant jelly that would be put on biscuits.' The words came tumbling out of Ivan as his enthusiasm to share his discoveries took hold. 'And a form of custard like the one I've prepared here, which is flavoured with – can you guess?'

Suddenly it felt as though I were taking part in an obscure, late-night BBC2 quiz show. I was determined to get the answer right. There was the faint trace of something at the finish – fleeting, mercurial, elusive … 'Cinnamon! But very subtle.'

'Spot on.'

'So here we've got custard, jelly, sweet wine, syllabub, crunchy biscuits and comfits. Pretty much all of the ingredients that go into a trifle.'

'Exactly, Heston. Sometime before 1751 some wag decided it would be a great idea to put them all together in one bowl.'

I laughed. Ivan's encyclopedic knowledge and photographic memory often unnerved me. 'How can you be so accurate?'

'Because I've got the fifth edition of Hannah Glasse's *The Art of Cookery Made Plain and Easy*, which includes a recipe for a layered trifle that brings together all the elements in one dish. I used the book this morning to make the base.' He indicated a large bowl in which sat a layer of pale yellow custard. 'That's a 1740s Delftware punchbowl, exactly what they would have served trifle in. Now all it needs is the finishing touch – a syllabub, which by this period was very different from the unattractive liquid we made earlier. It had become trifle's crowning glory.'

He disappeared into the kitchen once more and returned with another large bowl, a wooden drum sieve and what looked like a carved wooden ceremonial mace. 'In here I've got equal parts wine and single cream, mixed with lemon juice and spices. We need to put air bubbles into it.'

I stuck the mace head into the liquid and rubbed it back and forth between my palms. Bubbles began to speckle the surface, but it was hard, slow, dispiriting work, so I was grateful when Ivan informed me that someone had invented the Syllabub Pumping Engine – a set of bellows with a perforated metal cube attached to the nozzle. A few pumps and the bubbles increased in number and size, rising steadily closer to the rim of the bowl with each huff of air.

'I've seen modern chefs at demos using pumps to get a better foam. There's nothing new under the sun, is there?'

'The more you read, the more you realise that advances in cookery aren't revolutions, they're evolutions,' Ivan said. 'Now you lift the bubbles on to a sile and let them drain overnight.' He began gently spooning bubbles on to the wooden sieve.

'But you're going to say "Here's one I made earlier".'

'Exactly. I have one that has been draining for twelve hours.'

Food historian Ivan Day shows me the effects of the Syllabub Pumping Engine.

I could see how creamy it had become. The texture was now firm and fluffy. 'It reminds me of ricotta or mascarpone.'

'People would already have eaten a big, heavy set of meat courses, so they wanted their cream to be very light,' Ivan explained as he scooped it on top of the custard in its punchbowl.

'How strange that what began as a light dish ended up being added to more cream.'

'Yes. Fascinating, isn't it?' He put a final dab of syllabub in place, then straightened up and stepped back. 'There you have it – an authentic eighteenth-century trifle … '

It was a truly wonderful creation. I was eager to try that range of textures on my tongue. My mouth watered just looking at it. I reached for a spoon.

' … of course, Hannah Glasse recommends you strew different-coloured nonpareils over it. Care to make some comfits?'

My hand went back to my side. 'Sure.'

By the fire was a three-legged stool above which swung a wide, low-sided copper pan suspended on chains that hung from the ceiling. Ivan dragged a brazier of glowing charcoal underneath the balancing-pan and signalled that I should sit at the stool. 'The little, pale grey flecks in the pan are caraway seeds coated first in gum arabic to seal in the natural oils, and then in sugar syrup. They've had twenty coats already, but they need more. Spread them around the pan with your fingers to get them warm, then I'll add some syrup.'

The granules clumped to my fingers once the ladleful of syrup was poured in. I kept rubbing them off my hands and moving them around the pan until the heat evaporated the water in the syrup and the sugar crystallised on the surface of the seeds, making them a loose powder again. Ivan added a second ladleful. 'You can increase the amount as time goes on,' he encouraged.

It was nonetheless an incredibly time-consuming procedure. The comfits would need fifty coats in all, with drying periods after every ten coats. Labour-intensive and painstaking in its attention to detail, the process reminded me of several techniques used at the Fat Duck. (There really is nothing new under the sun.) I had no doubt that the end result would benefit from the care that went into its preparation.

It was great to get stuck in, to sit as someone would have sat 300 years earlier, with the same aching back perhaps, cooking by touch and feel. This kind of historical exploration always gives me a thrilling sense of connection to other cooks across the centuries, and a renewed awareness of the debt cuisine owes to the past. These comfits, for example, might have gone out of fashion – the word is no longer common parlance, and little children no longer carry a box of them in their pocket, as Lewis Carroll's Alice did – yet they were obviously the ancestor of the hundreds and thousands that now decorate super-market trifles.

'I hope you've got some comfits you made earlier as well. I want to try that trifle exactly as it would have been in 1751.'

Ivan smiled and produced a plate with not only a pile of sugared caraway seeds, but also knobbly white cardamoms and red, torpedo-shaped fennel seeds, the colours the result of natural colourings added to the last few coatings. 'Here, I think you've earned the right to strew the nonpareils. Make sure you do it in the eighteenth-century style – elegantly.'

I scattered over the comfits and crumbled ratafia biscuits. 'I think I've done it in more of an abstract style … '

'More like Tracey Emin's *Unmade Bed*, I'd say. But let's eat it anyway.'

I dug a spoon right down to the bottom, keen to get an idea of the hidden layers, popped it in my mouth and chewed. Ivan did the same. I could see him watching me intently, trying to gauge my response.

'How many would this serve?' I said, keeping him on tenterhooks.

'About twenty-four people. Why?'

'Because you might need to make some more. It's absolutely deli-cious. Trifle's usually thought of as something cheap and nasty. A bowl of gloop. But this has a range of distinct flavours and textures – a real complexity. There's a great sense of contrasts in the experience of eating it. It's rich and creamy but it also has a real lightness. I can see the value of soaking the biscuits in sherry. And then there's the wonderful crunch of the comfits on top.'

'Yes. That's the bit I really like,' said Ivan, as if it were a guilty pleasure.

'That caraway freshness is extraordinary. And I think it's given me a great idea involving a molecule called carvone that comes in two mirror-image forms, like Tweedledum and Tweedledee.'

'Well,' said Ivan, looking at the table crowded with books, bellows, wine glasses, biscuit shards, sieves, jelly, flagons of sack and half-eaten syllabubs, junkets, creams and custards, 'it has been a bit of a Mad Hatter's tea-party.'

ORAL HIJINKS

The Centre for Food Sciences at Wageningen University in the Netherlands provided a sharp contrast to Ivan Day's Cumbrian cottage (though, as it turned out, it was no less of a mad tea-party). Instead of being in a traditional kitchen, I was standing in the Restaurant van de toekomst (Restaurant of the Future), and Jon Prinz was explaining how this half-built university canteen-cum-research lab would eventually have banks of video cameras recessed in the ceiling to monitor people's eating habits, and weighing scales set into the floor.

I had come to expect this kind of thing when visiting Jon, an oral physiologist who investigates the way we deal with food once it is in our mouths. He is brilliant and barking mad in equal measure. In the past he has made me chew gum while listening to a crunching noise on headphones, and fed me food containing what he called 'particles', but which you or I would call sand. Jon's inventive, devious mind also makes him something of a wind-up merchant. The black T-shirt he was wearing, with its white outline of a gorilla, turned out to be an example of this. Shocked colleagues suggested it was a deliberate reference to Bokito, the gorilla who had escaped from Rotterdam Zoo a month earlier and run amok, injuring several people and terrorising those who had barricaded themselves into the zoo's restaurant.

'Come on, Heston. Let's talk custard,' said Jon, ambling towards the stairs. 'I've got something interesting to show you.'

He led me to the department's brand-new experimental tasting room. Seven people were seated around an octagonal table. In front of each was a laptop on which to record reactions, and a black globe on a tall, thin stand – a motion-sensitive camera to assess facial activity.

'It's impressively state of the art, Jon.'

'But that's not the best bit. Watch this.' He pressed a button. There was a motorised whine and out of the table rose metal partitions, segmenting the table into eight sections and effectively screening each volunteer from the next. 'It prevents the subjects from inadvertently influencing each other's responses. Today they'll be tasting five different custards to see which is the creamiest. There's a chair spare … if you're interested?'

Apprehensive, I took my place at the table. The last time I had worked with Jon he had suddenly pounced on me and wedged an expandable clamp in my mouth. Fortunately, this time he appeared carrying a tray with eight spoons of custard on it, and lifted one towards my mouth.

'Here comes the train into the tunnel. Open wide, Heston.'

I remembered that Jon had once been a dentist. An image of Laurence Olivier in *Marathon Man* threatening Dustin Hoffman with a dental pick and asking 'Is it safe?' came to my mind unbidden. I pushed it to one side and swallowed.

Custard. With no tricks. Thin and medium creamy with a perceptible vanilla flavour.

Jon fed all eight of us, then returned with a second set of spoonfuls. This time the mixture had an impression of thickness, certainly. It was colder, but was it creamier? Hard to tell, and I'd get no help from my fellow guinea pigs: the partitions proved extremely efficient, allowing only disembodied sounds, the clank of metal on teeth.

Spoonful three was where the kind of strangeness I had been expecting crept in. It had a perfumed aroma that reminded me of some baby product or other, perhaps even nappies. It was unpleasantly claggy in the mouth. The spoons had been carried in on a tray flecked with foam. What had Jon been serving up? It seemed creamy at first, but this gave way to a gummy, sticky aftertaste.

The fourth spoonful was equally puzzling: clean, creamy, at first enjoyable, but then becoming more eggy, with a starchy endnote. It left me with a weird sensation under the tongue at the back of the mouth. I wanted to try all four again, now I had some basis for comparison.

The fifth and final spoonful had a gritty crunch. Sand. He had done it to me again!

'OK,' said Jon. 'Thanks for doing that, everybody. Let's have a show of hands for who found number one the creamiest.' He needed to go no further: eight hands were raised. 'Numbers one and two were exactly the same,' he explained, 'except that the first was warmed. Number three was sprayed with starch, number four with oil. And as for number five … ' Did his bushy moustache conceal a grin? 'We added very fine, edible polystyrene spheres to it.'

The other guinea pigs filed out, looking slightly shell-shocked. I hung back to get an explanation of the results. Jon settled into the taster's chair next to mine and began playing with the gas-operated height adjuster. Hisssss. Suddenly he was a foot higher than me.

'So, Jon, the warm one was perceived as the creamiest. Why is that?'

'You know how on a cold day metal feels cold but wood feels warm?' Hisssss. Now I was looking at the top of his head. 'That's to do with thermal conductivity. Heat doesn't travel through wood particularly effectively. And, like wood, fat has low thermal conductivity. It too tends to remain warm, so the brain has come to link fat and warmth.* Warming custard fools the brain into thinking there's more fattiness, and hence creaminess, in it. And, oddly enough, that seems to work better than spraying the surface with oil.' Hisssss. I was face-to-face with the outline of a gorilla.

'What was the reason for the starch with its strange aroma?'

'Sometimes custard's too smooth, too slimy. Starch roughs up the surface, moving the perception of it from slimy to creamy.'

'And the crunchy custard?'

Hisssss. He was level with my eyes. 'You know, it only takes a grain of sand to turn a dessert into a desert.'

---

* Fat is an essential energy store for animals, and scientists are keen to find out how far detection of it might be hardwired into us. Recent studies have furthered the idea that, as with salty, sweet, bitter, sour and umami, fat is a taste that is chemically detected by receptors in the taste buds, though this is hotly disputed.
   Jon suggests that it is possible that the lips' acute sensitivity to heat is similarly geared to fat detection. Our ape-like ancestors didn't have access to cookers, and ate everything at ambient temperature. Therefore the lips weren't needed as an early warning system for hot food. Perhaps, then, their primary purpose was to distinguish warm-feeling, fat-rich foods, such as avocado, from cold foods that are low in fat, such as apple.

CUSTARD'S LAST STAND

Jon's high-tech tasting table had lent his creaminess experiment the atmosphere of a gameshow. To finish off, he gave three quickfire demonstrations of how food reacts in the mouth that were more like warped magic tricks – with me as the unwitting volunteer from the audience. On the table in front of me were a cup of water, a cup of custard and a tampon. 'Take a spoonful of custard, Heston,' Jon encouraged, 'and swallow until you think it's all gone.'

I did as I was bidden.

'Now drink the water, then spit it back into the cup.' It was cloudy, opaque. A second cup of water produced similar results. 'This shows that food doesn't simply disappear down the throat as you eat. The first bite produces a coating in the mouth that can remain for up to ninety minutes.'

'That must reduce our perception of flavour.'

'Yes, and it also means that the first bite gives the most lasting impression.'

This has significant implications for cooking and eating. The only part of the meal that is tasted 'cleanly' is the first bite. Moreover, flavours that are slow to release are likely to be overshadowed by that first impression. 'What can I do to break down that coating quickly?'

'Something with starch in will do it.'

Desserts such as gateau St Honoré use a whipped cream with starch called chiboust. Even as I began thinking about it, I could see chiboust as part of my trifle – it has plenty of creaminess but it is also delight-fully light, allowing other flavours to come through.

'Swallow another spoonful of custard.' Jon broke in on my thoughts. He was on to his next trick. 'Now stick out your tongue.' He beckoned the camera in close. 'You can see that, although the custard is gone from the front of the tongue … ' (The director and researcher nodded solemnly as they viewed the monitor. I had become a lab rat.) ' … it is still there at the back. The tongue has several kinds of projec-tions on it called papillae. At the front are fungiform papillae and filliform papillae. The middle third, however, are only filliform papillae. They have little hairs that hold on to the custard, allowing flavour molecules to break off and rise up to the olfactory bulb situated behind the nose – which is where we detect flavours.'

This seemed to offer fascinating possibilities for flavour release but there was no time to question Jon because he was already bearing down on me with more custard.

'OK, this is the last spoonful but one. Remember how it tastes because I'm about to clean your tongue with the most absorbent thing I can think of.'

He placed the tampon on my tongue, told me to close my mouth and wait for thirty seconds before removing it. The TV crew were enjoying this. The camera zoomed in as I sat there with the string dangling out of my mouth, as though I were swallowing a mouse and had got as far as the tail.

'Now you've got a nice clean tongue, try one more spoonful of custard.'

'Amazing. It's much richer. Perhaps sweeter too.'

'That's possible. What's happened is that a layer of mucus has been removed from the mouth so that the food reaches the taste receptors far quicker. It's a neat experiment that really gets its point across and doesn't need any fancy equipment.'

'It's nice to finish with something you can try out at home ... '

Trifle Serves 6

Like Black Forest gateau, trifle became a question of architecture and layers, of building a construction where each part supported the next physically as well as gastronomically. As with the BFG, the huge number of possible combinations made it a lengthy process of trial and error. Although I wanted to draw in the dish's history as much as possible, several classic features of the dish were in the end regretfully set aside. Junket simply turned out too messy, making the trifle look slapdash and unappetising. Traditional syllabub, on the other hand, didn't give the richness I was looking for. Eventually we came up with a series of layers that really worked, and that contained both tradition and innovation. Introducing saffron to the custard gave the look of a shop-bought trifle – the kind we all remember as kids – and tapped into an old custom of flavouring dishes with the spice. The comfits, candied angelica and crystallised rose petals provided a topping that I reckon would have made sense to Robert May.

The inclusion of olive purée he might have found more surprising, but this had its own logic, starting from a strawberry dish I had developed for the Fat Duck. Strawberries and black pepper are a classic Italian combination. Thinking about that peppery aspect led me to play first with the notion of strawberries and olive oil, and then with the idea of strawberries and olives themselves. The result worked fantastically well and has become a popular feature of the Fat Duck's tasting menu. Since the trifle contained strawberries, it seemed likely that adding olive purée would enliven it by adding an unexpected flavour profile.

Special equipment
Piping bag, food processor or mixer, digital probe, large tin can with a hole drilled in the base and the drill bit still attached using a washer and nut, muslin-lined bowl, hand-held blender, atomiser

Timing
Total time about 8 hours.

For the syllabub mixture
35g dry cider _ 25g vermouth _ 20g unrefined caster sugar _ peel and juice of ½ unwaxed lemon _ 125g Bodega Tradición Palo Cortado sherry _ 4g leaf gelatin _ 6–8 ladies' finger sponges _ 12 amaretti biscuits _ 24 small/medium strawberries, hulled _ 20g fructose

For the strawberry juice and syrup
1.5kg hulled and quartered strawberries _ 200g fructose

For the strawberry jelly
reserved strawberry juice _ 5g leaf gelatin _ 25g orange blossom water _ juice of ½ lemon _ reserved trifle glasses

For the olive purée
150g pitted black olives (Kalamata olives work well) _ 45g icing sugar

For the saffron custard
100g whole milk _ 200g double cream _ ½ packet (about ¼g) of saffron _ 100g (about 6) egg yolks _ 55g caster sugar _ 2g leaf gelatin, soaked in cold water

For the puff pastry rounds
200g icing sugar, sifted _ 375g puff pastry

For the caraway biscuits
150g unsalted butter _ 100g unrefined caster sugar _ 50g ground almonds _ ½ tsp salt _ 1.5g baking powder _ 125g plain flour _ seeds from 1 vanilla pod _ 10g caraway seeds, lightly toasted _ 45g (3) egg yolks

For the mascarpone cream
2 egg yolks _ 20g unrefined caster sugar _ 50g Bodega Tradición Palo Cortado sherry _ 8g tapioca starch (available from Asian grocers) _ 125g full-fat mascarpone cheese _ 100g whipping cream, whisked to soft peaks and chilled

For the comfits

500g sugar _ 200g water _ 3g natural green food colouring _
3g natural red food colouring _ 3g natural yellow food colouring _
40g caraway seeds, toasted _ 40g fennel seeds, toasted _ 40g
coriander seeds, toasted _ icing sugar

For the rose-petal confetti

2 organic red roses _ 50g egg whites _ 25g gum arabic (available
from Holland & Barrett) _ 2.5g rose water _ sugar

For the candied angelica

200g fresh angelica twigs (about 8 twigs 6cm long) _ 200g sugar _
200g water

For the candied almonds

50g Spanish Marcona almonds, cut into quarters _ ¼ tsp table salt _
10g unrefined caster sugar

For the final assembly

reserved dessert glasses _ reserved olive purée _ reserved
strawberry syrup _ reserved caraway biscuits _ reserved saffron
custard _ reserved puff pastry rounds _ reserved mascarpone
cream _ reserved candied angelica _ reserved comfits _ reserved
rose-petal confetti _ reserved candied almonds _ popping candy _
orange blossom water in an atomiser _ Pedro Ximénez sherry, to serve

MAKING THE SYLLABUB MIXTURE

1. Put the cider, vermouth and sugar in a pan and bring to the boil.
   Allow to cool to room temperature.
2. Add the lemon peel, lemon juice and sherry and stir together.
3. Weigh 150g of the liquid into a small pan and add the gelatin. When
   the leaves have softened completely (bloomed), place the pan on
   the hob and heat gently to dissolve them.
4. Place the sponges and biscuits in a bowl. Pour the warm gelatin
   mixture over them and allow to soak in for 10 minutes.
5. Meanwhile, quarter 6 of the strawberries and cut the remaining
   ones in half.

6. Toss the strawberries with the fructose and allow to macerate for 20 minutes.
7. Gently stir the soaked sponges and biscuits together and divide between 6 dessert glasses that are 8cm in diameter and 10cm deep. Press the mixture down with the back of a spoon to create an even layer 1cm thick.
8. Place the cut sides of the halved strawberries in a ring against the wall of the glass, pressing them firmly in place and packing them together tightly.
9. Take the pointed end of each quartered strawberry and press it into the soft cake layer so that it stands upright.
10. Place the glasses in the fridge for at least 1 hour to allow the gelatin to set.

MAKING THE STRAWBERRY JUICE AND SYRUP
1. Place the strawberries and fructose in a heat-resistant bowl and cover tightly with clingfilm.
2. Create a bain-marie by filling a medium-sized pan one-third full with water. Bring to a simmer and place the covered bowl of strawberries over the pan without actually touching the water. Steam for 4 hours, checking the water regularly and topping up if necessary.
3. Remove the bowl and allow to cool completely with the clingfilm still intact.
4. Transfer the strawberry mixture to a muslin-lined bowl. Tie the corners together to create a bag and hang this above the bowl.
5. When the bag has stopped dripping, transfer the juice to a pan and reduce over a medium heat until you have 500g of liquid.
6. Remove from the heat and allow to cool.
7. Reserve one half of the liquid for use in the strawberry jelly. Return the other half to a small saucepan and reduce to a thick syrup. Leave to cool.

MAKING THE STRAWBERRY JELLY
1. Combine the strawberry juice and gelatin in a pan. When the gelatin has completely softened, place the pan over a medium heat, bring to a simmer and dissolve the gelatin.

2. Remove the pan from the heat and add the orange blossom water and lemon juice. Allow to cool to room temperature.
3. Remove the trifle glasses from the fridge. Transfer the cooled strawberry juice to a measuring container with a spout and divide the liquid between the 6 glasses. It should come halfway up the sides of the strawberries.
4. Place the glasses on a tray and return to the fridge so that the gelatin can set.

MAKING THE OLIVE PURÉE
1. Combine the olives and icing sugar in a food processor and blend to a smooth purée, scraping the bowl regularly.
2. Transfer the purée to a piping bag and reserve in the fridge.

MAKING THE SAFFRON CUSTARD
1. Put the milk, cream and saffron in a pan and bring to the boil, watching that the mixture does not boil over, and simmer for 4 minutes. Remove from the heat.
2. Meanwhile, whisk the egg yolks and sugar together in a mixing bowl, then slowly whisk in the saffron cream. Return this mixture to the pan.
3. Heat over a low temperature, stirring constantly until the mixture reaches 75°C/165°F. Hold the mixture at this temperature for 2 minutes, using a digital probe to check that the temperature remains constant.
4. Stir in the gelatin and quickly cool over ice.
5. Transfer to a storage container and cover with clingfilm directly touching the custard to prevent a skin forming. Store in the fridge until ready to use.

MAKING THE PUFF PASTRY ROUNDS
1. Preheat the oven to 200°C/400°F/Gas 6.
2. Dust a work surface with a generous handful of the icing sugar and place the puff pastry on it.
3. Scatter more of the icing sugar on top of the pastry and roll it out as thinly as possible, working the sugar into the dough. As you work, move the pastry around in quarter turns and add more icing

sugar as necessary to prevent it sticking. It should eventually measure 20 x 35cm.

4. Line a baking sheet with parchment, then place the rolled-out pastry on it. Cover with another sheet of parchment and one or two baking sheets to weigh down the pastry and prevent it from rising.

5. Place in the oven for 10 minutes. Check to make sure it has browned evenly. If not, return to the oven for a few more minutes.

6. When done, remove from the oven and lift off the coverings. While the pastry is still warm, use an 8cm cutter to cut out 6 circles. Allow to cool, and reserve for the final assembly.

MAKING THE CARAWAY BISCUITS

1. Put the butter and sugar in a food mixer and cream together for 5 minutes.

2. Add all the dry ingredients, including the vanilla seeds and caraway seeds, and continue to mix until incorporated thoroughly.

3. Add the egg yolks one at a time until incorporated and a dough forms.

4. Remove the dough and wrap in clingfilm, then chill in the fridge for at least 1 hour.

5. Cut out a piece of parchment the same size as your baking sheet and place on a work surface. Sit the dough on the parchment and cover with another sheet of parchment.

6. Roll the dough out to a thickness of 1mm. Place in the freezer until completely chilled through.

7. Preheat the oven to 150°C/300°F/Gas 2.

8. Remove the top sheet of parchment from the chilled dough and place in the oven for 10 minutes, or until golden brown.

9. Remove from the oven and immediately cut out 5cm circles from the cooked dough, using a pastry cutter.

10. Allow to cool completely and reserve the biscuits for the final assembly.

MAKING THE MASCARPONE CREAM

1. Combine the egg yolks and sugar in a small mixing bowl using a hand-held blender.

2. Place the sherry and tapioca starch in a saucepan over a medium heat and whisk constantly for 2–3 minutes.
3. Pour the sherry mixture into the yolks while mixing with the hand-held blender until fully incorporated.
4. Add the mascarpone to the bowl and whisk until thoroughly combined.
5. Fold the whipped cream into the mascarpone, then cover and refrigerate for at least 2 hours.
6. Transfer the cream mixture to a piping bag with a medium-sized straight tip and return to the fridge.

MAKING THE COMFITS

1. Place the sugar and water in a pan and bring to the boil. Using a digital probe, boil the syrup until it reaches 108°C/226°F.
2. Remove the syrup from the heat and divide between three small bowls.

My pastry chef, Jocky, making comfits using a hairdryer and a coffee can bolted to a sander.

3. Add one of the food colourings to each of the bowls and stir to incorporate.
4. Place the caraway seeds in a can attached to a drill and turn it on at a low speed. Use a piece of tape to hold down the trigger and keep the drill in constant motion.
5. Begin to add the green syrup to the seeds about a tablespoonful at a time while pointing a hairdryer set on a medium heat into the can at all times. As the syrup begins to dry and harden around the seeds, add more syrup. If the seeds begin to clump together, turn the drill off, then break them up with your fingers and add a bit of icing sugar.
6. Once the caraway seeds are coated with a shell of the syrup (about 30 minutes), remove them and repeat the process with the other seeds. Use the yellow syrup for the fennel and the red for the coriander.

MAKING THE ROSE-PETAL CONFETTI
1. Gently remove the petals from the roses, discarding any that are damaged.
2. Place the egg whites, gum arabic and rose water in a bowl and mix together using a hand-held blender.
3. Wearing gloves, coat each of the petals with a thin, even layer of the egg white mixture.
4. Toss the rose petals in a bowl of sugar one at a time to coat evenly. Place on a sheet of parchment as you finish them.
5. Before the petals have a chance to dry completely, use a hole punch to create confetti from them. Allow this to dry completely before using in the final assembly.

MAKING THE CANDIED ANGELICA
1. Clean the angelica twigs and use a small knife to peel away any fibrous strings, as you would on a stick of celery.
2. Quickly blanch the twigs in boiling water and plunge into an ice bath.
3. Place the sugar and water in a saucepan and heat until the mixture reaches 106°C/223°F.
4. Place the angelica twigs in this syrup and allow the mixture to cool to room temperature.

5. For the final presentation remove the twigs from the syrup and slice into 30 sticks about 15mm long.

PREPARING THE CANDIED ALMONDS

1. Place a sauté pan over a medium heat and add the almonds, stirring continuously until lightly roasted.
2. Sprinkle in first the salt, then the sugar, and stir constantly as they become a caramel and coat the nuts.
3. Tip the almonds on to a parchment-lined baking sheet and cool to room temperature.

ASSEMBLING THE FINISHED TRIFLES

1. Remove the dessert glasses from the fridge and pipe a dollop of olive purée in the centre of each one. Using the back of a spoon, make an indentation in the purée and cover with an even coating of the strawberry syrup.
2. Place a caraway biscuit on top of the purée and press down gently to straighten the layers.
3. Spoon in a layer of the saffron custard about 15mm thick, and tap the glasses gently on the work surface to flatten the custard.
4. Place a round of puff pastry on top of the custard, again pressing down gently.
5. Pipe the mascarpone cream up to the rim of the glass by making individual dollops.
6. Garnish the cream with 5 pieces of angelica per portion, a sprinkling of the comfits, the rose-petal confetti, pieces of the candied almond and a little popping candy.
7. Spray the tops of the trifle with a few spritzes of the orange blossom water. This can also be sprayed lightly in the room as the trifle is served.
8. Serve the trifles with a glass of Pedro Ximénez sherry.

Food Safety

Salmonella, *E. coli*, botulism … It often seems as though there's a new food scare every week. The scare stories show that it's absolutely vital to establish a proper and effective hygiene routine in your kitchen. One of the major causes of food poisoning is cross-contamination: the transferral of bacteria from one foodstuff to another. Below I will outline the best practices for preventing this.

But the scare stories can also encourage a culture of fear. Remember the listeria hysteria of the late 1980s, which prompted many people to avoid soft cheese altogether? The ultra-cautious approach would see us reduced to a diet of overcooked meat and hard-boiled eggs, with no access to mayonnaise or chocolate mousse. Half the world's greatest culinary pleasures would be denied us. Fortunately though, freedom of choice means we are still able to eat meat on the bone and cheese made from unpasteurised milk.

We should celebrate that freedom by exploring the marvellous ingredients the world has to offer, but we also need to live up to the responsibility of our choices: find out where your food comes from and how it is made and handled; search out suppliers and artisans who care about what they are doing and take the trouble to get it right. These are simple actions that go a long way towards minimising any risks involved. And reinforce this by ensuring the food stays safe when it is being prepared in your kitchen.

Wash your hands regularly using a bactericidal hand cleaner.
Busy as they are, your hands are one of the most effective ways of carrying bacteria from one food to another. Wash them not only when you first enter the kitchen (and, of course, after touching the waste bin or pets) but also after touching raw meat, fruit or vegetables. Extra care needs to be taken with foods that won't be cooked – salad, fruit, bread, etc. – because there'll be no opportunity for transferred bacteria to be destroyed by heat.

Clean work surfaces, cutting boards and knives after each task with a spray sanitiser that both cleans and disinfects.
After your hands, utensils are probably bacteria's best means of spreading across the kitchen. (Professional kitchens have separate colour-coded chopping boards for meat, fish and vegetables. It's a good practice to get into at home as well.) Your sense of smell is a good ally in making sure this has been done properly. If a knife or a sieve smells of the last thing you used it for, it needs further cleaning.

Regularly wash, disinfect or dispose of wiping cloths and dishcloths.
These too can be breeding grounds for bacteria. The best approach is probably to use kitchen paper where possible. Cross-contamination is lessened if you use different cloths for different jobs: one for wiping worktops, one for drying hands, one for drying dishes, etc.

Store raw meat so that it can't touch or drip on other foodstuffs.
Keep it separately in sealed containers on the bottom shelf of the fridge. Don't store it alongside other foodstuffs, and keep raw meat separate from cooked meat. Take care when defrosting meat in the fridge: the liquid produced can spread bacteria if it drips.

Take care when handling eggs.
The outside of a chicken's egg can carry a lot of bacteria, so treat it with the same vigilance as you would raw meat.

Try to complete each stage of a task before going on to the next.
If you're peeling and chopping onions, peel the lot and discard the peelings, then clean the work surface before you begin to chop. You'll not only lessen the potential for cross-contamination, but also enjoy a more methodical and orderly kitchen.

Equipment

Eating is one of the few things we do that draws on all of our senses at the same time. Cooking, similarly, is above all about touch, taste, smell, sight and sound – sniffing out the aromas that tell you a herb has released its essential oils; watching the colour-change penetrate the surface of a seared steak or slice of tuna; hearing the noisy bubbling of butter in the frying pan cease as the last of its water content departs. The eyes, ears, nose, mouth and fingers are the really essential tools of the cook's trade, and no amount of fancy equipment can replace them. Nonetheless, there are a few, largely inexpensive, pieces of hardware that should be part of any cook's arsenal.

THERMOMETERS

Temperature is of vital importance in cooking, and two pieces of equipment will help make you master of it. First, I'd recommend an oven thermometer: it's amazing how inaccurate oven dials can be, and how much heat can be lost through an open oven door or the introduction of a cold roasting tin. Cooking at the wrong temperature, even by a few degrees, is probably the easiest way to mess up a meal. An oven thermometer will ensure that, if a recipe calls for 200°C, you're able to reach and maintain that temperature.

Second, a battery-operated digital probe is the best way of achieving perfectly cooked meat, fish and pastries, an ideal that in itself should be justification for having one. As the recipes in this book show, cooking meat, for example, is a complicated juggling act of trying to reconcile the different temperatures at which meat browns, tenderises and totally dehydrates. A digital probe takes the heartbreak out of this.

SCALES

Accurately measuring ingredients is as vital to successful cooking as regulating temperature, yet scales are often no more accurate than oven thermostats, especially where small amounts are called for. Make sure you have a good set of scales that is accurate even below 100g. (To test them, take a pat of butter, cut off 50g – often the wrapper is marked at 25g intervals – and weigh it.)

To find a reliable set, it is worth consulting scalemagazine.com. The Jennings CJ300 is a good, relatively inexpensive model.

EQUIPMENT ONLINE

Most of the recommended items are available in any good kitchen shop. However, should you have any difficulty in obtaining them, the following online stores stock good versions of each.

Continental Chef Supplies
The Courtyard, South Hetton, South Hetton Industrial Estate,
County Durham DH6 2UZ
Tel: 0808 1001 777
www.chefs.net

Hansens Kitchen Equipment Ltd
306 Fulham Road, London SW10 9ER
Tel: 020 7351 6933
www.hansens.co.uk

Nisbets
Fourth Way, Avonmouth BS11 8TB
Tel: 0845 1110285
www.nisbets.co.uk

Pages
121 Shaftesbury Avenue, London WC2H 8AD
Tel: 020 7565 5959
www.pagescatering.co.uk

Atomisers: available from Boots, www.boots.com

Blowtorches, goggles, paint guns, protective gloves: obtainable from almost any hardware store, DIY shop or builder's merchant.

Digital probe: available from www.cooper-atkins.com

Dry ice: the best site I have found for getting (gloved) hold of dry ice is http://ind.yara.co.uk/en/products_services/dry_ice/. They will supply a minimum of 10kg of dry ice in 1kg slabs (it's the slabs you want, not the pellets). It has no real shelf life and you can't store it in your freezer, so you need to have it delivered as near as possible to the day you want to use it. Keep it in its original container and, as it evaporates, stuff newspaper into the gaps that develop between the slabs.

Food mixer: where mentioned in recipe methods, a Kenwood Major mixer was used. See www.kenwoodworld.com for a list of stockists.

Pacojet: available from www.pacojet.com

Pizza peel: a short-handled peel can be bought in many professional cookware stores (see also page 476).

Sausage equipment: available from www.naturalcasingco.co.uk

Soda siphons: available from www.johnlewis.com

Sous-vide appliances: available from www.grantsousvide.com

Vacuum-seal storage bags: available at many department stores, and can also be found at www.spacebag.com

Wood-effect painting tool (basically a small paddle with a wood-effect rubber stamp around the leading edge): available at art shops and some DIY stores.

Suppliers, Restaurants & Other

Useful Addresses

General Information

Farmers' markets
www.farmersmarkets.net

Food Standards Agency
www.food.gov.uk

Meat suppliers
www.aubreyallen.co.uk
www.laverstokebutchersshop.co.uk
See also Jack O'Shea's, page 474.

Organic farming
www.soilassociation.org

Slow Food movement
www.slowfood.com

Speciality produce from France
Chef to Chef Direct Ltd,
40 Woodend Drive, Ascot,
Berkshire SL5 9BG
Tel: 01344 874266 (no website)

Spices
www.seasonedpioneers.co.uk
www.steenbergs.co.uk
www.thespiceshop.co.uk

Suppliers by area
www.foodloversbritain.com

Vegetable supplier
www.fresherway.com

Roast Chicken & Roast Potatoes

L'Arche Cafeteria
Autoroute 39,
L'Aire du Poulet de Bresse
Tel: 00 33 (0)3 85 76 30 97

Georges Blanc
Tel: 00 33 (0)4 74 50 90 90
www.georgesblanc.com

Boucherie Trolliet
102 Cours Lafayette,
69003 Lyon
Tel: 00 33 (0)4 78 62 36 60
www.boucherie-trolliet.com

C. Lidgate (Bresse chickens)
110 Holland Park Avenue,
London W11 4AU
Tel: 020 7727 8243

Label Anglais (Bresse chickens)
S.J. Frederick & Sons,
Temple Farm, Roydon,
Harlow, Essex CM19 5LW
Tel: 01279 792460
www.labelanglais.co.uk
See also: www.pouletbresse.com

MBM (potatoes)
Glenthorn, March,
Cambridgeshire PE15 0AW
Tel: 01354 652341
www.mbm.uk.com

Chicken Tikka Masala

Malik's Tandoori Restaurant
High Street, Cookham,
Berkshire SL6 9SF
Tel: 01628 520085
www.maliks.co.uk

Moti Mahal
3704 Netaji Subhash Marg,
Daryaganj, New Delhi,
Tel: 00 91 11 2327 3661

Spice market
Khari Baoli Marg
Old Delhi

Zaika
1 Kensington High Street
London W8 5NP
Tel: 020 7795 6533
www.zaika-restaurant.co.uk

Contractors Plant & Tool Hire
Skates Farm, Skates Lane,
Pamber Green, Tadley,
Hampshire RG26 3AB
Tel: 0118 984 3123
www.contractorshire.co.uk

Peking Duck

China Tang
The Dorchester,
53 Park Lane, London W1A 2HJ
Tel: 020 7629 9988
www.thedorchester.com

Da Dong Roast Duck Restaurant
Nanxincang International
Building, 22 Dongsi Shitiao,
Dongcheng District, Beijing
Tel: 00 91 10 5169 0328

Quanjude (Hepingmen branch)
14 Qianmenxidajie,
Xuanwu District, Beijing
Tel: 00 91 10 6302 3062
www.quanjude.com.cn

Silver Hill Foods
Emyvale, County Monaghan
Tel: 00 353 47 87124
www.silverhillfoods.com

Wangfujing night market
Dong'an Men Dajie
(Wangfujing underground station)

Steak

Empire Diner
210 Tenth Avenue,
New York, NY 10011
Tel: 001 (212) 243 2736
www.empire-diner.com

Gray's Papaya
2090 Broadway,
New York, NY 10023
Tel: 001 (212) 799 0243
www.grayspapaya.com

Katz's Delicatessen
205 East Houston Street,
New York, NY 10002
Tel: 001 (212) 254 2246
www.katzdeli.com

Pedigree Meats (Longhorn steaks)
Huntsham Farm,
Goodrich, Ross-on-Wye
Herefordshire HR9 6JN
Tel: 01600 890296
www.huntsham.com

Peter Luger, Inc.
178 Broadway,
Brooklyn, NY 11211
Tel: 001 (718) 387 7400
www.peterluger.com

Robert's Steakhouse
Penthouse Executive Club,
603 West 50th Street,
New York, NY 10036
Tel: 001 (212) 245 0002
www.penthouseexecutiveclub.com

WD-50
50 Clinton Street,
New York, NY 10002
Tel: 001 (212) 477 2900
www.wd-50.com

Smoked sea salt: available from the Anglesey Sea Salt Company (www.seasalt.co.uk) and Waitrose

See also:
www.beefyandlamby.co.uk
www.eblex.org.uk

Spaghetti Bolognese

Antica Trattoria della Gigina
Via Stendhal 1, 40128 Bologna,
Tel: 00 39 051 322 300
www.trattoriagigina.it

Osteria Francescana
Via Stella 22, 41100 Modena,
Tel: 00 39 059 210 118
www.osteriafrancescana.it

La Pasta di Aldo
Via Castelletta 41,
62015 Monte San Giusto, Macerata
Tel: 00 39 0733 53105
www.lapastadialdo.it
La Pasta di Aldo has no representative in the UK, making it difficult

to obtain, and there's
no spaghetti in the range.
The best alternative is:

Rustichella d'Abruzzo SpA
Piazza Vestini 20,
65019 Pianella, Pescara
Tel: 00 39 085 971 308
www.rustichella.it
This brand is available in some
delicatessens and online at
www.guidetti.co.uk

Chilli con Carne

DC 101 Annual Chili Cookoff
11th & New York Avenue NW,
Washington DC
www.dc101.com
www.kidneywdc.org

International Chili Society
www.chilicookoff.com

Dry ice: see page 470

Hamburger

Bouchon Bakery
3rd Floor,
Time Warner Center Mall,
10 Columbus Circle,
New York, NY 10019
Tel: 001 (212) 823 9366
www.bouchonbakery.com

Burger Joint
Le Parker Meridien,
118 West 57th Street,
New York, NY 10019
Tel: 001 (212) 245 5000
www.parkermeridien.com

Jack O'Shea's
11 Montpelier Street,
London SW7 1EX
Tel: 020 7581 7771
www.jackosheas.com

Louis' Lunch
261–3 Crown Street,
New Haven,
CT 06510
Tel: 001 203 562 5507
www.louislunch.com

Shake Shack
Madison Square Park,
Madison Avenue at 23rd Street,
New York, NY 10010
Tel: 001 212 889 6600
www.shakeshacknyc.com

Bangers & Mash

Crombie's of Edinburgh
97 Broughton Street,
Edinburgh EH1 3RZ
Tel: 0131 556 7643
www.sausages.co.uk

Ludlow Marches Food and Drink Festival
Stone House,
Corve Street,
Ludlow,
Shropshire SY8 1JY
Tel: 01584 873957
www.foodfestival.co.uk

MBM (potatoes)
see page 472

Piperfield Pork (Graham Head)
The Dovecote,
Lowick,
Berwick-upon-Tweed,
Northumberland TD15 2QE
Tel: 01289 388543
www.piperfield.com

Smoked olive oil:
www.organicsmokehouse.com

See also:
www.sausagefans.com
www.sausagelinks.co.uk
www.sausagemaking.org

Fish & Chips

As far as fish suppliers go, there's no substitute for a good local fishmonger. If you have trouble finding one in your area, try www.foodloversbritain.com

A Salt and Battery
112 Greenwich Avenue,
New York, NY 10011
Tel: 001 (212) 254 6610
www.asaltandbattery.com

Cecil & Co (fish supplier)
393 Liverpool Road,
London N1 1NP
Tel: 020 7700 6707

James Knight of Mayfair
(fish supplier)
67 Notting Hill Gate,
London W11 3JS
Tel: 020 7587 3070
www.james-knight.com

Marine Conservation Society
Unit 3, Wolf Business Park,
Alton Road, Ross-on-Wye,
Herefordshire HR9 5NB
Tel: 01989 566017
www.mcsuk.org
www.fishonline.org

Marine Stewardship Council
www.msc.org

MBM (potatoes)
see page 472

Sea Fish Industry Authority
18 Logie Mill, Logie Green Road,
Edinburgh EH7 4HS
Tel: 0131 558 3331
www.seafish.org

White rice flour:
Doves Farm rice flour is available at supermarkets and at www.goodnessdirect.co.uk. Otherwise, try www.thai4uk.com

Fish Pie

Colchester Oyster Fishery Ltd
Pyefleet Quay, Mersea Island,
Colchester, Essex CO5 8UN
Tel: 01206 383758
www.colchesteroysterfishery.com

Cape Clear Fish Shop
(fish supplier)
119 Shepherd's Bush Road,
London W6 7LP
Tel: 020 7751 1609
www.capeclearfishshop.co.uk

Kingfisher (Brixham) Ltd
(fish supplier)
Torbay Business Park,
Woodview Road, Paignton,
Devon TQ4 7HP
Tel: 01803 553232
www.kingfisherbrixham.co.uk

**Sono Seaport
Seafood Restaurant**
100 Water Street,
South Norwalk, CT 06854
Tel: 001 203 854 9483
www.sonoseaportseafood.com

Topcatch (fish supplier)
The Stoep,
Dartmouth Road,
Paignton
Devon TQ4 6LQ
Tel: 07768 704899

Pizza

L'Antica Pizzeria da Michele
Via Cesare Sersale 1–3,
80100 Naples
Tel: 00 39 081 553 9204
www.damichele.net

Antimo Caputo Srl ('00' flour)
Corso San Giovanni a Teduccio 55,
80146 Naples
Tel: 00 39 081 752 0566
www.molinocaputo.it
See also:
www.nifeislife.com for '00' flour

Il Pizzaiolo del Presidente
Via dei Tribunali 120,
80138 Naples
Tel: 00 39 081 210 903
www.ilpizzaiolodelpresidente.it

Pizzeria Brandi
Salita S. Anna di Palazzo 1–2,
(Via Chiaia), Naples
Tel: 00 39 081 416928
www.brandi.it

Pizzeria La Notizia
Via Caravaggio 53–55,
80112 Naples
Tel: 00 39 081 714 2155
www.pizzaconsulting.it

Malt syrup: Clearspring Japanese
brown rice malt syrup is available
from www.goodnessdirect.co.uk

Mozzarella: Garofalo Mozzarella
di Bufala is available at Waitrose
and online

Smoked sea salt: see page 473

See also:
www.fabflour.co.uk
www.fornobravo.com
www.pizzamaking.com
www.woodstone-corp.com

Risotto

Acquerello
Tenuta Colombara,
13046 Livorno Ferraris,
Vercelli
Tel: 00 39 0161 477 832
www.acquerello.it

Cracco-Peck
Via Victor Hugo 4,
20123 Milan
Tel: 00 39 02 876 774
www.peck.it

Gli Aironi
Risi & Co Srl,
Strada delle Grange 8,
13100 Lignana, Vercelli
Tel: 00 39 0161 344 025
www.gliaironi.it

Ristorante Gualtiero Marchesi
L'Albereta,
Via Vittorio Emanuele 23,
25030 Erbusco, Brescia
Tel: 00 39 030 776 0562
www.marchesi.it

Tenuta Val del Serpe
13040 Lamporo,
Vercelli
Tel: 00 39 0161 481 0653

Black Forest Gateau

Amedei Srl (chocolate)
Via San Gervasio 29,
56020 La Rotta (Pontedera),
Pisa
Tel: 00 39 0587 484849
www.amedei.it
See also:
www.seventypercent.com
for chocolate

Café König
Lichtentaler Strasse 12,
76530 Baden-Baden
Tel: 00 49 (0)7221 23573
www.chocolatier.de

Call Caterlink Ltd
(Amarena Fabbri cherries)
Callywith Gate Industrial Estate,
Launceston Road, Bodmin,
Cornwall PL31 2RQ
Tel: 01208 78844
www.caterlink.co.uk

Confiserie Kaffeehaus Gmeiner
Hauptstrasse 38,
77704 Oberkirch
Tel: 00 49 (0)7802 2629
www.chocolatier.de

Franz Fies GmbH (kirsch)
Schwarzwalder,
Edelobstbrennerei,
Kastelbergstrasse 2
77704 Oberkirch-Ringelbach
Tel: 00 49 (0)7802 4445
www.fiesbrennerei.de

Treacle Tart & Ice Cream

Hampton Court Palace
East Molesey,
Surrey KT8 9AU
Tel: 0844 482 7777
or 020 3166 6000
www.hrp.org.uk
The activities section of the
website gives details of when
you can visit the kitchens to
see Tudor cookery at first hand.

Tate & Lyle plc
Sugar Quay,
Lower Thames Street,
London EC3R 6DQ
Tel: 020 7626 6525
www.tateandlyle.com

Waltham Place Farm
(milk for ice cream)
Church Hill,
White Waltham,
Berkshire SL6 3JH
Tel: 01628 825517
www.walthamplace.com
The gardens, shop and tearoom
are open on specific days from
May until September. They are
well worth a visit.

Dry ice: see page 470

Glucose syrup: obtainable from
some supermarkets, or online
from www.jane-asher.co.uk or
www.squires-shop.com

Baked Alaska

Delmonico's Restaurant
56 Beaver Street,
New York,
NY 10004
Tel: 001 212 509 1144
www.delmonicosny.com

Chlorinated flour: available
from Overseas Buyers Club,
www.obcusa.co.uk

Dry ice: see page 470

Trifle

Ivan Day
Historic Food, Wreay Farm,
Shap, Penrith,
Cumbria CA10 3LB
Tel: 01931 716266
www.historicfood.com

Heston's Restaurants

The Fat Duck
High Street,
Bray,
Berkshire SL6 2AQ
Tel: 01628 580333
www.fatduck.co.uk

The Hind's Head Hotel
High Street,
Bray,
Berkshire SL6 2AB
Tel: 01628 626151
www.hindsheadhotel.com

Bibliography

This is not an exhaustive list by any means. I've tried to include books that seem to me to be definitive in their field, along with others that provide a great starting point for further exploring particular areas covered in this book.

GENERAL

_ Simon Hopkinson and Lindsey Bareham, *The Prawn Cocktail Years*, Macmillan, 1997
_ Laura Mason and Catherine Brown, *Traditional Foods of Britain: An Inventory*, Prospect Books, 2004
_ Sri Owen, *The Rice Book*, Doubleday, 1993
_ Jeffrey Steingarten, *The Man Who Ate Everything* and *It Must've Been Something I Ate*, Review, 1999 and 2002

HISTORY

_ E.N. Anderson, *The Food of China*, Yale University Press, 1988
_ Lizzie Collingham, *Curry: A Tale of Cooks and Conquerors*, Vintage, 2006
_ Andrew Dalby, *Food in the Ancient World*, Routledge, 2003
_ Alan Davidson, *The Oxford Companion to Food*, OUP, 1999
_ Felipe Fernandez-Armesto, *Food: A History*, Macmillan, 2001
_ Theodora Fitzgibbon, *The Food of the Western World*, Hutchinson, 1970
_ Jean-Louis Flandrin and Massimo Montanari, *Food: A Culinary History*, Columbia University Press, 1999
_ Nicola Humble, *Culinary Pleasures: Cookbooks and the Transformation of British Food*, Faber & Faber, 2005
_ Jane Renfrew, Maggie Black, Jennifer Stead and Peter Brears, *Food & Cooking in Britain* (series), English Heritage, 1985
_ Gillian Riley, *The Oxford Companion to Italian Food*, OUP, 2007
_ Colin Spencer, *British Food*, Grub Street, 2002
_ Reay Tannahill, *Food in History*, Three Rivers Press, 1988

_ C. Anne Wilson, *Food & Drink in Britain*, Academy Chicago Publications, 2003

SCIENCE

_ E. Aberle, J. Forrest, D. Gerrard and E. Mills, *Principles of Meat Science*, 4th edn, Kendall Hunt Publishing, 2001
_ S. Afzalinia, M. Shaker and E. Zare, 'Comparison of Different Rice Milling Methods' in *Canadian Biosystems Engineering*, vol. 46, 2004
_ Peter Barham, *The Science of Cooking*, Springer, 2001
_ S. Beckett, *The Science of Chocolate*, Royal Society of Chemistry, 2000
_ H.D. Belitz, W. Grosch and Peter Schieberle, *Food Chemistry*, 3rd revd edn, Springer, 2004
_ E. Bennion and G. Bamford, *The Technology of Cake Making*, 6th edn, Springer, 1997
_ G. Calvert, C. Spence and B. Stein, *The Handbook of Multisensory Processes*, MIT Press, 2004
_ Rita Carter, *Exploring Consciousness*, University of California Press, 2002
_ Stanley P. Cauvain and Linda S. Young (eds), *Baking Problems Solved*, Woodhead Publishing, 2001
_ Stanley P. Cauvain and Linda S. Young, *Technology of Breadmaking*, Aspen Publishers, 1999
_ C. Clarke, *The Science of Ice Cream*, Royal Society of Chemistry, 2004
_ T.P. Coultate, *Food: The Chemistry of Its Components*, Royal Society of Chemistry, 2002
_ Mariette DiChristina (ed.), 'Secrets of the Senses: How the Brain Deciphers the World around Us' in *Scientific American*, vol. 16, no. 3, 2006
_ W.P. Edwards, *The Science of Sugar Confectionery*, Royal Society of Chemistry, 2000
_ P.J. Fellows, *Food Processing Technology: Principles and Practice*, Woodhead Publishing, 2000
_ A.-L. Ferry, J. Hort, J.R. Mitchell, D.J. Cook, S. Lagarrigue and B. Valles Pamies, 'Viscosity and Flavour Perception: Why Is Starch Different from Hydrocolloids?' in *Food Hydrocolloids* 20, Elsevier, 2006
_ G. Hasenhuettl and R. Hartel, *Food Emulsifiers and Their Applications*, Chapman & Hall, 1997

_ R.A. Lawrie, *Meat Science*, Woodhead Publishing, 1998
_ Robert T. Marshall, Richard W. Hartel and H. Douglas Goff, *Ice Cream*, Kluwer Academic/Plenum Publishers, 2003
_ Harold McGee, *On Food & Cooking*, Hodder & Stoughton, 2004
_ D. Nelson and M. Cox, *Lehninger Principles of Biochemistry*, 3rd edn, Worthn, 2000
_ J.B. Rossell (ed.), *Frying: Improving Quality*, Woodhead Publishing, 2001
_ Yoko Takechi (ed.), *The Fifth Taste of Human Being: Umami the World*, Cross Media, 2005
_ E. Ziegler and H. Ziegler, *Flavourings: Production, Composition, Applications, Regulations*, Wiley-VCH, 1998

BRESSE CHICKENS

_ Quentin Crewe, *Foods from France,* Ebury Press, 1993

CHOCOLATE

_ Sara Jayne-Stanes, *Chocolate: The Definitive Guide*, Grub Street, 2005

DOUGH

_ Raymond Calvel, Ronald L. Wirtz and James J. MacGuire, *The Taste of Bread*, Kluwer Academic/Plenum Publishers, 2001
_ Jeffrey Hamelman, *Bread: A Baker's Book of Techniques and Recipes*, John Wiley & Sons Inc, 2004

FISH

_ Bernadette Clarke, *Good Fish Guide*, Marine Conservation Society, 2002

HAMBURGERS

_ John T. Edge, *Hamburgers & Fries: An American Story*, G.P. Putnam's Sons, 2005

ICE CREAM

_ Caroline Liddell and Robin Weir, *Ices: The Definitive Guide*, Grub Street, 1995

MEAT

_ Bruce Aidells and Denis Kelly, *Bruce Aidells' Complete Sausage Book*, Ten Speed Press, 2000
_ Hugh Fearnley-Whittingstall, *The River Cottage Meat Book*, Hodder & Stoughton, 2004
_ Donald MacPherson, *Tender, Tasty Beef – Every Time*, report sponsored by the Royal Highland and Agricultural Society of Scotland and the Royal Smithfield Club, 2003

PIZZA AND PASTA

_ Nikko Amandonico, *La Pizza*, Mitchell Beazley, 2001
_ Marcella Hazan, *The Essentials of Classic Italian Cooking*, Macmillan, 1992
_ Claudia Roden, *The Food of Italy*, Chatto & Windus, 1989

POTATOES

_ Alex Barker and Sally Mansfield, *Potato*, Lorenz Books, 1999
_ Lindsay and Patrick Mikanowski, *Potato*, Grub Street, 2005
_ Alan Romans, *The Potato Book*, Frances Lincoln Publishers, 2005

TRIFLE

_ Ivan Day, 'Further Musings on Syllabub, or Why Not "Jumble It a Pritie While"?' in *Petits Propos Culinaires* 53, Prospect Books, 1996
_ Ivan Day, 'The Art of Confectionery'; go to www.historicfood.com
_ Helen Saberi, 'Whims and Fancies of a Trifle Lover' in *Petits Propos Culinaires* 50, Prospect Books, 1995
_ Helen Saberi and Alan Davidson, *Trifle*, Prospect Books, 2001

Acknowledgements

I'd like to thank all the chefs who devoted their time, energy and imagination to showing me some amazing food, especially Georges Blanc, Massimo Bottura, Ernesto Cacialli, Enzo Coccia, Carlo Cortesi, Carlo Cracco, Wylie Dufresne, Volker Gmeiner, Thomas Keller, Adam Perry Lang, Gualtiero Marchesi and Hiroshi Sudo.

I'd also like to thank the many people who indulged my fascination for how things work and patiently answered all my questions: Alimuddin Ahmed and his family, Michele Antony, Alison Ashman, Professor Jim Atkinson, Fred Austin, Victoria Barr, Dan Bauer, Fred Bell, Laurent Berthelin, David Blagden, Celine Brattinga, Harold Bult, Enzo Caldarelli, Dr Gemma Calvert, Carmel and Alberto, Eugenio, Carmine and Antimo Caputo, Chris Carter, Emile Castillo, Vinod Chadha, Christian Chotard, Dino Ciccarelli, Ian Clark, the Big Boys at Contractors Plant & Tool Hire, Richard Coraine, Sandy Crombie, Tom Dixon, Da Dong, Luigi and Maria Donnari, Marion Donnelly, Dewey Dufresne, Fabian, Tracy Falcone, Simone Farris, Hans-Peter Fies, Andrew Francis, Deambrogio Franco, Luca Gardini, David Gasston, Michael Gianmarino at Lombardi's, Professor Lynn Gladden, Amanda Glover, Professor Penny Gowland, Alan Griffiths, Professor Laurie Hall, Claire Harrison, Lucien Harthoorn, Graham Head, Ferne Hudson, Liu Hui, Ajay Kumar, the Lassen family, especially Jeff, Lee and Ken, the Lewis family at Orleton Farm Shop, Monica Lee, Clinton McCann, Gary McDowell, Dr Mick Mantle, Dr Luca Marciani, Marcel Meinders, Michael Mitchell, Jos Mojet, Theresa Mullen, Dr Douglas Neil, Serge Nollent, Dr Rob Osterbauer, Davide Ostorero, Jim and Monica Parker, Peter Pattrick, Gianluigi Peduzzi, Michele Perinotti, Nicky Perry, Carlo Maria Ricci, Rinaldo Rondolino, Jody Storch, Cecilia and Alessio Tessieri, Maurice Trolliet, Dennis Turcinovic, Mike Wall, Amy West and Professor Steve Williams, along with Matt and Nicky at A Salt and Battery, the team at Waltham Place Farm – Chris Stevenson, Vinnie McCann, Val Turner, Beatrice Krehl, Steve Castle, Suki Mann and Nicky and Strilli Oppenheimer – and everyone at Peter Luger, Brandi, Da Michele and Solania.

A number of people readily joined in with recipe exploration, offering resources and advice: Tim Sieloff at the American Institute of Baking; Stella Cook at Campden & Chorleywood Food Research Association; Professor Julian Vincent at the University of Bath; Professor Malcolm Povey at the University of Leeds; Professor Francis McGlone and the department at the University of Nottingham; Bernard Mense; Nick 'The Fish' Wilson at Cape Clear; Robin Hancock at Wright Brothers Oysters; and the perfumier Christophe Laudamiel. I'm very grateful to all of them. In addition I would like to acknowledge the invaluable assistance of all the Steele family at Silver Hill; Malik Ahmed at Malik's; Ringo Chan at the Dorchester's China Tang; Sanjay Dwivedi at Zaika; and of course Jack O'Shea.

Neither this book nor the TV series could have happened without enormous behind-the-scenes work by a number of drivers, fixers, coordinators and translators. I'm especially indebted to Irene Agrillo, Paolo Benzi, Damon Bundschuh, Dario Canciello, Frank Dunne, Isabelle Faure, Adam Gill, Neelima Goel, Shenny Italia, Irene Junge, Ramesh Kumar, Jodie Penfold, Venetia Phillips, Hong Qian, Faye Rogafki, Sanjay, Deirdre Traynor, Gabriel Walsh and Tan Yadong. I'd also like to thank all the farmhands, factory workers, sous-chefs, waiters and waitresses to whom I wasn't introduced but whose hard work, professionalism and enthusiasm underpin everything described in this book.

Filming was often gruelling, but the teams at the BBC made sure it was fun as well. A massive thanks to Gary Hunter for making all this happen and allowing me to gain a good friend in the process. For the first series of *Perfection* I owe a lot to Michael Massey, whose energy, determination, encouragement and imagination were the linchpin of the project. He was skilfully backed up by Andrew Fettis, whose expertise and inventiveness contributed much to the programmes, and by Dawn Lake and especially Peter Strachan, who did some great filmwork under difficult circumstances.

For the second series I owe a lot to Melanie Jappy, who brought a real passion and commitment to the production, and masterminded the series' shape; David Robertson, who directed with a combination of keen focus and good humour that made the experience extremely rewarding; Ben Finney, who provided top-notch research and became an invaluable guide for the direction each programme should take; Jon

Sayers, who filmed in the Netherlands with the enthusiasm of an old hand; and David Pembrey and Roger Houston, who skilfully finessed the logistics of moving us all across the globe. Thanks, too, to Eddy Andres, Mike Fox, John Gillan, Claire McMahon, Christina Schultz and the many soundmen who waited patiently through fluffed lines, usually with one knee wedged in a blast chiller and their head in the armpit of the photographer: Douglas Kerr, James Baker, Alex Sullivan, Wu Yanbo, Subbu Subramanian, Paul Nathan, Stephen Atherton and, especially, Richard Coles. I'm grateful to Juliet Hadden for taking the legwork out of some of the paperwork; and special mention must go to Emma Robertson: her research skills, recipe testing, food knowledge and devotion to the cause are second to none.

I'm also grateful to everybody who helped make the studio sessions run smoothly, in particular Lou Abercrombie, Kate Adam, Eleanor Bailey, Robin Brigham, Luis Carreola, Maree Cochrane, Abi Fawcett, Tim Green, Lisa Harrison, Tara Kane, Paul Keyworth, Fiona Llewellyn, Chris Meed, Steve Moss, Andy Muggleton, Lucie Parker, Jo Pratt, Micky Reeves, Tanya Severn, Rudi Thackray, Maria Ttofian, Frank Webster, Joe Wildman and Andy Young.

Several experts have been generous with their time and ideas. I'm indebted to Professor Peter Barham, Professor Tony Blake, Ivan Day and his assistant, Louise Rostron, Harold McGee, Dr Bernard Mackey, Professor Don Mottram and Dr Ann Marie Friend, Jon Prinz, Professor Charles Spence, Jeffrey Steingarten, Professor Andy Taylor and Rachel Edwards-Stuart, Robin Weir, and doctors Terry Sharp and Sam Millar. Their limitless curiosity helped to form many of the ideas in this book.

I've had a fantastic publishing team whose passion was a vital part of this book's creation and development. My agent, Zoë Waldie, had the vision and determination to bring the project to life in the first place. My publishers, Mike Jones and Richard Atkinson, provided the enthusiasm and encouragement necessary for its completion. The text was edited with great intelligence, sensitivity and patience by Emily Sweet, Mary Instone and Trish Burgess, and production director Penny Edwards went to superhuman lengths to transform it into a book. Thanks must also go to Bronwen Jones, who read and commented on early versions of the manuscript, and to Rachel Calder at the Sayle

Literary Agency, Monica Brown at Lotus PR and Johnny Dawes of Raw World.

Peter Dawson and Myfanwy Vernon-Hunt at Grade Design did a wonderful job of designing the paperback edition of the book. Two superlative photographers also made a vital contribution to the look of the book: Simon Wheeler, whose uncanny ability to capture the spirit of the action was matched by an acerbic wit that made it a pleasure to travel with him; and Andy Sewell, who has a great eye allied to the bloody-mindedness needed to get the right picture. Most location sessions ended with him demanding 'Just one more, Heston' (it never was just one) while forcing me to hold up some ingredient as though it were Yorick's skull. I shan't miss it, but I'm glad he put me through it.

Many of my staff at the Fat Duck and Hind's Head went way beyond their duties in providing assistance. Thanks must go to my head chef, Ashley Palmer-Watts, and my pastry chef, James 'Jocky' Petrie: without them to help steer the mother ship, this book would not have been possible. My head of development, Kyle Connaughton, and Chris Young not only worked tirelessly on recipe experimentation, but also took supporting roles in the TV series – I can't thank them enough for doing both things with determination and inventiveness, and making me laugh a lot in the process. Mary-Ellen McTague, Dominic Chapman and Jonny Lake energetically tested, tasted and discussed – their input was essential to the project, as were the dedication and hard work of all the assistants in the research kitchen, especially Otto Romer, Max Billet, Matt Marcus, Mayla Bagano and Sam Fahey-Burke. Finally, the organisational skills of Roisin Wesley and Melissa Lyons were the only thing that allowed me to juggle a hectic film schedule and still find time to cook. Thank you.

Index

Figures in **bold** refer to recipes

bird flu 18n, 86
bitter taste 323
Black Angus cattle 107, 209
Black Forest gateau 365, 375, 376, 385–7,
   388–97
   cherries 379
   chocolate 366, 374, 386, 389
   Kirsch and Kirsch cream 379–80,
      381–5, 389, 393
   mousse 378, 379, 389
Blagden, David 255, 259
Blanc, Alexandre 32
Blanc, Elisa 27
Blanc, Frédéric 32
Blanc, Georges 25, 27–8, 29–33, 81
Blanc, Jean 27
Blanc, Jean-Louis 27
Blanc, Paulette 27
Blanc, Virginie 27
Blue Belle potatoes 34
Bocuse, Paul 25
Bologna 131, 134–5
   Antica Trattoria della Gigina 135–8, 141, 151
Bon Repos farm, near Viriat, France 22–4
bonito 324
Bottura, Massimo 138–42, 374
bouillabaisse 324
bouillon 324
   basmati-infused chicken 356, **357–8**
Bresse chickens 21–4, 31, 32, 33
brill 255, 256, 258
   deep-frying 259
Brillat-Savarin, Jean-Anthelme 21
brining chickens 39, 40–41, 65
brisket 213, 215
Brisse, Baron Léon 425
broccoli, cooking 39, 40, 43
bromelain 113n
Broun, Heywood 400
Bruise potatoes 261–3
Buontalenti, Bernardo 400
burgers *see* hamburgers
butter, gelled 248, 251

Cacialli, Ernesto 308, 309
Caldarelli, Enzo 316, 321
calpains 125
Campden & Chorleywood Food Research
   Association 434
capsaicin 170, 171, 174

Caputo, Eugenio 304, 305, 307–8, 312
   flour 305, 307–8, 318, 319
Caputo mill, Naples 304–5, *306*
caraway biscuits 458, 462
Carême, Antonin 377
Carnaroli rice 336, 342, 345, 347–9, 355
carpetbag steak 104
Carroll, Lewis: *Alice's Adventures in
   Wonderland* 399
carrots, glazed 39, 40, 43
cashew nut butter 64, 66
Castillo, Emile 205–6
cathepsins 125
Cather, Willa 427
celeriac 39
cellulose 341
Chadha, Vinod 47–51, 53
Chaissac, Gaston 350
Chan, Ringo 90
Chapel, Alain 25
Chapman, Dominic 36
Charles I, of England 400, 401
Charles II, of England 400
Charlotte potatoes 34
chateaubriand 103
Chianina cattle 141
chiboust 455
chicken 17–18
   best types 20–21
   blanching 39, 40, 41
   Bresse 21–4, 31, 32, 33
   brining 39, 40–41, 65
   chicken and frogs' legs 33
   chicken tikka masala 45–6, 48–51,
      53–5, **63–9**
   cooking on skewers 57n
   garlic rubs for 64, 65
   marinades for 60–62, 63
   oysters and chicken oysters 33
   poulet à la crème 28, 29–30, 32–3
   roast chicken 28, 29, 30–32
   roast chicken and roast potatoes **39–43**
   tandoori chicken 58–9
chilli 52, 171
   effects scanned by MRI 174–6
chilli con carne 157–8, 162–4, 166, **184–93**
   exploring with gas chromatography 180–83
   finishing touches 178–80
   and side dishes 176–8
   see also International Chili Society

Jersey cows 403–5
Jiménez de Quesada, Gonzalo 19
John Dory 255, 256
   deep-frying 258–9
Johnson, Lyndon B., US President 158
Juliette potatoes 34, 245

Kalm, Pehr 103
Kansas City steak 104
Keller, Josef 365
Keller, Thomas 206–9
Kentucky, USA: state dish 158n
ketchup 324
   mushroom 125, 126, 127–8, 325
Kettilby, Mary: A Collection of Above
   300 Receipts 414, 416
'kiki' and 'bouba' 172, 174, 176
King Edward potatoes 34, 36, 38
Kirsch 379–80, 381–5
   cream 379–80, 388, 389, 393
kiwi fruit 113n
Kloeck, Gerd 91
Knight, James (of Mayfair) 254–5
Kochhar, Atul 53
Köhler, Wolfgang 173
kombu 324
korma 54
Kurti, Nicholas 424
   'The Physicist in the Kitchen' 430–31, 433

Label Anglais chickens 20
lactose 341
Ladenis, Nico: My Gastronomy 364, 376
Lady Claire potatoes 34, 36, 244–5, 261–2
Lady Olympia potatoes 34, 244
Lady Rosetta potatoes 34, 245, 260–3
Lang, Adam Perry 117–19, 121, 123
langoustines 275–6, 277, 278
Large Whites (pigs) 235
Lassen, Jeff 198, 199, 200
Lassen, Ken 198
Lassen, Lee 198
Lassen, Louis 197–8, 199
Lebowitz, Fran 102
leeks 39
lemon sole 255
Leo V, Emperor 226
lettuce
   iceberg 125, 129, 203
   Romaine 39

Levinson, Barry: Diner 109–10
Lewis, C. S.: The Silver Chair 227
Lincoln, Abraham 427
Linda Dick chickens 20
Lindt, Rodolphe 372
liquid nitrogen 405–6, 407
lobster, Norway 275
Longhorn cattle 122
Louisiana, USA: state dish 158n
Low Sizergh farm, Lake District 445
Ludlow, Shropshire 227
   Food & Drink Festival 227–30
Luraschi, Felice: Nuovo cuoco Milanese
   economico 334
Lyon, Les Halles de 24–7

McCann, Clinton 428, 430
McGee, Harold 355
McGlone, Francis 175
McTague, Mary-Ellen 36
madeleine biscuit base 389, 391
Maillard reactions 125
Malik's restaurant, Cookham 53–5
Mallory, George 263
Mantle, Dr Mick 60–62
marbling 108, 118, 122, 123, 211–12
Marchesi, Gualtiero 349–53, 352
Margherita, Queen 298, 300
Marigliano, Pasquale 316
Marine Conservation Society 257
Marine Stewardship Council 257
Marinetti, Filippo: La Cucina Futurista 139
Maris Piper potatoes 34, 36, 38, 244, 245, 261–2
Marmite 324
Martino, Maestro: Libro de arte coquinaria 334
masala/masala sauce 45, 64, 67, 68
mascarpone cream **458**, **462–3**
May, Robert: The Accomplisht Cook
   446, 447, 457
MBM, Little Snoring 34–6, 243, 260–61
meat
   collagen in 259
   hanging 107–8, 237
   storing 467
   from stressed animals 236–7
   see also beef; pigs; pork sausages
Medici, Catherine de' 400
Melody potatoes 245
melon 113n
melon seeds, toasted 64, 67